*Culture in a
Post-Secular Context*

Culture in a
Post-Secular Context

Theological Possibilities in Milbank, Barth, and Bediako

Alan Thomson

PICKWICK Publications • Eugene, Oregon

CULTURE IN A POST-SECULAR CONTEXT
Theological Possibilities in Milbank, Barth, and Bediako

Copyright © 2014 Alan Thomson. All rights reserved. Except for brief quotations in critical publications or reviews, no part of this book may be reproduced in any manner without prior written permission from the publisher. Write: Permissions, Wipf and Stock Publishers, 199 W. 8th Ave., Suite 3, Eugene, OR 97401.

Pickwick Publications
An Imprint of Wipf and Stock Publishers
199 W. 8th Ave., Suite 3
Eugene, OR 97401

www.wipfandstock.com

ISBN 13: 978-1-60608-504-2

Cataloguing-in-Publication data:

Thomson, Alan.

Culture in a post-secular context : theological possibilities in Milbank, Barth, and Bediako / Alan Thomson.

xii + 288 pp. ; 23 cm. Includes bibliographical references.

ISBN 13: 978-1-60608-504-2

1. Postmodern theology. 2. Post-postmodernism. 3. Secularism. 4. Milbank, John. 5. Barth, Karl, 1886–1968. 6. Bediako, Kwame. I. Title.

BT40 T465 2014

Manufactured in the U.S.A.

Contents

Preface | vii
Acknowledgements | ix
List of Abbreviations | xi

Introduction | 1
1 Theology and the Neutrality of Culture | 11
2 Challenging the Neutrality of Culture | 48
3 John Milbank and a Theological Account of Culture | 93
4 Milbank, Violence, and Idealization | 132
5 Karl Barth and a Theological Alternative | 175
6 Kwame Bediako and an African Alternative | 224
Conclusion | 269

Bibliography | 279
Index | 289

Preface

CHRISTIAN THEOLOGIANS AND MISSIOLOGISTS frequently refer to the concept of culture but do not usually generate definitions for it, relying instead on those offered by the social sciences. Underpinning this reliance is the assumption that culture is a theologically neutral concept. Recent critiques of the secular paradigm from scholars like Charles Taylor, John Milbank, and Jacques Derrida indicate this assumption might be problematic, a suggestion that throws doubt on the tactic theologians and missiologists are using. Implied in these recent critiques is the possibility that definitions of culture participate in and embody dispositions potentially antithetical to the Christian framework. If this is indeed the case then the process of reliance just described should perhaps be re-examined and the relevance of these borrowed definitions for Christian theological purposes carefully assessed. In particular, such critiques suggest the need for generating specifically Christian understandings of culture to guide theological scholarship.

The bulk of this book pursues this goal. While resources for this are admittedly slim, which is perhaps not surprising given how prevalent the borrowing strategy is, there are nevertheless good if somewhat surprising possibilities available. For example, John Milbank's critical engagement of the secular is accompanied by an alternative constructive proposal that relies in part on a tradition in which the theological nature of culture is stressed. The work of Giambattisto Vico proves to be an important moment in the development of this perspective, one that strongly influences Milbank. Other possibilities also exist. For example, the Reformed tradition has a long history of engagement with culture under the guise of Dutch neo-Calvinism, although it is suggested that the richest engagement comes in the work of Karl Barth. Despite apparently strong contra-indications, Barth develops a rigorous description of culture that rivals Milbank's for theological depth, sophistication, and applicability.

Preface

If left here it would seem that culture is an exclusively Western concept, yet it is a discussion involving a global constituency, hence insights generated from the non-Western world also need to be examined. One particularly apt example comes from Africa, where the Ghanaian theologian Kwame Bediako has undertaken an analysis of the African context that relies in part on a specifically theological understanding of culture. This understanding is grounded in a more general African emphasis on the inherent religiosity of humanity, a core element of much African Christian anthropology. Culture, as a refraction of this underlying anthropology, is therefore largely understood in theological terms.

If the critical and constructive proposals outlined above can be sustained then it is suggested that theological and missiological references to "culture" should no longer take their lead so strongly from the social sciences. What is required instead is a specifically theological engagement with the notion of culture that seeks to properly recognize and account for the religious character of this world. Milbank, Barth, and Bediako outline three ways this might be achieved, and provide in the process three models for ongoing appropriation and development by the Christian community.

Acknowledgments

THIS BOOK IS THE culmination of a long and sometimes arduous journey completed in large part because of the generous provision of time and resources by others. The initial idea for the thesis came in the winter of 2002 while living in the married quarters at the Bible College of New Zealand (now Laidlaw College). I fondly remember this time and am grateful to my fellow students for making the study of theology so much fun. While our many discussions might now appear incidental to the current book, they were central to its early shape. Especially formative however were my interactions with Laidlaw College staff, in particular I am grateful for the courses offered by Steve Graham, Dr John Hitchen and Dr John Roxborogh. Under their expert tutelage I received invaluable, ongoing guidance into the missional life of the church that has now blossomed into a love for the church in mission, to which a proper understanding of culture is essential.

Still, the initial proposal might even now be languishing had not the University of Otago offered financial assistance through their doctoral scholarship program. I was also privileged to receive from the Humanities department a travel bursary that enabled me to attend an essential conference in Rome. I greatly appreciate the financial support I have received from the university. I would also like to extend my thanks to university staff, especially those in the Theology department who have always been very efficient and supportive, and to the remote services staff of the university library who dealt so effectively and patiently with my many requests and enquiries.

Over the years there have been many who have shown an ongoing interest in my progress. I am very grateful for the significant input into my life so freely given by Doug McConnell, Paul Whales, Richard Starling, Kevin Hapi, and Andy Edwards. I have also benefited enormously from my chats with Paul Whiting. His learned ear and sage advice helped to refine certain ideas quite considerably.

Acknowledgments

Without doubt the people with the greatest direct influence on this book came in its getation as a doctoral thesis under my two supervisors, Professor Ivor Davidson (formerly of the University of Otago, New Zealand and now at the University of St Andrews, Scotland) and Dr Roxborogh (recently retired from Knox Centre for Ministry and Leadership, New Zealand). I want to thank them for their vigilant supervision and constant encouragement. Through the years they have added immeasurably to my learning, a great part of which is now embodied in this book. I have benefited enormously from their influence.

I also owe a large debt of gratitude to "the olds" for their unfailing support, especially for helping with the children, listening to my "outrageous" ideas, even when they did not understand these "new" concepts, and for giving such assistance to our family. I therefore thank the late Les and late Beryl Whales (nee Butler), and the late Dot Whales and Mike Whales. Their help and constant faithful dependence on Jesus Christ has been inspirational and I hope to honor this influence by refracting it through my own life. My mother, Pauline Thomson, has been a solid rock throughout, assisting in all manner of ways. Without your assistance this would not have been possible.

Finally, I cannot adequately express the depth of my thanks to my family for their help and many sacrifices. Emma, Joel, and Caitlyn have all grown up in the shadow of this book, first as a thesis and now in its published form, bearing with gracious good humor the amount of time I spent away from them. Similarly, my wife Carole has always stood by me, constantly offering encouragement despite the many privations that inevitably accompany a return to study after time spent working. The completion of this thesis was dependent on this support hence it is dedicated to my family. Thank you.

Abbreviations

TST   John Milbank, *Theology and Social Theory: Beyond Secular Reason*. Oxford: Blackwell, 1990.

WMS   John Milbank, *The Word Made Strange: Theology, Language, and Culture*. Oxford: Blackwell, 1997.

BR   John Milbank, *Being Reconciled: Ontology and Pardon*. London: Routledge, 2003.

RO   Radical Orthodoxy, the loose knit "movement" cohering around the work of John Milbank, Catherine Pickstock, and Graham Ward.

CD   Karl Barth, *Church Dogmatics*. Edited by G. W. Bromiley and T. F. Torrance. 5 vols. in 14 parts. Edinburgh: T. & T. Clark, 1936–75.

CD 3   Karl Barth, *The Doctrine of Creation*. Vol. 3 in 3 parts of *Church Dogmatics*. Edited by G. W. Bromiley and T. F. Torrance. Edinburgh: T. & T. Clark, 1958–61.

CD 4   Karl Barth, *The Doctrine of Reconciliation*. Vol. 4 in 4 parts of *Church Dogmatics*. Edited by G. W. Bromiley and T. F. Torrance. Edinburgh: T. & T. Clark, 1956–69.

CD 3/1   Karl Barth, *The Doctrine of Creation*, Vol. 3, Part 1 of *Church Dogmatics*. Translated by J. W. Edwards, O. Bussey, and Harold Knight. Edited by G. W. Bromiley and T. F. Torrance. Edinburgh: T. & T. Clark, 1958.

CD 3/3   Karl Barth, *The Doctrine of Creation*, Vol. 3, Part 3 of *Church Dogmatics*. Translated by G. W. Bromiley and R. J. Ehrlich. Edited by G. W. Bromiley and T. F. Torrance. Edinburgh: T. & T. Clark, 1960.

Introduction

"[W]hen we contingently but authentically make things and reshape ourselves through time, we are not estranged from the eternal, but enter further into its recesses by what for us is the only possible route."[1]

JOHN MILBANK

THE CONCEPT OF CULTURE aims to explain in some way human living, yet it seems strangely disconnected from such a goal when explored in the context of theological discussions. This is to say, the term is seldom linked in a *structural* way with distinctively theological doctrines it might otherwise seem intimately connected, such as creation, (theological) anthropology, ecclesiology, and the incarnation. Of course, these doctrines are not absent from theological discussions of culture; on the contrary they are usually closely connected to it. However, it is notable that while in some way coordinated with culture, these doctrines are seldom if ever used to define what culture *is*. In other words, even though these doctrines are often connected to and associated with the term "culture" they are not considered constitutive of it. Culture as a concept, as distinct from how it may be used, notably lacks a distinctively theological foundation.

This becomes clearly evident when considering how the term "culture" enters theological discourses. It will be argued below that in the normal course of such discussions culture enters as an already defined, pre-formed entity. Even before theologians and missiologists begin to work with the concept its contours and content are already established. Much like many commercial builders, theologians and missiologists are working with prefabricated material, formed and shaped elsewhere that are then appropriately

---

1. Milbank, *Being Reconciled*, ix.

slotted in. There is some leeway regarding placement, but the builders have limited scope for shaping the pieces, usually only doing so in order to facilitate a good fit.

In one respect this construction analogy can be usefully extended. Each prefabricated piece is, in and of itself, neutral in as much as it is a subsidiary component of a much larger design. Certain bespoke details may have a significant influence on the overall design or express an idiosyncratic feature, but even then most pieces contribute to the finished product in a collective and nondescript manner. Aside then from specifically engineered highlights, each piece is an anonymous contributor to the overall effect. Culture tends to act in a similar way, forming a neutral component of theological projects, usefully contributing to the final goal but in a relatively anonymous sense. At certain times it is a highlight feature, for example when a theologian like H. Richard Niebuhr undertakes a study on "Christ and culture." Yet upon closer examination, even these examples, as will be shown, conceive the term in its pre-fabricated form.

This is perhaps best revealed by considering how culture is defined. For example, despite culture forming a central theological topic in his discussion, Niebuhr does not ask how culture might be *theologically* constituted and therefore defined. The theological doctrines of most relevance, as noted above, are simply not called upon to assist in the definitional task. Neither does he draw from a theological heritage in which this type of analysis has been important. Instead, as will be seen in chapter 1, he turns to the social sciences for a pre-existing definition of culture, using one of their definitions that he then suitably adapts or nuances for his purposes. There are, of course, a number of good reasons for such a strategy, not least that theologians can take advantage of an existing *lingua franca* that then allows participation in wider discussions and the chance to engage a broader audience.

Nevertheless, while useful for these good purposes such a strategy is always inherently in danger of so identifying with the *lingua franca* that it no longer acts as a vehicle of translation or an instrument for external engagement but becomes instead the standard and constitutive language of the term. Again this might be thought a reasonable proposition if culture were indeed the neutral construct it purports to be. Determining the validity of the claim to neutrality is therefore crucial, a task that necessarily requires an inspection of how culture has been defined prior to its arrival in theological discussions. This in turn requires a careful examination of the underlying foundation giving rise to the various definitions of culture, and in particular an assessment of this foundation's presumed ability to grant to culture the status of neutrality it is assumed to hold. That culture is usually appropriated from the social sciences is a critical clue for determining which foundation needs analyzing, indicating that the meaning and status of the term is derived from the secular framework now routinely guiding the social sciences.

Chapter 1 prepares the ground for this task by empirically establishing what has already been argued, namely that theologians and missiologists do indeed treat culture in the way just described. Here sufficient evidence is found to suggest Christian scholars generally accept culture to be a structurally neutral concept available for theological appropriation without the need to engage in a specifically theological, structural analysis of it. As already hinted, these scholars approach their task in this way for a range of positive reasons, but these should be assessed against the possible losses accruing from inattention to theological underpinnings for the term.

Chapter 2 then examines the viability of the neutrality thesis by determining the legitimacy of the underlying secular claim. Contrary to expectations this claim is found wanting because it does not issue from any intrinsic or inherent basis. The secular perspective certainly offers *an* account or description of the world, but this turns out to be only one particular account of reality, one grounded in a decision to accept an immanent rather than transcendent perspective as the objective basis for all of reality. This decision is based in an exercise of sheer preference since it springs from only one *possible* objective basis for reality (and is therefore not simply *the* objective basis). There exists at least one alternative paradigm offering a different measure of what counts as objective, one that must be, in some way, accounted for. The claim to neutrality is therefore revealed as a biased rather than objective claim.

The rest of the book is concerned with considering the potential inherent in one particular alternative paradigm, and hence can be characterized as exploring post-secular possibilities. More specifically it seeks to tease out the contours of a Christian theological perspective on culture. In this constructive mode the discussions of culture undertaken by John Milbank, Karl Barth, and Kwame Bediako are carefully considered. The first two in particular might seem unusual choices given that they are more usually categorized as exponents of counter-cultural analysis. Milbank's Augustinian emphasis on the sinfulness of *Civitas terena* (City of Man) does not seem a promising basis on which to secure a positive account of culture. Barth seems an even more difficult proposition given that his antagonistic attitude towards culture is a regularly rehearsed feature of discussions on his theology, his love of Mozart registering a seemingly minimal affirmation in the shadow of his determined advocacy of divine sovereignty and *Diastasis* (separation).

On closer inspection however, these portrayals turn out to be inadequate caricatures that have failed to grasp the sophistication and complexity of the understandings of culture they supposedly represent. This is, of course, in part at least, a reflection of the widespread lack of attention paid to specifically theological ways of defining the concept of culture. These theologians have been read in one way and not another precisely because of an implicit bias, one this book seeks to overcome. A full response to this issue is therefore a product of the whole book hence this must simply remain a bald assertion for now, one awaiting vindication in the course of discussion.

Milbank's argument in *Theology and Social Theory* provides important grounds for initiating the constructive element of this book, laying out one possibility for what a Christian post-secular description might look like. The third chapter therefore pays careful attention to the writings of Milbank, though its focus is less on the more popular elements of his corpus than on his earlier agenda-setting doctoral dissertation and post-doctoral work. In the two publications arising from these studies Milbank sets out a description of a Baroque cultural theology as (pre-eminently) expressed by Giambattista Vico. This is explored before considering how this has subtly but pervasively influenced Milbank's later writing. What emerges is the suggestion that Milbank in his more popular works is slowly outlining something like a contemporary Vichian cultural theology, or what amounts to a theological description of culture.

The fourth chapter then engages this Milbankian framework critically, carefully considering the efficacy of his proposals given the numerous critiques it has attracted. The initial treatment is broad, investigating the various ways others have interacted with his ideas as a whole. The larger portion of the chapter then narrows the focus, concentrating in particular on his ecclesial suggestions for it is here that Milbank's primary resources for pragmatically addressing culture are located. Of considerable interest in this regard are the many critiques the supposed idealized character of his ecclesiology has attracted, a nexus of considerations that can be representatively treated through careful attention to Gillian Rose's substantial critique. She engages Milbank across several levels, most notably on the practical aspects that a theological description of culture needs to be attentive to.

While the second half of this chapter recognizes some validity in this critique, it argues that Milbank offers important resources that, with further development and refinement, could successfully counter the charge. His notion of "judicious narratives," coupled with his arguments regarding Gothic and complex space and his description of Christian Socialism would seem to provide the required "space" for a Christian understanding of culture that is more than the amorphous escape or overly theoretic idealization with which he is usually charged. Milbank, seen through this lens, is instead proposing, in admittedly idealized terms, a practical engagement that is already found in diverse situations around the world.

The fifth chapter then shifts focus. Having established the case for a theological description of culture it then asks if it is also necessary to assert that Milbank's version or model of Christian reason is the only possibility. Is there really only one Christian account of reality offering resources for describing culture in a specifically theological way? In contradistinction to Milbank's supposed captivity of Christian reason a case is made that Karl Barth offers a plausible alternative. Barth gives a sometimes similar, yet importantly and strikingly different account of culture that is rooted in an alternative conception of the Christian framework.

The chapter paints the broad panorama of Barth's project, describing the key elements of his writings pertinent to the question of culture. In this discussion both his negative and positive views on culture are described. The negative perception represents the way Barth's views have traditionally been presented, embodying and perpetuating his emphasis on *Diastasis*. This is clearly seen, for example, in his critical assessment of the idea of worldview. By contrast to this popularized understanding of Barth, the positive locus is not well known, having only recently received any explicit recognition. A few scholars have begun to deconstruct the negative cultural prejudices to discover within Barth a vibrant, positive and deeply theological account of culture. This perspective will be described and then integrated with his critical proposals in order to propose a theological alternative to Milbank's model.

The final chapter pursues a similar but expanded line of inquiry to the preceding one by asking whether models of Christian reason and reality are the sole domain of any one cultural sensibility. It asks, therefore, whether the Western focus characterizing the approaches presented by Milbank and Barth offer the only resources for conceiving a specifically Christian description of culture. The African theology promulgated by the late Kwame Bediako suggests otherwise, offering an important series of insights that not only align at critical junctures with those generated by both Milbank and Barth but which move beyond them in certain ways. This presents a description of culture in its international guise, by way of an African proposal that situates the discussion within the church catholic.

At this point it is worth taking a little time to explain the rationale behind the selection of these specific theologians over others and, because this is in turn a function of the overall aims of this book, to explain the rationale behind the shape of the book as a whole. This book is shaped by four key questions, with the first and second being closely related. First, is the concept of culture theologically neutral? This question is a challenge to the normativity of secular conceptions of neutrality; a challenge taken up by increasing numbers of contemporary scholars. From amongst these scholars two in particular stand out as candidates for engagement given the importance of their respective projects—Charles Taylor and John Milbank.

Both propose a primarily negative view of secularity and both build their cases in similar ways. Taylor, for example, explicitly aligns himself with Milbank at several points.[2] Taylor's own interest, as he goes on to argue, is not to disrupt the Milbankian and associated genealogies but to complement them by noting Milbank's inattention to the processes by which secularization became a mass phenomenon. Milbank, he argues, rightly notes shifts within the elites but not those within the broader population and neither is he sufficiently attentive to some of the counter movements and resistances. What both Milbank and Taylor also voice is the view that secularity could be understood otherwise. This is where Karl Barth becomes particularly helpful as this expresses a central plank of his understanding of culture. Barth is arguing for humanity to be recognized as inherently secular, though he conceives secularity very differently from how it is normally understood. He suggests that being a creature, living and flourishing within creaturely confines, is what defines secularity. True secularity is merely the recognition that we are just creatures and nothing more. The secular, for Barth, is therefore that space in which we are what we were always intended to be—creatures under God.

The problem with Taylor's proposals is that he fails to offer a comprehensive theological alternative in the way both Milbank and Barth do. For this reason this book focuses on Milbank rather than Taylor. Also, although Barth is strong in terms of his constructive proposals, he is weaker for critical purposes hence Milbank becomes the prime instrument for critiquing traditional cultural understandings. His constructive proposal then becomes the initial answer to the second question animating this book: determining whether viable Christian theological alternatives exist that could replace the current secular models of culture. Milbank's project is one such possibility hence the book moves on to outline and then describe his proposals. At this stage Milbank has become the central character, offering the primary deconstructive move and the corresponding reconstructive possibility. The book could easily have remained here and explored at considerable length

---

2. He explicitly aligns himself with Milbank, Hauerwas, and so on in tracing the emergence of the secular as a negative from late scholasticism forwards, see Taylor, *A Secular Age*, 295, 773ff. At p. 774 he explicitly acknowledges Milbank's account of Duns Scotus as the fount of the anthropocentric shift.

Introduction

the Milbankian proposal, however it is at least equally important to demonstrate that Christian theological alternatives exist.

The third question driving this book therefore was whether other Christian traditions offered potentially compelling alternatives to that set out by Milbank. One notable dialogue partner here could have been Roman Catholicism however the Anglo-Catholic nature of Milbank's theological sensibility meant much of this material was already engaged at some level. What was a much more interesting possibility came in the Reformed outlook of Karl Barth. While received opinion would seem to preclude the viability of this suggestion, careful examination of his project reveals an intriguing insight—Barth had at various stages articulated a sophisticated theological understanding of the concept of culture. When these various statements are taken in concert with aspects of the architecture of his thought, it is clear that he offers a viable alternative to the Milbankian proposal hence Barth becomes an important conversation partner.

One fair question the reader might raise concerns why Barth is not allocated the same space granted Milbank in this book? Some might even ask why Barth did not form the sole character within it given his extensive theological output and his seminal influence on Protestant theology in the twentieth and early twenty-first centuries. These are entirely fair questions to which there is not a finally satisfying response other than authorial predilections of two kinds. First, Milbank deals consistently and directly with the *contemporary* secular framework in a way Barth does not (Schleiermacher and those following in his footsteps being his primary target). The aim of this book is to deal with the contemporary situation and given that Milbank is writing directly into the current context, his project is the more proximate.

This objection is not insurmountable as Barth necessarily deals with secular constructions of reality in his writings, however a full enough analysis of his work to render it suitable for both the critical and reconstructive purposes of this book would render it almost exclusively a study of Barth's view of culture. Such a task would then preclude pursuit of the third and fourth questions set out in this section, both expressing one of the key goals this book sets out to achieve: do multiple, distinctively theological, models of culture exist?

The third question in turn suggested the desirability of a related, fourth question. If theological alternatives existed within the Western tradition then might not other possibilities be present within the broader ambit of global theologies? In some respects this is the most difficult question to answer since the focus is not only on the theological proposals being offered but also on underlying differences in context that might impinge on the suggestions being put forward. While not fully encompassing of the range of differences, there is a need to address not only the theological proposals but also the philosophical underpinnings guiding them. Kwame Bediako offers an exciting possibility in this respect, not only because he is an alternative to Milbank and Barth but also because his Western education eased the contextual difficulties a little, allowing for a more direct comparison than might otherwise have been the case.

One of the very interesting aspects of reading scholars from outside of the Western framework is the way Western assumptions become questions rather than assertions. Bediako's proposal is in some ways just as much a response from the particularities of the African philosophical context as it is the result of his Christian theological reflection. The chapter on Bediako therefore attempts to refract something of this "peculiarity" of the contextual framework he is writing within and the chapter should therefore be read with this in mind. The assumption of neutrality is here rendered contextual rather than objective as a matter of normal engagement, an insight that strengthens the basic case being presented by this book.

Having briefly outlined what the book intends to cover it is also necessary to explain a little about what it does not seek to do. Certain readers will note the lack of attention paid to the resurgent field of Natural Theology. In some ways this might seem a significant oversight given what might at first appear to be a degree of affinity between the interests of theologians writing on culture and theologians writing on Natural Theology. It is perhaps fair to admit that Natural Theology offers a way into the question that is quite suggestive. For example, working from the doctrine of creation through to culture seems on the face of it to resonate with aspects of the argument being outlined here. However, there are a number of reasons why this topic is not and could not be pursued here.

Primary amongst them is the way it would fundamentally alter the contours of this discussion, resulting in the pursuit of an entirely different set of questions through an altogether different framework of analysis. Milbank and Barth are usually understood as contesting the legitimacy of Natural Theology hence the book would have centered at some stage on resolving or explaining this tension. At root, this would entail engaging the question of underlying assumptions. This book takes its lead from scholars such as Gadamer, MacIntyre, Wittgenstein, Milbank, and Barth, all of whom operate with a broadly non-foundational framework. By contrast, Natural Theology usually involves some form of broadly foundationalist philosophical paradigm expressed in some version of critical or scientific realism. This is not to say Natural Theology is still in the comparatively naïve Enlightenment forms Barth was encountering, however it is to say that the framework guiding this book is not compatible with the roots of Natural Theology.

Introduction

One further factor to be taken into account is the lack of a major Natural Theologian dealing extensively with the question of culture as it presents itself in contemporary discourse. In fact, Alister McGrath, one such significant theologian, readily admits at one point that this represents one of the three key aspects distinguishing his project from Milbank's—that Milbank had decided to follow the cultural route rather than the natural science one. Natural Theology therefore represents perhaps a second or third phase of the project initiated through this book rather than a core element of the present book.

One last aspect of this should also be mentioned. In Milbank it is arguable that resources exist for thinking through the relationship with Natural Theology differently, perhaps even for rethinking some central elements of Natural theology. Milbank is not actually dismissing modernity *per se* but is sharply contesting the form it currently takes. His critical project is arguing that "modernity" could have been very different, that it could have taken an alternative, Christ-centered form. He is essentially suggesting that an alternative modernity can be envisaged and is still available for appropriation. It is not that science as currently conceived and pursued is "wrong," but that it has been shaped and molded by a narrative privileging a certain, highly rational form of thinking to the exclusion of any other. There are intriguing possibilities associated with his attempts to redress the balance here, particularly for Natural Theology; however such an exploration would wander very far from the considerably more limited aims of this present work.

To conclude this particular discussion, a word must be said about the role of the social sciences in all of this. As the immediately preceding comments intimate, Milbank is often misread, and this book could potentially be misunderstood for similar reasons, as contending against and therefore as seeking to displace the social sciences. In a sense this is accurate, however everything hinges on the sense in which this is understood. This book does not dispute, in presumed accord with Milbank's own perspective, the validity of much of the empirical work undertaken by the social sciences. Instead, it argues the need to rethink the formative assumptions guiding the empirical process, not just in terms of the interpretation of empirical data, but perhaps even more so relative to the data initially collected.

Neither anthropological nor sociological insights, for example, should be dismissed out of hand or otherwise ignored. However presented, and irrespective of the agenda they may be temporarily attached to, there lurk within these insights an empirical component that requires explanation and appropriation in some shape or form. Social scientific research is legitimate, and continues to be so even under the critical agenda presented at various stages within this book. This correlates closely with Milbank's own desire, expressed most cogently when he argues in *Being Reconciled* (BR) "In this

9

sense, my sequence on gift constitutes also a sequel to *Theology and Social Theory: Beyond Secular Reason*. Compared with the latter volume, the engagement is much more positive in character: however, nothing here is being retracted—rather I am concerned to learn from social theory in its more historical, ethnographic and less ideological aspects."[3]

What is not admitted, however, is that contemporary social scientific explanations with roots in versions of rationalism *necessarily* provide the *best* explanatory framework for analyzing and understanding the underlying data. This does not in itself mean social scientific explanations are excluded since at times they may well offer the best possible way to conceive the situation under discussion. Rationality is here being opened up to a larger field of possibilities, and to an alternative frame of reference, rather than being dismissed or circumvented.

Throughout this book all forms of rationality privileging contemporary modernist or post-modernist forms of empiricist or philosophically positivist foundations are contested. They are held accountable for their presumption of exclusivity, for seeking to assert the primacy of critical engagement over any other form of encounter. It is suggested that far from this kind of perspective, what is needed is an encompassing understanding of rationality. Some, for example Milbank and Pope Benedict, argue for an understanding that covers "faith and reason." Only in this expanded view of rationality, they suggest, can be found a plausible, comprehensive explanation of reality or of its various aspects.

---

3. Milbank, *Being Reconciled*, xi.

Chapter 1

Theology and the Neutrality of Culture

H. RICHARD NIEBUHR, PERHAPS the most influential theological commentator on culture of the latter half of the twentieth century, considered the theological engagement of culture to be "the enduring problem."[1] One way to read David Bosch's magnum opus *Transforming Mission* for example is as an account of how "in each historical epoch of the past two millennia the missionary idea has been profoundly influenced by the overall context in which Christians lived and worked."[2] This notion of missionary idea can be described as the attempt to ensure that Christians "with creative but responsible freedom, prolong the logic of the ministry of Jesus and the early church in an imaginative and creative way to our own time and context."[3] Each of the six epochs he examines work in very different ways to resolve the culture problem, birthing in each case theological paradigms that have currency for the duration of the epoch but which then fade in the face of new circumstances (albeit there are usually elements of continuity).

Niebuhr notes this quality of perpetual irresolution, considering it a reflection of the "irreconcilable tension" at the heart of the relationship between Christ and the world, one perennially confronting humanity as it participates in a strategy it understands only dimly; lieutenants following the orders of a captain in whose mind alone the strategy has final form. Some sense of the difficulties he is attempting to encompass is given by Rudolf Bultmann when he points out the relationship consists of the "paradox of the Christian as an eschatological and historical being . . ." as well as "The paradox of Christ as

1. Niebuhr, *Christ and Culture*, 1–44.
2. Bosch, *Transforming Mission*, 349.
3. Ibid., 181.

the historical Jesus and the ever-present Lord."[4] This nexus of paradoxes is rendered more complex because the role of the church must also be factored in, itself existing paradoxically "as the eschatological entity . . . between the 'no longer' and 'not yet.'"[5] In Bultmann's writings the overarching relationship is therefore examined through several synonymous pairings: faith and history, history and eschatology, theology and cosmology.[6]

While many interesting comparisons could be made between Bultmann and Niebuhr it is the terminological question that is the most striking for the purposes of this discussion. Whereas Bultmann conducts his analysis through overtly theological terms, Niebuhr grants prominence to the relatively new word culture, a word lacking the theological pedigree Bultmann's choices enjoy. Robert Webber, for another example, examines the same relationship Niebuhr is considering but uses "world" (*kosmos*) instead of culture, with all of its rich biblical pedigree. Webber undertakes an exegetical study that discovers two primary biblical meanings for "world."[7] The first is a positive perspective in which creation (and recreation in Christ) is affirmed while the second is a negative one that captures the deleterious effects of the fall throughout creation (spiritual beings included). The term is likewise present throughout Bosch's work where it functions in much the same way.[8] In his analysis the positive element is historically less prevalent, only recently recovered as an emphasis. This implies the historical dominance of the pejorative model.[9]

The question this brief analysis raises is why the word culture is the most appropriate term through which to engage this topic given that it lacks the theological heritage or overt biblical grounding of other terms, such as "world."[10] This is especially relevant given that words embody worlds of meaning, as Raymond Williams argues (for which, refer the next chapter); hence it is worth pausing to carefully consider the implications stemming

---

4. Bultmann, *History and Eschatology*, 152–55.

5. Bultmann, *Theology II*, 155ff. for the soteriology nexus and p. 203 for the ecclesial statement.

6. History is Bultmann's synonym for culture, hence he describes history as the field of human actions which is distinguishable from nature, refer Bultmann, *History and Eschatology*, 138ff. The theology and cosmology pairing can be found in Bultmann, *Theology II*, 144ff. The faith and history pairing come from the title of his concluding chapter in the book entitled with the other pairing: Bultmann, *History and Eschatology*, see 138ff.

7. Webber, *The Church in the World*, 15–19; Appendix A (ibid., 279–82).

8. Bosch, *Transforming Mission*.

9. Ibid., esp. 376–78, compare use of culture 291–98.

10. The lack of historical heritage is debatable of course. Niebuhr, for example, essentially argues it reaches back and envelops prior terms and hence, by logical extension, it carries forward their respective heritages.

Theology and the Neutrality of Culture

from this seemingly innocuous semantic change. There are of course benefits that accrue, such as the ability to actively engage with external (non-Christian) interlocutors for whom (as will be seen) the term culture is part of normal discourse; as well as for the purposes of internal discussions given that Christians also participate in, because they inhabit, this "normal" discourse. This present chapter is not concerned, however, with elaborating this positive assessment since the prevalence of the term culture in theological discussion already speaks to these constructive possibilities.

In what follows the basic premise is that insufficient attention has been paid to one particular negative implication and to assessing whether this represents an appropriate or unacceptable cost for using the term, or at least for using it as it is currently deployed. It is further argued that it is only through a satisfactory resolution of this issue that the term culture can reasonably be appropriated for theological purposes. The key matter to be placed under the microscope is the reputed neutrality of the concept of culture, a reputation that has led to a widespread, hence general pattern of engagement with the term culture by theologians and missiologists. It is then argued that this general pattern is enacted through three primary modes: explicit, active, and passive deferral.

The "general pattern" refers to a process of deferral whereupon theologians treat the term culture as a neutral construct. In the face of the presumption of neutrality theologians and missiologists defer to the expertise of social scientists as the specialists knowledgeable about culture. As already noted, this inevitably leads to culture becoming a largely unexamined datum inputted into theological projects on the presumption such insertion does not significantly affect their underlying foundations.

This general pattern of deferral is achieved through the three primary modes of engagement noted earlier. The first, active mode, refers to those who select an anthropological or sociological definition of culture after a debate over the respective merits of competing definitions. While rigorous and active, the candidate definitions are nevertheless all selected from the pool of options offered by the social sciences. In the second, direct deferral mode, theologians adopt a definition or definitions drawn directly from the social sciences. In most cases the definition is selected from amongst those offered by socio-cultural anthropologists.[11]

---

11. This brings up a significant delimiter for this study. Some balance needs to be struck between the competing interests of comprehensive coverage and deep engagement in a context of proliferating interest in the concept of culture. In view of all this the remainder of this thesis will focus its attention on cultural anthropology, taking this as a representative discipline of the social sciences.

The final mode is the passive one. Here the term culture is used without further explanation or clarification, amounting thereby to a tacit deferral to social scientific constructs in light of the dominant position these disciplines have in the contemporary intellectual milieu. To commentate on culture today usually means speaking in an anthropological idiom.

The point of distinction between these three approaches amounts to little more than the degree to which the theologian is involved in selecting the specific concept of culture to be relied on. While the differences between these approaches are important, and will be addressed below, for now it is important to note their underlying similarity. When taken together these approaches constitute the general paradigm for theological engagement with the concept of culture: deferral to social scientific explanations. It will be argued against this pattern that the paradigm is actually characterized by two inter-related thrusts: the already noted deferral to social scientific descriptions, and a concomitant, fundamental disengagement from the need for a *theological* definition of culture. This chapter sets out to demonstrate the presence and prevalence of the first thrust, while the question of disengagement forms the subject pursued in the next chapter.

The primary role of this chapter therefore is to establish and document the presence of this general pattern in each of its three modes by way of representative examples. Hopefully the diversity of contexts, theologians, and theological projects surveyed is enough to strongly suggest albeit not exhaustively chronicle the prevalence of this pattern. The first mode to be considered is the active one.

Active Deferral

In this mode the theologian, rather than expecting readers will simply accept their use of any one particular definition for culture, makes public some of the arguments behind their choice of definition. This is ordinarily achieved by bringing competing articulations of culture into direct and apparently competitive debate over the merits of two or more differing definitions so as to determine the ideal one.

Kathryn Tanner's work exemplifies this category, engaging the task of definition by competitively considering two core social scientific models that constitute perhaps the most prevalent set of social scientific definitions. Kevin Vanhoozer's variation is also well worth noting, hence some attention will be paid to his work. This analysis of Tanner and Vanhoozer is very useful not only for understanding the active group of approaches but also the content the passive modes (outlined below) tend to gravitate towards.

Theology and the Neutrality of Culture

Kathryn Tanner

The first third of her book *Theories of Culture* is concerned with describing Tanner's understanding of culture whereupon she effectively reduces almost two centuries of discussions to three core movements that are then trimmed to two central models. The three movements essentially describe consecutive historical developments that at a broad level also describe the maturation of cultural anthropology. By describing it in this way Tanner is able to map these movements to wider philosophical changes, the two final models constituting a contemporary anthropological dialogue between modern and postmodern sensibilities.

Tanner begins with an introduction to the modern, or perhaps "traditional," anthropological understanding of culture. She argues the contemporary term is rooted in distinctive German, French, and English notions of *Kultur*, civilization and culture respectively, as developed under the influence of various eighteenth- and nineteenth-century intellectual movements. In the late nineteenth century aspects of these developments were woven together under the auspices of a burgeoning interest in what is now called cultural difference, an interest stimulated by colonial and missionary impulses.[12] The rise under modernity of the traditional understanding is briefly recounted; brevity that sacrifices nuance in order to describe a broadly consensual synthesis she considers more useful for theological purposes.[13] Against a complex and variegated background of interweaving social theories Tanner sets out a concise definition,[14] one delineated through a nine-point description, presented here with slight variation for stylistic reasons:

1. A human universal

2. of diverse patterns

3. that vary between social groups

---

12. This description picks up one of two emphases for the early roots also represented a countervailing sensibility to the modern construct developed under anthropology and based in *Kultur*. Culture as an evolutionary paradigm, somewhat *la civilisation* but particularly as developed under the English romantic tradition (though its interest in combating what the Germans described as *Zivilisation*, the industrial revolution, masked this somewhat) continues to influence.

13. For a similar discussion but one giving primacy to roots in Cicero's use of *cultura animi*, an agricultural metaphor picked up in the Renaissance by Thomas More and Francis Bacon, amongst others, see Gorringe, *Furthering Humanity*, 3–9.

14. Against this must be weighed Kroeber and Kluckhohn's eschewing of a similar approach—Fox and King, *Anthropology Beyond Culture*, Foreword, xvi.

4. for whom it describes an entire way of life
5. that has been built upon consensus
6. and which acts to constitute or build human nature
7. and is therefore a form of social determinism
8. but which is also a human construct
9. and is therefore contingent (could have been otherwise)

As this shows, cultures are generally considered incommensurate wholes, their unifying cores "often identified in ideational or mental terms, for instance, as a characteristic set of norms, values, beliefs, concepts, dispositions, or preoccupations . . . the informing spirit of a whole way of life . . ."[15] Culture is therefore understood to be "*the meaning dimension of social life* . . ."[16] and is consequently distinguishable from social behaviors in that it is the "ordering principle" of such behaviors, and therefore of society generally. It is the blueprint or control mechanism that guides social actions.[17] This controlling and integrating function imposes a sense of societal coherence, in turn implying a similar coherence within the concept of "culture" itself. Identifying a single unifying factor behind this coherence has been very difficult prompting a wide variety of possibilities to be suggested.[18]

Further, behaviors are understood to be comprehensible mainly with reference to surrounding context, especially to the specific environment it is situated within but also to the wider societal context that condones and supports it. Deriving the "imaginative universe" such behaviors emanate from has led to a highly localized approach. This emphasis on particularity has also contributed to a truncated notion of time, to a temporal particularity in which the focus is on synchronic rather than diachronic analysis. The genealogy of a specific behavior is therefore not as important as the contemporary justifications for its continued existence.

---

15. Tanner, *Theories of Culture*, 30–31. Refer also to p. 35 for discussion of how cultures are distinguishable by their offset from other cultures.

16. Ibid., 31.

17. In 1958 there was a landmark agreement reached between Kroeber and Parsons regarding the appropriate partitioning of anthropology and sociology. Effectively the meaning dimension was assigned to anthropology while social behaviors became the purview of sociology. Such neat demarcations are finally arbitrary and empirical work is never so clean cut. Refer for some discussion on this to Fox and King, *Anthropology Beyond Culture*, Foreword, xvi.

18. The most common notions include central motifs, semantic logic, integrating beliefs, structural logic and/or function, the choice usually depending on the specific epistemological sub-foundation being brought to bear.

Tanner then moves on to examine elements of recent critical engagements with this modernist understanding, from which she derives a reconstructed postmodern cultural framework that then deeply informs her new agenda for theology. This postmodern critique is not a monolithic engagement, stemming instead from a series of interrelated though independently sourced critiques drawing from historical, literary, and social scientific roots, amongst many others. Again Tanner engages them concisely, noting the presence of six major impacts upon the traditional definition and explanation given above.

First, members of an individual culture do not engage life from within a holistic understanding of their culture; rather life is pragmatically encountered, with cultural understandings only being "partially applied." Although an encompassing view of the culture may exist, it does so only from the privileged perspective of the anthropologist. The "whole" is only achieved by the anthropologists using three key distortions: hypostasizing individuals; allowing the part to representatively stand in for the whole; and by dehistoricizing social behaviors.[19]

Second, the existence of cultural coherence is queried because social behaviors are only seen as integrated by the application of a peculiarly Western aesthetical need for such integration. The resulting interpretive framework, it is argued, does not exist in reality. Too often cultural informants are induced into theoretically oriented responses that belie the pragmatics of their lives. In practice the neat dividing lines of theoretical constructs are rent asunder when confronted by the complex economy of interrelationships present in daily social discourse.[20]

Third, and in part derivatively from the preceding two points, it is difficult to sustain the notion of consensus so prevalent in the modern definitions. The Western anthropologist, aesthetically inclined towards integration, tends to look for commonalities. Three mechanisms in particular serve to reinforce this: the already mentioned tendency to hypostasize individuals; the use of generalized, statistically common features; and reliance on powerful informants. Taken together these operate to suppress divergent perspectives and stories. Further, deep cultural values often have a vague quality to them, a characteristic that can tend to foster the appearance of consensual support.

Against this appearance of broad consensus must be noted the existence of sometimes deep divisions bespeaking widely varying degrees of

---

19. Refer for example to the challenge offered by biological metaphors to individualism, Kallenberg, *Live to Tell*, 17–20.

20 James, Hockey, and Dawson, "Introduction".

consent. Anthropologists often miss an important element of this because of their tendency to intellectualize and objectify social behaviors, missing in the process "the power dimension of meaning."[21] They have a consequent inattention to the power struggles present in the post-structuralist gap between cultural forms and their meanings.

Fourth, and again partially derived from the preceding, the notion of culture as a key to social order is queried. The presence of deep fissures in cultural coherence, as outlined above, coupled with the existence of various forms and degrees of coercive legitimation raise significant doubts about the locus of societal order. Instead of being found in the consensual community of meaning advocated by the modern view, postmoderns point to the power wielded by elites as the substantive factor in societal order. Allied to this, there is a sense in which culture is divorced from human agency in the modern view. Culture becomes "an already constituted force for social order simply waiting to be imposed upon or transmitted externally to human beings who passively internalize it or mechanistically reproduce it."[22] Problematically the factors and agencies that gave rise to this force are still active, continuing to alter the cultural edifice, and consequently the cultural adherents. Strong notions of social determinism are therefore highly questionable.

Fifth, the idea of an assumed cultural stability is questioned. Culture is a flow rather than a given; it exists in a constant state of flux. The factors that historically contributed to the present structures still play a significant role. External factors certainly contribute to this; however the main changes tend to come from internal forces. This may happen by way of previously suppressed perspectives reasserting themselves, or through cultural innovation. Further, there is a natural sense of instability in the human agency driving cultural forms. These forms are constantly subject to reinterpretation and to being reapplied, often differently, within the ever-changing milieu of daily life. Culture is therefore a complex and variable phenomena subject to all the foibles inherent in human social interactions.

Sixthly, Tanner argues that understanding cultures as sharply defined, spatially determined bounded sets is no longer tenable or necessary. Cultural boundaries are fluid and permeable, as evidenced by the increasing impact of globalization. Anthropology is now conducted in the context of global processes that militate against the hypostasizing or reifying effects of the modern approach. Further, consideration must also be given to the historical processes that have always been at play, and which continue to influence cultures. In other words, there is a need to pay far more attention

---

21. Tanner, *Theories of Culture*, 47.
22. Ibid., 50.

to diachronic analysis. Ultimately however, the presentation of cultures as discrete, equal entities is unmasked as a tacitly complicit force in the continuing disparities of global power and economics, a subtle tool for glossing inequalities. For postmoderns it is also revealed as an inherently ethnocentric mechanism, albeit a more subtle and complacent form than the evolutionary model that previously held sway. The very act of "defining" a culture assumes the advantage of a superior perspective.

In conclusion, Tanner argues that while much has substantively changed, little has structurally changed. The modern definition still stands, though now as a considerably chastened and humbled conversation partner. The modern definition has "been decentered or reinscribed within a more primary attention to historical processes."[23] Attention to these processes leads to the breakdown of culture as a static, synchronic object and the emergence of culture as a deeply historic process of tension-filled negotiations; an ongoing process that demands a much more provisional and minimalist descriptive approach. In summary, cultural identity is a more fluid, relational concept than previously thought, perhaps better depicted through the metaphor of "style" than the biological metaphors of a previous generation.

As the preceding demonstrates, Tanner specifically defers to anthropology for definitions of culture. While she does outline a debate between competing definitions there are two important aspects of this worth commenting on. First, the debate is engaged entirely *within* the overarching frame of anthropological discussions. There is no specific attempt to subject the notion of culture to structural theological critique or engagement. Second, the debate is a staged one that operates as a legitimating device for the preferred option she was always already pursuing; the debate was always in the service of presenting a specifically postmodern anthropological articulation of culture.

At this point it is worth noting intrinsic difficulties with her project from an intra-anthropological perspective. Christoph Brumann, for example, has castigated culture critics for their tendency to erect essentialist, reifying, "straw cultures" as the classical model they then rally against for its tendency towards "boundedness, homogeneity, coherence, stability, and structure whereas social reality is characterized by variability, inconsistencies, conflict, change and individual agency . . ."[24] He argues instead that most definitions in the classical mould are agnostic on these points, rendering them investigative avenues rather than settled conclusions.[25] Some of

23. Ibid., 56.
24. Brumann, "Writing for Culture," 1.
25. Ibid., 4.

the implications flowing from this critique will be charted in more detail in the next chapter, however for now it can ironically be noted that Tanner is susceptible to the very critique that in the first place motivated her identification with the postmodern position.

Kevin Vanhoozer

In 2005 Kevin Vanhoozer wrote *The Drama of Doctrine: A Canonical-Linguistic Approach to Christian Theology* in which he sought to both critique and extend George Lindbeck's postliberal cultural-linguistic theology, taking it in a different, dramatic direction.[26] At the heart of his proposal is the Canonical-Linguistic approach expressed in two parts. The first is *scientia*, a process of biblical exegesis in which the emphasis is placed on the polyphonic dramatic quality of Scripture rather than on just its cognitive propositional characteristics. This poetic proposal is then supported by the second part, *sapientia*. Here the aim is to understand the bible as "*prosaic wisdom*: practical reasoning incarnated in ordinary communicative practices. The challenge of prosaic theology is to move from the prose of Scripture to the prose of contemporary culture."[27] It is this practical wisdom that then forms his understanding of contextualization, the movement between text and context he calls dramaturgy.

Vanhoozer asserts elsewhere in the *Drama of Doctrine* that it is culture that "sets the stage, arranges the scenery, and provides the props that supply the setting for theology's work."[28] Culture, a term he uses interchangeably with "context," is defined at two points in his book. The first time it is referred to as "the beliefs, values, and practices that characterize human life together at a particular place and time."[29] The second is an affirmation of Lindbeck's proposal that culture is "the sum total of ways of living that is handed on from generation to generation."[30] Perhaps unwittingly these two definitions provide both a synchronic and diachronic "take" on the term that is defined in an anthropological manner.[31]

26. Lindbeck, *The Nature of Doctrine*; Vanhoozer, *The Drama of Doctrine*.
27. Vanhoozer, *The Drama of Doctrine*, 310. Emphasis original.
28. Ibid., 129.
29. Ibid.
30. Ibid., 309.
31. Refer for example to the categories catalogued in Kroeber and Kluckhohn, *Culture*. See also the typologies offered by Bodley, *Cultural Anthropology*, Winthrop, *Dictionary*. In each case something strikingly similar to Vanhoozer's proposals are central to the anthropological definitions canvassed.

Theology and the Neutrality of Culture

Vanhoozer is attentive however to the possibility that there may be problems with this construction of the concept. In one of his early footnotes he comments "Lindbeck is particularly indebted to Ludwig Wittgenstein's philosophy of language and to Clifford Geertz's cultural anthropology, an indebtedness that prompts one again to wonder whether, and to what extent, theological prolegomena should be properly theological."[32]

By 2007 it is quite possible to see the suspicion guiding this comment beginning to bear fruit in his work. It was during this year that he put together a collection of essays prepared by some of his students to theologically address the topic of culture. This anthology was headed by Vanhoozer's introduction, entitled "What is Everyday Theology? How and Why Christians Should Read Culture."[33] This is an impressive treatment of the subject that may come to represent something quite seminal for its kind. He essentially outlines a contemporary restatement of Tanner's discussion, though attempts to ground it in a more distinctively theological prolegomena.

In terms of defining culture he adopts a broadly chronological schema though his emphasis is really on a thematic presentation. He begins with Tylor's seminal definition (to be addressed in the next chapter) before turning to Tanner's "modern" construct, which in turn gives way to Clifford Geertz's formative analysis, itself challenged by a semiotic position whose innate tendency towards holism is then suitably challenged by Tanner's postmodern posture.[34] Culture, against this background, finally emerges as that which is *"made up of 'works' and 'worlds' of meaning."*[35] As a work culture is what humanity does with the raw material of nature, namely the production of cultural texts—and these are worlds. Worlds are "lived worldviews," active engagements that both inculcate and express a "meaningful environment." In short, "Cultural texts project worlds of meaning that invite us in and encourage us to make our home there."[36]

In what he develops from this Vanhoozer makes striking advances in something like the direction this thesis is advocating. The constructive moment giving rise to this suggestion can be found in his taking up the notion of culture as spiritual formation, reading culture as "projecting ideal forms for our spirits."[37] This almost Platonic note expresses both a creative

---

32. Vanhoozer, *The Drama of Doctrine*, 10 n. 10.

33. Vanhoozer, "What Is Everyday Theology?"

34. Ibid., Refer pp. 24–26 for this and regarding Tanner see esp. notes 24 and 33 on pp. 255 and 256 respectively

35. Ibid., 26, emphasis original.

36. Ibid., 27.

37. Ibid., 31.

and teleological understanding of culture. Something of this mood is also evident during his discussion of Tillich's mantra, religion as the "substance of culture" and culture as the "form of religion," in which he asserts the inherently transcendent nature of culture.[38] In these and other ways Vanhoozer considerably advances the discussion, providing important hints towards thinking more carefully about culture as a structurally theological phenomenon.

Yet despite these important hints Vanhoozer is not yet presenting or necessarily heading directly towards a fully theological analysis of culture. The suggestions he promulgates may be birthed in theological considerations but are grafted onto a foundation built in the social sciences. Hence, for example, he espouses the virtues of an Augustinian system of signification but places it under the tutelage of modern semiotics.[39] In the next section of his discussion he dissects the "modern" commitment to signifying "system" (tacitly embracing Augustine thereby) by the same postmodern analysis Tanner used.[40] His point of origination and therefore his overall orientation towards culture (and this alone) is not ultimately theology and its attributes, but anthropology and its empirical evidence. His definition of culture does not emerge from an ultimately theological analysis but a social scientific one in which the basic competitive structure encountered in Tanner is re-presented, though now with a distinctly hermeneutical twist that shifts the emphasis towards a third preferred model—a broadly semiotic one.[41]

Direct Deferral

This form of the general pattern is similar to the active one in that it involves an explicit deferral to the social scientific framework. It differs in that it does not debate which definition should be deferred to. Instead the theologian concerned has previously selected their preferred understanding from the range of options offered by anthropology, sometimes explaining the choice but more often not, before presenting it in their work with an accompanying description. Implicit in this approach is a perhaps unrealized autonomy from both anthropological and theological debate. The definition is presented as if culture were in all actuality constituted in specifically this way and no other. It acts as a totalizing narrative. This is of course a common occurrence for innumerable words across discourses of all kinds.

38. Ibid., 33.
39. Ibid., 25.
40. Ibid., 26.
41. Ibid.

Theology and the Neutrality of Culture

However, in view of what has already been said about culture this approach now seems to warrant more careful consideration.

The following sets of examples are split between systematic theologians and missiologists. This becomes an important distinction here only because the character of their engagements is quite different. As will be shown, missiologists exhibit a more ambiguous and interactive relationship with the social sciences than systematic theologians. One could suggest various reasons for this, ranging from the effects of specialization through to culture's ostensibly ethnographic and therefore empirical character. However explained, it is nevertheless clear that distinctive attitudes have developed.

Theological Examples

A particularly interesting example occurs in a recent series of articles in *The International Journal of Systematic Theology* by Robert Jenson, broadly entitled Christ as Culture. It is the first one, "Christ as Culture 1: Christ as Polity," that deals in particular with the question of culture, or more specifically with how it relates to the title "Christ."[42] The other two articles investigate distinctive aspects of the overall argument but do not directly address culture again, or at least do not offer treatments that diverge from the central point established in the first article.

In his initial article Jenson begins by commenting

> Let me adduce two standard definitions of culture, from different branches of social theory. We may say that a culture is the mutual behavior of a group in so far as this behavior is sustained by teaching and not only by genetics and physical ecology. Or we can say that a culture is the mutual behavior of a group of persons in so far as this can be abstracted from those doing the behaving, as in itself a coherent system of mutually determining signs.[43]

Here Jenson unequivocally places his project within the broad ambit of social theory so perhaps unsurprisingly he goes on to describe the church as itself a culture, one that "like any community, is responsible to cultivate her culture, and can lose her identity if she does not."[44] This ecclesiological anchoring of his understanding of culture is but a platform for he then notes

---

42. Jenson, "Christ as Culture 1."
43. Ibid., 323–24.
44. Ibid., 324.

Culture in a Post-Secular Context

> Now—coming at last to the matter of these essays—if the church is the body of Christ, that is, if the church is the availability of Christ in and for the world, and if this body of Christ, the church, is a culture, it follows that Christ is a culture. And the sense of the "is" in "Christ is a culture" will be the sense in which each of us must say that he or she "is" his or her body.[45]

The argument that follows is sophisticated but what is important is the central place accorded a social scientific definition of culture, and the consequences that flow from this, especially for Christology. While having sympathy for his intent, the result is to imbue the heart of the Christian enterprise with a social scientific gloss that then flows through into the rest of his theological project. For example, he goes on to suggest "Augustine's 'polity of God' is not a polity only in heaven; it is—however imperfectly—a polity now, and just so in conflict with other polities, with what Augustine called the 'earthly polity', the polities of this age as a class. Which is of course simply to say again that it is itself a polity, also in this age."[46]

It is doubtful that Augustine would fully recognize the nature of the polity being adduced here, however this comment is particularly interesting for another reason. So far it has been suggested that Jenson is building on social scientific understandings of culture that are predicated on the essential neutrality of the social scientific understandings. This means that not only all instances of distinctive community and polity but the church and Christ himself, precisely as *totus Christus*, are all together *equally* arrayed as cultures. Here the full effects of the last sentence of the previous quote become evident. Just as each polity participates equally in being a "polity," taking on every aspect of what being a polity is, then so also every culture participates in what being a culture is, as this concept has been defined by social theory. Each of the cultures just described are therefore all equally subsumed within the objectifying gaze of the social sciences. If all are equally cultures then so too are they all equally examinable in cultural, hence social scientific terms.

The significant implications of this argument can really only be intimated here because it is the overarching purpose of this thesis to argue the contrary view. While Jenson's analysis represents an admirable attempt to articulate an important description of Christ it nonetheless fails to escape its originating foundations and therefore remains captive to them. Jenson does not envisage the possibility that in making culture the controlling category of his analysis he is concurrently subsuming Christ within an alternative paradigm of understanding. If culture is indeed inherently a theologically

45. Ibid., 325.
46. Ibid., 329.

directed and shaped construct then his framework requires considerable rethinking.

An important and highly influential theologian also appearing in this category is H. Richard Niebuhr. In 1951 he outlined a series of solutions to what he termed "the enduring problem" or the many-sided and confused debate about how Christ and Culture should relate to each other. These solutions were ostensibly arrayed as a neutral taxonomy although Niebuhr's preference for the transformer option was considered by many an open secret.[47] For a long time his treatment of Christ and culture has been seminal, deeply informing the views of many of his contemporaries and more especially scores of students, and a great many theologians from succeeding generations. He still remains an important figure to engage with despite criticisms that attack core structural issues in his presentation.[48]

Niebuhr begins by observing that neither the cultural nor Christian poles are easily reducible; both exhibit significant variety and can consequently only be defined in tenuous fashion. Yet these supposedly tenuous definitions, despite their inherent reductiveness, are not similarly tenuous in application. They are applied in his work as controlling paradigms that anchor his project, and their specific articulation is therefore critical for his taxonomy. For our purposes two aspects of his description of culture are of particular significance, especially when taken together. First, Niebuhr borrows directly from the anthropologist Bronislaw Malinowski when defining culture as "the 'artificial, secondary environment' which man superimposes on the natural."[49] He goes on to suggest, "Though we cannot venture to define the 'essence' of this [concept] culture, we can describe some of its chief characteristics."[50] These characteristics are then listed: it is inherently social; purposeful in terms of human achievement; based in values; which are good for humanity; and which are realized in temporal and material ways; which must therefore be conserved; and, he finally notes, it is pluralistic.[51]

Second, he comments "A theologian's definition of the term must, in the nature of the case, be a layman's definition since he cannot presume

---

47. Refer for example to Peter Gathje's discussion of Yoder's objections, supported by Hauerwas and Willimon and countered by James Gustafson; Gathje, "A Contested Classic," 30.

48. Ibid., rehearses the main contours of the discussion.

49. Niebuhr, *Christ and Culture*, 32. In this he is quoting from the work of Malinowski, refer for example Malinowski, *A Scientific Theory of Culture*.

50. Niebuhr, *Christ and Culture*.

51. Ibid., 32–39.

to enter into the issues raised by professional anthropologists . . ."[52] It is a description "of the phenomenon without theological interpretation . . ."[53] This does not imply for him an elimination of such interpretation but a relegation of it in terms of priority; it is a secondary step. When presented in this manner culture becomes a raw datum or resource that is then available for theological engagement, but an engagement that has one critical circumscription. There is no theological ability to penetrate the notion of culture itself, no means by which a theologian can get beneath or behind the raw material of the definition.

Culture, as anthropologically defined, is in this framework a technically developed resource that must be accepted as presented. For Niebuhr, the professional theologian does not have the technical ability to encroach on the professional arena of anthropology in order to query their technical pronouncements. There is no need to trace the outlines of the heritage this view springs from for the classic modernist approach to enquiry, predicated on the presumed objectivity and neutrality of scientific discourse, has already been well enough rehearsed in postmodern critiques.

For Niebuhr the entire category of culture is therefore controlled by a neutral, anthropologically-defined denotation behind which there is no substantive theological access and in which there is no correlative theological implication. He effectively defers to the then increasingly "scientific" discipline of cultural anthropology for a description of one of his two key terms. Not surprisingly this grants the anthropological definition a pervasive presence in his otherwise theological discussion. Both have influenced mission thinking by asking it to think carefully about culture, hence what follows is an attempt to further this goal.

Missiological Examples

The missiological discussion of this model is separated out for extensive treatment not primarily because it is a significant counterpart to the preceding theological analysis, though it is this, but because it is a considerably more complex frame of reference. Where theologians are largely positive about or affirming of social theory in their engagements, missiologists tend to be more ambivalent in the wake of a strong negative view promulgated by a significant coterie within the discipline.

Cultural anthropology has been in conversation with missiology since its inception, animated from the beginning by shared concerns that often

---

52. Ibid., 30.
53. Ibid.

gave rise to a context of mutual dialogue.⁵⁴ The early, though not always reciprocal, contributions are numerous; Bishop Robert Codrington's study of the Melanesians, especially his analysis of *mana*, is a central example, as is the work of Edwin Smith, missionary to South Africa and former president of the Royal Anthropological Institute. In later Roman Catholicism the mutual nature of the conversation has been particularly fruitful, with the influential *Anthropological Quarterly* representing the interests of Catholic anthropologists while the "Vienna School" of Father Wilhelm Schmidt provided another exceptional platform for discussion, including that based around the journal *Anthropos*.⁵⁵

The influence of linguistic anthropology would become highly significant as a catalyst for dialogue, with the Summer Institute of Linguistics providing a seminal framework and scholarly home. Eugene Nida, for example, bequeathed Dynamic Equivalence theory to missiology while Kenneth Pike's extensive work in tagmemic linguistics has been foundational for much mission work. The influential journal *Practical Anthropology* (which later became absorbed by *Missiology*) was begun and maintained by missiologists trained in linguistics, most notably by successive editors William Smalley and Charles Taber.⁵⁶ Not surprisingly then there are a plethora of missiological authors offering positive affirmations of anthropology, approving anthropological definitions of culture and embracing in the process the trialogue between theology, anthropology, and mission.⁵⁷

One very influential figure has been Paul Hiebert. As Darrell Whiteman notes, Paul Hiebert has been seminal in missiological discussions of culture and contextualization.⁵⁸ From amongst his most prominent literary outputs it is probably *Anthropological Insights for Missionaries* that has proven most central for readers, scholars and practitioners alike.⁵⁹ In this book

54. Hiebert, "Missions and Anthropology," 166.

55. Refer Smalley, "Anthropological Study," 4ff.

56. Hiebert, *Anthropological Reflections*, 9. He is historically inaccurate however in according the work of Gleason, Pike, Nida, et al. the status of first substantial contact between mission and anthropology, refer above for details of earlier contact. It is more accurate to record them as the first substantive linguistic anthropologists. Harvie Conn comments that these early threads all contributed to the emergence of a new cross-disciplinary discipline, missionary anthropology, refer Conn, *Eternal Word and Changing Worlds*, 138ff.

57. Here Paul Hiebert makes use of Harvie Conn, who specifically develops the notion of a trialogue with particular emphasis on the missiological connection, refer Conn, *Eternal Word and Changing Worlds*, 10, 46 and esp. 128, 130, Hiebert, *Anthropological Reflections*, 10–15.

58. Whiteman, "Anthropological Reflections" esp. 54–60.

59. Paul G. Hiebert, *Anthropological Insights*.

Culture in a Post-Secular Context

he argues the relevancy of anthropological insights for missionaries, suggesting that they can aid the missiological endeavor and associated research both theoretically and practically. In the practical sense he thinks it provides tools important for the process of exegeting contemporary culture, while in the theoretical sense it contributes towards a holistic or comprehensive understanding of people and societies, an advantage he tries to ensure deeply informs his overall approach to the contextualization process.

Hiebert carefully delineates this approach by first describing what it is not. He eschews popular reductionistic models because they bifurcate the physical and spiritual elements of humanity; and argues against stratigraphic approaches for their lack of full integration and implicit secularizing tendencies. He instead contends for a holistic perspective where "We must learn what theology and the sciences have to teach us about people and weave these insights into a comprehensive understanding of human beings."[60] In such an anthropocentric model anthropology is unsurprisingly the integrating human science that shows "how the various insights each discipline brings relate to each other . . ."[61] It is the primary mediating discipline, providing "us with insights into various structures of empirical reality."[62] This is not to say Hiebert is advocating a purely immanent project for he is decidedly not, rather he reserves for theology the central role of providing "an overall picture of the building, the builder, and key events in its history."[63]

What is of particular interest here is the way culture is then handled. Hiebert moves on to devote the next two chapters to various aspects of the gospel's interactions with culture. When defining culture he frames it in distinctively anthropological terms, defining it as "'the more or less integrated systems of ideas, feelings, and values and their associated patterns of behavior and products shared by a group of people who organize and regulate what they think, feel, and do.'"[64] The effects of this definition can be seen in Hiebert's final depiction of his model, which he suggests consists of a complex interplay between the Evaluative, Affective and Cognitive features that characterize his understanding of World View. These all work together to form a foundation that builds into and therefore heavily

---

60. Ibid., 26, also refer pp. 23–26 for his descriptions of the other models.
61. Ibid.
62. Ibid., 27.
63. Ibid.
64. Ibid., 30. Refer pp. 30–56 for a fuller description and discussion of this definition.

Theology and the Neutrality of Culture

influences all of the various sociocultural aspects, of which religion is one.[65] This is the critical step.

For Hiebert, anthropology reports on the empirical reality of cultural constructs of which religion is just one of the elements *within it*, providing information that then forms a neutral datum for missiological engagement. In this theoretical aspect Hiebert is broadly in line with the various authors described above. Culture is a category defined by social theory that is then used and manipulated by theologians and missiologists for their particular purposes as if it had no bearing upon the theological nature of the underlying project. In this respect the neutrality of culture as a concept defined anthropologically is simply accepted. Hiebert does not envisage in this process the ability to theologically peek behind the anthropological veil in order to discern a specifically theological understanding of what culture is.

Equally important in missiology is the work of Charles Kraft who perhaps best describes his perspective on culture, anthropology, and the social sciences in *Anthropology for Christian Witness*, though his seminal work remains the earlier *Christianity in Culture*.[66] The later work is more interesting however because in it he specifically deals with a critique of the earlier book that provides an interesting set of insights.[67] In his earlier publication Kraft had stated that culture was, in and of itself, a neutral structure that people inhabited, representing a tool or map available for human use, but one that does not predetermine the ethics of use. This bears a striking familiarity with some of the models already encountered, especially Hiebert's.

Sherwood Lingenfelter challenged this view.[68] He suggested culture was in fact deeply implicated in the presence of inequalities, representing a conduit for the pervasive presence of unequal power relations. People are active agents in the construction of culture and construct it in line with their own individual or group interests. Others become entangled in the various "social images" perpetrated by these social constructions, which thereby imprison them in structures deeply antithetical to Christian principles. Lingenfelter argued that Jesus Christ challenges not only these systems but all of the structures that give rise to them. For him the gospel inherently contradicts culture.

To the contrary, Kraft argues, "People are *not* determined by cultural structuring . . ."[69] It is notable that this statement is less emphatic than his

---

65. Ibid.
66. Kraft, *Christianity in Culture*, Kraft, *Anthropology for Christian Witness*.
67. Kraft, *Anthropology for Christian Witness*, 33–36..
68. Lingenfelter, *Transforming Culture*.
69. Kraft, *Anthropology for Christian Witness*, 34.

previous ones because he is aware that, in retrospect, his earlier views may have been too magnanimous; peoples' choices have a greater effect than he had previously thought. Cultural structuring may actually be influenced such as to negatively skew the playing field, leading to a tendency for people to choose inappropriate behaviors. However, "this fact is a comment on the nature of persons, not the nature of the structures within which we function."[70] For him cultural structures are infected by sin but not intrinsically so; they are ultimately influenced by people and it therefore remains a fundamentally people-oriented problem.

Two further points are central to Kraft's proposal. First, he makes a distinction between society and culture, or what he also describes as personal behaving and cultural structuring.[71] In this there is a radical inversion of cultural determinism, the so-called superorganic (structuralist) view.[72] He argues there is no power in cultural structures to impel conformity; people behave as they do because they choose to. Even habitual patterns are founded on initial choices that are then constantly refreshed; each choice or refreshing in equal measure an opportunity to choose otherwise, albeit the conditioning tends to solidify over time.

Second, Kraft takes up the language of worldview as a way of describing "the culturally structured assumptions, values, and commitments/allegiances underlying a people's perception of reality and their responses to those perceptions."[73] He considers worldview a structural element of culture and therefore, in the same way as culture, considers it *not* to be determinative of behavior. Underlying structures are neutral in and of themselves, and are therefore not structurally inclined relative to sin one way or the other; they are instead directed by people towards particular perspectives.

Kraft initially received a lot of critical attention in missiological literature from his target audience, though attitudes have since thawed considerably.[74] Throughout the period of initial suspicion, and at considerable personal cost, Kraft managed to continue articulating a comprehensive vision of a missiology grounded in the appropriation of anthropological insights. In common with Paul Hiebert, Kraft is arguing that culture is a

---

70. Ibid., 35.

71. Ibid., 36–38.

72. Refer Wan, "A Critique of Charles Kraft." He argues Kraft is a functionalist. This commentary represents perhaps the best reflection on Kraft's reception to date, including within it the authors' own journey from a negative perspective to an embracing one, as testified to by some of his later works on ethnohermeneutics.

73. Kraft, *Anthropology for Christian Witness*, 52, refer 51–68 for his discussion of worldviews.

74. Wan, "A Critique of Charles Kraft."

neutral construct whose content is determined by people, and therefore whose direction or shape is not intrinsically related to its underlying conceptualization or articulation.

These two missiologists, Paul Hiebert and Charles Kraft, have considerably advanced the case for accepting the efficacy and value of an anthropological perspective on culture. They both conceive of it as an important input into the theological process of contextualization, providing critical information for understanding the culture side of that engagement. As was most clearly articulated by Kraft, anthropological definitions of culture are considered inherently neutral accounts of underlying human structures and hence as a necessary tool for understanding the various interactions encountered therein.

These two examples embrace generally positive views about the relationship between anthropology and theology however others argue for varying amounts of negative correlations Harvie Conn argues that the relationship was never especially friendly. Instead of the mutual dialogue of enrichment the theological proponents of anthropological theory portray he presents an at times warlike relationship, one steeped in an old antipathy, an "angry dialogue" that stems from unresolved (perhaps unresolvable) eighteenth-century tensions.[75] He suggests Enlightenment rationalism confronted and effectively, if not always obviously, dispensed with Christian supernaturalism—to the particular dismay of Evangelical scholars.[76] The shared concerns and consequent dialogue noted in the positive perspective above have therefore always been shadowed by an underlying uncertainty and at times outright rejection of the way the early tensions were apparently resolved. The abiding suspicion has been that the "resolution" was founded in a rationalism that orientated and circumscribed supernaturalism such that it was tacitly, and often explicitly, obviated.[77]

An introduction to the negative view has already been provided through Lingenfelter's objections, but other more extensive treatments exist. In what now seems an irenic analysis Charles Taber, *To Understand the World, to Save the World: The Interface Between Missiology and the Social*

---

75. Paul Hiebert terms it a love/hate relationship born from intimacy and brotherhood, refer Hiebert, "Missions and Anthropology," 165 and 178.

76. Conn, *Eternal Word and Changing Worlds*, 46ff.

77. The following discussion could also have been conducted under the auspices of "contextualization," though space precludes this. This would have seen Shoki Coe and Liberation theologians, for example, arrayed over against David Hesselgrave and other similarly conservative Evangelicals as representatives of a positive and negative view respectively. Harvie Conn, for example, notes the central role of contextualization, see Ibid., 128ff.

Sciences calls for a "penetrating and critical understanding of the social sciences . . ."[78] Amongst other things his work focuses on two aspects of the relationship. First he queries the apparent monopoly anthropological and sociological categories have on the definition of central features of the missiological landscape. Importantly he is not querying the dominance of social science constructs *per se* but of specific social science disciplines as against other disciplines. There is, he argues, a distinct tendency to ignore economics and political science, even when they may afford a better understanding of key cultural elements.

His second concern is more pertinent and prefigures aspects of the critique being offered in this thesis. He notes a tendency for missiologists to naively imbibe the premises of cultural anthropology through an uncritical incorporation of social science theory into missiological theory and practice.[79] He argues that by their very nature, their avowedly scientific disposition, the social sciences are predicated on an enlightenment perspective ideologically centered in rationalism. Overly simplistic recourse to such theories fundamentally impacts the framework of missiological discussions, leading to the potential for competing presuppositions within the bedrock of key missiological premises. Taber argues missiologists need to be more sophisticated in both their awareness of this fundamental distinction and in the way they allow this insight to characterize their interactions with the social sciences.[80]

Whereas Taber draws back from recognizing an explicit disjunction between theology and the social sciences the New Zealander Bruce Nicholls, in *Contextualization: A Theology of Gospel and Culture*, is not always so inhibited.[81] He argues the need to acknowledge the existence and importance of supracultural factors in the contextualizing process. These are factors arising from the reality of the spiritual realm, a realm only perceived through the eyes of faith not science. From this foundation he sounds a similar though more strident and discordant note of caution to that offered by Taber, positing the fundamental inability of secular anthropological and sociological theories to render an intelligible account of these supracultural factors. For Nicholls human culture is not the passive and neutral entity the social scientists depict, the fall and consequent universal degradation

---

78. Taber, *To Understand the World, to Save the World*, 2.
79. Ibid., 30ff for example.
80. Ibid., 48ff.
81. Nicholls, *Contextualization*. Nicholls is admittedly a difficult person to pigeonhole since his negative rhetoric is offset by a much more liberal personal stance, as his ecclesial background testifies to. In what follows attention is paid to the specific outlook presented in his work on contextualization with the proviso that he now adopts a much more ecumenical perspective. My thanks to John Roxborogh for these observations.

precluding any such conclusion. Culture is therefore not the value-free structure envisaged by Kraft. Instead, for Nicholls, every perspective on culture necessarily presupposes a particular view on human nature and the natural/supernatural relationship.

Using Mbiti as his primary interlocutor Nicholls presses his case against the possibility of cultural neutrality. Mbiti, according to Nicholls, calls for African culture to "extend its hospitality to the Gospel as an honored guest that, hopefully, may stay for many centuries and millennia as the case may be."[82] In stark contrast Nicholls delineates the encounter as essentially conflictual in nature, with culture the scene of a supernatural conflict between the kingdoms of God and of Satan. Culture, as a human product, is a structure built on choice but Nicholls understands the operation of choice quite differently to Kraft. He argues culture always contains within its contemporary forms the decisions people have previously made, especially those regarding this supernatural conflict. This renders it inherently, hence structurally, oriented by these decisions. He then argues that the pervasive effects of the fall are determinative. The gospel can never be understood as an honored guest of culture for "it is always its judge and redeemer."[83]

Nicholls consequently distinguishes two levels of contextualization—cultural and theological. The cultural realm refers to the surface levels of culture, or the institutions, traits, artifacts and other observable phenomena that constitute it. This, according to him, is the level at which anthropologists and sociologists can and should operate. By contrast, the theological level refers to the deep structures of cosmology, worldview and values, a level he thinks should be the peculiar domain of the theologian.[84] It is these deeper structures, those which Kraft suggests are neutral, which Nicholls suggests the gospel should, and in fact does target (even if theoreticians fail to acknowledge this).

What is not entirely evident from this discussion of the positive and negative perspectives described above is the relative weight or influence these two respective positions have on missiological discussions. It is perhaps fair to suggest that missiology has grown to embody a predominately positive view of anthropology that in some places borders on a consensus.[85] The voices directly protesting this state of affairs, as opposed to those

82. Ibid., 15.

83. Ibid.

84. Ibid., 24.

85. Consider, for example, the constituency of Steve Bevans various models of contextual theologizing, per Bevans, *Models*. This is also perhaps not surprising given that by 1978 Paul Hiebert could suggest "anthropological assumptions now pervade much of modern western thought . . ." Hiebert, "Missions and Anthropology," 165.

uttering cautionary words, are a distinct minority all too easily dismissed because of their rather overt affiliations with fundamentalist theological positions (here understood in a pejorative sense). Scholars like David Hesselgrave, Byang Kato, Don Carson, and so on form this latter, deeply embattled constituency. It is hoped that this thesis may contribute somewhat to an at least partial vindication of their underlying impulse, even if it does so in a way that also critically engages some of their core elements.

So far discussion has concentrated on two modes of engagement that have in common an explicit deferral to social scientific, or more specifically anthropological, definitions of culture. This is not the only way the relationship can be conceived however. A large segment of the theological encounters with the term culture are conducted in a quite different way. It is time now to turn to the passive mode and consider the various manifestations of this approach.

The Passive Mode

This mode is both easily explained and readily recognized so not too much attention will be paid to it *per se*. The analysis of this approach will focus on just two examples, one drawn from theology and one from missiology. Particular attention however will be paid to the notion of passivity and what this entails in terms of how readers are being asked to engage with the idea of culture. The central contention is that in the absence of a specific denotation for the term the currently prevalent models of culture become the *de facto* basis for understanding the term, raising in the process the question of which models this brings to the fore. The argument made here is that social scientific models, and in particular anthropological ones, are the most logical sources to fill the void given their contemporary domination of the field.

The passive approach can be quickly dispensed with in its primary form because it is no more than the use of the term culture without definition or explanation. In theological publications this approach is particularly notable in the work of systematic theologians, perhaps especially and surprisingly so in introductory texts. Stanley Grenz in *Theology for the Community of God*, for example, provides a discussion of theological method during which the question of culture is raised, but in which no definition is subsequently provided.[86] In similar fashion Millard Erickson's highly influential *Christian Theology* proceeds by discussing culture under theological method but is equally shy regarding its content; he too fails to define it.[87]

86. Grenz, *Theology for the Community of God*, 14ff.
87. Erickson, *Christian Theology*, 62–84.

Both authors move on to use the term and associated words repeatedly throughout their respective works but provide no further explicit information as to the meaning or content they thereby intend.

This raises the question of where such meaning comes from, of how a reader determines an understanding of the term culture when it is not explicitly defined. This sort of question has been most actively considered by scholars in the field of hermeneutics, especially in the groundbreaking work of Hans Georg Gadamer.[88] He provides a useful analytical tool for beginning to explore how such meaning arises in his application of Martin Heidegger's notion of fore-structured understanding. He describes Heidegger's framework as follows: "a person trying to understand a text is prepared for it to tell him something. That is why a hermeneutically trained consciousness must be, from the start, sensitive to the text's alterity."[89] Sensitivity to the alterity of the text is achieved in the realization that one should be "aware of one's own bias, so that the text can present itself in all its otherness and thus assert its own truth against one's own fore-meaning."[90]

The presentation of "textual otherness" that Gadamer describes has two dimensions. In terms of the text itself it involves the ability of the material being read to arrest the reader, to interrupt their fore-understanding by way of a specific signal that calls into question what Gadamer calls the "tyranny of prejudice." The signal, or what Gadamer terms the "interruption," is a textual indication that there either is or may be an alternative meaning intended from that which the reader may already have in mind. On the side of the reader it requires an attentive openness, a willingness to suspend putative fore-meanings in the presence of such a signal. Given these conditions, a signal such as an explicit definition and attentive openness to it, the reader is alerted to the author's intent that they should follow their lead rather than simply subscribe to their own implicit inclinations. If, as was noted above, there is no such signal or interruption indicating some intra-textual meaning/s for culture, then what definition pertains?

Before considering this further, one more element must be brought into the discussion, namely an understanding of mutual participation, or of how text lacking an interruption is read. Reading for understanding is predicated in part on a reasonable expectation that in the normal

---

88. In the translator's preface to his most important publication Weinsheimer and Marshall offer the following tribute: "Truth and Method is one of the two or three most important works of this [twentieth] century on the philosophy of humanistic studies. The book is powerful, exciting but undeniably difficult . . . it gathers the ripe fruit of a lifetime's reading, teaching and thinking." Gadamer, *Truth and Method*, xi.

89. Ibid., 271.

90. Ibid., 271–72.

course of engagement with a contemporaneous culturally aligned text the reader would be participating in a common frame of understanding with the author. James McClendon, arguing for slightly different purposes but identifying the same underlying attribute, notes that in oral communication "Uttered words are not mere labels changeable at will, but constitutive speech acts that engage their users in networks of practice . . ."[91] In other words the speaker (and hence author) builds a world of understanding in which the hearer (reader) participates, but where there is a high degree of contextual commonality between author and reader then a significant amount of what is spoken or written may be considered self-evident. That is, they do not require explanation because they fall within the boundaries of a common pre-formed understanding.

In a similar vein to McClendon, but more pertinently for textual hermeneutics, Kevin Vanhoozer says much the same thing in his analysis of the role genres play in writing. These he considers analogous to Alasdair MacIntyre's notion of "practice," hence he suggests "a given genre embodies a social expectation, an expectation that the hearer/reader will respond appropriately . . ."[92] Genre is in this view an element of "cultural rationality," a rule-governed "socializing practice" guiding interlocutors into a process of mutual participation. Quoting Carolyn Miller he notes "Form shapes the response of the reader or listener to substance by providing instruction, so to speak, about how to perceive and interpret; this guidance disposes the audience to anticipate, to be gratified, to respond in a certain way."[93] This means that a mutual pre-formed understanding will be determinative for meaning in the absence of any signal or interruption disrupting it.

It is the case therefore that in this absence, of a signal or some interruption indicating a changed context, or a shift from the set of "reasonable expectations," the reader participating in the same cultural environment as the author will assume the author is intending nothing more than the meaning the reader already had in mind before reading. Therefore, in the absence of a signal the text inevitably succumbs to prejudicial fore-meaning, to what is effectively a semi-autonomous reading.[94] It is not entirely autonomous because the shared context of meaning constrains creativity and genre, as a rule-conducted practice, acts to broadly circumscribe the range of acceptable interpretations. This formal description sets out a process that actually

---

91. McClendon and Murphy, *Witness 3*, 297.
92. Vanhoozer, *The Drama of Doctrine*, 215.
93. Ibid., referring to Miller, "Genre as Social Action,": 159.
94. This use of prejudice accords with Gadamer, *Truth and Method*, 268ff.

Theology and the Neutrality of Culture

remains hidden since it expresses the largely unconscious attribution by the reader of meaning to the various words used by the author.

As the foregoing demonstrates, this unconscious attribution of meaning does not occur in a vacuum. It happens within the context of an overarching framework or paradigm that forms the theoretical structure guiding and directing the diverse range of social, economic, political, scientific, and so on, networks gathered within it.[95] In the West, as has already been discussed in the introduction, the prevailing paradigm is the secular perspective. It is therefore this secular frame of reference that is the primary producer and maintainer of meaning for late twentieth- or early twenty-first-century Western thinkers. It is from this pool of candidates that all of the examples discussed in this chapter are taken. This is therefore the context from which definitions of culture are likely to be drawn. Even amongst theologians this is highly likely as extraordinarily few of them undertake to *theologically* define culture (which is why a recovery of tradition is so central in the later chapters of this thesis).

At this point some preliminary description of what this paradigm might consist of is important in order to understand the form of meaning production being envisaged. Taylor is useful, summarizing the general shape in a way that closely resembles the account to be given in the chapters to follow.[96] According to him the presiding paradigm is a coalescence of 'closed world structures' (paradigmatic ways of thinking) constructed on two strongly related premises—that the natural world can be separated from the supernatural and then further, that the natural world can be inhabited without recourse to the supernatural, and hence can exist autonomously.[97] From one angle this represents Taylor's modern moral order not only legitimated now but become the normalized state of the West; a hegemony resourced by the powerful normalizing narrative of secularity that has taken upon itself the ability to position all other discourses. In this secular context it is the material, humanistic and rational narratives that hold sway, hence the prominence of the scientific.

---

95. For a discussion of "paradigms" indicating their usefulness and limitations refer Bosch, *Transforming Mission*, 183–89. Note in particular the constellation of correlates he gathers at p. 185. Something of the sweeping generalization of these broad categories is in mind here.

96. Refer especially Taylor, "What Is Secularity?"

97. The influence of both Wittgenstein and Heidegger are clearly evident throughout Taylor's description hence something like Wittgenstein's language games is at play in the closed world structures, as is Heidegger's sense of such structures having no requirement for transcendence, see Ibid., 57–60.

Culture in a Post-Secular Context

The sway of the secular narratives is not as complete or embedded as this description makes it seem. As Taylor indicates so well it is an intersecting discourse, a narrative of narratives, one that is actually deeply ambiguous and fraught, filled with claims and counter-claims. Further, the counter-claims are not just promulgated by those preferring supernatural explanations; they are just as vociferously presented by materialist and other thinkers. One only has to think of Martin Heidegger, Slavôj Žižek, or post-structuralism to entertain this thought.[98] The production of meaning is therefore exceedingly complex and the malleability of culture allows this complexity full reign within its precincts. Each major philosophical theory has its correlate understanding of culture. Perhaps unsurprisingly it is this very complexity, accompanied as it is by a significant proliferation of meanings, which creates the conditions needed for the emergence of simplicity in meaning.

In the face of the increasing avalanche of meanings for the term "culture" a natural process of simplification seems to have been triggered whereupon the vast range of meanings are ruthlessly sifted, *lex parsimoniae*. The law of parsimony (as manifested in Ockham's razor) is usually invoked within the sciences to adjudicate between two theories making the same prediction. In this case the one involving the simplest structure (whether stylistically or ontologically, though preferably both) is favored. Something like this happens with culture as well, with only a few of the myriad definitions gaining traction in the world at large. Tylor, Geertz, Kroeber, and so on offer examples of exactly this kind of enduring definition.

The key point here is that culture is now generally defined relative to only a few models that have penetrated deeply into the Western consciousness. Social sciences such as cultural anthropology and sociology, along with closely aligned crossover disciplines like cultural studies, and various other related sub-disciplines, are the dominant producers and promulgators of these meanings and have therefore become the most important purveyors of understandings of culture in the contemporary West. Their dominant models are everywhere, infiltrating almost all of the scholarly disciplines and popular outlets such that they have gained center stage in the popular imagination.[99] Something of this prevalence and penetration has already become evident in the various examples given in this chapter. In the normal course of engagement therefore it can be readily assumed that a Western reader of Western texts reading the word "culture" without an interrupting

---

98. Refer for some discussion of this point to ibid., 74–75.

99. Note for example the degree of infiltration suggested by Robert Borofsky in Watson, "Archaeology, Anthropology, and the Culture Concept": 684. For a more extensive commentary refer Brumann, "Writing for Culture," 9ff. For example, he notes the emergence of a "'culture cult' in civic society . . . ," to quote Jack Eller.

definition would rely on one of these few populist social scientific understandings to fill the definitional gap.

The "populist" qualification is important as the culture concept is quickly becoming an ever more abstract and amorphous construct increasingly divorced from its roots in the social scientific discipline of anthropology. The anthropologist Christoph Brumann, for example, argues "Whether anthropologists like it or not, it appears that people—and not only those with power—*want* culture, and they often want it in precisely the bounded, reified, essentialized, and timeless fashion that most of us now reject."[100] Notwithstanding this Brumann still acknowledges the presence of both an anthropological anchoring and voice within these models, though the shape and extent of these insights remains contentious, especially in light of "cultural fundamentalisms."[101] The framework offered by Kathryn Tanner above perhaps best illustrates the shape of two plausible populist outlines still anchored in and reflective of core anthropological sensibilities.

So far the discussion has concentrated on what could be called a purely passive approach, a fairly self-evident category of deferral as found in Grenz and Erickson. Not all passive approaches are so inert, exhibiting such a total disengagement from the definitional task. Some writers make use, however unwittingly at times, of implied meanings. In these cases no explicit definition for culture is given but the term is used in such a way that it is clear the author probably has some particular underlying meaning/s in mind. In these cases the context of use is important because it provides the reader with clues that trigger a signal, one suggesting the author has an intention in mind that might interrupt the readers' fore-understanding. This initial reaction is tempered however by a lack of certainty and clarity such that the signal becomes weak or scrambled. This causes the reader to examine the text with a heightened sense of anticipation that is then never finally resolved by the text itself, forcing the reader to fall back on their fore-understanding, and a semi-autonomous reading ensues anyway. This type of approach is best seen by way of example; hence the illustrations below demonstrate this 'weak' version of the passive model.

In 1991 Thomas F. O'Meara, Professor of theology at the University of Notre Dame, wrote the second of a two part analysis of nineteenth-century German theology *Church and Culture: German Catholic Theology, 1860–1914*. O'Meara's intent, as clearly indicated by the title, was to commentate on the relationship between philosophy and theology through the

---

100. Brumann, "Writing for Culture," 11, emphasis original.

101. Ibid., 12, and p. 10 for the term cultural fundamentalism, derived from Verena Stolcke.

latter half of the nineteenth century, tracing its course through the work of five major German Catholic theologians. It is in his words, "a narrative of theological struggles and directions, and a presentation of major exemplary theologians."[102] This narrative turns out to be the story of theological engagement, both positive and negative, with German modernity. He argues that this modernity has indelibly shaped the theologies that emerged; each theology reacting to, addressing and consequently marked by the "style" of the epoch in which they were produced. An epoch is German culture as it presents itself within a short, specified time period. When these epochs are chronologically linked together into a single temporal procession, the changing face of German culture as a whole is described over the approximately fifty years he is investigating. An understanding of culture is therefore central to his project.

Contrary to expectations however a close reading of the text fails to reveal a single explicit definition of culture. There are hints and inferences but in the absence of a definite cohering center these become relatively isolated intimations that tend to point the reader in several different directions. The first such direction is towards an amalgam of philosophy and religion, hence he comments he is interested in "fundamental theology, that intersection of philosophy and religion, which in the last analysis involves the cultural expression of faith."[103] His interest, he comments further, is primarily in the intellectual development of theology as it traversed modernity and how "faith—with reserve and critique—could express itself through modernity."[104] In this use culture is dealt with almost entirely as a philosophical predicate, one reducible in the end to a peculiarly German modernity (with a hoped for theological twist). Yet O'Meara also uses the term culture in other contexts that would seem to indicate some other meaning should be invoked.

He more clearly indicates the possibility of culture in his reference to a "cultivated bourgeoisie," a concept he overtly twins with *Bildung* and hence with *Kultur*, though this is rather cryptically signaled by referring to culture in "the German sense of that word."[105] This is an ambiguous reference since there is no single German sense to refer to but two and it is not entirely clear that he is even *necessarily* linking with the dominant one. What the link with *bildung* does is to focus attention on just one of these two aspects of the *Kultur* framework, eschewing in the process the other one: the *Volk* sense

102. O'Meara, *Church and Culture*, 3.
103. Ibid., 11.
104. Ibid.
105. Ibid., 15.

Theology and the Neutrality of Culture

of nationalism heralded by Herder and Fichte. He concentrates instead on that aspect dealing with elitist ideals such as notions like high art, philosophy and so on embody. This is most clearly illustrated by examining the synchronology he provides as an appendix, where the culture column refers almost exclusively to major European examples of literature, art, and music.

A third prospect for his definition of culture comes when he delineates an historical understanding that is much more in the *Volk* tradition, though a somewhat reduced philosophical variation of it. He describes the period he is covering as a succession of epochs, each distinctive in method, outlook and philosophy; each interacting with and engaging through Germanic society in the context of various important historical socio-political events. Classicist, Idealist, Romantic, and Baroque philosophical influences, in particular, intertwine with political events throughout the period, with varying degrees of continuity and discontinuity, interspersed by periods of transition, all of which are finally drawn together and merged into a single, cohesive philosophical narrative.[106] This menagerie of influences, reminiscent in some ways of contemporary culture theory, is however reduced to an almost purely philosophical patina such that the three "cultural alterations" separating the period before 1830 from that after it amount to no more than three distinctive shifts in philosophical positions.[107]

It could conceivably be argued that this last option is a reflection of his interest in *Kultur* in the elitist sense captured by *bildung*, hence to culture as the best of humanity (taking philosophy as the highest ideal of culture). In this respect the relative dominance of philosophical descriptions over social or historical ones may be expected. But he also seems to have in mind a much more expanded understanding that seeks to take into account the influential effects of internal German politics, international relations (especially as they refracted the political machinations of the Roman Catholic Church), along with the impact of significant changes in social structures, wealth distribution, and so on. In these sections a much less philosophic intent is in view, with a more pragmatic perspective being clearly evident instead, one more in line with a *Volk* perspective on *Kultur*.

The important point in all this however is not to determine whether he adequately describes German culture or the course of its interactions with theology, but to decide whether he offers a definition of culture. At no stage is an explicit definition given and it is not possible to infer a single, dominant understanding given that he deals to some extent with both aspects of *Kultur*. Perhaps the elitist paradigm expressed through his *bildung* emphasis

106. Ibid., 11–24.
107. Ibid., 15.

might qualify as a controlling definition, yet his attempt to deal with the *Volk* aspect remains enigmatic. He seems to sense its importance but fails to finally resolve its relationship with his philosophic emphasis. The meaning of the term "culture" is therefore left hanging. There are some interrupting signals provided by the references to elitist models and/or to philosophy however these do not clearly present themselves as encompassing definitions of culture.

The three signals described above are each sufficient to alert the reader to the possibility that a specific meaning for culture is intended however the very presence of three distinctive signals rather than just the one is sufficient to create confusion. In the absence of a definite definition the reader is likely to resolve the confusion by placing their emphasis on the signal that seems most prominent. This is problematic for two reasons. First, no clear definition is offered for any of the three possibilities. Theologians, who generally lack specialist backgrounds in the theory of culture, are therefore likely to rely on their fore-understandings for determining meaning, and these are likely to consist of the prevalent, contemporary social science models. Second, the subtle nuances O'Meara is struggling to bring to bear are likely to be lost in this process, subsumed within the dominant model in almost all cases (the exceptions being those having some significant familiarity with culture theory).

One further problem needs to be addressed here as well. O'Meara's presentation deals with an historic situation in which the ways of framing the discussion have since been superseded (note the demise of *Kultur* in recent times). Contemporary theory on culture was developed, at least in part, from each of the three strands of meaning suggested above, and has moved well beyond them since.[108] This presents contemporary readers, in the absence of a specific definition, with a strong temptation to simply substitute an existing meaning for the term culture, hopefully encompassing thereby the various subtleties and nuances O'Meara is attempting to describe. The intermixing of politics and social considerations with the strong elitist component leads to the possibility of deriving a definition from sociology or cultural theory but an overarching anthropological meaning is also entirely feasible. Either way the probability of deferring to one such appropriate contemporary definition must be considered very high.

Another example in this category comes from missiology. Also in 1991 David Bosch penned one of the most significant missiological works of recent times, *Transforming Mission: Paradigm Shifts in Theology of Mission*. This work

---

108. Refer for example to the descriptions of lineage provided by Gorringe, *Furthering Humanity,* and Tanner, *Theories of Culture*.

Theology and the Neutrality of Culture

not only attempted to survey church history but also aimed to transform contemporary understandings of it by setting it within a specifically missionary context. The sweep of Christian history is recounted as a progression through "successive missionary paradigms," though it would falsely characterize his project to render this successive progression a simple linearity.

Bosch is instead careful to note "at no time in the past two millennia was there only one single 'theology of mission' . . . different theologies of mission do not necessarily exclude each other; they form a multicolored mosaic of complementary and mutually enriching as well as mutually challenging frames of reference."[109]

In terms of the word culture however he is considerably less careful in his descriptions. A close read of his book reveals no specific definition for it and neither does it reveal an outline for any of the cognate terms he refers to, such as context, world, nations, socio/economic/politico-cultural, and others. His major section on culture, entitled "The Gospel and Culture," does not define it and neither does he take advantage of his discussions on contextualization or "The Church and Its Context" to denote it.[110] There is throughout his work no particular effort made to define what culture is, to describe what the mission of the church is encountering and engaging with in the delimiting sense implied by the notion of definition.

Having said this it is nonetheless clearly evident that his understanding of this locus of engagement is not thereby fractured or unknown. There is a strong sense of purpose permeating his work that infuses his understanding of culture and its cognates with a particular, identifiable, even if only sporadically noted flavor. For example, during his discussion of inculturation Bosch notes "culture is an all-embracing reality . . ."[111] This cannot be attributed to him in a simple manner however as it occurs in a section where he is summarizing the perspective offered by adherents of inculturation. The tone of the surrounding context certainly indicates his basic affirmation of it but this is not thereby a clear-cut definition. Further, the nature of this characterization is granted its particular shape by the argument it is situated in. Bosch is contending against a view that seeks to isolate individual aspects of culture from their surrounding elements, and it is against this background that he asserts the totalizing nature of culture.

Looking elsewhere in *Transforming Mission* slightly different understandings can be observed that at times militate against the statement noted

---

109. Bosch, *Transforming Mission*, 8.

110. Ibid., 291–98 for "Gospel and Culture," 420–32 for Contextualization, and 192–96 for "The Church and Its Context."

111. Ibid., 454.

above. For example, Bosch argues "Any individual Christian's understanding of God's revelation is conditioned by a great variety of factors. These include the person's ecclesiastical tradition, personal context (sex, age, marital status, education), social position (social 'class', profession, wealth, environment), personality, and culture (worldview, language, etc.)."[112]

Here his understanding of culture is separated out and distinguished from a number of other important constitutive elements of human sociality. Culture is therefore more circumscribed than it was above, limited to notions like worldview and language. Admittedly these are wide and encompassing constructs in their own rights but not so wide as to include the apparently more personal attributes of individual context, social position and personality. In this section of his discussion Bosch then goes on to delineate the influence of culture on religion before again seeming to curtail and differentiate the meaning in a similar way.

Elsewhere he describes a correlate of culture that is somehow linked with (this is never clearly described) yet ultimately extraneous to culture that he terms the "general frame of reference" with which people have grown up. This is said to include "their overall experience and understanding of reality and their place within the universe, the historical epoch in which they happen to live and which to a very large extent has molded their faith, experiences, and thought processes."[113] Curiously this is again distinguished from "personal, confessional, and social differences." It is actually this notion of a "general frame of reference" that then comes to dominate his overall exposition rather than culture *per se*, primarily because it becomes directly linked with his central emphasis on paradigms. In essence a paradigm expresses an epochal general frame of reference.[114]

There is therefore some confusion within the detail of Bosch's account as to what culture is, again arising from the lack of explicit definition. It would be overly pedantic however to consider this a fundamental confusion for in the broad sweep of his treatment it would seem that culture, worldview, general frame of reference, and paradigm are all used somewhat interchangeably, in each case with what seems to be a relatively consistent content. In this there is a progression over the uncertainty present in O'Meara. A distinctive and coherent understanding is discernable; the language of worldview and frames of reference providing important clues as to how his use of the term culture should be treated.

---

112. Ibid., 182.
113. Ibid., 183.
114. Ibid., 183ff.

While a fundamental confusion may be absent there is nevertheless still no specific direction or indication given as to how this content should be understood. To take just an anthropological view, for example, there is little indication of which of the many possible anthropological understandings is uppermost in his mind. Readers are unable to easily determine whether he is taking a primarily structural, functional or conflictualist view (all of which can be read into, and out of, his framework). Taking into account his concluding chapters it is even plausible to suggest he is advocating a generically postmodern perspective, a less defensible but still possible contention that nonetheless remains susceptible to multiple interpretations. Discerning which of these he would support would be difficult. In a context of confusion such as this something like the reader mechanism activated by O'Meara's work is likely to also be activated here. The reader tacitly falls back on their prior understandings for a definition to fill the lacuna Bosch has left.

The preceding discussion has offered two examples of the passive approach in its slightly more active form of implied meaning. O'Meara demonstrated an approach in which even the broad contours of his understanding were difficult to see; largely leaving it to the reader to provide the content. In the meantime Bosch entertained a more sophisticated treatment that broadly indicated his views but which then failed to ground this in a more specific schema of understanding. The reader had considerably more guidance than was offered by O'Meara but the lack of identifiable depth meant a similarly difficult task in determining the more precise frame of reference he had in mind. Once again the reader is required to fill in the blanks and is therefore most likely, in a contemporary context dominated by social science models, to refer to these for assistance.

It might be objected that this has been an overly pedantic analysis of these two scholars given that both have indicated to some degree a perhaps legitimately broad set of parameters with which the reader must cohere. There is some value in this observation since the general intent of their use of the term seems reasonably clear. However, it only seems so clear because of the application of fore-understanding. Further, even if the objection were to be granted it reflects primarily on the merits of assigning these examples to a passive rather than more active category of engagement. What is not at issue here is the presence of a deferral to social scientific models. Whether taken at their most explicit or taciturn, there is in these examples a distinct lack of any specifically theological definition of culture and a consequent deferral to social scientific frames of reference.

A General Pattern of Engagement

The preceding has demonstrated by way of specific case studies the presence of a general pattern of theological engagement with the concept of culture, one in which theologians tend to somewhat passively, or at least semi-passively, defer to social scientific constructs. The variety of examples hints at the popularity of the method, highlighting the presence of this perspective across a diverse assortment of scholars (systematic theologians, missiologists, historians, and post-modern scholars). Space does not permit a fuller treatment however these are by no means isolated cases; the methodology abounds. Many of the examples were influential scholars in their fields, Niebuhr and Kraft to name just a couple, that nonetheless could have been supplemented by other equally prominent authors and practitioners. Further, examples could have been multiplied by extending the analysis to Roman Catholic scholarship, for example Tracey Rowland's *Culture and the Thomist Tradition* exposes something of this same framework within recent papal encyclicals.[115]

Rowland explores what culture might look like when viewed theologically. She is not alone in this, calling on a long history of Catholic social engagement resources relevant to her task of outlining a specifically Thomist articulation of culture. In some ways Roman Catholic thought has moved considerably ahead of Protestant thinking in this area. On the Protestant front, the dissenting opinions noted in the direct deferral mode above provide a primarily negative impetus towards such a perspective, offering little in the way of constructive proposals that are not always already implicated within the same framework they are contending against.

This is not a claim intended to suggest that other Protestant scholars always argued similarly for good examples of positive and articulate responses in a very different vein exist. It is a central premise of the remainder of this book that not only in Roman Catholicism but also in Protestant heartlands there may be found powerful resources for thinking through culture from a specifically theological perspective. The picture painted above is of a dominant, comprehensively adopted pattern that is nevertheless not an entirely pervasive one. In the chapters that follow some significant nonconformist perspectives will be tapped for insights.

To this point the need for an alternative, specifically theological constructive proposal has not yet been established, it has only been hinted at. In the next chapter this hint is enlarged into a full critique. The prevailing pattern of engagement described above is subjected to close scrutiny by a critique querying whether this pattern of deferral is theologically warranted.

---

115. Rowland, *Culture*.

Before engaging with this however the feasibility and credibility of a religiously grounded critique needs to be established as the secular nature of the contemporary intellectual context putatively disparages even the possibility of such a thing. This is formulated in a general way that disputes the purity of the secular construct, demonstrating in the process both the efficacy of the religious perspective and the tendentious nature of the secular claim to being simply given. With this general principle established the critique offered by John Milbank is then engaged.

Chapter 2

Challenging the Neutrality of Culture

THE INTRODUCTION SUGGESTED THAT many theologians and missiologists adopted a hermeneutical stance towards culture, treating it as a neutral construct whose use rather than mode of construction or nature was the primary concern for theologians. This theory was then empirically examined in the previous chapter where various representative examples from a wide range of theological and missiological contexts were considered. In each of the cases examined the hermeneutical stance was found to not only be the primary approach adopted but the only one. The tentative conclusion drawn from this analysis was that the hermeneutical theory is an accurate depiction of an approach enjoying what appears to be significant popularity. The extent to which this perspective is present across the theological disciplines can only be determined by further empirical investigation but for now there is sufficient evidence to suggest the probability it is widespread. If this is the case then it prompts a follow up question—is culture by its nature a neutral concept or is it instead dependent on some biased presentation of reality potentially antithetical to the theological outlook?

This question places the emphasis very differently from normal theological treatments in that the relatively simple hermeneutical considerations are replaced by a considerably more complex inquiry centered on the nature of culture itself. Such an approach means paying attention to the concept rather than its terms of use, delving therefore into its processes of construction, structures of meaning and underlying ontology (presuming for now the validity of this sort of talk). A theological investigation conducted along these lines must try to bring the full density of culture into view, a strategy that not only penetrates deeply into the nature of culture but one which also engages the myriad concepts associated with it. This complex mutuality of relations is a wide-ranging set of associations bridging the humanities and sciences. Raymond Williams captures the difficulties here when he observes "Culture is one of the two or three most complicated words in the English language."[1] In a sense this is surprising because it seems counter intuitive to suggest we struggle to understand that with which we are most intimately connected, after all, "Culture, however we define it, is central to everything we do and think."[2] Yet careful examination of the term reveals, as Williams goes on to point out, an underlying confusion about the "everything" it supposedly defines.

On the one hand, it straightforwardly represents its primary etymological root in Latin descriptions of the process of cultivation.[3] This sense is most clearly evident in physical sciences like microbiology where, for example, a "germ culture" is cultivated, or in medicine where bacterial, tissue and viral cultures are grown. On the other hand, a range of alternative meanings have grown up in light of the metaphoric applicability of this root to various aspects of human life. Slowly and somewhat sporadically these metaphoric applications emerged and matured until around the sixteenth century when they accelerated through a complex and often very convoluted process of evolution into the higher levels of abstraction characterizing it today. The complexity of its post-sixteenth-century genealogy is significantly compounded by its complicated transition through multiple European languages. The parallel developments and eventual melding of French *civilization*, German *Kultur* and English culture, each a contested discussion in its own right inhabited by multiple clusters of meaning, are behind the manifold and sometimes competing English understandings characterizing contemporary Western discourses.[4]

According to Williams these metaphoric understandings can be gathered into three main clusters of meaning. The first takes its lead from the notion of growth implied by the etymological analysis above, applying

1. Williams, *Keyword*, 76. The title of most complicated, according to Williams, belongs to the corollary of culture, nature.

2. Ostry, *The Cultural Connection*, 1.

3. The root Latin word is *colere*, which has meanings ranging from cultivation to worship and inhabiting to protecting. *Cultura* picks up the cultivating aspect, hence culture derives from nature rather than the more popularly considered obverse, though it also takes on somewhat the idea of worship. See for example, Eagleton, *The Idea of Culture*, 1–2.

4. For a German review representative of the sorts of complications involved in each tradition refer Gadamer, *Truth and Method*, 8–17. For a concise overview from a theological perspective see the beginning of Tanner, *Theories of Culture*. For an anthropological overview refer Kuper, *Culture*.

the process of cultivation to human development. Plato's description of wholesome craftsmen dwelling in idyllic pastures captures the sense being conveyed here whereupon through proper tutelage undertaken in an environment conducive to the intended results, people can mature such that they exhibit the harmonious grace of right living.[5] The second group of meanings is quite different and corresponds primarily with what contemporary anthropology addresses, namely the whole "way of life" of a people, as first intimated in distinctive ways by both J. G. Herder and G. F. Klemm. This cluster not only encompasses whatever it is that separates humanity from nature but more importantly that which divides humanity into its distinctive groupings. The third and final sort of meanings gather around a variation on the first cluster in that it refers to the result of the civilizing process and hence to the various artifacts that are taken to constitute a "cultured" outlook—eminent pieces of fine art, great literature, and so on. It refers by extension also to the attitude towards life such exemplary works as these induce.

Williams and a Vulgar Understanding of Culture

Having narrated a relatively standard genealogy of culture Williams then seeks to introduce a novel adjustment. He asserts that the diverse range of meanings just identified only become problematic if one is constrained by disciplinary requirements. Scholarly studies of culture, he suggests, have mainly proceeded by examining the concept through disciplinary lenses, leading to a pattern of specialization that has tended to narrow the parameters of discussion along parochial disciplinary lines. Individual disciplines have been inclined to elevate one of the core clusters of meanings over others and pursue this as if it were culture writ large. For example, that which is "cultured" (Williams' fourth meaning) has become of special interest to cultural theorists, while culture as a "way of life" (third meaning) is most closely associated with anthropologists. In each case the selected emphasis tends to take on an enlarged role, becoming the central paradigm guiding in a dominant way the ongoing investigations of each discipline while also effectively acting to block a comprehensive disciplinary mutuality that might lead to the development of a cross-disciplinary meaning.

There is of course an important sense in which specialized inquiries are a necessary component of the definition process, an integral element in the ongoing investigation of what the term culture means. The very existence of the current range of plausible meanings is a result of such inquiries.

5. Jenks, *Culture*, 22.

Williams forestalls this objection by arguing his target is not specialization *per se* but the unfortunate (and for him far too widespread) tendency to rely on this specialty emphasis as the *primary* mechanism for defining culture. Such an approach cannot help but produce fragmentary results that perversely truncate understanding by foreclosing the possible range of meanings. As Williams' notes "It is clear that, within a discipline, conceptual usage has to be clarified. But in general it is the range and overlap of meanings that is significant."[6] This logically sets the overlap as the true goal towards which students of culture need to be heading—establishing a definition of culture that encompasses the full range of meanings the term evokes in this sense.

Williams adverts here to the notion of *actual* usage, or what he describes as the "vulgar" fullness of the term, as representing the best way of achieving this. He argues it is only in the context of common parlance that the term exhibits its flexibility and variety, through which can be seen some indication of the full range of meanings it embraces. Somehow culture in this vulgar state is able to incorporate within itself each of its meanings separately, indivisibly yet holistically. This suggests to Williams the possibility that each supposedly individuated use of the term noted by the specialist approach of academics is not invoking a distinctive meaning *per se* but is rather addressing a particular convergence of the elements that constitute culture from amongst a common pool of possible elements.

The notion of convergence is used by Williams to refer to more than some temporary gathering of elements for he has in mind a longer-term collocation of underlying elements in what is otherwise a constantly shifting array of interactions. Any particular meaning of culture is therefore a somewhat consistent conceptual solidification of these fluid relations into some specific and significant arrangement. The four core meanings described above are examples of such convergences, ones that have over time proved fairly fixed in nature. This of course implies the potential (even probable) presence of other as yet undiscovered arrangements and equally suggests the possibility of some overarching explanation that might allow these various arrangements, in either their fluid or solidified forms, to be related to each other in some convincing theoretical and empirical manner.

On this basis Williams not surprisingly suggests culture resists reduction to any one of the descriptions yet given for it, or even any particular class of them, for each of these are only parts of a greater whole. Culture is instead the totality that encompasses these various descriptions, along with any other possible configurations of the constituent elements. Defining the concept should therefore become the attempt to chronicle this totality; encompassing

---

6. Williams, *Keywords*, 80.

thereby the fullness of the social and living space humanity inherits and continuously negotiates. Specialist investigations are useful in clarifying individual components of this space but should finally serve the superintending process of developing a comprehensive understanding of culture.

William's epistemological argument can be given a distinctly medieval twist in a move that also philosophically formalizes it by aligning it with the similar structure set out by Giambattista Vico in the early eighteenth century, itself borrowing from classical Greek formations. Vico too advocates the need for a vulgar wisdom (*sapienza volgare*) founded on common sense (*sensus communis*), while arguing also that it requires supplementation, but not supplanting (the bedeviling temptation he argues ensnares the Epicureans and Stoics alike), by the philosopher's esoteric wisdom (*sapienza riposta*).[7] As Robert Miner notes in his commentary on Vico, the argument is that "Vulgar wisdom is the original source of true doctrines about the nature of humanity. The role of the philosopher is to strengthen vulgar wisdom, to make it explicit and purge it of error."[8] In terms of William's proposal then the social scientist can be considered analogous to the philosopher in the effort to refine the vulgar findings Williams seeks to first unearth.

Vico is an especially useful dialogue partner because he not only offers a congenial framework and structure for William's contentions but presents from within the context of his own analogous background a diagnosis of the condition Williams is trying to address. This in turn leads Vico to suggest a remedy that might, with the aid of a contemporary expositor of Vico, show how the dilemma could be resolved. The rest of this chapter will take up both these aspects, beginning with the question of diagnosis initially by briefly setting out the situation as Vico might conceive of it, before considering at more length changes within the contemporary context that pave the way for the proposal to come. The second half of the chapter then begins to engage with the process of resolution by considering the Vico inspired work of John Milbank. This leads into an extended analysis that occupies the attention of the following two chapters.

To begin with Vico then, he argues that modernity (as he experienced it in the eighteenth century) is a severely debilitated construct because it holds an entirely inadequate, bordering on non-existent, appreciation of the need for *ars topica* (topical arts), impelled in large part by its dogged determination to exalt the *ars critica* (critical arts—or the equivalent of rational thinking today). The art of rational examination is certainly vital

---

7. Miner, *Vico*. See also p. 131 where Vico understands Descartes and Spinoza to be fundamentally Stoic in orientation while identifying Locke, Hobbes and Gassendi as Epicurean.

8. Ibid., 132.

Challenging the Neutrality of Culture

for specifying the particularities of things he suggests but it is the art of generating topics that first brings to attention and then appropriately arranges whatever it is that needs such specification. As he argues, "Topics discovers things and piles them up. Criticism divides the pile and removes some of it: and thus the topical wits are more fertile, but less true; the critical ones are truer, but are sterile."[9] This admirably expresses the intent Williams is arguing towards in his call for a return to a vulgar account of culture. The specialized investigations of individual disciplines arise from and perpetuate a rational approach founded on the primacy of the *ars critica*. This has proven inadequate, as Vico foresaw, in that it failed to comprehensively encompass and therefore begin to truly articulate the fullness of what culture is.

In the rhetorical language of Vico, Williams is advocating the need for a conjoint structure of esoteric and vulgar wisdom in which concepts are first examined by the creative and ordering function of *ars topica* before the rational *ars critica* is deployed. This is quite different from contemporary practice in which the rational (or critical) aspect is to the fore with the topical category notably lacking. It is argued therefore that this latter element must be recovered. This is not easy however since as Robert Miner argues,

> What actually motivates the purveyors of the *ars critica*, Vico holds, is not the disinterested pursuit of truth, but the particular desire to rewrite the curriculum from the anti-rhetorical perspective that reduces eloquence to sophistry. By including only the texts and topics they favor, and thereby eliminating humanistic disciplines that train the mind in ways that cannot be quantified, Cartesian pedagogies may be unmasked as ideologies that seek to promote and perpetuate their own power.[10]

Before commenting further it is worth pausing to note that Vico does not read modernity through the Cartesian matrix alone, he also understands the significant and quite different legacy encountered in the experimental scientific heritage bequeathed by Bacon and Galileo.[11] It is worth noting that this critical element of his engagement is prosecuted against both the Cartesian and empirical streams, albeit only one of them is under examination above.

---

9. Quoted in ibid., 5.
10. Ibid., 4.
11. Ibid., 5.

Gadamer and the Element of Sheer Preference

As inheritors of the successful application and propagation of the anti-rhetorical agenda that Vico sought to contend against, contemporary scholars are deeply if often unwittingly influenced by its now subterranean but no less powerful presence. Envisaging and then constructing an alternative agenda is extremely difficult because of the dominance of this paradigm, but not impossible, as Hans-Georg Gadamer demonstrates when he undertakes an analysis along lines strikingly similar to those advocated by Vico. He argues in his seminal work *Truth and Method* that experiences of art, of philosophy, and of history are all "modes of experience in which a truth is communicated that cannot be verified by the methodological means proper to science."[12] By this declaration Gadamer prepares the way for a project of "philosophical hermeneutics" that seeks to assert the validity of these "other" truths despite their existence outside the normal legitimating parameters and protocols of the natural sciences.

At first encounter this project seems to be an attempt to indict harder versions of logical positivism or objectivism, however his goal is considerably more ambitious, targeting, on the one hand, Cartesian epistemology of which inductive methodology is just one (admittedly primary) presentation and, on the other, German Speculative Idealism. It is especially this former framework that carves off the experiences mentioned above from what constitutes truth in order to allocate them a role in the less certain and accordingly less reliable realm of the human rather than natural sciences. Gadamer critiques this partitioning process, suggesting instead a broadly Kantian schema in which the truth claims of the "human sciences" are argued to exist beyond, and hence bring into view, the outer limits of Cartesian rationality.[13] Truth in this structure becomes something considerably broader than that envisaged by Cartesian certainty.

Gadamer deals extensively with Wilhelm Dilthey's attempt to bridge the gap between the human and natural sciences, using it as an example of the more general posture of philosophy. Dilthey had sought to hold in tension the twin goals of Cartesian certainty and "knowledge in life" (experiences of art, philosophy, and history), or the "other" Gadamer is targeting. Unfortunately he succumbed to the priority of the former by suggesting all reflection had to pass through the Cartesian chamber of doubt in order to assure certainty, which, as Gadamer notes, amounts to no more than "a description of the special ideal of scientific enlightenment[;] . . . [one] little

12. Gadamer, *Truth and Method*, xxi.
13. He explicitly acknowledges this lineage, refer ibid., xxxiii.

compatible with a reflection immanent in life . . ."[14] By subjecting all truth claims to this requirement Dilthey ended up releasing the tension such that the rational polarity was able to assimilate its counterpart "life-philosophy."

Gadamer argues against this pressing of everything into the singularity and therefore universality of rationality because it does not allow other forms of certainty and doubt due place. He seeks to circumvent this process in part by adopting a phenomenological approach reshaped in critical ways by early aspects of Heidegger's project.[15] He conjoins this thrust with an emphasis on tradition, and in particular on recovering core elements of the classical tradition which post-enlightenment thinkers had supposedly left behind. This *ressourcement*, or return to and appropriation of original sources, is exemplified by his recovery of the neglected Aristotelian notion of *phronesis* (practical knowledge); a requirement first signaled vital for the hermeneutical task by Heidegger.[16] This, despite its different terminology and focus, is strikingly similar to the Vico and Williams contentions outlined above.

What is so useful about Gadamer however is the way he makes clear what the others only obscurely suggest, namely the presence of an anterior moment of decision that shapes all such proposals. This is most clearly articulated in an essay completed in 1965, hence after the first edition of *Truth and Method*, but which was attached to the second edition as Supplement I "Hermeneutics and Historicism."[17] Here he surveys the various options for grounding an account of hermeneutics before, perhaps surprisingly, commenting on the advantages offered by a "theological metaphysics." He openly argues it represents a viable way around the hermeneutic problem he is addressing. Notably the theology he refers to is shaped by Schleiermacher and Bultmann (who theologizes Heidegger) rather than Barth.[18] In the end Gadamer does not consider it a realistic alternative because it entails an objectionable reliance on "the order of creation, which thus remains an ordering prior to all human projections."[19]

What Gadamer brings to the surface here is the element of sheer preference determining the ontological foundation funding his methodological choice. His decision to rely on immanence rather than transcendence is not

---

14. Ibid., 231. Gadamer discerns in Dilthey's personal life a similar tendency he calls his "personal secularization process," embodied by his movement from Christian faith to philosophy, refer p. 232.

15. Gadamer's foreword to the second edition makes this lineage clear, refer ibid., xxv–xxxiv, equally explicit is his discussion at p. 526 and then at p. 556.

16. Ibid., 536, see also his discussion at pp. 310–21 but especially that at pp. 18–21.

17. Ibid., 507–45.

18. Ibid., 527. Compare this with his discussion at p. xxxiii.

19. Ibid., 527.

derived from any indubitable process of logic arising from the inherent rationality of reality but is rather driven by a personal inclination.[20] This is, of course, a stark depiction of the decision but it nevertheless strikes close to the intent Gadamer is expressing. He could have, had his predilections run otherwise, pursued the theological trajectory and constructed an altogether different hermeneutical project except that his proclivities were already shaped by the direction intimated by his teacher Heidegger, and it was down this path that he chose to tread.

This same, equally decisive junction presents itself before this book and interestingly there are two very good reasons for following the lead of Gadamer when analyzing culture. First, his conception of hermeneutics addresses itself directly to culture. He presents a tightly framed theoretical structure in which the hermeneutic decision becomes equally (hence more than analogously) a cultural one. It is a choice as to how culture should be analyzed but more importantly, as to how it should be understood.[21] That it is more than an analogous relationship is made clearer by noticing the way Gadamer constructs his hermeneutic account on a historicism conceived ontologically rather than instrumentally.[22] The historical emphasis is placed on his conception of *Erlebnis*, taking it as an aesthetic experience that "stands for the meaningful whole of life."[23] Life is a central concept in his project perhaps best understood through Husserl's notion of "life-world," "the pregiven basis of all experience . . . [which] is always at the same time a communal world."[24] Gadamer's implicit but foundational focus is culture through and through.[25]

---

20. Ibid.

21 Admittedly in *Truth and Method* culture is not rendered an explicit focus in anthropological terms but culture is nevertheless clearly evident at a surface level in numerous ways. It is present for example in the collocation of themes he deals with, hence his epistemology accounts for the natural and human sciences in the context of *Bildung* (which he calls "culture" but which is unfortunately not linked with any corresponding emphasis on *Volk*). He also refers to the importance of *Sensus Communis* and practice, and locates his entire project (as is well known) in the realm of tradition and therefore in history and language. The Vico comparison is well warranted considering the overlap of interests displayed in just this list, refer Miner, *Vico*.

22. He describes his approach as being founded on "the ontological universality of understanding . . ." that is "a theory of the real experience that thinking is." Refer Gadamer, *Truth and Method*, xxxiii–xxxiv.

23. Ibid., 61.

24. Ibid., 239.

25. Note also his commentary on the social sciences at the beginning of his afterword, ibid., 555ff.

The second attraction Gadamer offers is an unusually strong theological interest only suppressed by choice rather than necessity. Like John Milbank, Gadamer is attracted to an Augustinian Neo-Platonism that is aligned with an interest in the Trinity as a process within God, for it is here that he finds a linguistic boundary or limit necessitating analogy.[26] In myriad other ways their respective projects correspond, as can be seen by their joint interests in linguisticality, retrieval of rhetoric, Aristotelian *praxis*, gesture as language, recovery of the classical framework, and so on. Gadamer in fact emerges as one of the few non-theological commentators to be depicted positively by Milbank in his seminal work *Theology and Social Theory*. Milbank conceives of him as writing philosophy that is not good as philosophy *per se* but which is great "as theology, because Gadamer seeks to articulate (like the present book, but unlike Derrida) an original, necessary and ongoing supplementation which is not yet violent and subversive in relation to the original . . . [but] presents itself (a very long way from Heidegger) as a secularization of the aesthetics implicit in the Christian doctrines of the Trinity and incarnation . . ."[27]

It is this secularizing tendency that finally rules Gadamer out as a primary dialogue partner for this book because Milbank outlines similar arguments that are expressly theological in orientation (hence they are altogether different) and it is down this transcendent route that this book travels. Nonetheless Gadamer is useful as an introductory figure because his brand of post-Cartesian anti-foundationalist critique prefigures in important ways some of the theological suggestions that will be entertained by this book. In particular Milbank's counter-history subverting the reigning secular paradigm is founded on a similar overcoming of the forms of "foundationalism" Gadamer so heavily critiques in Dilthey: objectification (Cartesian certainty) and experiences ("life" as described by either Dilthey or Husserl).[28]

The Secular

Several times already the notion of the secular has been referred to but has not yet been defined, an important exercise because there is some variation in meaning between scholars. Following William's lead it is worth commenting on popular use for here a rough and ready approximation of meaning

---

26. See, for example, his views on this in an interview conducted towards the end of his life, Gadamer and Grondin, "Looking Back with Gadamer," 92–93.

27. Milbank, *Theology and Social Theory*, 423.

28. Gadamer, *Truth and Method*, 241–42; Milbank, *Theology and Social Theory*, 384.

is found that seems to adequately characterize the term as it is generally presented. Such use indicates it represents something like the antithesis of religion, referring to a space or institution somehow devoid of sacred or spiritual endowment or encroachment.[29] It is most often used this way, at least in the West, to refer to the political arena, describing for example a public domain ruled by consensual tolerance rather than some form of theocracy. It often finds expression in the active removal of partisan religious perspectives from influential policy forming or implementation roles in public governance. Perhaps the best way to exemplify this framework is to point to the contrast between a Western neo-Liberal democracy like the United Kingdom and broadly Islamic states like Saudi Arabia who are guided by Sharia.

Charles Taylor offers a more formal characterization of this meaning in his adoption of John Rawls' "overlapping consensus."[30] Taylor argues it implies the maintenance of distance, whereupon the public arena, represented by the various organs of government, is established such as to deal equally with *all* religious sensibilities. This can only be achieved by ensuring a distance over and against the various faiths, creating thereby a public space that is a free flowing, intersubjective arena of exchange, one built on tolerance. Freedom is also thought to inhabit this circumscribed field of negotiation and secular social cohesion is therefore built here. Religion is not therefore *simply* excluded since, as Taylor goes on to note, every particular perspective has the ability to speak within the arena, and not only this but can do so using language appropriate to their particular perspective. Nevertheless each such perspective (including every faith) is always subject to a greater mandate, to the prevailing ethos that allows these free interchanges to occur, or what Taylor calls the "Modern Moral Order."

The Modern Moral Order is not coterminous with but is founded on seventeenth-century conceptions of natural law, as mediated in particular by Grotius and Locke. The contractual society these two architects dreamed of has slowly evolved and developed through a process Taylor calls the "long march."[31] The contemporary product of this now four-century long march is

29. Cauchi, "The Secular to Come," 1. He suggests "the concept of the secular thus carries within itself a view of itself as total and pure . . ."

30. Taylor, *A Secular Age*, 532. See also Brittain, "The 'Secular' as a Tragic Category," 151ff. for an explanation of Taylor's phrase and for a description of how Talal Asad develops his critique of secularism through it.

31. The "long march" refers to the slow inculcation of new practices and modifications of old ones, whether initiated through the slow processes of evolution, developments improvised in the face of new situations or introduced suddenly, usually by the elites. Refer Taylor, *A Secular Age*, 176. It is strongly reminiscent of Raymond Williams "long revolution," refer Williams, *Culture and Society*; Williams, *The Long Revolution*.

Challenging the Neutrality of Culture

the modern Western democratic nation state. This modern secular state and its social concomitant emerged from the "social imaginary" of the late medieval synthesis by way of a convoluted process involving myriad influences acting in sometimes very subtle ways in order to effect the transformation.[32] This complex historical process refracts a fundamental shift in the West in which the age of public spaces inhabited by God (hence religion) gave way to the contemporary milieu where they are not. This is often characterized in Weberian terms, as disenchantment, as the shift from a religious to an autonomous foundation for public engagement.

In the earlier religious model the full range of communal and personal activities were conducted in the light of religious considerations. Viewed institutionally, the cultic cohabitated with and was determinative for the political along with all the other aspects of the social imaginary. None of the constituent elements of society operated independently of this; they were instead arranged and ordered relative to cultic requirements. By contrast, the autonomous model prescribes a public space in which the religious is relegated to a separate privatized sphere (which can be a significant political influence nonetheless, as the United States model demonstrates) that substantially curtails its public role. Each mode of public engagement (the political, economic, educational, and so on) is therefore conducted without formal reliance on, or *necessary* reference to, God or even ultimate considerations. These modes and their supporting institutions are instead guided by "internally consistent rationalities," a phrase Taylor decodes as the Modern Moral Order.

This is arguably the primary model people have in mind when referring to the secular but it represents only one of three models Taylor has identified.[33] A second cluster of meanings Taylor observes involves the emptying of religion from even the private realm of life, hence the extinguishing of religion as such from society. This is more than the consequent decline in the general religious sensibility of a people accompanying the change in public ethos noted above. It entails instead the demise of religious practice as a symptom of an underlying withdrawal from faith commitment. Rather than chronicling a loss of communal belief as such, though this is a

---

32. Taylor, *A Secular Age*, 159ff. The terminology "social imaginary" is deliberately preferred over "social theory" because it also encompasses the other than theoretical ways people imagine and enact the social, hence it "is that common understanding which makes possible common practices, and a widely shared sense of legitimacy." Taylor, *A Secular Age*, 172.

33. Note also the rise of the term secularisms, some examples of which strongly dispute the "standard" model just outlined. For a concise discussion refer Seitz, "A Review of Secularisms."

corollary, it testifies to a widespread turn away from God, faith, and religion in the private sphere. It describes the long noted empirical evidence of a series of declines related to religion chronicled in parts of Western Europe: in church attendance, belief in the effectiveness of prayer, belief in the existence of God, and so on. This is a distinguishing feature of European secular frameworks, as opposed to the lively religious sensibility characterizing the North American model.

It is the third and final group of meanings however that Taylor finds most interesting and towards which he directs his substantial writings. This definition captures the sense in which religious belief is no longer the axiomatic heart of Western society but is instead an embattled minority option amongst many. It is an increasingly minority position because individuals are now able to choose to believe in any of a number of faiths, or more commonly they choose not to believe at all and often people are now living without any exposure to or knowledge of faith as such. It is also an embattled option because it is confronted by a systemic suspicion. If tolerance and neutrality are both posited as the highest values then faith is perforce the inferior way that must always be militated against in case it attempts to subvert these supreme values, which of course it does.

What interests Taylor most about this third option however is that it represents something considerably more sophisticated than the simple dichotomy of belief versus unbelief the preceding tends to suggest. The secular in this view represents changed conditions for living. Previously in the Latin West the human condition was typified by a naïve belief in transcendence—the world was enchanted. Now it is characterized by disenchantment, but this has not simply slipped into an opposing yet equally naïve unbelief. It has led to reflexivity, a process primarily enabled by the emergence of a humanist perspective that no longer saw human flourishing as something dependent on exterior fulfillment. It saw instead the possibility of an immanent "fullness" of living, one that could flourish without reference to transcendent *telos*. This, quite naturally, leads to the associated possibility of deriving a truly materialist account of human living, a gateway through which non-humanist but equally materialist possibilities have also since traveled.

A core contention of this book, as has already been commented on, is that the secular is not and can never be the purveyor of true neutrality. Taylor provides the crucial hint why, supporting here the similar view presented by Gadamer, when he renders it a lived condition built on immanent presuppositions as opposed to the previous transcendent ones. It is constructed on the basis of a preference. What hides this anterior decision from view now is the historical process of development noted above, for it has been accompanied by a codification of this decision into the social fabric guiding everyday living and thinking in the West and now beyond. The decision now exists as an embedded condition for believers and non-believers alike, forming the taken-for-granted background that generally remains invisible in the sense Heidegger captures through his notion of "pre-ontology."[34] The secular construct has come to form the whole context of understanding from within which the West presently operates. While it is not necessarily overtly anti-religious, though it often is, it is certainly non-religious, and both these in a thoroughly religious way.

This pre-ontological character of the origins of the secular means the process of historical change outlined above is now commonly articulated through what Taylor calls a "subtraction story." This generally understands the secular to be an articulation of something always latent *within* humanity, hidden for a long time by a primitive context of enchantment now removed through the emancipating efforts of the humanists and their descendants. According to this story the secular was always central to human flourishing, forming an integral element of human development and in particular of the transition from primitivism to sophistication. Over against this depiction, Taylor suggests the secular is a human invention, something constructed and maintained by the desire to find answers on the immanent rather than transcendent plane. It is therefore not an integral element of the human condition but a learned, contingent pattern of thinking—a practice unique to the context from which it emerged.[35]

Mark Cauchi aptly describes this when he comments "Moreover, because with religion comes religious-identification and thus cultural-identification, the shedding of religion is the shedding of false and artificial culturally-constructed identities, casting the secular [therefore] as a culture- and identity-neutral and so universal humanist space."[36]

Just a little earlier in his discussion he suggests framing the issue in terms of the following question—granted the thoroughly and utterly comprehensive religious *saeculum* of the sixteenth century, where does one stand in order to critique the religious? It is perforce a space that has been created for this very purpose, one Cauchi argues was constructed on essentialist and humanist grounds and accompanied by a process that involved peeling back the artificial layers of culture and religion to reveal the supposed underlying essence of humanity, that which has been inappropriately

---

34. Taylor, *A Secular Age*, 3, 13 for this use of pre-ontology and background.

35. Ibid., 22. See also Milbank, *Theology and Social Theory*; Miner, *Vico*, who notes, for example, MacIntyre's call for a "subversive history" that provides an alternative geneaology, refer p. xiii.

36. Cauchi, "The Secular to Come," 4.

"colonized" by religion and culture.[37] Cauchi therefore offers a version of Taylor's subtraction story.

Part of what the preceding establishes is the extent to which the current intellectual climate of the West is established on and expressive of secular inclinations. Extending beyond this, it is worth noting that it is conventional in such a context to consider religion an object of inquiry, one that secular thinking can attempt to penetrate and comprehend. From the religious perspective this is received as the domestication of religion by an aggressive secular framework that can only engage religion in this way because it privileges some other supposedly more basic foundation. As Newbigin comments, echoing Vico's earlier quoted position, "Gladstone was surely right when he pointed out that the Roman Empire could give equal tolerance to all religions just because it could be quite adamant about something much more important than religion . . . namely, the veneration of the emperor."[38]

In a general way this conclusion has already been nascently anticipated at various points within contemporary secular discourses, especially though not only in philosophical and social scientific discussions. It is especially noticeable amongst postmodern writers who have for some time been discussing an irruption of the religious in their work. That this is more than a sporadic or isolated effect is indicated not only by the increasing attention being paid to the so called "turn to religion" but also by the significant influence of some of the individuals involved. Exploring this terrain is useful because of the possibility it might open up an avenue for pursuing the theological possibility being proposed by this book.

A Ground of Possibility: "The Turn to Religion"

Graham Ward suggests "Religion is, once more, haunting the imagination of the West."[39] This implies it was somehow absent for a time, and in a sense it was, or at least seemed to be. For quite a while it appeared entirely reasonable to suppose, along with Feuerbach, Freud, and Hegel, that philosophy had shaken free of the shackles of religious primitivism to embrace with gratitude the reign of pure reason—transcendent considerations having been expunged from the immanent realm. Humanity, now apparently freed from its enslavement to transcendent dependence (whether this be to ancient myths, classical gods, or the Christian God), was finally able to

---

37. Ibid.
38. Newbigin, *Foolishness to the Greeks*, 131.
39. Ward, *True Religion*, vii.

Challenging the Neutrality of Culture

autonomously pursue a fully material exploration of the world. On the back of phenomenology, empiricism, logical positivism, scientism and myriad other supporting positions this triumphal assertion marched across the Western landscape and staked its claim.

Behind this stark depiction is a useful caricature that reveals the core impulse behind the sensibility over against which Ward positions religion—unfettered, autonomous reason. But perhaps Ward can be seen as conceding too much if he is suggesting or can be taken as implying that reason has enjoyed an untrammeled reign, as if Hegel's now infamous hubris (as regards reason) had appropriately gauged the intellectual climate. Yet this is historically inaccurate as Kant's comparatively humble perspective demonstrates. Reason in the Kantian mode relied on a Cartesian rationalism that placed its "reliance upon reason as man's chief guide to a knowledge of reality . . ." but this was nevertheless accompanied by a corresponding noumenal reality "so constituted that mortal men cannot apprehend it through sensuous intuition or even grasp its essential structure through reason."[40] The phenomenal is therefore always shadowed by this noumenal realm such that reason never quite becomes unbounded or completely autonomous but rather always remains subject to limit, a limit Kant conceived of in religious terms.[41]

Friedman argues the point well. Kant understands philosophy to be "a map for the world which we see, for the moral law which we feel within us, and for our aspirations as rational creatures situated in a world of sense. This is as far as philosophy can go."[42] What it cannot do is reach beyond the empirical, sensual world; or probe further than the sensuous context of the human condition. Beyond these boundaries reason enters into a strange and unfamiliar realm that it lacks the resources to adequately understand. This does not mean reason is entirely deficient, as if completely without the ability to say something about the non-material context. What it does mean is that as reason travels further into what for it is unknown terrain, it increasingly relies on intuition for navigation rather than rationality, a move that comes at the expense of both its internal integrity and external effectiveness. According to Kant then, the non-material realm is properly ruled over by

---

40. Greene, "The Historical Context and Religious Significance of Kant's Religion," xxxviii–xxxix.

41. None of this is an attempt to deny the difficulties present in the Kantian account, Kant is being used in order to rebut the suggestion that religion has not retained an enduring role in philosophy. For a good discussion of the problems with the Kantian description see Firestone, "Rational Religious Faith and Kant's Transcendental Boundaries."

42. Friedman, "Hypocrisy and the Highest Good," 521.

religion which alone has the imaginative capacity necessary for exploring the region of the unknown.

For Kant, admitting this constraint on reason registers as wisdom, the recognition that human reason has limits that need to be acknowledged and respected.[43] For Hegel by contrast this final appeal to religion on the part of reason is read as failure, the espousing of "a failed teleology, a mere collection of imaginary ends which cannot be realized."[44] Kant's account of reason only discloses to Hegel an essential deficiency because in the end reason construed in this way repudiates itself, abdicating in favor of *mere* belief. But is this really an abdication or is it perhaps the prudent exercise of *sapientia*, a wise decision in the face of human limitation? Friedman argues the latter, finding in Kant's position a Socratic wisdom that admits into its core a realistic appreciation of ignorance. "There are things we must believe, for the adoption of these beliefs is the only way we can make sense out of what we know, which seems painfully inadequate and what we must do, which seems painfully impossible."[45]

From this small foray into a well-known debate between Kant and Hegel it is clear that religion is present at some level in both of these highly influential traditions. What Hent de Vries argues for politics is equally applicable here: "A political philosophy and a philosophical politics situate themselves in the wake of the founding event, from whose religious origin and meaning they must necessarily depart, that is, turn away. But paradoxically, this turning away just as much conserves and commemorates the original event, which it (thinks it) supercedes . . . it remains faithful to what it betrays, thereby revealing a full-fledged aporia . . ."[46]

What is happening in contemporary philosophy is therefore less a renewed haunting than an overt (re)turn of religion to intellectual

---

43. In a summary of Chris Firestone's chapter the editors Vanhoozer and Martin comment "On the proposed reading, Kant in his Third Critique indicates that we must go beyond theoretical and moral philosophy to considerations of teleology, aesthetics, poetics and religion in order to resolve the tensions arising from the attempt to harmonize his response to the question 'What ought I do?' in the Second Critique with that to 'What can I know?' in the First, to stabilize the relations between practical and pure reason." Vanhoozer and Warner, "Introduction," 4.

44. Friedman, "Hypocrisy and the Highest Good," 516.

45. Ibid., 522.

46. de Vries, "Miracle of Love," 242–43. Note also his discussion at p. 250 and then at p. 266 where formal features of religion survive through equivalencies and analogues in the "new dispensation." His article argues very similarly to the proposal presented in this chapter.

respectability.[47] Certainly this is the language by which it is more popularly described in the wider humanities and within deconstruction philosophy.

In the case of the former group of disciplines, to discuss the role of religion in the wider ambit of Western thinking, scholars in literary and cultural studies are moving away from naïve forms of secularism, inscribing in their place forms of reason bearing striking similarities to the Kantian model outlined above.[48] The role of positive revelation is still widely abjured; hence the notion of religion at play is different from the Christian variant (somewhat) guiding Kant. Nevertheless it is the case that religion and reason are now actively, if somewhat delicately, negotiating the terms of a possible future partnership within the humanities.[49] The form this partnership might take is difficult to discern but perhaps Hegel might have methodologically, though not substantively, affirmed the possibility of these two potential partners no longer inhabiting the space of simplistic antithesis.[50]

Turning to deconstruction philosophy, an interesting dynamic is beginning to emerge in which a possible shape for the partnership is increasingly coming into view. John Caputo provides a useful introduction in his *Philosophy and Theology*.[51] He locates the turn to religion in three preceding shifts that were instrumental in instigating the postmodern mood itself, arguing "The upshot of the shift effected by the hermeneutical-linguistic-paradigmatic turn is to introduce the idea of *seeing as*, which functions like something of a third term . . ."[52] This hermeneutical third way mediates the excessive claims of either faith or reason by showing to each their inherent reliance on the other. For example, reason always "involves an ongoing faith and trust in its ensemble of assumptions and presuppositions which func-

47. For a suggestion of how to understand the nature of this turn refer Putt, "Poetically Negotiating the Love of God," 488. For a discussion for and against the use of the term "turn" refer de Vries, "Miracle of Love," 41ff.

48. For an example from literary studies capturing the emergence of this kind of sensibility on a wider scale refer Jackson and Marotti, "The Turn to Religion in Early Modern English Studies." For a collection of essays treating this theme from within culture studies refer Mendieta, *The Frankfurt School on Religion*.

49. It is perhaps worth imbuing the term negotiation in this particular context of the discussion between religion and reason, with the more specific Derridean sense of an eternal reciprocity and anticipation. Refer for example to the discussion in Putt, "Poetically Negotiating the Love of God," 494–95.

50. The attribution of the thesis-antithesis-synthesis triad to Hegel is now routinely criticized for not quite capturing the process Hegel envisaged. What he seems to have intended is a higher "sublation" drawing from within the problem itself rather than from anything external to it. This use of antithesis tends towards something of this Hegelian meaning.

51. Caputo, *Philosophy and Theology*.

52. Ibid., 56, emphasis original.

tion like a set of anticipatory fore-structures that enable us to make our way around . . ."[53] It is on these grounds that Caputo formulates his own core thesis, namely that philosophy and theology are not really different types of structures but are instead differing forms of faith. While they are related, these forms nevertheless exhibit distinctive traits hence philosophy upholds an indeterminate or common faith that has as its foundation the underlying presuppositions common to all human endeavors while religious faith is distinguished by its determinate and confessional nature.[54]

Caputo demonstrates this distinction by comparing and contrasting the pre-modern Augustine with the post-modern Derrida. Augustine professes a faith in God and very particularly defines who this God is, professing Him (in conjunction with the community of believers to which he belongs) as the Christian God. Derrida by contrast espouses a "religion about which nobody understands anything . . . ," one always referring to some constancy that nevertheless fails to take determinate shape or rest in some specific translation.[55] It has been suggested that this amounts to a "constantly negotiated . . . endlessly translatable . . . endlessly substitutable . . . polynominal . . . semiotic multiplicity . . . that results in a plurivocity of divine naming, which, in turn, results in the postponement of any absolute divine transcendental signified . . . [where] one loves God in a state of undecidability . . ."[56]

Arthur Bradley considers this less a "turn" in Derrida's writing than a consistent outworking of an always present impetus now shadowing, through Derrida's influence, deconstruction as a whole. He suggests Derrida has steadily pursued over the years a "progressive de-materialization and re-transcendentalization . . ." of his originary aporia.[57] He agrees with Bernard Stiegler's assessment that this movement effaces the empirical, historical pole through which the aporia must pass, skewing Derrida's project towards a transcendental emphasis that births the quasi-religious, ethical position discerned by Caputo.[58] Bradley then joins ranks with not only Stiegler but also Richard Beardsworth in recognizing the juncture this

---

53. Ibid., 56.

54. Caputo describes them as "two kinds of interpretive slants," rendering the distinction an hermeneutical rather than ontological one, refer ibid., 57.

55. Ibid., 59ff., p. 62 for the quote.

56. Putt, "Poetically Negotiating the Love of God," 495.

57. Bradley, "Derrida's God," 28, see also p. 37.

58. A considerably more subtle though complex discussion, demonstrating the way Derrida's notions of alterity and an "irreducible" faith hinged on sociality rather than religion, contribute towards his ethical position can be found in Cauchi, "The Secular to Come," 11–13, see also p. 15.

Challenging the Neutrality of Culture

places deconstruction at. Down one avenue is empiricism and its "technical" future while along the other is religion (of some form).[59] Derrida has chosen the latter.

The shape of the religious turn in Derrida's deconstruction is therefore somewhat ethical and phenomenological and hence quasi-religious in a searching, exploratory sort of way, a way that might be said to characterize the turn in its general appearance. It is not a return to the naïve structures of the pre-moderns, rather it represents a post-critical appropriation of religious language and sensibilities that is still forming and cohering itself. For at least some of its adherents it seems to be aimed towards a post-secular theology that looks increasingly Christian in orientation, even if this may finally prove a step too far. In this, it can be suggested, space has opened up for the possibility of shaping a form of Ricoeurean "second naiveté," "a renewed encounter with the historic Christian faith that takes seriously where we have come from historically."[60]

Vanhoozer and Martin have edited a book that examines precisely this question at length. In *Transcending Boundaries in Philosophy and Theology: Reason, Meaning and Experience* they along with others interrogate the divide between theology and philosophy, seeking a way to move beyond it that genuinely enters into something like the Ricoeurean space mentioned above while maintaining a respect for the inherent dignity of both disciplines. They discern three primary strategies for addressing this problem: externally reconceptualizing the terrain; an immanent pressing to the limits; or a combination of the two. While all three possibilities appear somewhere amongst the essays they include in the collection, one seems to them particularly useful—the reconceptualization strategy.[61]

This strategy is evident in Aristotle, Kant, and Hegel who each embrace an essentially dialectical approach. While this is executed in quite different ways by each it is nonetheless the same in that it works "to develop a new conceptual framework in terms of which familiar intellectual boundaries may be seen in a new light, and thereby as less fundamental than they were previously thought to be."[62] The Kantian framework, with religion at the end of reason, expresses the tenor of this tactic in one of its modes. Other considerably more aggressive modes have since emerged, as can be

---

59. Bradley, "Derrida's God," 40 n. 14. See also p. 38 n. 2 for a list of references testifying to the widespread nature of the turn. For a description of this same choice rendered on a much wider scale, and correspondingly crafted in more generalized terms refer Taylor, *A Secular Age*, 768–69.

60. Middleton and Walsh, *Truth Is Stranger Than It Used to Be*, 173.

61. Vanhoozer and Warner, "Introduction," 2–3.

62. Ibid., 1.

seen in Pope Benedict XVI's now (in)famous 2006 Regensburg address. In this speech the Pope argues that reason separated from faith is inherently impoverished, becoming little more than a caricaturing shadow of itself. He advocates instead a grander account of reason, one in which reason finds its place *within* rather than over faith. Vanhoozer and Warner note the primary role narrative plays for exponents working in this vein, in particular the seminal role played by counter-narratives; Charles Taylor's genealogical approach is their exemplar for this.[63]

This book proceeds along broadly similar lines, although its locus is in the account offered by John Milbank rather than Charles Taylor. Milbank not only describes the emergence of the secular sensibility but adjoins it with an alternative Christian narration, an alternative modernity as he sometimes describes it, that shows how Western intellectualism could have (and still could) tread a different path, one centered in Vico rather than Descartes. To begin exploring this terrain it is worth returning to the original question faced by this chapter in order to consider how the conception of culture embodied in the previous chapter fares at the hands of Milbank's critique. This time however the broad paradigm developed above is investigated through the specific example of the pattern noted in chapter 1.

A Theological Objection to the General Pattern

In chapter 1 it was argued that a general case existed whereby neither theologians nor missiologists considered the concept of culture a theological topic; in view of which they were inclined to appropriate social scientific and hence secular descriptions of the concept for their theological purposes, even if only passively. Dissenting opinions did exist however for various reasons these failed to gain a hearing and were consequently relegated to the margins of the discourse. The purpose of the remainder of this chapter is to consider again the core doubt guiding this contrary view, although to do so in a different way. The aim here is to critically assess the implied reliance on social theorists in the suspicion that such a strategy is not as warranted or efficacious as is commonly thought.

Against the general pattern of deferral the following analysis presents a theological objection that is a particular case of the broad critique established above. This addresses concerns over the tacit assumption that appropriating existing definitions from other disciplines is possible because of an essential compatibility between these articulations and the theological uses to which they are put. This assumption in turn relies on both frameworks

---

63. Ibid.

trafficking in ideas developed through either essentially similar frames of reference, or ones at least structurally amenable to each other. But this raises a question: should not such a fundamental presumption be subjected to rigorous scrutiny? It is argued here that the default position of the general paradigm must of necessity and urgency be carefully examined in light of the religious element the secular has till now ruled out of play.

Raymond William's argument that culture is a word containing within itself worlds of meaning is pertinent. Culture brings with its use not only the denotation being explicitly invoked but a long *social* history. This development, precisely because it is always socially attuned, is constantly shaped and molded, in subtle and not so subtle ways, by a continuous process of interaction with prevailing patterns of thought. Any particular articulation of culture will usually reflect quite closely the mores of the time, and the concomitant rendering of the world and reality these are derived from. The core of the theological argument presented below is that on examination the social scientific descriptions of culture turn out to be based in an immanent framework consistent with the general sensibility built and nurtured by the secular as described above. In view of this, such descriptions should *initially* be considered antithetical to the transcendent underpinnings of theological projects. At the very least the possibility that culture might not be the theologically neutral product social scientists depict it as should be entertained.

This proposition needs to be carefully conceived, however, since the missiologist Charles Kraft, for example, suggested a distinction between the inherently neutral *nature* of culture and its subsequent non-neutral humanly directed *use*. By contrast theologians like Nicholls vociferously proclaim the thoroughly antithetical nature of culture. Far from Kraft's conception of innate neutrality, and hence little or no intrinsic *telos*, Nicholls considered culture to be always already bent towards human proclivities for evil; intrinsically directed towards "this world" rather than Christ. In the following it will be argued that in a sense Nicholls was right, at least in as much as he saw the need to get behind the abstraction Kraft was working with. In this respect it is not a case of culture being a neutral datum or object that is then subsequently directed by human desires because it is at all points intimately intertwined with both human behavior and nature.

Yet it is not appropriate to simply extol the virtue of Nicholls approach *per se* because there is an underlying complexity that he does not seem to fully allow for in his thesis. He achieves his critique only by connecting culture directly to the fall with the corollary that non-Christian culture is thoroughly and unambiguously evil, but he does so in a way that requires this "type" of culture to be separated from the Christian "type" of culture. Further ambiguity in his use of the term culture arises from his tendency to conflate non-Christian culture with culture as such in his struggle to articulate how culture relates to the universal church (and hence to Christian culture). In this respect there seems present in Nicholls an unwarranted reliance on a dualist construct rooted in and gaining its impetus from the very foundations Nicholls is so assiduously arguing against.[64]

The key question requiring attention however remains the one prosecuted by Nicholls; determining whether anthropological constructs of culture are in fact theologically neutral, although the approach advocated here seeks to avoid the metaphysical entrapment characterizing Nicholls response. This can only be achieved by staging a direct confrontation with the secular construct and the various means by which it seeks to capture alternative frameworks; hence this is the major emphasis of what follows. There are a number of ways this could be achieved but perhaps the most helpful is to consider a worked example. For this purpose Kathryn Tanner's previously described work *Theories of Culture: A New Agenda for Theology* proves a useful description against which can be placed John Milbank's slightly older *Theology and Social Theory: Beyond Secular Reason*. Tanner is taken here as paradigmatic of the general pattern of engagement outlined in the previous chapter, a pattern characterized by deferral to the social scientific definitions of culture promulgated so successfully by sociocultural anthropology, while Milbank presents the counter position advocated by this book.

As discussed Tanner begins by describing a modern or classical account of culture that is defined by the following nine point outline, listed with slight variation for stylistic reasons:

1. A human universal
2. of diverse patterns
3. that vary between social groups
4. for whom it describes an entire way of life
5. that has been built upon consensus
6. and which acts to constitute or build human nature
7. and is therefore a form of social determinism
8. but which is also a human construct
9. and is therefore contingent (could have been otherwise)

Against this model she sets a synopsis of recent critical analyses that are broadly gathered under the postmodern sensibility. As already described,

64. For an example of the sort of captivity envisaged here refer Murphy, *Beyond Liberalism and Fundamentalism*.

these critical engagements query key presuppositions considered constitutive of the classical model, such as holism, coherence, consensus, societal order, stability, and boundedness. She finishes by arguing that while these critiques are significant, they have not irreparably damaged the culture concept; rather they have strengthened understanding of it, allowing it to continue standing though now as a much more provisional and open construct.

The Problem of Expertise

Three methodological points stand out about Tanner's proposal. First, the possible definitions she decides between are drawn only from sociocultural anthropological categories. Second, she follows a quite specific process by which two competing anthropological accounts are compared and contrasted before one is shown to be preferred as the apparently superior option. Third, the entire discussion is undertaken for a specifically theological rather than anthropological purpose, namely to support her call for an "everyday theology." It is argued here that this last point has its genesis in a prior, unstated decision that forms the ground upon which the other two aspects are not only established but warranted. This decision is the choice to defer to experts.

In one respect this is unsurprising as it is one of several characteristic features of the contemporary trend towards academic specialization.[65] Each discipline has over time marked out and delineated its boundaries (even if only because of disciplinary isolation), seeking to establish thereby an academic territory over which it has dominion, a position granting it a consequent right to the gathering and promulgation of the specialized knowledge contained therein.[66] Operating through a loose system of reciprocal arrangements the various disciplines both assert and accept this right, sometimes quite overtly but usually fairly passively.[67] There are of course always breakout works that challenge this systemic network of allegiances but in the normal course of events each discipline remains largely content to operate within the broad boundaries of this process (albeit constantly pressing these boundaries). Underpinning the success of this enterprise is "a

---

65. For a defence of specialization in an otherwise critical engagement refer the discussion in Shumway and Messer-Davidow, "Disciplinarity," 214.

66. In large part this arose because "the university enabled disciplinary practitioners to achieve cognitive exclusiveness over their regions of the academic world. These practitioners relied not on licensing but on credentialing . . ." Refer ibid., 207. This article provides an excellent historical description of the emergence of disciplinarity before critically engaging with the notion.

67. Ibid., 208.

differentiating activity called 'boundary-work' . . . [that] entails the development of explicit arguments to justify particular divisions of knowledge and of the social strategies to prevail in them."[68]

In theology this right of specialization cedes to theologians the ostensible ability to speak about God in authoritative terms while correspondingly granting to other disciplines the reciprocal right of authority over their own subjects.[69] However much this may be an idealization it is nevertheless an effective description of the relationship currently existing between theology and the social sciences, as the previous chapter argued. There arises from this state of affairs a general question over whether theology's use of external expertise is a warranted strategy. Tracey Rowland, in her book *Culture and the Thomist Tradition*, examines this question from the Roman Catholic perspective, with the aid of Alasdair MacIntyre, in her essay "The Epistemic Authority of 'Experts' and the *Ethos* of Modern Institutions."[70] Her focus is on the rising influence of external experts on Roman Catholic institutions. She contends that such influence cannot be accepted uncritically for there is an appropriate need to discriminate between experts on the basis of the epistemic authority they rely on, not least because this authority profoundly shapes the advice they present.[71]

Tacit in this contention is recognition that there is no single authoritative foundation with universal validity but instead a plurality of possibilities, each of which engenders and nurtures practices consistent with its underlying ethos. Alasdair MacIntyre, for example, identifies one such foundation in what he terms emotivist ideology, the dominant ideology guiding Western thinking today that he considers a now pathological and ultimately pernicious foundation with regard to identity and moral agency. As he notes, it tends to spawn Machiavellian, utilitarian social networks that are often perversely considered institutionally virtuous but which are actually far from the human flourishing envisaged by his own choice of foundation, Aristotelian Thomism.

Rowland consequently argues "the only 'experts' whose authority may be legitimate are those who see through the ideological quality of such practices, and who continue to base their judgements upon a pre-modern

---

68. Ibid.

69. This is a necessarily malleable concept for the boundaries are more fluid in some disciplines than others. Refer the excellent discussion in ibid., 208–10 especially.

70. Rowland, *Culture*, 53–71.

71. This effect can be seen, for example, in the scientific ability to garner "the cognitive authority that Western cultures grant to interpreters of nature and producers of truth . . . ," Shumway and Messer-Davidow, "Disciplinarity," 210.

Challenging the Neutrality of Culture

tradition of practical reason, including the virtue of prudence."[72] Such experts should be, she argues, those involved in the Thomist "virtue-engendering" and "virtue-requiring" *practices* MacIntyre advocates. Relying on experts schooled in this epistemic foundation ensures the Roman Catholic Church creates an internally consistent institutional framework fostering virtuous practices in harmony with the revelational foundation it takes its lead from. For her this means allowing a (certain strain of) Thomist reason to permeate every aspect of the church's life. In short, she advocates Catholic institutions engendered and infused by a sacramental *ethos* congenial with its revelatory roots.[73]

In order to better understand the implications of this perspective a more complete account of what MacIntyre means by practice is required. This comes in his book *After Virtue: A Study in Moral Theory* where he defines it in the following terms:

> By a "practice" I am going to mean any coherent and complex form of socially established cooperative human activity through which goods internal to that form of activity are realized in the course of trying to achieve those standards of excellence which are appropriate to, and partially definitive of, that form of activity, with the result that human powers to achieve excellence, and human conceptions of the ends and goods involved, are systematically extended.[74]

This understanding of practice is then aligned with his accounts of both narrative and tradition to form the foundation on which he constructs his ethical theory.[75] The best way in which to conceive the framework he establishes can be found in the most common metaphor scholars use to demonstrate the concept of practice—the game, adjusted appropriately for MacIntyre's emphasis on virtue. In this vein he is arguing that expert participation in a practice (game) for the sheer sake of that practice (game), rather than for exterior benefits like power, money or fame, engenders virtue.[76] It

---

72. Rowland, *Culture*, 69. In similar vein Shumway points out the ability of feminist critiques to "see through" the hard sciences, revealing them as social practices amenable to social science investigation. He goes on to highlight the presence of a distinctive "disciplinary regime" that works to instil habits (close to MacIntyre's practices) considered conducive to its discplinary *ethos* into its disciples, Shumway and Messer-Davidow, "Disciplinarity," 211.

73. For a radical call along these lines refer Pickstock, *After Writing*.

74. MacIntyre, *After Virtue*, 187.

75. Ibid., 186–87.

76. He defines virtue as "*an acquired human quality the possession and exercise of which tends to enable us to achieve those goods which are internal to practices and the*

can be likened therefore to tennis whereupon the player competes for the sheer love of the game, with the intention of becoming expert at playing tennis rather than with the aim of using this expertise for some other goal like money or fame.

The game metaphor is also useful because it points quite directly towards one of the central roots from which practice theory springs, namely "Wittgenstein and the Cambridge 'ordinary language' tradition (e.g., Cook Wilson, G. E. Moore, J. L. Austin) . . ."[77] Wittgenstein's deployment of the language-game is an important foundation not only for MacIntyre but for all adherents of the "practice turn" in contemporary theory.[78] This turn is pursued by a relatively loose cadre of scholars interested in the way the notion of practice gets beyond the stultifying dichotomies endemic to so much philosophy and social theory, especially the Cartesian and Kantian subject/object divide.[79] The link between Wittgenstein and this later application of his work is rather straightforwardly established by noting how he conceives a language game as a "form of life," meaning by this only a small variation on the notion of practice described above.[80]

This is an important link because Wittgenstein has attracted a number of criticisms that have correlate implications for the idea of practice. One in particular requires attention for present purposes, namely Wittgenstein's inadequate attention to the diachronic features of language games. As Christopher Lawn argues, his "language-games" are fertile accounts of language but only in a synchronic way, making it difficult for him to link his present language-games to past ones. There is, in short, a lack of historicity.[81] This argument has been most prominently advanced by Jürgen Habermas whose comment is worth quoting at length:

> Language spheres are not monadically sealed off but are inwardly as well as outwardly porous. The grammar of a language cannot contain a rigid designation for its application. Whoever has

---

lack of which effectively prevents us from achieving any such goods." Ibid., 191, emphasis original.

77. Pilario, *Rough Grounds of Praxis*, 85.

78. For a good discussion refer ibid., 73ff. See also p. 541 where he argues "We have shown that the sociological 'turn to practice' is rooted in the Wittgensteinian emphasis on language and language game . . ." This sociological conclusion applies equally to MacIntyre because he earlier argues at p. 82 that "MacIntyre's project in fact is to ground ethical theory in sociology since, in his account, any claim of moral philosophy falters when it has not spelled out its social embodiment."

79. Ibid., 74–75.

80. Ibid., 541 for this argument, and n. 21 for the reference in Wittgenstein.

81. Lawn, "Wittgenstein."

learned to apply its rules has not only learned to express himself but also to interpret expressions in this language. Both translation (outwardly) and tradition (inwardly) must be possible in principle. Along with their possible application, grammatical rules simultaneously imply the necessity of interpretation. Wittgenstein failed to see this; as a consequence he conceived the practice of language-games unhistorically.[82]

One of the dangers Habermas seems to envisage Wittgenstein courting here is an over-determined synchronic emphasis in which language-games become fractured and atomized activities devoid of mechanisms that can account for either historical change or cross language-game engagements. To address these two difficulties Lawn recruits Gadamer, paying particular attention to his use of "horizon" and "prejudice." Lawn errs slightly when describing Gadamer's notion of horizon by aligning it too closely to an individualized perspective since Gadamer also has the sense in which "Everything contained in historical consciousness is in fact embraced by a single historical horizon. Our own past and that other past toward which our historical consciousness is directed help to shape this moving horizon out of which human life always lives and which determines it as heritage and tradition."[83]

Nevertheless it is a good appropriation for by his use of horizon, whether conceived individually or communally, Gadamer is able to fully gather up the past, while prejudice becomes the mechanism that accounts for change because it acknowledges the way language is both productive and creative. The hermeneutical process Gadamer uses these elements in describes enquiries that are conducted on the basis of a conscious foregrounding of what Heidegger called fore-understandings (prejudices). This allows the inquirer to begin their interrogation, or questioning of things, in an (at least somewhat) transparent way. This foregrounding process is then ideally coupled with an attitude of openness to the strangeness, otherness or alterity of what is being encountered such that the prejudices (fore-understandings) become malleable and pliable, as in turn does the horizon of understanding and hence what is called the hermeneutical circle is formed.[84]

Lawn goes on to argue that Wittgenstein does make an attempt to "thematize the continuity of tradition," using the idea of "custom" to capture the regularities of language. Unfortunately this fails to convince Lawn because the past still seems to register as inflexible bedrock impervious to

---

82. As quoted in Ibid., 284.
83. Gadamer, *Truth and Method*, 303.
84. Ibid., 268ff.

contingent concerns.⁸⁵ An alternative possibility from a Protestant perspective that enacts something like Gadamer's approach (despite disavowing Gadamer's overall project) in a Wittgensteinean structure is offered by Kevin Vanhoozer in his recent *The Drama of Doctrine: A Canonical-Linguistic Approach to Christian Theology*.⁸⁶ As will become clear, Vanhoozer is effectively presenting a species of the practice turn, using one of its correlate conceptualizations "performance."⁸⁷ As Sherry Ortner suggests "For the past several years, there has been a growing interest in analysis focused through one or another of a bundle of interrelated terms: practice, praxis, action, interaction, activity, experience, performance."⁸⁸

For Vanhoozer the interplay between the past and the present is a central issue, one he engages by considering the relationship subsisting between tradition and Scripture. He is especially concerned about a new and growing Protestant tendency towards a focus on tradition that eclipses the normativity of Scripture, handing interpretation over to interpretative communities at the expense of an appropriate emphasis on authorial intent.⁸⁹ In his theo-dramatic terms, this means that performance is privileged over script. Vanhoozer finds in George Lindbecks' cultural-linguistic model an exemplar of this emphasis on contemporary performance and hence appropriates this label to represent the position he is contending against. By contrast he develops what he calls a canonical-linguistic model where the script "is both *transcript* of the theo-drama—the divine once-for-all 'command performance'—and a divine *prescript* that commands performance by others (e.g., the church)."⁹⁰

A little later Vanhoozer argues "*canonical-linguistic theology means being instructed by, being apprenticed to, and participating in the communicative practices that comprise the Scriptures.*"⁹¹ This use of practice is similar to MacIntyre's, especially since it is imbued with a similar notion of virtue in that an internal good is envisaged, and "That good is *God with us; life with God*—in a word, Jesus Christ."⁹² Vanhoozer also anchors his

85. Lawn, "Wittgenstein," 292.

86. Vanhoozer, *The Drama of Doctrine*. See pp. 211ff. for his use of Wittgenstein and pp. 157–58 for his critical engagement with Gadamer.

87. Ibid., 165ff. for his reliance on performance and 211ff for his invocation of practice.

88. Quoted at Pilario, *Rough Grounds of Praxis*, 74.

89. This deliberately invokes the work of Stanley Fish. Refer to Vanhoozer, *The Drama of Doctrine*, 169 for a critique of the Fish position.

90. Ibid., 167, see also pp. 179–85. Emphasis original.

91. Ibid., 211. Emphasis original.

92. Ibid., 219. Emphasis original.

account in a specific social situation, namely the covenantal relations that persist between God and His people such that God socializes (canonizes in Vanhoozer's terms) His people into a covenantal "way of being," that is into what is structurally the equivalent of Wittgenstein's "form of life."[93] He then argues that "Those who become skilled in covenantal capacities achieve excellence in worship, theology, and ethics alike."[94] In short, they become the equivalent of what MacIntyre calls *virtuous*.

Vanhoozer further develops this structure by way of an account of theology as dramaturgy that is then overlaid with a description of its performance, at which point a further interesting correlation comes into view.[95] He is outlining here a structure akin to what the French sociologist Pierre Bourdieu calls *habitus*, an arrangement that also bridges the Wittgenstein and Gadamer problem outlined above. According to Daniel Pilario *habitus* is "embodied history, internalized as a second nature and so forgotten as history . . ." that also exhibits what Chomsky calls a "generative grammar."[96] In other words, it is "born in a particular situation and is reactivated in another historical circumstance. It is thus capable of infinity of possible action . . ."[97] In this respect it is both a "structured structure and structuring structure" that therefore creatively enacts through "regulated improvisations."[98] In this outline an overt similarity to another well-known formulation can be seen: N. T. Wright's frequently employed construal of the Bible as an unfinished script. Wright argues the Bible is analogous to a recently discovered but incomplete Shakespearean play that must be enacted by "highly trained, sensitive and experienced Shakespearean actors, who would immerse themselves in the first four acts, and in the language and culture of Shakespeare and his time, *and who would then be told to work out a fifth act for themselves.*"[99]

Bourdieu explores his account of practice through the subsidiary concepts of habitus, capital, and field.[100] This is useful because it breaks down the concept into its constituent parts, one of which is particularly important

93. Ibid., 219–20.

94. Ibid., 220.

95. Vanhoozer devotes Part Three of *Drama of Doctrine* to a discussion of the dramaturge and the concluding Part Four to the question of performance.

96. Pilario, *Rough Grounds of Praxis*, 134.

97. Ibid., 135.

98. Ibid., 135 for the structuring label and p. 235 for the improvisation one.

99. Wright, "How Can the Bible Be Authoritative?" See also Middleton and Walsh, *Truth Is Stranger Than It Used to Be*, 179ff. Also refer Bartholomew and Goheen, *The Drama of Scripture*. These last two offer good discussion and a six act alternative.

100. Pilario, *Rough Grounds of Praxis*, 173–76 explains this.

for present purposes, namely "field." While the notion of field is deployed for his explanation of power relations it also effectively operates as a soft account of incommensurability. Bourdieu concentrates on elaborating field in its instrumental aspects however it can equally be taken as a structure in its own right, especially as it intersects with *habitus*. Pilario offers valuable insight when explaining how these two structures intersect. He turns to the game metaphor noted above, arguing "each card-player, for instance, by the mere fact of playing the card-game, is convinced that the game is worth playing—a conviction present only among the players of one specific game-field."[101] As he goes on to note, farmers are not interested in hair-splitting logic and neither are philosophers especially concerned about rainfall patterns, each is instead focused on their own considerations.

This is not a hard and fast rule for there are of course cards that traverse game-fields, and the fields also prove porous in the face of ordinary language use.[102] However, the "'fields' are 'relatively autonomous social microcosms' whose structures serve as the constraining mechanism in the game their occupants play."[103] Another constraint is offered by the notion of rules because these regulate the game. It is important to note however that *habitus* represents a learned, lived engagement in which the participant gradually gains a "feel for the game." They so imbibe the rules over time that these highly structured conventions become more like guidelines that can be creatively engaged with, a process he terms "regulated improvisations" or which are more generally referred to as strategies.

In this sort of context the role of the exterior expert becomes clearly delineated for they equate to the "impartial spectator," becoming what T. E. Lawrence picturesquely but pejoratively characterizes as "'a man sitting in an armchair' [as] against 'a man entirely taken up in his task.'"[104] It is in fact this sort of approach that Bourdieu is particularly keen to dispute for it hinges on the ability to escape the exigencies of life, to distance oneself from the game in order to play another game in which there are no real stakes, just conjecture, pretend and play.[105] This theoreticist stance is not an irredeemable position however since Bourdieu's intent is not to excise such activity (and thereby the whole academy) but rather to point out the need to

---

101. Ibid., 160.

102. It is tempting to suggest Raymond William's vulgar approach is heading in this direction, which it is, but not in the way Bourdieu envisages for this transgresses his view of the "Thersite principle"—that the perspective of the ordinary citizen offers insight. Refer ibid., 220–21.

103. Ibid., 160.

104. Ibid., 204.

105. Ibid., 219.

consciously factor in the implications of this perspective into the analysis, perhaps by acknowledging and redeeming the role played by the various fallacies attending this perspective.[106]

What becomes clear from Bourdieu's approach is that the problem of external expertise is an issue of bias in which the expert by the very nature of their distance from the social object they are scrutinizing objectifies it, but does so without then accounting for this effect. The difference between the theoretical gaze and the in-game perspective of participants must therefore be explicitly addressed. Yet in Bourdieu there is also a second, causal perspective that attempts to press against this relatively irenic view of the issue. The objectifying tendency is in large part grounded in an Enlightenment based view of rationality that universalizes reason (as was shown above). Against this he posits a contingent *"Realpolitik* of Reason" that is radically grounded in history but also distinct from history in that it reflects the "forces and constraints," "conflicts and pressures" present within history rather than the operations of history *per se*. This does not equate however to the seemingly similar formulations presented by Foucault since it is always mediated by the dual constraints of collective purpose and the norms and methods of the field.[107]

It is not necessary to delve further into his views here since the critical point for present purposes resides in why he chose to anchor his project in the forces of history rather than anywhere else. Really there was nowhere else for him since by an anterior decision he had limited himself to the immanent plane. In his own words he works in the presumption that "reason did not fall from heaven."[108] But, it might be argued, what if it had? While he does well to highlight the parochial nature of reason he nevertheless assumes in the process the universal sway of both the game-theory itself and the immanent perspective that founds and legitimates it. But, what if reason were not located in impersonal, political force as Bourdieu and (tacitly) Wittgenstein argue, but is instead something "from heaven" as Vanhoozer and Wright contend, and therefore something only really explainable in its relation to whatever is transcendent?

Here the horns of dilemma that had already confronted Gadamer present themselves also before Bourdieu and a choice is demanded. Bourdieu

---

106. Pilario argues Bourdieu identifies three main fallacies in three separate domains—scholastic epistemocentrism (knowledge/science), egoistic universalism (ethics/politics), and aesthetic universalism (aesthetics). All of these are ultimately expressions of "the intellectual's 'dream of omnipotence' . . ." Refer ibid., 220–25, 224 for the quote.

107. Ibid., 225–30.

108. Ibid., 225, quoting Bourdieu.

follows the same path as Gadamer but again this must be seen as the operation of sheer preference. There is no superintending, Archimedean point of observation available to humanity from which to look down upon and adjudicate the case. If this were so then the dilemma utterly dissolves in the face of this superior perspective. Instead, the human condition is such that humanity must contingently explore its way forward, embarking on an uncertain journey in which the decision over how to understand rationality presents itself as a fork in the road. The route in either direction is unknown hence it amounts to a considered wager or gamble on the more likely prospect. Vanhoozer chooses differently from Bourdieu and Gadamer by placing his wager overtly on revelation and the promise it suggests is contained in the transcendent option, a gamble this book also makes. What follows is therefore an attempt to work out an understanding of culture that is oriented by a transcendent rather than immanent perspective.

Here a small excursus is required as the foregoing, and so also the discussion surrounding Gadamer above, suggests the situation hinges on some sort of pure wager in which genuine uncertainty is courted. This is not entirely true for there are real grounds for preferring the Christian rather than secular option, even if bias seems to be entertained by this admission. John Milbank most concisely and directly points out the reasons involved when he argues it "is *not* really an ungrounded decision, but a 'seeing' by a truly-desiring reason of the truly desirable . . ." which appeals "to a certain bias towards reason rather than unreason . . ."[109] As he goes on to note, the choice really narrows to one between cold and warm reason, between nihilism and unreason on the one hand and a divine reason on the other.

Reversion or a turn to a transcendent perspective does not mean however that the various methodological tools developed by the alternative perspective cannot be used, on the contrary there is quite likely to be some degree of methodological cross-over since the same task is being pursued in each case.[110] For instance it is instructive to append an element of Bourdieu's analysis to the position adopted by Rowland. She argues that the Roman Catholic institutional *ethos* should derive its "authority from principles of the Aristotelian-Thomist tradition of practical reason . . ."[111] Bourdieu's reflexive model offers an intriguing possibility here in that the second of his three types offers a way to envisage and conceptualize Rowland's argument on a grander scale. His first type involves the social agents in self-examination in an attempt to locate themselves in the social

---

109. Milbank, *Theology and Social Theory*, xvi. Emphasis original.
110. For an argument along similar lines refer ibid., xiv–xv.
111. Rowland, *Culture*, 57.

space relative to their class, sex, race and so on. The third tackles the myth (*illusio*) of objectivity in which the agent seeks to take cognizance of the implications stemming from their choice to engage in a theoretical and contemplative way (the theoreticist stance met above). The second however is concerned with social or structural reflexivity in which an attempt is made to recognize the way

> Each field is characterized by the pursuit of a specific goal, tending to favor no less absolute investments by all (and only) those who possess the required dispositions (for example *libido sciendi*). Taking part in the *illusio*—scientific, literary, philosophical, or other—means taking seriously (sometimes to the point of making them questions of life and death) stakes which, arising from the logic of the game itself, establish their "seriousness," even if they may escape or appear "disinterested" or "gratuitous" to those who are sometimes called "lay people" or those who are engaged in other fields.[112]

Inserting "account of reason" wherever "field" appears (and appropriately adjusting for the change of context) makes the point. The question then turns to unmasking the *illusio* involved, the task to be engaged in the discussion below. This means returning to the description of reason Bourdieu sought to dispute in order to trace out from it the alternative path offered by the transcendent perspective.

Engaging again with the writing of Tanner is informative for this purpose, offering through its encounter with the work of John Milbank the opportunity to consider this issue by way of an example, though now with a much more critical eye towards the foundations being relied upon.

A central claim Tanner makes is

> The most basic contribution that an anthropological understanding of culture—postmodern or not—makes to theology is to suggest that theology be viewed as a part of culture, as a form of cultural activity. Most contemporary theologians would admit as much. Theology is something that human beings produce. Like all human activities, it is historically and socially conditioned; it cannot be understood in isolation from the rest of human sociocultural practices. In short, to say that theology is a part of culture is just to say in a contemporary idiom that it is a human activity.[113]

---

112. Pilario, *Rough Grounds of Praxis*, 217, quoting Bourdieu.
113. Tanner, *Theories of Culture*, 63.

The essential logic here is fairly obvious. Theology is a human activity that is therefore a form of cultural activity and accordingly is a part of culture. Culture is the object of anthropological investigation and consequently theology is an aspect of culture upon which the professional anthropological gaze may reasonably be turned. Theology, in short, is an object available for anthropological examination.

John Milbank and a Theological Critique

John Milbank, in *Theology and Social Theory*, addresses similar considerations when he comments

> theology has rightly become aware of the (absolute) degree to which it is a contingent historical construct emerging from, and reacting back upon, particular social practices conjoined with particular semiotic and figural codings. It is important to realize that my entire case is constructed from a complete *concession* as to this state of affairs, and that the book offers no proposed restoration of a pre-modern Christian position.[114]

Milbank seems to cede here the cogency of the logic Tanner is relying on. Theology is a human activity subject to all the influences inhering in this particularity and its narrative construct. Both Tanner and Milbank therefore agree on the contingent nature of theology: theology is a human production subject to sociocultural influences.

This agreement however is almost entirely superficial because the grounds of commonality do not extend beyond this bald statement; Milbank immediately goes on to comment "However, there is a very common perception amongst theologians that once this concession is made, most of what is to be known about social processes in general and the sociohistorical 'aspects' (an unwarranted qualification) of Christianity in particular, must be learned from social scientists."[115] Here are early intimations of what will be a wholesale rebuttal of the need for theology to rely on social scientific expertise. The hint provided by Rowland and MacIntyre is now being writ large across the canvas of secular history for it is the secular that Milbank identifies as the underpinning foundation requiring attention.

Milbank initiates a thoroughgoing attack on the very foundations of the Secular, along with its complicit social theories. His central argument is that social theory does not spring from an "innocent, genial inspiration,"

114. Milbank, *Theology and Social Theory*, 2.
115. Ibid.

instead it is a specific theological construct built upon a particular confessional foundation.[116] The bulk of Milbank's substantial argument in *Theology and Social Theory* is genealogical, concerned with unearthing this foundation in order to reveal its true nature; a nature ultimately resting on two interrelated roots, the one pagan and the other heretical.[117] The former is derived from "the Machiavellian Moment," which Milbank describes as "the astonishing re-emergence of pagan political and philosophical time no longer as a makeshift, nor a Thomist preparation for grace, but rather as something with its own integrity, its own goal and values, which might even contradict those of Christianity."[118]

The latter root, by contrast, is described as heretical because "the institution of the 'secular' is paradoxically related to a shift *within* theology and not an emancipation *from* theology."[119] Milbank brings these two thrusts together when he suggests that "the Machiavellian field of power is constructed by a partial rejection of Christianity and appeal to an alternative *mythos*."[120] These roots do not of course stand alone; they are shored up by a comprehensive web of supporting and interlocking theses gathered around this central, controlling paradigm.

Milbank then pursues four consequent goals through *Theology and Social Theory*. First, delineating the historical iterations and development of this Machiavellian field, particularly with respect to its social scientific manifestations; second, describing and challenging the underlying ontology of violence it is predicated on; third, proposing an alternative participatory ontology based in peace rather than violence; and fourth, demonstrating how this peaceable ontology can be outworked through an appropriately developed ecclesiology.

Tracing the complex arguments with which Milbank analyses each of these four goals is beyond the scope of this chapter, however the central points can be demonstrated through an example quite central to Milbank's

116. Postmodern theorists are not entirely unaware of this, though many theologians are, creating the perverse situation in which "'Theology accepts secularization and the autonomy of secular reason; [but] social theory increasingly finds secularization paradoxical, and implies that the mythic-religious can never be left behind. Political theology is intellectually atheistic; post-Nietzschean social theory suggests the practical inescapability of worship." Ibid., 3.

117. The form of genealogy Milbank relies on here has definite connections with the Nietzschean understanding but is actually derived from the very much earlier work of Giambattisto Vico, refer for example John Milbank, *The Early Metaphysics;* and Milbank, *Language, Law and History*.

118. Milbank, *Theology and Social Theory*, 21.

119. Ibid., 29, Emphasis original.

120. Ibid., 21.

case. Milbank suggests Heidegger proposes a description of ontological difference that considers the iterations of being, that is various instances of 'a being', as suppressions of Being itself. Milbank argues "The idea of an inescapable ontological 'fall' (*zug*) is . . . the transcendental support for Heidegger's nihilist version of historicism, and the very heart of his philosophy. Yet it is a thoroughly questionable notion."[121]

He argues the difference between "a being" and "Being" need not be understood through some notion of obliteration or concealment (being as a reduction of Being), though this is one possibility. It can also be read, and Milbank argues better read, as an exhibition of Being and therefore not as a rift from Being but rather as an enjoining with it. Heidegger's notion of being is therefore revealed as no more than one particular alternative, but also as one that is specifically developed through an immanent discourse. In this Heidegger is not engaged in a neutral maneuver but a bolstering and stabilizing effort that inherently accords primacy to the immanent possibility. It therefore always acts to suppress transcendence and consequently actively obscures from view the other already encountered option: transcendence. Ontological violence is for Milbank a possibility but it is only one of at least two feasible options. In short, despite appearances, Heidegger is not in pursuit of the only possible option. Preference is elided, or only really occluded, in Heidegger's analysis, but in the end plays a pre-emptive, premier role.

Milbank's analysis of Heidegger's account of Being/being leads him to examine the theologian whom he along with many others considers the author of the initial displacement within reason by which this option became viable, namely Duns Scotus.[122] Scotus, Milbank notes, argued the univocity of Being such that "Being" was no longer distinguishable from "being," the two designations instantiating the same meaning. This conjoining of being with Being had the effect of immediately separating reason and theology while concurrently laying the foundation for prioritizing the former over the latter because associating God with Being no longer provoked a hierarchical separation. The resulting priority of reason would in time find its fulfillment in the autonomy offered by nihilist discourse as the Aristotelian hierarchy Scotus relied on for theological structure eventually gave way to absolute diversity. Deleuze and Derrida, Milbank argues, joined univocity of being with non-hierarchical equivocity such that the utter dissolution of hierarchy was finally achieved and a ceaseless flux ensued.

---

121. Ibid., 300.

122. Caputo, *Philosophy and Theology*, straight forwardly narrates Duns Scotus as the root, refer p. 76 n. 5, whereas others describe it in more incremental terms refer, for example, Taylor, *A Secular Age*, 295.

As Milbank later comments "By these sorts of arguments one can begin to expose the element of sheer preference in the fundamental ontologies of Heidegger, Derrida and Deleuze."[123] In contradistinction to their suggestions he argues "By contrast, I am suggesting the possibility of a *different* ontology, which denies that mediation is necessarily violent. Such an ontology alone can support an alternative, peaceable, historical, practice."[124] At root Milbank asks, "is the nihilist philosophy of simultaneous univocity and equivocity more demonstrably 'fundamental' than the Catholic philosophy of analogical difference?"[125] His emphatic response is that it is not, albeit this relies on an important restatement of the classical analogical framework.

At this stage there is neither the need nor space to penetrate further into his fascinating suggestions for an analogical alternative, or what he terms a participatory ontology. The key point requiring attention has already been established, namely that at each step the nihilist framework (capturing both modernity and postmodernity in this description, the latter therefore effectively construed as ultra-modernity), along with the prior though still currently vigorous Kantian schema, is constructed and then buffered, hedging itself against the theological, hiding from itself and others the truth that is just one preferred *theologia* from amongst several. The secular *mythos* is therefore not *the* truth but is instead unmasked by Milbank as "a post-Christian paganism, something in the last analysis only defined, negatively, as a refusal of Christianity and the invention of an 'Anti-Christianity.'"[126] It is, in short, a grafted alternative, a perverse simulation.

Until now these ontological foundations, along with their associated theological lineages, have been assiduously hidden from view, submerged under an aggressive secular project of legitimation conducted through the unstinting, ramifying effects of "rationality." The secular maintains this stance by managing rival religious sensibilities, localizing them in the marginal area nominated "value"; that area of the secular that functions as the protected and treasured, but distant, ethereal lodge of "irreducible humanity":

> Sociology's "policing of the sublime" exactly coincides with the actual operations of secular society which excludes religion from its modes of "discipline and control," while protecting it as a "private" value, and sometimes invoking it at the public level to overcome the antinomy of a purely instrumental and goalless

---

123. Milbank, *Theology and Social Theory*, 306.
124. Ibid. Emphasis original.
125. Ibid., 303–4.
126. Ibid., 280.

rationality, which is yet made to bear the burden of ultimate political purpose.[127]

The Secular jealousy guards the marginalization of religion because "What is refused here is the idea that religion might enter into the most basic level of the symbolic organization of society, such that one would be unable to extract a 'society' behind and beneath 'religion.'"[128] If this refusal were to fail then society, and by implication culture, would be recognized as religiously narrated entities.

As Milbank later notes "sociology is only able to explain, or even illuminate religion, to the extent that it conceals its own theological borrowings and its own quasi-religious status."[129] Because these roots have remained hidden theologians have largely ceded the primacy of the "social" and unwittingly been forced into a *de facto* defensive position that has hindered their ability to recognize the thoroughly religious nature of the secular claim.

Milbank's critical contentions in *Theology and Social Theory* therefore form around the charge that this refusal of the religious does fail; that the function of the social as a privileged metadiscourse is only vindicated by "the illusion of a 'social fact', which can be contrasted with religion defined in such a way as to confine it and yet preserve it, in an irreal sublimity."[130] Far from being an "innocent, genial inspiration . . . we can now see that the emergence of the concept of the social must be located within the history of 'the secular', its attempt to legitimate itself, and to 'cope' with the phenomenon of religion."[131]

At this point Tanner's argument can be considered much more clearly in light of Milbank's thesis. Tanner, Milbank might argue, respected the authority of anthropological expertise because she did not recognize the theological underpinnings that founded it. Tanner was not, as she supposed, relying on a privileged discourse of rationality that objectively described the social. Instead she was unknowingly courting a quite specific theology; inviting into her project, through the notion of culture, the central tenets of a distinctively anti-Christian paradigm. Far from bolstering her theological agenda it reverses the agenda and turns it into another complicit construct in the ongoing history of secular legitimation, even if only through a complacent acceptance of the secular status quo—here one might invoke some passive sense of a Kuhnian rear-guard action as appropriately descriptive of her role.

127. Ibid., 106.
128. Ibid., 109.
129. Ibid., 52.
130. Ibid., 110.
131. Ibid., 102.

Contrary to Tanner's expectations then contemporary social scientific articulations of culture are not innocent children of ethnographic research; they are primarily molded and shaped through their filial relations with the social sciences. Social theory as an expression of secular reason provides an interpretive network that engenders and perpetuates theories which in turn act to ensure the continued persistence of the secular schema. This is of course a much more subtle operation than this bald statement of it implies for it is not the overt, consciously pursued agenda implied here, it is instead the expression of a tacit but supremely confident assumption that the secular is the only viable option. A corollary of this operation is the need to appropriately locate, and thereby cope with, any and all potential rival foundations, such as the Christian sensibility.

Tanner quite openly embraces the domesticating function just described, defining her engagement of culture as an attempt to

> locate theology in a very particular place on the cultural map. Theology from an anthropological point of view would be something like what nineteenth-century scholars called a "positive science," [which involves] . . . thinking about theology as a part of some specific, communally shaped way of life, with all the full-bodied and concrete comprehensiveness that the expression "way of life" conveys from an anthropological point of view.[132]

This mechanism of "locating" theology is subtle but definitive, and expresses also the tenor of Tanner's engagement with Milbank. She does not directly encounter him, in the sense of tackling him *on his own terms*, but instead reads him through the grid of the social and relativizes or "locates" him on this basis. She envisages Milbank as an advocate of a Christian *form* of society rather than as challenging society *per se*; construing him therefore as espousing just a version of the social.[133]

Yet it is precisely this process he sets out to critique. Milbank is not advocating distinctions in the form of society, but is deconstructing the very notion of society, at least in its secular narration, by presenting its various contemporary descriptions as manifestations of the coercive legitimating structures of the secular. There is no autonomous notion of society that can be divided up into forms or versions, only particular kinds of *mythos*; religiously narrated understandings of human sociality that underpin distinctive social formations. The secular confession is one, and, as Milbank argues, the Christian another.

132. Tanner, *Theories of Culture*, 67.
133. Ibid., 97–102.

Culture in a Post-Secular Context

As he notes,

> At best, these social scientific theories are but narratives which seek to locate the ultimate "meaning" of human history by telling a story with certain emphases, and to insinuate that certain precedent conditions for events really constitute sufficient (efficient or formal) causes. Theology purports to give an ultimate narrative, to provide some ultimate depth of description, because the situation of oneself within such a continuing narrative is what it means to belong to the Church, to be a Christian. However, the claim is made by faith, not a reason which seeks foundations. Surrendering this gaze to the various gazes of "methodological atheism" would not prove to be any temporary submission.[134]

Tanner's analysis of Milbank is therefore grounded in a category error, one that mistakes different ways of understanding the socius for variant ways of describing discourses occurring within the socius.

Gavin Hyman provides a useful way of understanding the Tanner and Milbank disjunction when he analyses Don Cupitt's comparable failure to properly engage Milbank. In Wittgensteinian vein he suggests Cupitt is pursuing the debate as if it were "one *within* a single framework rather than *between* two different frameworks . . . [and he therefore] . . . refuses its alterity and interprets it in terms of the very framework it is concerned to reject."[135] This misunderstanding, disingenuous or not, leads to a "confusion and distortion" that ultimately degenerates into polarization.

Wittgenstein, according to Hyman, in terms that clearly invoke Milbankian themes, conceives inter-framework disputes not as the grounds of reasoned argument, as it is for intra-framework discussions, but of persuasion and charm, or what amounts to propaganda; a rhetorical inducement to change from "one particular kind of vision of the moral and spiritual world" to another.[136] Milbank describes this as a process of outnarration; Graham Ward refers to it as cultural politics.[137] However labeled the underlying logic is simple, at least in its basest form. Reasoning is contextual in a quite specific sense, it is an internally validated logic wedded to a particular legitimating framework. When taken outside of this framework it simulta-

---

134. Milbank, *Theology and Social Theory*, 249.

135. Hyman, *Predicament of Postmodern Theology*, 53–54.

136. Refer ibid., 54–56. The phrase in single quotes being one he borrowed from Rowan Williams as recorded at p. 59.

137. Refer esp. Milbank, *Theology and Social Theory*, 1, 279, 330. See also Ward, "Radical Orthodoxy and/as Cultural Politics," 102–3.

neously steps outside of its authenticating context and takes up the more demanding posture of persuasion.

Milbank is not reasoning from *within* the socius, as Tanner imagines, instead he is engaged in charming persuasion.[138] In the process of achieving this goal he narrates the Secular as an outworking or consequence of human foible and the Christian, or at least a postmodern, neo-platonic Augustinian variant thereof, as an expression of divine intention.[139] This is not to say he resides in some self-deluding Archimedean point subsuming all frameworks, but that the Christian frame of reference, now wrestled from secular sublimity, is asserting itself as *at least* a comparable frame of reference for understanding and explaining the world to that offered by the secular.

The secular then, is not the expression of inherent universal rationalism it claims to be but is in fact the purveyor of a distinctly partisan description that is only as legitimate as its ability to persuade. This naturally raises the question of how it is possible to determine which discourse is to be preferred. Perhaps the best question to guide this endeavor at distinguishing between efforts of legitimating persuasion must ultimately be the place of humanity within the cosmos. In other terminology, the focus should be placed on how the world is ordered in each case and how each option handles the relationships subsisting between transcendence, reality, reason and humanity.

Milbank in *Being Reconciled: Ontology and Pardon* provides his only full essay concerned with culture as a specific problematic, entitled "Culture: The Gospel of Affinity." In this essay Milbank pursues in one particular section points pertinent to present concerns. He suggests "An ordering of the world in terms of essences and relative values is linked in some way to teleology and hierarchy, or else alternatively, to spatialization."[140] Essentially he is arguing that within the Western tradition the world has been understood and described through either of two lenses: teleology or immanence; a dichotomy that has birthed three consecutive models which have dominated the tradition's history.

The first has already been polemically overcome in Western intellectual history, relegated or consigned to the realm of pre-modernity as

---

138. A sense of Milbank's argument is contained in emergent studies on disciplinarity and rhetoric; a suggestive possibility that would directly tie Milbank's thesis to Rowland's earlier noted argument on experts. This cannot be pursued here as it moves beyond the boundaries of the current study; however refer for an example to Robertson, "Review," 765–66.

139. Milbank sometimes presents his views as "postmodern critical Augustinianism," refer for example to Milbank, "Postmodern Critical Augustinianism."

140. Milbank, *Being Reconciled*, 194.

a surpassed forerunner of later constructs. It expressed and embodied a cosmos oriented around transcendence that imbued the world with a distinctive sense of purpose. The second historical development was the birth around 1300 of "what Gilles Deleuze called 'the plane of immanence' . . . seen as consisting in a kind of fixed spatial grid. Although height had been lost, depth displaced height and there still persisted fixed natures, especially human nature."[141]

This particular expression of immanence is now labeled Modernity but represents both the culmination and ongoing perpetuation of a long process of spatial flattening. As secular reason began to take hold and assert its arrogated prerogatives it persistently sought to remove the remaining vestiges of external vertical influence. This emphasis on expunging transcendence did not initially extend to a complete removal of the "other," though it did curtail it to an alterity of depth principally expressed as internality. This development had not at this stage dropped the emphasis on the fixity of human nature characterizing its forerunner; hence there remains the enduring prominence of a spatial emphasis.

The third development, whether considered as the surpassing or culmination of the second, did however take the next step of replacing fixity with fluidity and, importantly, spatiality with pure eternal linearity. As Milbank notes, "In postmodernity, however, neither height nor depth remains, but only a shifting surface flux, because immanence is now conceived in terms of the primacy of time not space."[142]

Taking this Milbankian framework and mapping it onto Tanner's analysis establishes an important nexus of relationships. Tanner argues against a modernist construct by establishing the greater explanatory power inherent in a postmodernist framework. According to Milbank this maneuver never escapes the immanent plane but quintessentially expresses its continued evolution. The initial shift from transcendence to spatialization is here simply radicalized as flux. Tanner unwittingly places herself in a bind because the very foundation she bases her subsequent theological agenda on is intrinsically antithetical to this agenda and cannot but work assiduously and insidiously against it. More problematically it represents a foundation she cannot access and critique from within the confines of her own framework. Culture for Tanner is not an object finally available for structural theological reflection because its relationship to the transcendent pole of the divine/human frame of reference has been putatively displaced by the immanent context of analysis she relies on. This is not as such an overt displacement

141. Ibid.
142. Ibid., 194–95.

Challenging the Neutrality of Culture

of the teleological view of culture but is instead the inevitable consequence of the systematic reconstrual of the divine/human relationship perpetrated throughout the social sciences. Unfortunately it has significant consequences for her program because reconstructing culture on a firmly theological foundation concomitantly threatens to destabilize and deconstruct Tanner's theological edifice. This is in fact the concern attending to varying degrees all theological constructs formulated on the basis of or emanating from social scientific definitions of culture.

Tentative Basis for a Christian Alternative

While the primary concern of the foregoing has been essentially negative, establishing the neutrality of culture as a problematic requiring resolution, there is within the material already surveyed intimations of a positive agenda, a description of how theology might begin to articulate a specifically Christian account of culture. Milbank, for example, plots a constructive theology that not only argues "theology is itself a social science, and the queen of sciences for the inhabitants of the *altera civitas*, on pilgrimage through this temporary world" but which also consequently contends "It is theology itself that will have to provide its own account of the final causes at work in human history, on the basis of its own particular, and historically specific faith."[143]

Theology, Milbank is suggesting, must look primarily at itself if it wants to develop an understanding of the historical manifestations of these final causes, a claim that invokes and fills with Christian content the "turn to practice" explained above. He then identifies the appropriate locus for these manifestations in ecclesiology; the explanation of the actual, historical social behavior of the church constituted as "a distinguishable Christian mode of action . . . ,"[144] though not thereby a "tridentine deduction of Christian social teaching from Christian doctrine."[145] Theology, through ecclesiology, is concerned with specific, historical, socio-linguistic iterations of human sociality and living; in short, with culture.

Furthermore, these various iterations of the Christian narrative have to do with real, historical events that consequently have a regulative function over the rest of human history. Christians read all of history through the "interruption" of Jesus and the coming of his church, both of which are social events governing the understanding of all other social configurations. In other words, the church embodies the exemplary form of human

---

143. Milbank, *Theology and Social Theory*, 380.
144. Ibid.
145. Ibid.

community (a notion in need of the explanation to be given in later chapters) and it is against this text that other communities need to be read. As the exemplary form it is also necessarily the consummate expression of human living, or what may be called culture.

This ecclesiology is therefore grounded in a specific understanding of culture that renders it both the norm and expression of culture. It articulates the goal, always pointing toward the ecclesial intent outlined in Scripture, while also describing specific historical articulations that exemplify this intent. The historical story of the church is seen in this light as the story of human "culture" in transition towards authentic human community. This is idealized in Scripture, realized in the eschatological future, but is also always proleptic; present in what Milbank terms "judicious narratives."

The preceding charts some of the course ahead; however before this can be fully articulated some of the underlying assumptions giving it traction must be subjected to careful scrutiny. In particular the way the preceding levels the playing field, portraying the secular account of rationality as one grounded in immanence and therefore as no more likely a possibility than any transcendent account, though in fact representing a far less reasonable proposition. This last claim is the most difficult to empirically substantiate because validation can only really be achieved by providing a superior description of culture from the transcendent foundation. The existence of a widespread tendency to defer to social scientific descriptions seems to preclude this possibility, yet Milbank does propose an intriguing alternative built out of a reconstituted minority Christian tradition. The next chapter therefore examines this proposal and its implications.

Chapter 3

John Milbank and a Theological Account of Culture

THE PREVIOUS CHAPTERS HAVE argued that social scientific descriptions of culture are not the neutral, empirically based commentaries they purport to be for no such impartiality exists. It was argued instead that the attribute of neutrality was constructed, representing an ascription intended to establish and perpetuate the hegemony of one specific, parochial account of reason that had arrogated to itself the colonial privileges of universal application—this being the secular account. Reason in its classical and early medieval guises was never conceived autonomously for it was uniformly understood to derive from and be linked into a divine heritage. It was only after certain critical disjunctions were initiated, such as that in the notion of being by Duns Scotus, that it became possible to consider disowning this heritage, a task that saw, as Robert Miner notes, "the secularizing architects of modernity—Bacon, Descartes, and Hobbes—engage in the willful detachment of human *ratio* from divine *ratio*, and thus paradoxically inaugurate postmodern irrationalism and nihilism."[1]

In John Milbank's writings this disengagement of reason from transcendent roots is not accorded positive space for immanence is instead conceived as a parasitically derivative case; formed and postulated as a denial rather than affirmation. As denial it lacks true or substantive content and can therefore only ever tend towards a "state" lacking in content or substance, or in other words, towards the *nihil*. Nihilism is consequently the most basic "form" of immanence, though this is to immediately overstate

1. Miner, *Truth in the Making*, 127.

the situation in suggesting it possesses a character. Rather, it is constituted as formlessness, characterized by instability and movement; hence the celebrated postmodern obeisance to flux. Milbank's most basic argument is that the Secular, as denial, is inherently involved in a continuous process of devolution towards its truest state, nihilism and hence formlessness and void nothingness. Against this dismal possibility he seeks to array the plenitude of divine affirmation, the framework upon which he constructs his own ongoing project.

His *Theology and Social Theory* (TST) is perhaps best read through this positive emphasis since his entire presentation is an attempt to persuade readers of the ontological priority of peace this possibility entails. It achieves this in two stages. The first involves a critical genealogical dissertation that seeks to unearth the immanent roots of contemporary social scientific discourse while concurrently demonstrating the inescapably nihilist nature of its inner logic. The second, a smaller but perhaps more important section, has both a polemical and positive focus. Polemically, it is a continuation of the critical engagement initiated in the first section because it demonstrates, by way of comparison with its positive affirmations, the paucity of the immanent construct. Positively, it is an exercise in envisaging an alternative understanding of reality, one that takes the divine, peaceable origin of all things as the most basic presupposition upon which an articulation of the world can be based.

In some ways it is therefore better to read the second, constructive section first for it is this Christian alternative that funds the prior critical engagements. It is the existence of this stable alternative that grants Milbank the ability to negotiate his way through the web of epistemological and ontological (mis)perceptions woven together by the secular paradigm because it provides him an exemplar against which each aspect can be measured. Point by point he seeks to demolish the artificiality of the secular pattern, uncovering and unpicking those threads he thinks have been wrongly woven together. He can only do so because he has already been exposed to the natural and entirely more beautiful pattern formed by God. What emerges to view through this is the way the secular disposition not only lacks positive space, but is in fact always negatively geared because it is a distorted parody of the divine alternative it was built from. Not only this, but it is now actively but perversely attempting (and in immanent terms apparently somewhat successfully) to colonize the positive space of divine reason.[2]

This description of Milbank's project has proceeded along fairly standard lines of sympathetic delineation, outlining the broadest contours of

---

2. Milbank, *Theology and Social Theory*, xiv–xv, makes this especially clear.

Milbank's metaphysical pathways. Having sketched this section of his panorama it is now possible to examine his project with more care with a view to determining the extent to which his proposals offer the positive Christian account of culture this book suggests is there. At first glance this appears an implausible task because culture seems notably absent from his various discussions, and ostensibly so from TST altogether. As will be detailed below this apparent lack of reference is deceptive.

It will be argued that contrary to appearances Milbank cannot be properly understood without attending to his understanding of culture. In as much as he presents a postmodern critical Augustinianism he also offers a poetic cultural theology that exerts a powerful subterranean influence on his corpus. Paying attention to only his popular writings will miss this influence because he only sporadically treats them in overt fashion.[3] Instead, two largely overlooked but seminal books covering his doctoral and immediately post-doctoral writings are crucial.[4] It is in these books that his overall stance is first developed, and it is here that the sinews holding together his later writings are most clearly evident.

John Milbank and Culture

It is possible to trace what appears to be a growing interest in culture in Milbank's popular writings. From a minimal role in TST the cautious reader can find several essays in the WMS dealing with the topic before finding in BR explicit coverage within the introduction. Yet this apparent "growth" of interest in culture is not really an "emerging" interest in or "developing" recognition of the importance of culture. It is instead an increasingly clear articulation (for the reader rather than author) of what was *always already* informing his entire theological project. Milbank, it is suggested, already had a definite and well-formed conception of culture before the publication of TST, one that is consequently woven into the very fabric of it and everything since. This contention will be elaborated with the aid of Milbank's doctoral and post-doctoral work on Giambattista Vico, the entirety of which, it is suggested, is concerned with describing culture, and this as an inherently religious phenomenon.

---

3. To date he was authored or co-authored the following academic works (aside from poetry): Milbank, *Theology and Social Theory*; Milbank, *The Word Made Strange*; Milbank, *Being Reconciled*; Milbank and Pickstock, *Truth in Aquinas*; Milbank, Pickstock, and Ward, *Radical Orthodoxy*; Milbank, Ward, and Wyschogrod, *Theological Perspectives*.

4. Milbank, *The Early Metaphysics*; Milbank, *Language, Law and History*.

Culture in a Post-Secular Context

The preceding descriptions already give clear indications of the shape of this chapter. It will be divided into three main sections, the first concerned with providing a concise but careful description of Milbank's pre TST understanding of culture, drawing heavily on resources found in his writings on Vico. The claim to outline *Milbank's* view here is problematized though because these writings did not set out to elaborate Milbank's own views but to delineate his conception of Vico's perspective. There is therefore a need to discriminate between what is properly descriptive of Vico without further implications for Milbank and what of Vico's framework manages to enmesh itself within Milbank's own theology. The only way this can be done is by comparing the material on Vico with what then appears in Milbank's subsequent corpus.

The second section attempts this task by describing the more important "cultural moments" inhabiting Milbank's post Vico publications. In this respect the TST discussion is taken as the exemplar, offering the most difficult possibility because it is here that his conception of culture is most heavily masked. Yet careful attention to the way critical moments in his narrative are constructed is revealing, bringing out the subterranean influence his understanding of culture exerts on TST. At this point it starts to become clear exactly how important the Vico dissertation was for him and how truly Vichian in character Milbank's perspective is. This is only strengthened by examining his publications since TST where these same themes emerge much more clearly to view. The third section is a short concluding discussion that brings into view the central lineaments traced through the preceding two sections in an analysis of his later writings.

What this analysis most clarifies is the extent to which Milbank takes on board and then perpetuates the themes he discovers in Vico. This places on display the extent to which he might be said to continue the underlying heritage Vico represents. Inversely, it also potentially predicts the contours of his future writings as this same legacy clearly implies the pursuit of a specific goal: the elaboration of the full-fledged poetic "cultural theology" he finds in Vico, taking this as being, properly and fully, "theology."

Before proceeding it is worth noting that Milbank's oeuvre is dense and intricately layered hence concise exposition is challenging; innumerable vistas open to view as one proceeds through his work. The following cannot hope, in the space available, to canvas the entirety of his subtle arguments or offer a comprehensive discussion of his many interrelated maneuvers; hence the primary focus is placed on the central elements of his exposition, tracing how these inculcate themselves into his overall thesis. The dearth of critical engagement with Milbank's work on Vico should also be noted; it is not terrain that has been explored very well yet (as at least one Vichian scholar laments).[5] Even less remarked upon is the centrality of the cultural thesis to his ongoing work hence there is even less guidance available for traversing this material. It is to be hoped that further exploration into the intricacies of Milbank's contemporary rendition of poetic theology might be stimulated as this dependence is brought more into the public domain, especially given the degree to which it permeates his later writings.

Milbank on Giambattista Vico

Vico and Factum

Milbank's discussion of Vico was published in two volumes, the first corresponding to his doctoral dissertation, completed under the supervision of the Vico specialist Leon Pompa and consisting of an examination of Vico's metaphysical foundations, especially but not exclusively those found in *De Antiquissima Italorum Sapientia* (On the Most Ancient Wisdom of the Italians). The second, completed as post-doctoral studies, extended this analysis both diachronically and substantively by investigating Vico's application of his metaphysic in his later more practical writings, most notably in *Diritto Universale* (Universal Right) and the various versions of *Scienza Nuova* (New Science). The central themes around which this latter volume revolves are the interrelated, core issues of language, law and history, or what turns out to be culture.

Partly due to space, but primarily because of the way Milbank's subsequent writings address these issues, the ensuing will concentrate on the metaphysic discussions, though taking language as its prime paradigm. Some discussion of historiography is necessary in the course of outlining the language schema, but will be restricted to precisely this domain. Juridical comment will be even more limited though this does not accord with its importance. Sufficient comment will be made to indicate the framework of equity that necessarily guides Vico's metaphysical construct; and which plays such an important role in Milbank's later work. What will not be pursued however is any consideration of the practical legal ramifications Milbank describes other than as they directly intersect with and converge on the issues already under examination.

When coming to Milbank's early writings it is worth noting that he accepts at least one aspect of what is generally agreed amongst Vichian commentators; namely that Vico's early writings are centered in the *verum-factum* (true-made) axiom. As he then informs us however, he departs quite

---

5. Mazzotta, *New Map of the World*, 225 n. 6.

markedly from these commentators in two principle ways. First, he reverses the normal order of priority. Vico is not, he suggests, advocating the primacy of the true, with its historic tendency towards universalizing abstractions and reified *a priori* assumptions, for this is precisely what Vico vigorously contends against. Milbank therefore objects to those seeking to recruit Vico to the cause of Kantian universals, or who describe him in such terms.

According to Milbank Vico should instead be seen as developing a thoroughly theological formulation of *verum-factum-bonum* (true-made-good) in which the *factum* element registers a certain priority at all points, a schema that ultimately dismisses the philosophic universals as inadequate shadows of divine truth, at least in their classical Kantian form. This last comment intimates the nuance with which Vico appears to approach this issue. His dethronement of the universals does not directly translate into an equally encompassing rejection of reason, as might be expected. Reason is instead restructured and then placed in what he thinks is its rightful abode—the divinely crafted space carved out for it under Divine *ratio*.

The second major point of departure Milbank has from standard Vico scholarship is his restoration of the religious dimension in Vico. Religion is not cosmetic for Vico but fundamental, forming the heart of his perspective. For Milbank it is the central element of Vico's writings; that around which everything is built: the heuristic key for understanding him. Most scholars have described Vico's "new science" as if it were devoid of religious intent and empowerment, anachronistically treating the obvious religiousness of his writings as idiosyncratic expressions of the context in which he was writing. Against this view, Milbank argues, must be posited the irreducibly religious nature of Vico's account. Once a scholar restores this aspect to its proper dominant position then almost all of the perplexities attending analysis of Vico's work become resolvable, or at least more understandable. Vico was, he asserts, writing from a specifically theological perspective that subscribed to the priority of the transcendent dimension.

The following analysis will not focus its attention on the repatriation of a religious dimension in Vico as this will emerge abundantly to view as the argument proceeds. It will instead concentrate on describing the core elements of Milbank's restoration of the *factum* thesis for it is this that gives rise to an account of culture that then impels, it will be argued, Milbank's own subsequent writings. The central question presenting itself therefore concerns the nature and characteristics of *factum*; both in its own right and as interrelated to the rest of his theology. The most convenient point to enter into this discussion is through his description of language.

John Milbank and a Theological Account of Culture

Language

For Milbank it is the following passage from Vico's later works that quintessentially expresses the *verum-factum* thesis, forming the *locus classicus* that most deeply informs Milbank's description of him:

> But in the night of thick darkness enveloping the earliest antiquity, so remote from ourselves, there shines the eternal and never failing light of a truth beyond all question: that the world of civil society has certainly been made by men, and that its principles are therefore to be found within the modifications of our own human mind. Whoever reflects on this cannot but marvel that the philosophers should have bent all their energies to the study of the world of nature, which since God made it, he alone knows; and that they should have neglected the study of the world of nations which, since men had made it, men could come to know.[6]

Milbank finds in this passage a resonance with the prologue of John's Gospel in that "Vico invokes the Trinity, and his own metaphysics; just as in God there is an original word, an original relation, an original signifying, an original 'supplement,' so also in human culture, or the 'metaphysics of the human mind,' the origin *is* the projection of language, the already-begun development of the human future."[7]

Already it is evident that Milbank envisages the Vichian passage to be talking about culture but more particularly of culture as a distinctively religious phenomenon, hence we are immediately presented with an interesting chain of linkages: *verum-factum* (Vico's metaphysics); Trinity (the eternal and never failing light); culture (world of nations/civil society); language (modifications of our human mind); and lastly, origins (thick darkness).

Milbank summarizes, providing in the process a Vichian definition of culture, by noting that cultures

> have to be regarded as the work of human wills, operating more or less self-consciously, according to the imperatives of a partially grasped, immanent logic, emerging from the figurative use of language . . . the whole process is a response to and realisation of, divine revelation.[8]

There are two central components to this account of culture. First, it has its origins in the "figurative use of language" and second, its emergence

---

6. Milbank, *Language, Law and History*, 9.
7. Ibid., 21.
8. Ibid., 221.

is a response to divine revelation. Clarifying the first naturally leads into a discussion of the second hence this will be the order of engagement in what follows.

Milbank argues "the methodological key to human origins is that history has been made by human beings, and the origin which this points to has the unsurpassable character of a tautologous statement of the problematic—human beginnings are *human* beginnings, the origin of culture is cultural, the transition to history consists in the human making of language."[9]

Of course, this immediately raises a problem for we do not have direct access to these origins; a problem consisting of two central issues. First, there is the methodological question of reconstructing historical narratives when there is no beginning to refer to, especially when their elaboration is as much about what is revealed as what is concealed.[10] Vico circumvents this by noting that any given cultural point has emerged as the result of a succession of modifications. Any point can therefore serve as the entrée once the "most general grammar of the human text" and the mechanisms of concealment are known because with these three pieces of information (the point of entry, the dictating human grammar and the concealment mechanism—or conversely the modification process) it is possible to track back to origins.[11] Vico takes as the basic principles of his universal human grammar the triad of marriage, burial and providence and from this builds a "theogony-chronology" that systematically delineates human development.[12]

As Milbank notes, once the basic principles of the human grammar are identified "the genetic rule is then followed, and Vico begins with the most ancient surviving material (however it may be preserved) and gradually builds up a complex narrative of human development, forming a continuous history

---

9. Ibid., 17. Emphasis original.

10. "Decoding involves more than becoming aware of a truth about a past time of which the people at that time were themselves unaware. It involves also exhibiting exactly how past language worked to conceal its own characteristics. Once one has done this, then the narrative given by the historian does not just take the form of a tale of communication, of the passing on of an inheritance which is gradually added to through time; it also takes the form of a story of concealment (not usually deliberate) and exposure. But 'breaks in intention' do not only occur for Vico as conscious critical uncoverings: on the contrary, as we have seen, Vico posits cultural changes that are unconscious 'concealments of concealments' (the founding of cities, later the coming of philosophy). These also can be later decoded, thereby tracing precisely the route by which present application has deviated from original intent." (II, 188)

11. For this and the following refer Milbank's discussion of Vichian historiography, especially Milbank, *Language, Law and History*, 209ff.

12. Refer ibid., 211–12. Here he provides a chart and explanation of this theogony-chronology.

which we must read in the right order . . . if we are to follow the unfolding 'geometry' of history in its own peculiar logical sequence."[13]

Second, and more importantly, there is the problem of the obscuring mystifications characterizing primitive narratives. There is a need to penetrate these mystical descriptions in order to reconstruct the "real" primitive thinking beneath the mythical accretions, the thought the primitives were themselves unaware of. There is a sharp distinction made here by Vico between the Hebrew and pagan cases. The latter is thought to be inherently characterized by mystification, *pace* the former. Vico argues his case with reference to the mythical discourse of Jove, the progenitor of pagan language and culture.

Jove is the god of sky and was first noticed by feral humanity when thunderclaps boomed from the sky and lightening streaked across it. At this sight and sound humanity lifted its eyes and saw the sky as if for the first time. They recognized in the display of power and might an element of themselves that then became projected back onto the sky, animating it as a single divine body precisely expressing this projection in all its fullness, a projection rooted in violence and its corollary, restraint of violence.[14] Despite its obvious mystical intonations Vico deems it *vera narratio* (true narrative) in the sense that it expresses a *mythos* embodying a cosmology that expresses their experience of the world. It is a *mythos* that they fully inhabit. At base it is founded in a partially grasped root truth, the presence of God. The partial truth involved has implications, leading them, for example, to inaugurate a polity seeking after true justice.[15]

At the same time the myth is systematically untrue because it is constituted by and continuously gives rise to idolatry, divination and sacrifice. Most interesting for present purposes is the charge of idolatry for this is linked with the central feature of Vico's account of language—metaphor. Jove is considered a "poetic universal" that becomes fully identified with nature (sky) such that the idea that Jove might be behind, above, or beyond nature is eclipsed and he becomes trapped within the system of "nature" signification, becomes in fact *the* personification of it. This is an inherent reductionism rooted in the premature foreclosing of the initial religious metaphor, one that diminishes its constitutive human and divine elements: God idolatrously becomes entirely identified with nature while humanity is structured into relationship with nature rather than God.[16]

13. Ibid., 210.

14. Ibid., 38ff. "Thus gentile language is *constituted* as an original withholding of a force of destruction, and an inhibition of the unmeaning and bestial chaos of the giant's wanderings." Ibid., 9

15. Ibid., 40–42.

16. "Although this image is initially the product of metaphor, which Vico associates

Milbank therefore argues "The grammar of pagan language is then for Vico a self-obfuscating grammar which conceals the founding role of metaphor."[17] This is sharply contrasted with the Hebraic grammar because "they did not collapse the inferred speaking subject into his signs, but retained a sense of his absence along with a sense of his presence."[18] In other words, the original metaphor was not foreclosed, albeit there was oscillation, but was instead allowed to retain its essential tension between the presence and absence of God. Further, God in the Semitic depiction is not presented in terms of holding back chaos or of restricting anger but as instead gift, as founded in charity and hence as the "creator *ex nihilo*."[19] Here Vico is clearly mediating the effects of the fall on Hebrew thought, finding behind the law, which was erected as a consequence of the fall, an original grammar of peace.[20]

From this it can be seen that the question of origins devolves into a fundamentally religious issue centered on how to construe the context humanity inhabits. The primary instrument for expressing this situation is language, which in its initial state of emergence is inherently metaphoric. For example, in the illustration of Jove, the initial human elements are gesticulations, early humanity pointing to the sky in response to the sky's thunderous gesticulation. The pagan error is to render Jove fully present, closing down and making immanent the divine metaphor. What, then, does Vico think should have happened? To answer this it is necessary to consider his analysis of rhetoric.

---

with analogy, it passes over, in the very course of its production, by process of alienation, into *allegory*, which Vico associates with univocity . . ." Ibid., 51.

17. Ibid. This continues on to give intimations of the focus of Milbank's later attack on the Secular in TST: "Vico portrays this grammar as being also the structure of a society and religion which thinks in terms of 'inhibition' and a 're-channelling' of a primal chaos and a primal anger."

18. Ibid., 77.

19. "[T]he Hebrew God is not posited as restricted anger, but as 'original charity' (*De Const.* I, IV [4] [18]), not as the confiner of chaos, but as the creator *ex nihilo*. His meanings proceed, in consequence, not from a progressive restriction, but from an infinite source of donation. Thus the multiplication of meaning, in the case of the Hebrew God, can only be a confirmation of his infinite unity." Ibid., 78.

20. The Semitic language is based around law and hence the holding back of a primal anger and chaos but beneath it one can see the prospect of a peaceable alternative. "Their language *also* registers the notion of a *more primitive* meaning originally conceived as God's gratuitous creation of the world from a charitable and in no sense violent impulse. This meaning of 'gratuitous extension' is then disseminated throughout Hebrew language and culture." Ibid., 81.

Rhetoric

According to Milbank Vico was writing at a time when classical understandings of rhetoric, the art of persuasive speech, were constructed on the basis of the Aristotelian categories *inventio*, *iudicio* and *elocutio* (topics, judgment and ornamentation respectively) that had given way before the dialectic emphasis—the art of rational discourse—established by the sixteenth-century humanists. Their version of dialectic had sharply circumscribed the parameters of rhetoric by no longer treating *inventio* and *iudicio* as independent categories. They were instead, dependent concepts under the sway of dialectic. This left *elocutio* alone within the rhetorical ambit; and it was within this much diminished arena of Aristotelian embellishment that Baroque rhetoric sought to assert itself.

Baroque rhetoric is an important influence on Vico, distinguishable from the tradition of the humanists by its emphasis on and interest in "the need to find moral and intellectual significance in the formation of words themselves, and in the transformative capacities of 'conceited' language . . ."[21] It's emphasis was not on the ornamentation characteristic of *elocutio* but instead on understanding the underlying structure of language, albeit from within the reductive "decorative sphere" imposed upon it by the priority granted dialectic. It harbored, in short, a sense of ontological ambition. Vico's originality, Milbank suggests, is his restoration of the Aristotelian/Cicerian categories outlined above *in conjunction* with a continued emphasis upon a specifically Baroque rhetoric as it had developed *in isolation* from the two erstwhile classical categories of *inventio* and *iudicio* under the ambit of humanist rhetoric.

The process he envisages can therefore be explained in the following way. Initial investigations of any particular topic can only occur by way of "preliminary determinations." As Milbank notes "Unless one makes some preliminary determination of the matter in hand one will not know the appropriate scope and mode of consequent argumentation. The axiomatic consideration that perception must precede judgement is important, because perception is never a 'bare perception' to which we can apply a ready-made critical *schema*, but a perception which already suggests certain sorts of argument."[22]

The investigation is therefore never undertaken in an entirely naïve fashion but is instead initially pursued by way of pre-existing categories operating as indicators of plausible future arguments. This, in a nutshell, is the

---

21. Milbank, *The Early Metaphysics*, 281.
22. Ibid., 283.

classical role attributed to *inventio*. It involves the generation of suitable preliminary "topics" applicable to the subject at hand that provide suggestive ways of understanding or grasping hold of the subject or its components.[23]

These preliminary headings, Vico suggests, should be as exhaustive as possible, encompassing the field of inquiry so as to bring to the fore all aspects that are likely to have a bearing on the subject at hand. Only once these are as comprehensive as possible can the investigation proceed on a logical basis. After the initial foray the topical introductions will have given rise to corresponding insights that must then be assessed, a process of weighing the various elements relative to their importance for the topic at hand. This requires the exercise of good judgment, or what is classically called *iudicio*.

There is a certain "natural ordering" of these two aspects, *inventio* coming before *iudicio* (or what Milbank describes in a legal context as *topica* before *critica*, the respective terms being equivalent) for "When we are first aware of any matter—natural or cultural—we get to know it in a hazy sort of way that is highly concrete and basically perceptual. . . . Only gradually does it dawn on us that to establish this fact as a fact we must assess—what is equally fundamental in the evidence before us—the probabilities, circumstances and motivations involved."[24]

The juridical terminology is an apposite equivalency because in his discussion of them Vico establishes the temporal but not "ontological" priority of *topica* over *critica* given that at all times "*critica* is a moment within *topica* itself."[25] He continues by asserting that in any determination

> we have to do our best with the aid of existing categories to define a particular situation, and only this process of contingent decision will suggest to us an appropriate course of action. Judgement depends upon a relatively complete determination of a state of affairs, but there is no available scale for measuring such relative completeness. Judicial judgement then, is radically dependent upon the fragile (and corruptible) exercise of rhetorical *inventio*.[26]

23. This equates to Robert Miners discussion of Vico's attention to *ars topica* presented in chapter 2, and hence to Raymond Williams emphasis on a vulgar approach to culture.

24. Milbank, *The Early Metaphysics*, 284.

25. Ibid., 287.

26. Ibid. "Vico can give the limiting case for the perfect judgement which is simultaneously the perfect topical determination. It is, of course, the situation in which a particular matter is fully producible or reproducible: where *inventio* carries the sense of 'invention' rather than the sense of discovery, in accordance with *verum-factum*. This limiting case only occurs, with reference to the ethical sphere, in the case of God, and for this reason divine justice is 'geometric'; for God *prudentia* (or providence) is at

Accompanying this basic process is a distinctive method, or what Milbank terms *artes*, called *ingenium* (the inventive faculty of intelligence or imagination). It is this metaphoric mode of engagement that governs the development of argumentation and advances the processes of either discovery or invention. *Ingenium* expresses the originality or creativity of imagination or what is involved in moving beyond the initial generation of topics.[27] It involves "synthetic moves in which the mind is guided by its own generation of models and standards which are not simply given in the already constituted material world."[28] Here a quintessentially metaphoric process is brought to the fore because what is envisaged is an imaginative leap, one that springboards off the underlying elements.

For Vico this imaginative leap works when we find delight in the beautiful discourse that unfolds from the originality of its result. Delight is here connected not only with aesthetics but also reason for "we do not admire merely a new sound, nor a new picture which is conjured up before us. In our admiration we grasp the *causa* (reason) of the utterance.... The more the conceit opens before us a prospect of understanding or new science hitherto ignored, the greater is our delight."[29]

Concetti (conceit) therefore expresses the Baroque intent found in *acutezza* ("acute utterances") rather than the mere ornamentation evoked by the humanist approach.[30] These utterances are thought by Vico to simultaneously evoke *bellus* and *verum* (beauty and truth). Importantly, "*Bellum* [sic] consists in the *artificium* (or the *factum*) of the acute utterance, rather than merely in the subject matter which this utterance evokes..."[31] To an extent there is therefore an ornamental or embellishing aspect here however it is methodological rather than stative. In terms of *verum*, he notes "acute utterance constitutes not just a basic grammar (opening up for us a series of meanings) but also a basic logic (opening up for us a series of truths)."[32]

Having established this rhetorical framework there is, Milbank suggests, "one final ambiguity. The need for *artes*, or for method, reduces, for

---

one with a realised *poesis*... this situation remains as a defining goal for rhetoric, and to the degree it falls short, human affairs remain at the mercy of *fortuna*, chance discovery..." pp. 287–88.

27. Ibid., 297.
28. Ibid., 253.
29. Ibid., 292.
30. *Acutezza* is more specifically the "human ability to make penetrating and original utterances." Ibid., 278. At this point Milbank also discusses the derivation of *concetti* in Vico from the "conceptists" element of Baroque rhetoricians.
31. Ibid., 293.
32. Ibid., 294.

Vico, to the exercise of metaphorical ingenuity and the appeal to traditional lists of *topica*. But how do these two aspects—the latter the traditional classical role of *topica* and the former the new Baroque role of 'wit' or *acutezza*—precisely concur? Does not *actuezza* finally displace *topica*?"³³

On the contrary, they complement each other for as already noted they occur at different stages of the process. *Topica* represents a set of categories or topics that are building blocks increasingly refined over time. This refinement happens in two ways. First, elements of the stock become increasingly pertinent, as their use is further specified, while, second, the overall stockpile is built up, both aspects occurring through the continuous application of *acutezza*.

Upon reviewing this framework it becomes clear that a primary role for rhetoric has been established in human thought. Human culture originated in language about divinity and hence language was, and consequently always is, necessarily metaphoric in its nature. Metaphors open up new vistas of learning that are continuously adding to the existing epistemological stock, this stock forming the topics guiding new metaphoric explorations and the expansion of human horizons. But, Milbank suggests, Vico has in mind much more than this almost purely instrumental, epistemologically based role for rhetoric; he contends it has deep metaphysical implications: "philosophy gets assimilated to rhetoric. In *De Certa Facultate Sciendi* Vico makes no distinction between the role of rhetorical topics and the role of philosophic categories . . . Vico's accounts of topics in the *Institutiones* and his account of *genus* in *De Antiquissiam* are entirely homologous."³⁴

This aspect has been hovering in the background of the discussion but now requires some attention as the claim has important ramifications.

Metaphysics

When referring to "philosophic categories" Milbank has in mind the Aristotelian and Kantian universals. There are two key points to this. First, Vico is attentive to the need for maintaining the tension that inherently constitutes metaphor, for keeping the exploratory realm between its constituting elements open. Second, it was noted earlier that Vico understood pagan cultures to stem from and represent the early foreclosure of metaphor, the primary way he characterizes Western culture. It has a partially mitigating juridical outlook, based in metaphoric tensionality, which remains in

---

33. Ibid., 305.
34. Ibid., 308. This assimilation is conditional however, refer for example to p. 311.

pursuit of the path towards divine equity, but nevertheless is primarily pagan in orientation.

Against this background, in an argument that seeks to pursue the implications of specifically Hebraic thought, Milbank argues "By assimilating categories to topics Vico implies that all human concepts, however rarefied, are but moments in the process of metaphorical appropriation of the world."[35] Aristotelian and Kantian transcendental universals are included within this but their status as settled categories is disputed as impediments to the growth of knowledge; it is the nature of metaphoric thought to be constantly moving forward. They can, Milbank avers, be understood as codifications of metaphoric connections, but not thereby as static categories immune from change. These universals, traditionally considered *a priori*, are examples of metaphoric foreclosure and are therefore pagan in orientation. They represent *critica* solidified, fallen out of the influence of *topica* and then ossified by the illusion they were ultimate *topica*; a divine prerogative alone.

For Vico there is here a "crisis of human understanding" for as Milbank notes,

> If the analogous terms are treated as more ultimate than the constituting metaphors, and if they are taken as carrying more ontological weight, as denoting the final achieved list of categories under which things may fall such that particular "instances" included within their scope are once and for all reduced to species subdividing a genus in a univocal fashion then all is lost. This is where Vico parts company with Aristotle—the philosopher. If, on the other hand, the topics, categories, or analogous terms are used simply as "indices," or as the sources for new metaphorical connections, then for Vico human understanding is saved. Because categories as mere "topics" do not pass from being analogous terms to precise literal definitions, they advert to metaphors as performing the true defining work.[36]

This does not mean that Vico sees all discourse as figurative. He distinguishes between a primary discourse rooted in metaphorical relations and a secondary discourse that is both reflective and abstract but, as was argued for *critica* relative to *topica*, there remains interplay between reflective abstraction and metaphor that places the former at the service of the latter. Discourse is metaphoric but within it can be moments of solidification, of abstraction. Each such moment is valuable because it does "have specific gnoseological value in so far as it contemplates, directly, the general and

35. Ibid., 309.
36. Ibid.

generative *loci* of understanding, but whose task is also to encourage a return to the poetic efforts of *ingenium*."[37] Such moments serve to strengthen rather than eclipse the metaphor and while not stagnating can take up long term habitation "Thus, in his later writings Vico introduces the mediating category of 'poetic universal' which shows how the metaphors of primary discourse 'settle down' into the linguistic deposit to already play the role of analogous terms."[38]

Where the traditional philosophic universals tend to close down meaning, representing an unhelpful long-term prioritizing between polarities, topics remain open, guarding the space of tension always present in the metaphoric, and therefore securing the future potential within it. In this respect Milbank suggests

> Metaphysics is for Vico a reflection on the world where eloquence holds sway; but for the later Vico this reflection is in fact always already begun as the very thing which promotes eloquence in the first place—the hearing of the divine voice which is simultaneous with the first human response to divinity. For Vico eloquence is already a metaphysics, already a "speculation" about divine speech, and metaphysic itself remains an endeavor realized by eloquence.[39]

The question then arises as to what supports this metaphysical eloquence. Metaphor is a construct that seemingly requires no support as such. In its purely rhetorical mode meanings emerge from the metaphoric processes themselves, hence eloquence seems devoid of solid anchoring and the prospect of radical metaphysical subjectivity emerges, a form of Nietzsche's rhetorical illusion.[40]

Yet Vico has more in mind than this. Previously the inherent religiousness of original metaphoric engagement was established, suggesting thereby a potential underpinning that can be explicitly identified. The preceding discussions were, in the early stages, founded on a distinction between pagan and Hebraic constructs, the former foreclosing metaphor while the latter maintaining its tension. It is within the Semitic construct that an appropriate anchor begins to emerge. It only begins to emerge at this point because it represents a truly monotheistic construct whereas Vico's argument assumes a distinctively Trinitarian account.

37. Ibid., 335.
38. Ibid., 310.
39. Ibid., 312.
40. Rose, *Dialectic of Nihilism*, 109–10.

Trinitarian Anchoring

Humanity creates within an infinite yet circumscribed horizon of possibilities. Each making carves out space within this horizon but also leads into further potentialities that expand the horizon. The entire space, the infinite horizon, is nonetheless not entirely unbounded for it is divinely demarcated, an ultimate limit we cannot see. "For this reason the human making of the limits of its own finitude which constitutes our understanding is simultaneously the *revelation* of these boundaries to us by God. Yet if we apprehend these boundaries only *as* distinct finitude (as Descartes) then we fall into error . . ."[41]

It is on this foundation that Milbank's discussion of Vico turns to a consideration of his central metaphysical claim. Milbank suggests Vico draws the underlying thematics of human participation in divinity (an aspect anticipated here but covered below in the historical discussion) and the priority of the made (*factum*) rather than the true (*verum*) into an inseparable conjunction that pre-eminently expresses his rejection of the Platonic view. The Christianized version of Platonism some advocate conceives of human fabrication, either as artifact or understanding, as a dim imaging of some *preceding* original perfectly formed by God. Knowledge in this framework consists of an ascent from the human image or copy to a pre-existent divine reality.

In contrast Vico proposes knowledge is the continuing process of discovering both the limits of human making and the consequent opening up of new vistas, of new infinite but circumscribed horizons. "If, Vico reasons, it is the construction of a series of limits that gives human beings their concepts and at the same time opens out for them an infinite prospect of thought, then it is natural to conceive of infinite understanding as an infinite product, an infinite *opus* establishing an infinite 'limit.'"[42]

The ramifications of this are significant for it is no longer a case of Platonic retrospectives but of "the telos of the infinite *factum*" in which the key is anticipation rather than memory. Instead of imitating already constituted ideals humanity is projecting forwards, reaching towards divine completion. There is buried in this an assumption of divine creativity that must by its nature be not only *ad extra* but also *ad intra*.[43] God is therefore

---

41. Milbank, *The Early Metaphysics*, 111.

42. Ibid., 113.

43. "For God, operating in infinity, the two creations occur simultaneously and are complete in themselves, because the Creation *ad extra* exists simply as the infinite possible finite striving towards the infinite. For human beings however, creation *ad intra* is always dependent on creation *ad extra*, and neither are ever 'complete in themselves.'"

"primordially creative, creative in his very being, and not merely in relation to an external Creation."[44]

This places making at the heart of divinity itself and in particular, from the creaturely perspective, prioritizes making over truth. This specifically theological centralizing of *factum* strongly implies a correlate metaphysical positioning, and indeed Milbank finds that Vico presents *factum* as a transcendental, though not in the senses elaborated by the Classical, Kantian or post-Kantian traditions.[45] It is rather an alternative schema in which *factum* sits alongside *verum* and *bonum*. In each case they "may be predicated of anything whatsoever, but that no *predicans* can be adequate to the full meaning which the word suggests; so that for example everything is a unity, but only the unknown, infinite, God is absolute unity."[46] In the same way, all things are made (hence making is necessarily predicated of them), but "the only comprehensive making, the only thing that fulfils the predicate *factum*, is the divine *Verbum*."[47]

At this point all of the key elements of Milbank's understanding of Vico's poetic cultural theology have been described. In essence Vico presages the intent of this book in that he has, according to Milbank's analysis, already offered a theological description of culture of the type this book is seeking. More importantly however, it will now be argued that Milbank has perpetuated this schema, providing in his constructive proposal a strikingly similar set of propositions. What has been provided in the foregoing are a set of categories useful for determining the extent to which Milbank has (explicitly or implicitly) defined the concept of culture in distinctively theological terms. The next step is therefore to consider his subsequent writings.

Milbank's Later Corpus

Theology and Social Theory

TST was initially published in 1990 (predating the publication of Milbank's work on Vico) though this analysis draws from the 1993 paperback

---

Ibid., 180.

44. Ibid., 113.

45. The traditional medieval transcendentals are: *esse, verum, unum, bonum* and *pulchrum* (being, truth, unity, goodness and beauty). Milbank is careful when describing Vico's position relative to these and their modern, post-Kantian equivalents because "Vico's position should be assumed to possess its own integrity and not be seen as an intermediate stage between a medieval and a modern perspective." Ibid., 138.

46. Ibid., 33.

47. Ibid., 137.

version.⁴⁸ A later section will consider the influence of the second edition published in 2006, with particular emphasis on aspects of the new preface dealing with critics of the first edition. This discussion is particularly important because in the course of his rebuttal he more clearly delineates the cultural heritage he was drawing from when writing TST. For now however, the following will trace the slim but important references to the tradition described above in the earlier edition.

Milbank begins TST with an introduction that expresses an intention to deconstruct secular reason, a process necessarily requiring critical treatment of liberalism as a prolegomenon to his equally adversarial engagements with the dependent secular adjuncts of positivism, dialectics and difference. The summary given in the introduction is instructive for he discerns within liberalism the desire to create an autonomous space for humanity.⁴⁹ This desire, he contends, is rooted in the twin influences of envisaging a violent ontology only kept at bay by restriction (counter-violence); and an understanding of the human construction of the cultural world grounded in immanence rather than transcendence. His contrary contention, as already established above, is the more basic presence of a peaceable ontology in which human construction is instead perceived as an "opening up" to transcendence.

There are several indicators in this introduction that a basically Vichian account is being used by Milbank. The already mentioned reference to "human making," notably placed by Milbank at the core of the ontological problem, is readily identified, as is his explicit use of a counter-modernity whose advocates are revealingly listed as Vico, Hamann, Herder, Coleridge, Kierkegaard, and Blondel.⁵⁰ More opaquely present is a basic rehearsal of Vico's account of Jove, delineated by Milbank as an original violence now held in abeyance by a restricting counter-violence. The comparison is significant because Milbank then counters it in the same way as Vico, through a broadly Semitic paradigm of underlying peace. He pursues a Vichian inspired pagan versus Hebrew structure.⁵¹ This insight leads to a suspicion that more deeply buried yet is the pagan foreclosing of metaphor, a suspicion confirmed by the sharp contrast engendered by the already mentioned "opening up" into transcendence reference. The Vichian attention to metaphoric tensionality is therefore also present, albeit in a disguised way.

---

48. Milbank, *Theology and Social Theory*.
49. Ibid., 4.
50. Ibid., 4, see also p. 6.
51. Ibid., 5–6.

Culture in a Post-Secular Context

Delving deeper into the discussion, these Vichian influences are conjoined with a similarly rooted methodology in Milbank's expressed desire to adopt an "archeological" approach concerned with tracing the genesis of the situation.[52] This is often mistakenly understood by critics and supporters alike to be an idiosyncratic appropriation of the Nietzschean genealogical method, but it is actually much more Vichian in nature.[53] For Vico it was central that a "correct" rendering of history be propagated, a requirement that requires a tracing back to origins of the various developments history recounts. As noted above, the specific point of entry into history is secondary to the accurate identification of the operative human grammar and the relevant mechanisms of concealment. In this case Milbank pursues the grammar of providence and the concealment processes inaugurated by disguised theologies.[54]

Further evidence of a basically Vichian orientation can be found a little later in the introduction when Milbank suggests his perspective is based in "linguistic idealism." Commentators usually align this with Milbank's postmodern sensibilities; a fair identification in light of Milbank's oft-stated predilections for such a reading.[55] Yet this is not the only affinity and neither is it necessarily the most congenial. As has already been noted, Vico presages many elements of postmodernity, not least by his existing linguistic "turn" (an anachronistic description but it establishes the point). While the elements of postmodernity Milbank most aligns himself with are certainly conducive to his purposes, they are arguably not the primary source guiding his thought. For this, the relevant aspects of Vico's radically rhetorical outlook should be considered first, with the postmodern attributions considered contemporary expressions approximating or reaching towards this earlier framework. In this respect "linguistic idealism" is perhaps best understood as code for the Vichian rhetorical structure (or for something extraordinarily similar).

To finish the analysis of the TST introduction, it is worth noting Milbank's penultimate paragraph. Here he takes the opportunity to define his goal as the sketching out of "a theology aware of itself as culturally constructed . . . [that] picks up the shadowy hints of a 'counter-modern' position—historicist and pragmatist, yet theologically *realist*—as suggested

52. Ibid., 3.

53. Robert Miner's description of Vico's genealogy, already discussed in the preceding chapter, is pertinent, refer Miner, *Vico*, 3–9.

54. Milbank, *Theology and Social Theory*, 4–5.

55. Ibid., 5. For Milbank's inducements for this reading refer for example to his espousal of the label 'Postmodern Critical Augustinianism' in Milbank, "Postmodern Critical Augustinianism."

John Milbank and a Theological Account of Culture

by Maurice Blondel."[56] Milbank concludes with a summary statement that brings all of the foregoing together in such a way as to specifically align himself with the heritage Vico stood in, as the reference to Blondel makes explicitly clear, although this is already established through the various mechanisms outlined above. Most importantly it points to this heritage positively, as elaborating the Christian target Milbank is reaching towards in TST. In numerous even if sometimes relatively obscure ways Milbank injects into the introduction for TST significant allusions to the structure he had earlier found present in Vico.

Perhaps one of the clearest and most succinct statements of Vichian reliance, not just in TST but across his whole corpus, comes a little later in TST when Milbank positively appraises Hegel for his inclinations toward metacritique, as opposed to his dialectic moments. The notion of metacritique Milbank deploys here is intimately connected with his conception of Mannerist poetics and Baroque *poesis*, "or the idea that human making is not a merely instrumental and arbitrary matter, but itself a route which opens towards the transcendent . . ."[57] For Milbank, metacritique refers to "a denial of the possibility of Kant's critical endeavor, from a critical point of view that is a more genuine and secure one. This point of view is that of language."[58] Language is taken as the key vantage point because there is really no way to get "in behind" language, to discern either a natural or cultural "thing" that precedes it. In this respect the natural and cultural are inextricably enmeshed in and constituted (although the natural element is of course nuanced for its sheer givenness) by human expression. Milbank consequently argues "linguistic expression, like art, brings into being its own specific, new content; before language, humanity is simply contentless."[59]

He goes on to suggest language is non-referential but is instead teleologically ordered according to an "aesthetic necessity," or, what in more specifically Vichian inspired Milbankian terms, is a *concetti* (conceit) arising from *acutezza* ("acute utterances") that simultaneously evoke *bellus* and *verum* (beauty and truth). According to Milbank it is this "aesthetic necessity" that truly resists linguistic skepticism, providing through culture a route into transcendence not available to the introspection of Cartesian

---

56. Milbank, *Theology and Social Theory*, 6. The terminology "cultural construction" is to be understood in the distinctively theological and Vichian terms to be described below.

57. Ibid., 148.

58. Ibid., 151.

59. Ibid., 149. Something like the Geertzian thesis of pre-cultural humanity as "brute biology," or a "chaos of pointless acts" provides an equivalent description though he discerns a "stratigraphic ordering" not present in either Vico or Milbank.

Transcendental Idealism. The notion of culture operative here is described relative to "The words and works which issue from us, determine what we are, and act back upon us beyond the reach of our conscious intention." Milbank suggests that "The sum of these words and works comprises culture itself..."[60]

Milbank then links this "aesthetic necessity" with the "expressivism" of Hamann and Herder and thereby to a "Christianization of the Renaissance" that brokers a "counter modernity" in the Baroque tradition.[61] Further, the idea of a "stable and universal framework" elaborating "categories" adjudicating the "finite" is challenged by the analogical turn constitutive of the expressive tradition he is espousing. In this perspective these "categories" become the sources of analogical imagining that step beyond the finite and reach towards the infinite, or what he terms "speculative extrapolation from immanent teleology..."[62]

Milbank completes this section by commenting "the entertaining of a notion of 'aesthetic necessity' (as Kant himself best explains in *The Critique of Judgement*) presupposes a transcendent meaningfulness which conditions our linguistic performance such as to render it 'true,' although it can never itself be fully grasped in finite terms."[63]

It is this framework that then empowers his subsequent critique of Hegel. The three great Hegelian errors, of retaining the Cartesian subject, upholding the myth of negation and misconstruing infinitude, are held by Milbank to reflect the eminently secular characteristics of subordinating *poesis* (because now rendered instrumental rather than metaphysic) and of a reversion to an "inhibition of chaos" thesis. These are in turn reflected in his ethics (*praxis*) especially in the political sphere.[64]

In the short summary just outlined there appears a stunning collocation of themes already encountered in Milbank's analysis of Vico set out above. The entwinement of human making, metaphoric opening up, and culture; the description of "aesthetic necessity"; positing of a Baroque counter-modernity; categories as the source for analogical imagining;

---

60. Ibid., 150. This definition initially sounds something like what this thesis is disputing however at this point Milbank also suggests culture is intended as a representation of "the road to transcendence" but not one in which "the social order is a divinely revealed totality which is prior to the creative activities of human subjects." Instead, per p. 151, "revelation [is] ... our participation in the divine creative power of expression." In context, therefore, this is a thoroughly theological description.

61. Ibid.
62. Ibid., 151.
63. Ibid., 152–53.
64. Ibid., 153ff.

John Milbank and a Theological Account of Culture

challenging a subordinated *poesis*; and countering the "inhibition of chaos" theme, are all drawn directly from his Vico period. In language and arrangement he presents a structure that overtly (once revealed) deploys these Vichian resources for his purposes in a way that intelligently contemporizes Vico. In this description resides what might even be considered a consummate summary of Vico.

Elsewhere in his analysis of Vico Milbank had suggested "Vico is really carrying out a kind of re-writing of Augustine's *Civitas Dei* in extremely sophisticated critical and linguistic terms."[65] This specific attribution was not fully addressed above because it did not feature prominently (in terms of space rather than importance) in Milbank's analysis of Vico; he simply did not take the opportunity presented then to pursue this thought. Nonetheless it is clear that Milbank understood Vico to be elaborating a fundamentally Augustinian solution. In TST this Augustinian solution is overtly linked with a Baroque aesthetics in which "every detail (as Deleuze points out) is a 'fold' within an overall design, but the design itself is but a continuous unfolding, which reaches out ecstatically beyond its frame towards its supporting structure."[66] The "horizon" that always opens up into still more distant horizons, as Milbank avers in his treatment of Vico's coverage of this theme, finds its summit in "the infinite maximal tensional harmony of difference [that] has to be something persuasively communicated . . ."[67] This centering of the infinite in a metaphoric discourse necessarily renders his project a rhetorical one, as indeed he expressly admits, one he argues is guided by charity.

Elsewhere in his analysis of Vico Milbank described the lineaments of Vico's proposed Augustinian solution as follows:

> It is this notion of charity which sums up the entire metahistorical and theological basis of the *Diritto Universale*. Christianity, says Vico, proposes a metaphysical end which is also a social end . . . and this is superior to the civil end which was all that could be mooted by antiquity. Charity constitutes this transcendentally social end and it does so because it is, as Vico says, in faithfulness to scholastic tradition, a "supernatural virtue." It is something that human beings are only capable of through the special assistance of grace.[68]

---

65. Milbank, *Language, Law and History*, 89. Note also his earlier discussion at p. 6 and later one at pp. 171–78.

66. Milbank, *Theology and Social Theory*, 428–29.

67. Ibid., 430.

68. Milbank, *Language, Law and History*, 176. Vico understand this notion of grace in a specific way: "Charity belongs properly to God alone because it is an *infinite*

Here, it might be fair to suggest, is a reasonable summary of Milbank's "other city" in its human mode.

Not only is the Vico schema, with its religious conception of culture, central to TST but it is also at the heart of the whole range of Milbank's thought. His corpus is filled with references to the need for, explanation and augmentation of, this retrieval of a Baroque understanding of the culture concept. No major published work excludes it completely. Its position in TST has already been described, while in WMS it constitutes the core subject of the book. For example, Milbank describes Jesus Christ in this vein in his essay "A Christological Poetics." The title alone evokes the rhetorical emphasis outlined extensively above, with Christ being described along the metaphoric lines this evocation suggests. No less anchored in this schema is his description of the Holy Spirit in his "The Second Difference" essay. Here the application of an "aesthetic hermeneutics" model considers the Trinity as a rhetorical community in which the terms relate in the following reversible manner: "As the Spirit *is* only its relation to the origin through the Son, so subjective, aesthetic dynamics are entirely 'inside' textual, poetic dynamics..."[69]

His contribution to RO, entitled the "Theological Critique of Philosophy" also expresses this same basic structuring, as does his introduction to BR. Further, in various ways he describes its consequences through numerous of his articles, especially those dealing with ideas of public theology. There is no need to pursue the similarities with Vico any further since the basic case has been established and further analysis does little more than accrue more supporting evidence that is anyway present in various different ways below (in article or essay titles, content analysis, and so on).

What is proposed instead is the need to more purposefully consider the evidence in light of the central theme being developed by this book, namely the analysis of culture. In seeking to describe his conception of culture the most important Milbankian resource is WMS, especially the essays: "The Linguistic Turn as a Theological Turn," "A Christological Poetics," and pre-eminently "Pleonasm, Speech and Writing."[70] These treatises are consequently examined first before investigations of the resources noted above in RO and BR are pursued. In what follows a systematic exposition of his understanding of culture is undertaken that begins from his account of language and then slowly moves towards his liturgical conceptualization of culture. This has the

---

virtue—a will towards infinite creative good which only he can realise. Humanity shares in this virtue by willing the good of neighbours and those who are 'unseen'. And it is because charity always proceeds to some unexpected, unforeseen upshot, that it must always be aided by divine grace..." p. 177

69. Milbank, *Word Made Strange*, 188. Emphasis original.

70. Just in these titles Vichian rhetorical and language themes are clearly evident.

John Milbank and a Theological Account of Culture

advantage of presenting his diverse descriptions of culture in a coherent and cohesive manner that sets out its core building blocks while also demonstrating how they build into an internally consistent structure.

Language

Bishop Warburton, Milbank contends in his essay "Pleonasm, Speech and Writing," falls prey to an anachronistically errant post-structuralist construal from which he must consequently be rescued.[71] The key moment of this erstwhile analysis comes in the publication of a 1977 translation of Warburton's discussion on the origins of language (which first appeared in his 1738 *The Divine Legation of Moses*) that now emerges "removed from its original theological context . . . [and] smothered with critical commentary by Patrick Tort and Jacques Derrida."[72] To correct this twentieth-century error Milbank enlists the aid of three "alien Samaritans": Bishop Lowth (Warburton's opponent), Giambattista Vico, and above all Johann Georg Hamann. The key point is simple enough: Warburton's thesis of linguistic origins cannot be understood outside of the theological context and lineage it was developed in and articulated through, and this background must therefore be rehabilitated. The argument achieving this goal is a dense, complex analysis seeking "to indicate how other eighteenth-century writers, grappling with some of the same issues as the Anglican Bishop, suggest the possibility of a non-violent, non-deceptive grammar . . ."[73]

Milbank partially achieves his goal by setting out several competing theses on the origins of language. He begins with Warburton's outline of progressive development, which charts language's rise from roots in a "language of action" to the heights of figuration embodied by contemporary metaphoric discourse.[74] Warburton's target, in common with certain other eighteenth century writers, is to "refute enthusiasts for Egyptian, Babylonian and Chinese antiquity—hermeticists, Jesuits and others—who discovered in the symbolic writing of these ancient cultures evidence of a buried primordial wisdom, and traces of an original, universal revelation, which was none other than the first handing-over of language to human beings."[75]

---

71. John Milbank, "Pleonasm." Note this essay is a largely unchanged version (cosmetic matters excepted) of an earlier two part journal article: John Milbank, "William Warburton 2," Milbank, "William Warburton."

72. Milbank, "Pleonasm," 55.

73. Ibid., 79.

74. For the following outline see the discussion in Ibid., 55–59.

75. John Milbank, "The Linguistic Turn," 86. The other eighteenth-century writers

Culture in a Post-Secular Context

Warburton specifically tackles the Egyptian lineage described especially by Athanasius Kircher, arguing against the mystic discourse of such enthusiasts by contending instead that human language has its origins in actions; pictographical gesturing that over time gave way to conventional abridgements or hieroglyphs. This demythologization of the hieroglyphs, Milbank suggests, is essentially Lockean in nature, concerned as it is with defending the gradual growth of language against claims of solely revelatory origins.[76] The biblical Adam, according to Warburton, names the living creatures in a "rational sequence" predicated on "clear sense perception." In keeping with this naturalistic understanding, Warburton depicts language as growing from its initially small stock of root words progressively, developing under the influence of the tropes into more figurative forms.

This development sees the early customary abbreviations, or hieroglyphics, slowly evolve into ideography; language predicated on similitude expressed through a first curiological (pictorial) and then symbolic idiom. From this latter point it is but a short step to alphabetic development and thence onto the most figurative level of Warburton's schema—metaphor. Tropes are understood to mediate the transitions between the various stages of development and are conceived of as "innocent" in their function, which is to say natural. Language in this schema grew by moving through synecdoche (the whole evoked by a part) and metonymy (an attribute invoking the whole) through to metaphor.[77] In the course of this process there is a notable growth in figurative emphasis accompanied by an increasing distance within the figuration between its origin and contemporary expression. The original connections grow more remote as development into ideographical marks increases, resulting over time in *catachresis* or the forgetting of roots.[78] For Warburton the more extravagant elements of metaphor con-

---

pursuing similar themes are listed by Milbank on the same page as: John Woodward, Edward Stillingfleet, Samuel Shuckelford and Giambattista Vico, each of whom "borrow and adapt from the materialist theses of the 'triumvirate of demons'—Hobbes, Spinoza and Isaac de Lapéyrere—in the interests of a strictly Christian apologetic."

76. Ibid, Milbank, "Pleonasm," 59.

77. This natural development via the tropes is an element of the polemical aim of his writing as well. Vico, for example, proceeds in a similar vein to Warburton, chronicling the way pagan culture developed primarily through metonymy and synecdoche (metaphor being prematurely foreclosed) as a result of its advocacy of univocity, birthing therefore "a culture based not on 'prophecy' but on idolatry and divination." Milbank, "The Linguistic Turn," 108. Refer also p. 109 for discussion of the implications of univocity and "prophecy" (refer below for discussion of the sense in which "prophecy" is deployed here). See Milbank, *Language, Law and History*, 96ff., for a much more nuanced discussion that highlights the narrative features of metonymy more strongly while also highlighting an alternative hierarchy of tropes.

78. Milbank will later dispute this in the sense that while aspects may be forgotten

sequently become an ornamentation rather than structural requirement of writing.

In this respect Warburton stands within a long Aristotelian and somewhat Platonic tradition that dominated the understanding of metaphor right through until the early twentieth century. In summary this view defined metaphor as "an elliptical simile useful for stylistic, rhetorical, and didactic purposes, but which can be translated into a literal paraphrase without any loss of cognitive content."[79] Metaphor was generally considered a literary ornamentation or embellishment, though whether it decorated discourse artfully or deceptively was disputed.[80]

Problematically there is lurking in the background here "the shadow of ferality" or a Hobbesian loss of what distinguishes humanity from the animals: the loss of human distinction.[81] Accompanying Warburton naturalism therefore is what Milbank terms a "crude interventionism" that seeks to explain the origins of the names by which Adam named everything brought before him, and therefore language: God, to speed up the process, revealed the names to Adam.[82] As Milbank points out, this leaves Warburton open to the very charge he was seeking to levy against the enthusiasts, namely the mystification of language, though the mystifying element is now located in Hebraic rather than pagan roots. In responding to this question Milbank finds resources for dealing with twentieth-century post-structural concerns, or in other words, resources for staging a confrontation between the peaceable ontology of Christianity and the primordial violence of postmodern nihilism.

---

this in itself does not betoken a betrayal of the essential thrust. He suggests "pleonastic variation," repetition-with-variety, guards against this by holding tightly to the original concrete imagery. Milbank, "Pleonasm," 72, and p. 65 for an explanation of pleonasm.

79. Johnson, "Introduction," 4.

80. Ibid., 8–13. Here he discusses the medieval and modern influences that engendered a negative view of metaphoric expressions. Within the narrow confines of this stream there were also other functions for metaphor, with some commentators considering them examples of catachresis, or words temporarily filling lexical lacunas. Note for example the discussion in Black, *Models and Metaphors*, 35. See also Soskice, *Metaphor*, 61–64.

81. Milbank, "The Linguistic Turn," 87. Milbank goes on to argue that Vico embraces this Hobbesian semi-animality, this ferality, for apologetic purposes, finding in it the site of pagan origins.

82. See also Milbank's discussion of Johann Peter Sussmilch's defence of a related position in this regard: he attempts to close the gap between "the totally arbitrary and artificial character of language . . . and . . . its indispensability for thought . . ." by advocating a divine origination, refer ibid., 96.

Primordality of Metaphor

Milbank begins his response by turning his attention to the first of the two 1977 post-structuralist commentators on Warburton who take hold of this change in metaphoric theory and wield it against Warburton. Patrick Tort argues the primordality of metaphor, suggesting language is inherently metaphoric from its inception. As Milbank states it, "Tort points out Warburton's mistake in not realizing that the very *first* writing must have been *metaphoric* (in both generic and specific senses), because the very possibility of a system of signs is the evocation of one thing signified only through another thing signifying."[83]

This may be considered the second broad theory of "natural" origins; metaphor as a rival to the literalistic view espoused by Warburton. Milbank has elsewhere argued that positing any such originary metaphor necessarily excludes the possibility of a materialist critique. As he notes, it renders it "impossible to appeal to a basic, universal, natural norm that will still be a human norm."[84] Instead of this, and here he returns to the central theme governing the eighteenth-century writers as already noted in Vico, he argues there can only be either a pagan or Hebraic construal; "original metaphor implies either a primal personification of nature ('paganism') or else a primal response to nature as a personal address ('monotheism')."[85]

When describing this metaphoric conception it is the other post-structural critic, Derrida, who provides important guidance. Derrida argues the impossibility and arbitrariness of positing any first element because any such possibility never escapes the play of signs. For him "There is no such natural origin of language or culture, but only a paradoxical 'cultural origin of culture' (as much transcendental as historical) in the original metaphor, or the original relation of present signifier to absent signified."[86] This Milbank avers, is the original difference, différance or "supplement at the origin"

---

83. Milbank, "Pleonasm," 60. Milbank interestingly finds presages of post-structural thought already in Augustine, present as a highly modified (and still modifiable) form of Stoic theory of language in which the *lekton* (Augustine's *dicible*) occupies "a position within a system of signification. Thus they seem already to have recognized Saussure's category of the signified as something distinct from either conscious thought or extensional referent." Milbank is careful here to distinguish between Augustine's treatment of language as such, and his "doctrine of thought as 'inner word.'" It is only in the latter sense the Stoic *lekton* within Augustine allows the relational rather than substantive ontology suggestive of a cultural-linguistic framework. Milbank, "The Linguistic Turn," 89–90.

84. Milbank, "The Linguistic Turn," 106.

85. Ibid.

86. Milbank, "Pleonasm," 61.

John Milbank and a Theological Account of Culture

that guides Derrida's project.[87] For Milbank it constitutes an "unrestrained equivocation" that establishes a gap between nature and culture but only in an always ambiguous and illusory sense.

At this point of his argument a theme haunting its passage becomes clearer: there has been unfolding in his discussion the specter of language conjoining with culture such that they are rendered indistinguishable other than in a purely formal sense.[88] This view is increasingly ratified as Milbank turns his attention to the recovery of Warburton from the post-structural critique savaging him. When commenting on the first of his trio of rescuers, Lowth, Milbank argues "It is, however, Lowth's strictly formal attempt to position Hebrew poetry vis-à-vis the categories of classical rhetoric and poetics . . . which leads him to a new depth of cultural analysis."[89] Milbank finds in Lowth "a return to the Horatian, humanist themes of the fourteenth and fifteenth centuries of the poet as founder of the city and of culture."[90]

In the second of his heroes, Vico, Milbank makes even clearer the cultural theme while also conjoining the integration of language and culture with history. He suggests that for Vico

> all culture and all humanity begins with an original metaphoric tension—manifest through ecstatic bodily gesture—in which the world is symbolically grasped as the story of a divine power whose presence constitutes a teleological imperative for human beings. This is the first *written* narrative or fictional space—suspended between trace and deferral—which is then *inhabited* by men and women to produce history.[91]

Here culture is specifically identified as both theological and teleological. By the time he arrives at his elaboration of Hamann's role the theological cultural theme has explicitly moved to the forefront of the discussion. He notes that for Hamann there is at origin

---

87. Elsewhere Milbank has described this Derridean formulation as "the inescapbility of language" whereupon there is "no thought prior to the irreducible invocation of an absent signified through the 'difference' of the present signifier." Milbank, *Language, Law and History*, 87. Refer 86–92 for a discussion of Derrida relative to Vico.

88. Milbank elsewhere notes Martin Luther as essentially Baroque in nature (refer below for a treatment of the relevance of this appellation) for contending "the Incarnation into humanity was also an incarnation into language . . . ," Milbank, "The Linguistic Turn," 93.

89. Milbank, "Pleonasm," 63.

90. Ibid., 64.

91. Ibid., 73. Emphasis original.

> no pure *a priori*, but rather a metahistorical foundation which invokes (via encounter with the historical Jesus) acknowledgement of the writing, speaking God of Israel. This God, says Hamann, like Jesus in St John's Gospel "stoops to scrawl on the ground," and by this *kenotic* act of writing, creates the world and human history as a present sign whose concealment-revealment of the absent God is the possibility of man's free creative response which gradually unravels through time. At the same time God speaks the entire human text in the eternal Word and interprets it in the Holy Spirit.[92]

In these descriptions Milbank argues a "metaphoricity within analogous bounds" exists, but only within the metahistorical schema articulated above *as* it passes over into "an affirmation of faith."[93] Warburton is now not only rehabilitated in the face of post-structural misreading but also rendered extremely useful for understanding culture as a theological predicate. His framework, significantly altered by an admixture of Lowthian and Hamannian orality, still stands, now chastened, but nonetheless effective although his "crude interventionism" has now been superseded by Hamann's considerably more sophisticated if equally faith driven *philologia crucis*.

For Milbank then, Warburton remains structurally central because his notion of interventionism remains, albeit in a highly modified form. According to Hamann however, not only is human history constituted by a Warburton like grace-given "extra" but it is also gathered up in its totality within the divine *Logos*. In a further distinction, the initial constitution does not occur in the passive sense Warburton seems to envisage but is instead an expression of humanity's participation in divine creative activity (Milbank's Vichian Neo-Platonism coming to the fore here). Milbank depicts this through Warburton's categories pictorially, as a carpet woven hieroglyphically on its underside by a humanity that cannot see the complete pictography present above, yet nonetheless faithfully (after a fashion) representing the above because of a mystical harmony.[94] In this depiction can be seen

---

92. Ibid., 78. Emphasis original. This *kenotic* stance of Hamann is used in a positive sense here, displaying the extent to which Milbank is willing to travel this route with him. What Milbank is not prepared to concede is that it represents the general paradigm Hamann argues it to be: "If there *is* a fault in Hamann, then it might be that he tends to *replace* altogether a sense of an analogical ascent to God . . . with the notion of God's kenotic adaptation to us . . . ," Milbank, "Knowledge," 31.

93. For discussion of the formative influence of Berkley on this construct refer Milbank, "The Linguistic Turn," 97–105.

94. Milbank, "Pleonasm," 74–75 for discussion of the foregoing description.

the passage into faith mentioned above, rendered by "the idea that man as an original *creator* participates in some measure in creation *ex nihilo*..."[95]

From Poetry to Prophecy

In faith therefore it can be said that "By writing this hieroglyph humanity is constituted as human."[96] This statement contains within it a complex conjunction of ideas that require explanation for there is a diachronic component that must also be brought out. Milbank comments just a little later "The original hieroglyph, through its primary metaphoric reference, simultaneously retains the human past and projects the human future as a horizon of desirable action: 'the hieroglyphical Adam is the history of the entire human race in the symbolical figure.' Because all human existence is inscribed in this written narrative, it is impossible ever to arrive at total comprehension, or an absolute starting point."[97]

By this phrasing Milbank harks back to and clearly invokes elements of both Derrida and Lowth. Regarding Derrida Milbank had already commented "written signs (a category which here *includes* oral poetry) . . . are given the task of preserving temporal continuity. The inscribed signifier carries the signified as both the re-tension of the past and the pro-tension or projection of the future. This is the grammatical context for possible human action."[98]

There is, Milbank recognizes, a danger in adopting this view because it feeds into the totalizing equivocation of nihilism, a point Lowth can help to stabilize by casting the discussion in distinctly poetic terms (Milbank's parenthesis indicating the importance of this particular intercalation). Lowth argues the presence of an ontological faithfulness in oral poetry, one brokered by a pleonasm, or repetition-with-variety, that achieves diachronic constancy without thereby necessitating literalness.[99] This "mimetic

---

95. Ibid., 79. Emphasis original. See also Milbank, "The Linguistic Turn," 106

96. Milbank, "Pleonasm," 74. This pithy sentence answers very directly the Geertzian and anthropological question that arose in the previous chapter. Discussion of this and its fuller implications are delayed until the appropriate section of the final chapter.

97. Ibid., 75. This poetic idea of echo and anticipation is evident through his work. For example, in a brilliantly concise statement, he suggests "it is only our faint anticipation and then echo of a divine redeemed humanity, intelligently erotic, erotically intelligent, which *at all* distinguishes us as more than animal, more than *nihilistic*." Milbank, "Knowledge," 31. Emphasis original.

98. Milbank, "Pleonasm," 60.

99. Ibid., 65. This is essentially a process of 'regulated improvisation' as was noted in chapter 2.

capacity" allows for the preservation of the original concrete referent (approximating Derrida's re-tension) and can be coupled with the idea of a reciprocal echo (approximating Derrida's pro-tension and representing Lowth's adaptation of Warburton's diachronic figuration) to allow the poetic to give way to the prophetic.

For Lowth the concept of reciprocal echo represents the interplay occurring between two "temporally separated poles of comparison [that] are real natural-cultural events . . . [that] cast light on each other, increasing the topical potential, without one being a 'fictional' shell and the other a 'real' content."[100] This is what he terms a "mystical allegory," the fictional/real formulation distinguishing it from traditional and contemporary conceptions of metaphor. This means that the prophetic represents "the 'natural' genesis of new meaning from topical founts through time."[101] Elsewhere Milbank picks up Vico's terminology of 'narratives in brief' to describe this, succinctly characterizing it in the following terms: "In these conceptions linguistics is relocated *inside* poetics, and poetic categories *define* the first human *topoi*, the first spaces in which specifically historical recording, and *consequently* (this reversal is entailed) specifically historical action will be possible."[102]

This Lowthian based adaptation of Derrida's signifying paradigm not only anchors a concrete past referent, without falling into the trap of thereby identifying it, but also manages to demonstrate a way around the apparent necessity of Derrida's equivocation. As Milbank comments, "Here, as for Derrida, there is an infinite sequence of mutually clarifying signs, and never foreclosure; yet still the 'next sign' *as* subjective performance clarifies, to a degree, and therefore *actually* differentiates (within the 'identical') instead of delivering us to a postponed, ideal, self-identical, non-differentiated *nihil*."[103]

There is in this a certain free-play of imagination that is yet bound within what Milbank has termed the "totemic"—pre-alphabetic hieroglyphics. This "binding" can be termed a number of things, Milbank tending towards terms like "tradition" and "narrative imagination." However labeled it is a construal that does not stray beyond the always expanding conical bounds of plausible inference. In a suitable summary of the discussion to date Milbank suggests "a prophetic and typological culture cannot finally lose touch with these totemic beginnings as it does not seek to obscure its origins, nor the material and metaphoric genesis of its meanings."[104]

100. Ibid., 69.
101. Ibid.
102. Milbank, "The Linguistic Turn," 107.
103. Milbank, "Pleonasm," 71. First emphasis mine, rest original.
104. Milbank, "The Linguistic Turn," 111.

From Prophecy to Verbum

Having established the diachronic operation and "material" nature of culture it now remains to situate it as the specifically theological predicate it was described as above. As already noted humanity is constituted precisely as humanity by the initial creative activity of God and humanity's participation with this, the original hieroglyph thereby constituting and framing both history and language. Cultural objects, Milbank argues, "mediate to us ethical goals, natural realities and God as the permanent object of understanding..."[105] This repatriation of the eighteenth century theological framework is then deepened by Milbank when he notes the need for addressing culture "as an *integral* element of Christian being alongside contemplation and ethical behavior, rather than as a 'problem', external to faith."[106] In short it is now necessary to consider how culture should be understood relative to a Christian ontology.[107]

For this task it is Vico that is important in that Milbank pays particular attention to his obscure mantra *verum et factum convertuntur* (the true and the made are interchangeable/convertible). Milbank argues that for Vico *factum* is "*Verbum* in God," a saying he then relates through more standard theological terminology by noting "this is equivalent to saying that God in his creation *ad intra* in the *Logos* 'incorporates' within himself the creation *ad extra*, including human history."[108] By this means he is able to "get behind" the original metaphor to elucidate what amounts to Derrida's "supplement at the origin" or original difference (*Verbum* being "a primordial difference in the Godhead..."[109]). He then finishes by arguing:

> When *Verbum* is included as a transcendental, all the transcendentals are transformed into personal, intersubjective, Trinitarian categories: but this leaves us with more than a "social God" which might be open to appropriation by an ahistorical theology, it leaves us also with a *cultural* God. A Christian ontology that takes account of language and culture, will then be, more fully than before, a *Trinitarian* ontology.[110]

---

105. Milbank, "Pleonasm," 79.

106. Ibid. Emphasis original.

107. Milbank goes on to critique Thomism, and to a lesser extent Augustinianism, because they fail to account for culture, refer ibid.

108. Ibid., 80. It is on this point that some scholars register their protest, refer for example Luft, *Vico's Uncanny Humanism*, 31ff.

109. Milbank, "Pleonasm," 80.

110. Ibid. Just prior to this he argued that both Thomism (in particular) and Augustinianism were incomplete theologies for today because they neglected culture and

Culture in a Post-Secular Context

In his essay "The Linguistic Turn as a Theological Turn," comprising his contribution to the RO manifesto *Radical Orthodoxy: A New Theology*, this seems to be what Milbank is getting to, but never finally explains, in his presentation of theology as a "metaphysics/metasemiotics of relation, rather than a metaphysics of substance."[111] He suggests there "Just as, for structuralists, a novel is ultimately 'about' its self-constitution as a novel, so theology has only really been about its own possibility as theology, as 'divine language.'"[112] In this "Linguistic Turn" discussion the ontological linkage to the "Pleonasm" thesis is more strongly established by the ability to map corresponding concepts, hence polysemy describes the same perpetual process of Derridean like signification narrated above and differential substitution refers straightforwardly to the notion of "differentiation within the identical." Both essays, this analysis demonstrates, are finally based on the same ground: a Trinitarian metaphysic centered in culture (as mediated through language and history).

From Verbum to Donum

Some six years after WMS was published Milbank offered *Being Reconciled*, the first of a new series of projected writings aimed at exploring his constructive project from a somewhat different perspective. The preface of BR offers an extremely important, densely constructed summation and prefiguration of his theological endeavors. In the preface he suggests his prior emphasis had been on the perspective afforded by *verbum* (word); investigating Christian doctrine Christologically. In BR this focus is now left, not so much behind as under, built upon rather than left out, in order to concentrate on *donum* (gift), the appellation Milbank notes Augustine considered the "supreme name" of the Holy Spirit. Milbank is therefore pursuing the implications of accepting "gift" as a transcendental category; considering the issue of constructing a theo*pneumatics* rather than a theo*logy*.

This change of direction is in one sense not at all surprising. While it sets out a distinctive frame of reference it is nevertheless not a complete deviation from the ambiance of his preceding constructive work, it instead seeks to develop it in an alternative but consistent way: "The *methexis* of donation . . . complements the *methexis* of language."[113] Not only so with his

---

history, refer p. 79.

111. Milbank, "The Linguistic Turn," 111–12.

112. Ibid., 111. Refer especially his n. 91 on p. 120 for the outline of a more formal linking of the respective notions.

113. Milbank, *Being Reconciled*, xi. As will be discussed more fully below, *methexis*

John Milbank and a Theological Account of Culture

positive thesis, but equally as much with his critical engagement, consistency is maintained. Even within the preface to BR Milbank presses home a theological critique of philosophy that demonstrates both philosophy's underlying paucity and theology's plenitude. He argues, for example, "It will be noticed that I have adopted as organizing principles, not the philosophical transcendentals—truth, goodness, beauty, etc., but rather irreducibly theological ones: *verbum, donum.*"[114]

Such a view does not mean these philosophical categories lack relevancy for they are pertinent *in their own way*; rather he means to suggest they only ever partially identify what they intend to explicate precisely because of the context in which they were birthed and subsequently matured. Milbank does not therefore simply obviate them but instead demonstrates how they are appropriately filled out by a specifically theological context:

> *Verbum* adds to truth the liturgical performance of truth; likewise, *donum* adds to goodness a sacramental dealing with the world of objects (seen as both *anathemata* and sacrificial *donata*) as alone allowing the emergence of a subject who is not a mere *libido dominandi*.[115]

The theological context applied here is not a straightforward one however because it is represented by a metaphysical articulation that extends in one very important way beyond traditional categories. Central to Milbank's description is the term *methexis*, a "code" word, for want of a better description, which captures how he "has been primarily focused on participation, but in a new way."[116] *Methexis*, Milbank argues, is normally framed around a metaphysical vision based on "a sharing of being and knowledge in the Divine."[117] Problematically this conjoining of ontology and epistemology has usually tended to privilege the universal as against the particular, the metaphysic vision over relativizing contingency; a prejudice that contemporary philosophy has assiduously sought to reverse.

Against this "dismal" dichotomy Milbank raises the possibility that "participation can be extended also to language, history and culture: the whole realm of human *making.*"[118] Here the concluding themes of the

---

is his code for participatory ontology; *donum* represents gift; while language is invoked by *verbum*.

114. Ibid., x.

115. Ibid.

116. Ibid., ix. *Methexis* is a Greek theatrical term that centres on the notion of audiences participating in and improvising the actions of a ritual.

117. Ibid.

118. Ibid. Emphasis original.

"pleonasm" and "linguistic" essays are given full play. A truly Trinitarian ontology should not only be understood through the usual transcendentals of being and knowledge (the God who is and who knows) but just as much and more so through that of human making or *poesis* (hence the God who is "infinite poetic utterance," Jesus, *verbum*, *logos*). It is this background that animates the already noted suggestion: "Thus when we contingently but authentically make things and reshape ourselves through time, we are not estranged from the eternal, but enter further into its recesses by what for us is the only possible route."[119]

Culture as Liturgy

This "only possible route" is given shape by Milbank's reference to the precedence offered by theurgic Neoplatonism.[120] As for philosophy generally then so too for theuorgia: final fulfillment is found only in Christian practice, or more specifically in liturgy "since liturgy already assumes the descent of the Divine in and through our praise of the Divine."[121] What was partially seen and mystically experienced by the Neo-Platonists is given full if still mysterious form by the Christian practice of liturgy, and it is through liturgy that we enter ever deeper into the recesses of the Divine. Milbank therefore concludes "A metaphysics of the participation of the poetic at once envisages all true *poesis* as liturgy, and at the same time must itself be a contingent temporal liturgical performance as well as an expression of *theoria*."[122]

In summary, Milbank's theological framework is amenable to not only ontological and epistemological descriptions, the traditional patterns of depiction, but also, and intimately so, to cultural representation. Both *verbum* and *donum* can be arrayed according to culture, a construal primarily mediated by Milbank's notion of *methexis*. The term culture is preferred here over *poesis* because the latter provides only part of the picture; Milbank notes, "culture is not just about production (*poesis*). It is also constituted through exchange."[123] This is the distinctive contribution his concentration on gift

---

119. Ibid.

120. This phrase is rich with symbols, encompassing a set of perspectives gathered around both the idea of calling up and bringing about the epiphany of the Gods; and the notion of ritualistically uniting with The One by a process of dedication and mimickery.

121. Milbank, *Being Reconciled*, x.

122. Ibid.

123. Ibid.

John Milbank and a Theological Account of Culture

adds: a perspective that brings into full view the always lurking but never fully articulated element of exchange.[124]

Milbank goes on to suggest "Thus the notion of a participation of the poetic in an infinite *poesis* is to be complemented by the notion of a participation of reciprocal exchanges in an infinite reciprocity which is the divine *donum*."[125] Culture is constituted by both *methexis* and gift and is an integral element of both his theological and theopneumatological accounts. In short, Milbank's constructive project can be accessed through any of the three metaphysical loci (ontology, epistemology and culture), although comprehensively if only still partially understood through the interaction of all three. Any reduction of this triadic descriptive schema to some lesser mix of its component elements necessarily truncates understanding while concurrently dimming the distinctively Christian metaphysical vision that even if only dimly expresses but fully participates in the Trinity.

The Ecclesial Connection

One of the problems with this theoretical depiction of culture is that it seems divorced from the ethnographic iterations actually present in the world. Milbank is not unaware of this, commenting that the direction offered by *donum* not only complements his focus on *verbum* but also adds a positive sequel to the argument of TST, a follow-up that is based on a desire to "learn from social theory in its more historical, ethnographic and less ideological aspects."[126] He is careful to ensure this is not seen to represent a reversal or drawing back from his earlier critiques for they still stand, it instead demonstrates his recognition of the need for taking account of empirical evidence, for ensuring an open connection between theory and practice.

Milbank has already established the primary vehicle for this connection in TST: the church. He contends "theology itself will have to provide its own account of the final causes at work in human history, on the basis of its own particular, and historically specific faith."[127] Social theory for Milbank "is first and foremost an *ecclesiology*, and only an account of other human

---

124. That this aspect was always in the background is demonstrated by Milbank's suggestion that his argument in TST was a disavowal of the social sciences as always representing an arbitrary privileging of either "production over exchange (Marx), or else exchange over production (Durkheim), when in reality any such privileging is incoherent in terms of social ontology. We only exchange in producing; but equally only those in relation produce, and all productions involve exchanges." Ibid.

125. Ibid.

126. Ibid., xi.

127. Milbank, *Theology and Social Theory*, 380.

Culture in a Post-Secular Context

societies to the extent that the Church defines itself, in its practice, as in continuity and discontinuity with these societies."[128] To this point Milbank is entirely consistent with the notion of culture outlined above: culture represents the participation of human production and exchange in Divinity and is therefore expressed most completely in the liturgical context of the church.[129] Further, "the Church is already, necessarily, by virtue of its institution, a 'reading' of other human societies . . ."[130]

> In this fashion a gigantic claim to be able to read, criticize, say what is going on in other human societies, is absolutely integral to the Christian Church, which itself claims to exhibit the exemplary form of human community. For theology to surrender this claim, to allow that other discourses—"the social sciences"—carry out yet more fundamental readings, would therefore amount to a denial of theological truth.[131]

This ecclesial theme will form the primary topic of the next chapter, wherein a close consideration of his apparent ecclesiological weaknesses is undertaken. This attempts to anchor the foregoing metaphysical discussions in the pragmatic soil of everyday Christian engagement, considering in detail how the translation between theory and practice can or might take place. It will be argued that while Milbank is somewhat susceptible here he nonetheless provides surprising resources for dealing with the question of practical application.

The attempt to isolate a specifically "Milbankian" treatise on culture in the latter stages of this chapter only served to highlight much more strongly the Vichian character of his argument. Milbank has taken on board from the specific choice of Vico as the subject of his doctoral dissertation a heritage that decisively shapes his own theology. In some ways his project is less a "postmodern critical Augustinianism," though it is aptly described as that, than a "poetic theology," or perhaps a rhetorically oriented "cultural theology." These latter labels capture the specific theological heritage he draws inspiration from while also more sharply specifying his core long-term concerns. Milbank, it will be suggested, is elaborating an "alternative

---

128. Ibid.

129. A very ambitious and largely successful rendering of the liturgical surpassing of the entire philosophical project is found in Pickstock, *After Writing*. Space precludes treatment of this work however it offers an important companion to the Milbankian thesis being explored in this chapter, one, it should be noted, that was prepared under his direct supervision.

130. Milbank, *Theology and Social Theory*, 380.

131. Ibid., 388.

modernity" not founded on, for example, Kantian *a priori* assumptions, but on the notion that there really is no human structure preceding or "behind" human culture. There is instead a divine origination, and consequent teleology that is properly the subject matter for human investigation, which is nonetheless, through and through, a fully cultural enterprise, and it is to these features that Milbank, with Vichian insight, constantly points.

Chapter 4

Milbank, Violence, and Idealization

GRAHAM WARD HAS COLORFULLY depicted John Milbank as a hero striding through intellectual history, rescuing it from the grip of secular reason. In this vein Milbank has been critically revelatory and then, in turn theologically constructive. The cultural approaches elaborated in the first chapter were exposed by the Milbankian argument presented in the second chapter as unwitting accomplices in the manipulations of secular reason. The secular, as an anti-theology in disguise, was found in the second chapter to be working incessantly on the limitation of theology proper, relegating it to the sublime and hence locating it at the margins of public discourse. In the third chapter this now unmasked anti-theology was confronted by a constructive proposal that did not seek to usurp it so much as make plain its illegitimacy. This alternative or counter modernity was identified as a Vichian based "poetic" or "cultural" theology now transplanted largely intact into the late twentieth century by Milbank, who had imbibed it during the course of his doctoral and post-doctoral studies.

To this point his critical and constructive theses have been presented largely unhindered, without much thought given to potential problems that might suffuse or distort his framework. This chapter seeks to remedy this by considering at some depth critical encounters with his work. From an initially broad canvassing of his critics the field of engagement is subsequently narrowed to the issue of ecclesiology for it is here that Milbank locates his cultural schema in terms of its empirical manifestation. Even this represents an overly large subset to fully grapple with hence the critique is further refined by focusing on a single representative interlocutor—Gillian Rose. From the writings of this complex Judaic philosopher comes a sharp, highly concentrated criticism that nevertheless forces a response drawing from the whole of the Milbankian corpus. In order to concentrate on the specific cultural theme at the heart of this book the various metaphysical and more generally philosophical considerations this analysis inevitably runs across at various stages are dealt with briefly except to the extent they aid in considering the practical implications that form the specific loci of attention.

From this discussion it can be hoped that a more satisfactory ecclesiologically based description of culture emerges, one still steeped in Milbankian verve but more fully cognizant of its various weaknesses, especially in the realm of empirical validation. This entails narrating how the idealized ecclesiology commentators consistently identify in Milbank can be related to verifiable, locatable churches and hence how a universal account of culture can be grounded in particular instantiations that broker to the world what culture truly is and could be. The liturgical consummation of culture identified at the end of the last chapter is, of course, the appropriate response here, and this is therefore placed on display though only as the still incomplete and imperfectly constituted human making that participates in divinity in a unique, Christian way that is itself the epitome of divinely guided human attainment. If all of this is achieved then some considerable steps have been taken towards the possibility of elaborating a practical description of Milbank's description of culture to support the theoretical construct outlined in the previous chapter. It now remains to be seen whether this is indeed defensible.

Milbank and His Critics

Initial indicators of the likely long-term impact of Milbank's work quickly emerged after the publication of TST. Very soon after its release a special issue of *New Blackfriars* was dedicated to discussion of its contents, the scholars uniformly noting the magnitude of the thesis it presented. Fergus Kerr, for example, observed that its central premise was brilliantly simple but that "The book's dense scholarship and theoretical complexity are formidable . . ."[1] Graham Ward more prosaically acclaims it a "journey . . . [that] calls for epic heroism, as it passes through woods dense with philosophical thought and over chasms of vertiginous intellectual argument."[2] Aidan Nichols "finished this breath-taking book lost in admiration for the breadth of intellectual culture that lies behind it . . ."[3] In similar vein Flanagan comments,

1. Kerr, "Simplicity Itself," 305.
2. Ward, "John Milbank's Divine Commedia," 311.
3. Nichols, "Non Tali Auxilio," 326.

133

"It is a brave, tough, complex, dense and difficult work that should keep theologians, philosophers and sociologists wrestling with it, and with each other, for some time to come, . . . a ruthlessly pursued narrative . . . a ruthless philosophical tour de force."[4]

Such testimonies are not limited to this cadre of scholars, each of who may be considered broadly sympathetic to the movement that TST was the catalyst for, Radical Orthodoxy. Elsewhere a similar story unfolded. The journal *Modern Theology* also dedicated an issue to TST in which David Burrell described it as "an immensely ambitious work . . ." in which while "the thesis is relatively simple, its orchestration is stunning in scope as well as harmonics."[5] It is, as Rowan Williams notes, hard to discuss Milbank's work briefly, "An adequate review would have to be a kind of gloss, a Talmudic margin."[6] It is also worth noting that *Philosophy and Theology* dedicated issue 9 to a discussion of Milbank and TST in 1996, again with an appropriate range of remarks echoing similar sentiments to those already expressed here.

Gavin Hyman pauses a moment to take stock of the various comments made in the vein noted above, subsequently reporting "Milbank's project is marked by an intellectual brilliance and an impressively dense scholarship . . ." but that this particular chorus is now so often sung as to be almost commonplace yet "the frequency of their occurrence does not in any way detract from the truth of their import. In short, Milbank's challenge is formidable."[7] From a remarkable assortment of contexts markedly similar sentiments are expressed despite very diverse opinions on how well Milbank achieves his much-vaunted goals.[8] As Flanagan goes on to suggest, the sheer magnitude of the learning involved, and its engagement at such depth across so many disciplinary boundaries, means "criticisms of the work are likely to be specific and partial."[9]

---

4. Flanagan, "Sublime Policing," 334.

5. Burrell, "An Introduction," 319.

6. Williams, "Saving Time," 319.

7. Hyman, *The Predicament of Postmodern Theology*, 65–66.

8. Scholars from across the spectrum, irrespective of their degree of agreement with the underlying project, are similarly inclined to acknowledge the breadth, depth and imagination behind his work. Refer for example to liberal responses like that of Hedley, "Should Divinity Overcome Metaphysics?" For a sociological equivalent note Joas, "Social Theory and the Sacred."

9. Flanagan, "Sublime Policing," 335. As Aidan Nicholls notes, Milbank's thesis includes "virtually the entire contemporary intelligentsia of Western Europe and North America . . .," refer Nichols, "'Non Tali Auxilio," 327.

Milbank, Violence, and Idealization

In his review of Don DeLillo's monumental novel *Underworld* the literary critic James Wood makes an observation particularly germane and hence easily translatable to TST. He comments "The book is so large, so serious, so ambitious, so often well-written, so punctually intelligent, that it produces its own antibodies and makes criticism a small germ.... It is easy, and rightly so, for big books to flush away criticism."[10] John Milbank's TST is one such big book though it constitutes but one element in a much bigger ambition; a theological project writing historically and proleptically the true course of Western intellectual history. In keeping with the finale of TST, Milbank is now engrossed in the composition of a timely, well-written, serious constructive theological oeuvre that is slowly moving through the Trinitarian transcendentals identified in the previous chapter.

James Wood did not rest his review on the plaudit however for he continued his engagement with De Lillo's *Underworld* by suggesting "despite chapters of brilliance, [*Underworld*] does not gather its local victories as a book this large should. Instead it enforces relations between its parts which it cannot coax."[11] Wood sidesteps the epic effect the novel generated not by positing an equally comprehensive counter-vision but by subverting the grandiose effect, highlighting in the process the presence of an innate disparity between the overall discourse and its constituent elements. Just as the epochal achievement of *Underworld* is revealed as illusory, or at best partial, in either case as ultimately debilitating of its efforts to fulfill its promise, so too, Milbank's critics suspect, may Milbank ultimately prove susceptible to the slow gathering of adverse reports.

There are several primary loci for Milbank's critics. The first and most obvious is his explicit retrieval of Neo-Platonism, a topic broached by Luft's critique in the previous chapter but not addressed more fully until the next chapter. The second concerns his engagement with individual scholars, of which three have proven especially contentious. The first relates to Milbank's characterization of his theology as Augustinian in nature, in recognition of which he has self consciously styled his project a "Postmodern Critical Augustinianism,"[12] a position that has attracted widespread discussion.[13] By contrast to this affirmative Augustinian stance Milbank has taken strong exception to doctrines hinged on univocity, the separation of ontology and theology initiated by the second figure: Duns Scotus. Scotus is primarily

10. Wood, "Black Noise": 38.
11. Ibid. Wood is positively scathing of Delillo's next major effort *Cosmopolis*.
12. Milbank, "'Postmodern Critical Augustinianism.'"
13. Note for example the argument mounted by Breyfogle, "Is There Room for Political Philosophy in Postmodern Critical Augustinianism?" See also Cochran, "At the Same Time Blessed and Lame."

accused of placing "being" behind and consequently above divinity.[14] Scotus therefore becomes the primary villain in the Western philosophical and theological story, a position that is heavily contested by both Scotist and Liberal scholars.[15] The importance and contentiousness of this thesis was recognized by the journal *Modern Theology* in its dedication of the October 2005 issue to the role of Scotus in theology. Thomas Williams provides a specific example of how the alternative posture may be constituted,[16] though it is Kevin Hughes' summary article that is perhaps most important.[17]

The position of a third key theological player, Thomas Aquinas, is considerably more ambiguous. It is notable that Milbank does slowly move, or perhaps incline towards a generally positive perspective, culminating in his joint publication with Catherine Pickstock of *Truth in Aquinas* in 2001. Initially however, as seen in TST, Aquinas is at best only cautiously referred to, affirmed on the one hand for disturbing Aristotelian ethics but on the other hand found culpable for opening up the possibility of secular autonomy. As Milbank argues, "he has moved not very far down the road which allows a sphere of secular autonomy; nevertheless, he has moved a little, and he has moved too far."[18] The reading of Aquinas offered by both Milbank and Pickstock is perhaps one of the more controversial aspects of their respective projects,[19] prompting *Modern Theology* to set aside the October 1999 issue to cover this topic as well.[20] In Milbank it can be noted there is now a clear trajectory towards a much more positive assessment of Aquinas, although this must still be set in a context of fundamental dispute. As noted by Vico, Aquinas is still caught in the transcendental problematic that stems from prioritizing *esse*.

14. Refer for example Milbank, *Theology and Social Theory*, 303.

15. A debate Milbank thinks has been derailed by those opposing the identification of Scotus as the instrument of this change for this assertion actually predates his own use of it. For Milbank the real question concerns how this change should be assessed. Refer his substantial discussion in Milbank, *Theology and Social Theory*, xxv n. 41.

16. This issue of *Modern Theology* primarily focused on critical responses to an article provided by Catherine Pickstock entitled "Duns Scotus: His Historical and Contemporary Significance." Here again the close intellectual proximity of Pickstock and Milbank is important, despite small variations. Refer for example their joint position in Milbank and Pickstock, *Truth in Aquinas*. For the opposing view refer Williams, "The Doctrine of Univocity."

17. Hughes, "The *Ratio Dei*."

18. Milbank, *Theology and Social Theory*, 407, refer p. 359ff. for the discussion on Aquinas and virtue.

19. Allen, "Putting Suspenders on the World," 44.

20. Lash, "Where Does Holy Teaching Leave Philosophy?" See also Hemming, "*Quod Impossible Est!*"

There are also a great many other scholars critically encountered by Milbank, some positively so, who represent a second tier of importance, though each seminal in different ways for Western thinking. His treatments of Aristotle, Blondel, de Lubac, Deleuze, Derrida, Descartes, Durkheim, Foucault, Hegel, Heidegger, Hamann, Herder, Kant, MacIntyre, Marx, Nietzsche, Plato, Rahner, Vico and Weber all fall into this category. Beneath these are a whole host of other figures running the full gambit of the Western intellectual tradition, all taking their place in the reconstructed heritage Milbank offers. In this respect Ward suggests, regarding TST but used here with respect to his whole corpus,

> Analyses of individual secular thinkers and schools of thought only become meaningful within the movement of the whole book. They need to be read within the context of Milbank's overall design. Each analysis has its place in the grand narrative he is composing. Each analysis is subservient to this grand narrative. Because of this there emerges an element of distortion . . . an evident reduction of specificity . . . a necessary idealism, a necessary "violence" one might say, as Milbank retells the history of ideas within the Christian superstory.[21]

In a great many respects the lack of attention to Milbank's Vichian orientation has exacerbated the tendency to distort Milbank himself, to read his "distortions" as eclectic and therefore idiosyncratic retrievals from the Christian tradition, a point established in the previous chapter. The grand narrative Ward refers to is arguably not as well recognized as it could and should be. This is in part a reflection of Milbank's own overt drawing on postmodern resources at the expense of explicit attention to the always "postmodern" oriented poetic and rhetorical heritage he draws from and for which postmodernity turns out to be such a congenial host, again as was argued in the previous chapter.

In this quote from Ward, to return to the questions raised by Milbank's critics, Ward picks up a central theme running right through the corpus of criticisms congregating around Milbank's work. Ward later frames it this way: "Is there no violence in the Christian story that is ontological? Could not the incarnation, the resurrection, and Christ's miracles be described as examples of violence? How is violence to be understood?"[22] There is, he notes, an inherent violence in the very act of persuasion, in the necessary hermeneutical misreadings and misrepresentations it entails, an aspect he suggests Milbank has not properly accounted for. In short, he argues

21. Ward, "Divine Commedia," 311–12.
22. Ibid., 317.

Milbank does violence despite the peaceable ontology he ostensibly makes use of. The question of violence does not only arise as an innate feature of the rhetorical strategy Milbank adopts, for in quite a different way Rowan Williams ponders the totalizing nature of Milbank's "harmony." He asks where the tragic is in Milbank's schema; that space between the ideal and its pragmatic manifestation. Williams asks "whether the kind of ethic he so evidently wants doesn't require rather more attention to the tragic implications of contingency itself, if the peace it constructs is not to be totalizing and ahistorical."[23] He comments on the need for Milbank to clarify how he avoids "an undifferentiated or timeless model of ecclesial virtue."[24]

Aidan Nichols presses home the case by noting Milbank's supposed underlying call for the return of Christendom (a dubious claim to say the least), or at least an English variant modeled on "Richard Hooker's *respublica christiana*, at once, and, in the concrete, inseparably, Church and civil society . . . the second, evidently, prior to and summoned to transfigure the first."[25] There is, in this, no space for the secular hence the theocracy thereby instituted can only be mitigated by the appropriate operation of *caritas*. But, and it is a big but, the empirical record is against such a claim. "Were all members of the Church saints, such a régime of charity might suffice. But as the history of the Church, that mingled story of grace and sin, indicates, charity is not enough."[26] Historically there has always been a "remainder"; those who are not, and for that matter that which is not, gathered into the proleptic body of Christ. "The Church 'pro-exists' for all humanity; but in the meanwhile, before her mission is divinely completed, she must 'co-exist' with other aggregates of the human members of the creation."[27] But this points to only one side of the equation for as James K. A. Smith points out the underlying disjunction here is actually between Milbank's conflicting depictions of the church. On the one hand, he advocates the Augustinian distinction between *civitas terrena* and *civitas Dei*, while on the other, upholding an already graced nature that, Smith argues, conflates "humanity *en toto* with the community that constitutes the *ecclesia* . . ."[28] This, Smith

---

23. Williams, "Saving Time," esp. 325.

24. Ibid., 325.

25. Nichols, "'Non Tali Auxilio,'" 331. This claim is dubious because it seems to pick up on Milbank's dedication of TST to Christendom as a hermeneutic key for the book, though Milbank emphatically refutes this in the acknowledgements of the second edition, noting the dedication was not to the Middle Ages but to the Christendom Trust who in part resourced the book.

26. Ibid., 332.

27. Ibid.

28. Smith, *Introducing Radical Orthodoxy*, 258.

suggests, borders on Ward's blurring of the cities in *Cities of God* or, perhaps more pertinently, to Ward's "Displaced Body of Jesus Christ."[29]

From a quite different perspective Gavin D'Costa charges RO generally, in a critique Milbank is also highly susceptible to, with an idealized repatriation of historical ecclesial orthodoxy, one devoid of the violent practices the church participated or was deeply implicated in. In an argument closer to the preceding lineage, he goes on to charge RO with pursuing an "ecclesiological form of theology" that amounts to a "church theology, with no 'accountability' to any real church."[30] The root issue is the church "is too often an invoked and reified figure, with 'Eucharist' and 'liturgy' often magically dispelling all ills."[31] In reality, he reports, "Sociologically speaking, RO's church is not locatable."[32] It is not difficult to see Milbank as a key protagonist in this drama for D'Costa. In a highly nuanced analysis the then Anglican R. R. Reno, in contrast to Smith and D'Costa, argues from Catherine Pickstock's *After Writing: On the Liturgical Consummation of Philosophy* in what constitutes an equally Milbankian thematic,[33] that the "element of liturgy as participation in a divine community has a political and social analogue. Since nothing exists outside the embrace of divine purpose, the Christian vision necessarily gathers up the diverse aspects of human life into its analysis, looking towards a transformed way of living."[34]

Reno's problem is not with the theoretic espoused here therefore but with the already noted empirical problem of its application. He finds in RO a distinct tendency towards the ideal that is grounded in the very nature of the Anglo-Catholic identity to which its three main proponents adhere: Milbank, Pickstock, and Ward (Ward is clearly central though increasingly ambiguous regarding his affinities). Reno argues that for these three (and the denominational tradition they stand in) there are both cultural and theological reasons for why neither Roman Catholicism nor Anglicanism truly appeals. The former lacks an appropriate institutional basis and the latter a rich enough tradition. In the face of this problem Anglo-Catholicism was forced to construct its own heritage and identity out of medieval and patristic resources, but, importantly, not on the basis of historical practices but on the basis of an idealized and highly philosophical portrayal.

29. Ward, "Bodies"; Ward, *Cities of God*.

30. D'Costa, "Seeking after Theological Vision." Refer p. 356 for the first description, p. 358 for the quote and pp. 358–59 for examples substantiating his claim: Gerard Loughlin and William T. Cavanaugh.

31. Ibid., 356.

32. Ibid., 357.

33. Pickstock, *After Writing*.

34. Reno, *In the Ruins of the Church*, 70.

Such a background, Reno contends, plays itself out in the RO literature by way of an inherent idealization. He suggests "Radical Orthodoxy cannot invent the flesh and blood of a Christian culture and so must be satisfied with describing its theoretical gestalt, gesturing, in postmodern fashion, toward that which was and might be."[35] In at least one sense this is entirely the nature of the case. RO is a new entry on the theological stage and is consequently still establishing its program. It has no distinctive *ecclesial* habitat as yet (and perhaps never will), and consequently lacks strong institutional grounding. D'Costa in fact warns against essentializing it because "RO should not be treated as a homogenous animal, but more like a pack, most of whom are in pursuit of the same prey, though some are distracted by other quarry."[36] There is no distinctive flesh and blood with which to stitch it together, no specific, identifiable ecclesial institution around which it may be said to congregate, other than in the ad hoc ways of the Anglo-Catholic sensibility. Yet, curiously, given all of the foregoing critiques and observations, Milbank himself argues his apparently idealizing thesis is a "possibility that only becomes available if ecclesiology is rigorously concerned with the actual genesis of real historical churches, not simply with the imagination of an ecclesial ideal."[37] This comment does not occur in isolation either for it is central to his case in TST that ecclesiology is the true sociology and hence his thesis must necessarily be founded on the empirical record, a point he is not unaware of. As he argues, Augustine's *Civitas Dei* asserts the priority of an ontology of peace over one of violence as its basic principle, a principle that must then be "firmly anchored in a narrative, *practice* and a dogmatic faith, not in universal reason."[38] Clearly Milbank intends his project to be pragmatic in nature, anchoring its theory in the daily flow of life rather than in some obscure, idealized ivory tower kept quite apart from the realities of living.

The following discussion probes the apparent disjunction between Milbank's express intent and the very different actuality so many commentators seem to discern, a task that entails delving deeply into the aforementioned series of critiques. A consideration of the interplay between idealization, violence, and the church is therefore the central subject of this chapter which is charged with determining the extent to which the claims of his critics can be considered sustainable. From the outset it is worth admitting that on the surface the accusations appear to have merit hence

---

35. Ibid., 77.
36. D'Costa, "Seeking after Theological Vision," 357.
37. Milbank, *Theology and Social Theory*, 380.
38. Ibid., 390, emphasis mine.

they need to be taken seriously, yet as has already been demonstrated by the Vichian analysis, deep currents flow through the subterranean courses of Milbank's thinking that must also be addressed. When these are taken into consideration a different picture begins to emerge, one in which the supposed lacuna of his formal description of the church begins to take on a quite different shape, one that begins to turn the assessments of the critics back on them. What finally seems to shape Milbank's response is a refusal to limit the church to *particular* historical instantiations, a refusal his critics seem all too eager to refuse as they prosecute their cases with certain specific institutional structures already in mind.

This does not completely absolve Milbank however for his critics are at a minimum placing their finger on what seems to be a distinctive reticence in Milbank's otherwise aggressively pursued program. That he seems to hesitate when explaining how his project finally anchors itself in the ebb and flow of history requires explanation. In part it perhaps reflects an underlying problem the church catholic has always struggled with, as the current differences between Pentecostal or Emerging Church structures and those affirmed in Greek Orthodox or Roman Catholic churches amply testifies to. Perhaps also it refracts some underlying problems with Milbank's Christological understanding, his tendency to focus on universals coming at the expense of an appropriate treatment of the particular context. Then again maybe it must be finally admitted that Milbank, as D. F. Pilario wants to suggest, cannot cope with the "rough grounds of praxis" because his recovered "idealized ecclesial society" cannot cope with the complexity of contemporary society.[39] Perhaps what follows might begin to form a plausible response to these claims.

When considering how to best stage this discussion the problem of the sheer variety of critiques and their authors must be dealt with, otherwise there is the danger of finishing with a piecemeal, fragmented explanation that responds like a shotgun—firing at the whole body but missing the heart of the matter. From amongst those who have attempted some form of assault on Milbank's theological edifice only a few have mounted sustained campaigns that sought to engage from the foundations up. From amongst this group there has been one in particular who has entered into a sensitive, longer-term process of rigorous engagement that has issued a particularly strong challenge on the nexus of violence, idealization and pragmatic ecclesial practice. Gillian Rose, herself a formative Semitic influence on Milbank, becoming one of the few he positively appropriates from outside of the

---

39. Pilario, *Rough Grounds of Praxis*, 527.

intellectual heritage he relies on, mounts this challenge and it is therefore her oeuvre that resources the following discussion.

The Challenge of *The Broken Middle*

In *The Broken Middle* Gillian Rose offers a specific, searching critique of Milbank's project in a section entitled "New Jerusalem Old Athens: The Holy Middle."[40] Her target is his constructive program but primarily in terms of its relationship to his critical maneuvers.[41] She essentially argues that Milbank presents a tale of three cities, characterized respectively as Athens, Jerusalem, and Salvation. Athens is presented as the Greek *polis*, cast here as the sinful city; Jerusalem is the Judaic model of polity, presented as the heavenly solution; and then there is an interposed salvation city mediating the immanent frame.[42] In TST this basic structure is clearly evident in Milbank's discussion and reworking of Augustine's metaphor of two cities *civitas terrena* and *civitas dei*. Milbank presents Rome as the sinful city, birthed and steeped in endemic violence, only avoiding utter chaos by the staying hand of the *stator*, the divine limiter of violence. In contradistinction to this he proffers the peaceable fellowship of "the heavenly city," the "heavenly Jerusalem," our "true mother." This city reaches down with the hand of salvation to inaugurate and fund the earthly "city of God on pilgrimage," the "nomad city"—the third city.

As Rose narrates it, for Milbank this salvation city has two primary characteristics: pilgrimage and inclusivity, a description Rose notes "effectively destroys the idea of a city: its task of salvation deprives it of site; while its inclusive appeal deprives it of limit or boundary that would mark it off from any other city and their different laws . . ."[43] As will be noted below, Rose is always careful to ensure the presence of a concrete referent for her metaphors hence this is in part chastising Milbank for not abiding by the characteristics that physically delineate what constitutes a city.

---

40. Rose, *Broken Middle*, 277–307.

41. There is a degree of similarity in their critical movements. Vincent Lloyd, for example, notes the presence of essential parallels between *Theology and Social Theory* and Gillian Rose's *Hegel contra Sociology* and *Dialectic of Nihilism* that he considers suggestive of fundamental similarities, p. 697. He does not then go on to describe them but they minimally include locating the pivotal moment in Duns Scotus, see esp. Milbank, *Theology and Social Theory*, 302–3, and Rose, *Dialectic of Nihilism*, 104–7.

42. Rose, *Broken Middle*, 281; Milbank, *Theology and Social Theory*, 391–92.

43. Rose, *Broken Middle*, 281. Refer also Milbank's similar description of it as "a paradox, 'a nomad city' (one might say) for it does not have a site, or walls or gates." Milbank, *Theology and Social Theory*, 392.

Today's teeming megacities, Mexico, Cairo, Kolkata, and so on, are increasingly challenging such limitations with their rapid ghetto led expansion into surrounding, supposedly independent, areas. Cairo's encroachment on Giza and New Zealand's city of Auckland, a sprawling conglomeration consisting of not one but three cities, are cases in point.

It might be objected that this requirement of relative isomorphism misses the key point since Milbank's construct is really expressing the presence of two earthly "cities" that are necessarily presented as geographically dispersed collocations of like-minded citizens gathered according to entirely non-physical characteristics. The citizens of the respective earthly cities are in neither case walled in because they freely roam the world, walking at will through the interpenetrating interstices of their cities. How else can one describe such collections of individuals from all over the world when the membership status of any particular individual is something only available to God? The key is that while they are described in immanent terms, they nonetheless always remain oriented by an eschatological reference that constitutes their dominating paradigms, providing them with both their character and form. Of course there is somewhat more to this element of Rose's critique than this initial assessment suggests however the corresponding rebuttal is not without efficacy, as will become clearer a little later.

After this brief description of Milbank's proposal Rose then brings it into an illuminating dialogue with the ostensibly contrary views of Mark C Taylor; not, it should be noted, as a simple elision of differences, for their differences from each other remain, and fundamentally so. Instead, Milbank's theology of harmonious peace and Taylor's a/theology of Dionysian joy are brought together as parallel types of projects; arrayed as instantiations of the same structural tactic. According to Rose, both found and consecrate new Jerusalems as replacements for old Athens; holy cities that are in both cases, Rose contends, built on the same antinomian and ahistorical sands. They are not alone in this tactic for she notes the presence of four such structurally similar "holy" cities: "pagan (Heidegger), Davidic (Levinas), nomadic Protestant (Taylor), nomadic Catholic (Milbank) . . ."[44]

All four of these cities are described as postmodern political theologies, an appropriate appellation in many ways but one of particular interest because it points quite directly to Rose's central critique. Some care must be taken over this analysis for Rose is a complex and often misunderstood interlocutor.[45] Focusing on Taylor and Milbank, Rose argues

44. Rose, *Broken Middle*, 283.

45. On this aptitude for confusion regarding Rose's work refer for example Lloyd, "On the Use of Gillian Rose." Lloyd's article is primarily concerned with delineating how Tony Gorman (698–700, described as getting lost "in a tangle of intertextuality")

> Neither ecstatic affirmation vaunting its "totally loving the world," nor eschatological peace vaunting its continuity with untarnished ecclesial practice, display any middle. There are no institutions—*dominium*—in either: Taylor offers no exteriority; Milbank offers no interiority. Without command and without revelation, Taylor's ecstatic affirmation remains exiled in an interior castle; whereas, with Milbank's latinity of "sociality" and "charity," how could "peace" bequeathed as "harmonious" arise, without acknowledging the *polis* intruding into such vague sociality, without acknowledging eros and agape intruding into such tamed "charity"? In both cases, without anxiety, how could we recognize the equivocal middle? In fact we have here middles *mended* as "holiness"—without that examination of the *broken* middle which would show how these holy nomads arise out of and reinforce the unfreedom they prefer not to know.[46]

The basic thrust of this charge gains considerable clarity once the obscure term "middle" is clarified. This is not easy however as it is a genuinely obscure albeit well used term in her work. One veteran commentator on Rose, Vincent Lloyd, comments "This middle is the realm of 'law,' by which Rose means the social practices and institutions that compose our world."[47] In similar vein Christopher Brittain describes it as the space between concepts, the area of tension between opposing extremes. Against the tendency to collapse these extremes into simple dualisms Rose is advocating the need to reside within the in-between spaces in which most of life occurs. The mistake of Milbank and the others is their apparent desire to escape this space of equivocation:

> The denial of brokenness implies that pure Goodness and Truth are capable of being possessed in their fullness, and so there is no "middle" territory of contradictions, incompleteness and

---

and Graham Ward (700–703, accused of enlisting Rose "to support a project [from which] she would most certainly dissent") have both fundamentally misunderstood Rose on the few occasions they refer to her, and how Rowan Williams (703–5) has understood but not taken sufficient account of the implications arising from his analysis. This is perhaps not surprising given that one seasoned reviewer of her work politely calls it an indirect and obscure approach but with important enough substance to warrant a less severe and oblique rendition, before exasperation finally takes over and he concludes "Even erudition and provocation can begin to pall." Murphy, "Review of *The Broken Middle*."

46. Rose, *Broken Middle*, 284. It should be noted that her use of anxiety derives from Kierkegaard and retains his quite specific understanding. Refer esp. Lloyd, "On the Use of Gillian Rose," 698–700. See also Rose, *Broken Middle*, 89–100.

47. Lloyd, "On the Use of Gillian Rose," 699.

Milbank, Violence, and Idealization

imperfection. The "broken middle" has been transformed into a "holy middle" beyond the limitations of the messiness of communal living.[48]

But Lloyd and Brittain are also overly simplifying here, for the concept embraces more than the simple conceptualization of social order implied in these comments; it is also a metaphysical construct that characterizes any and all conceptual compositions of the world, social or not. The key is to understand how the middle is negotiated since it is inherently broken, representing a triune set of fragmenting "breaks between universal, particular and singular, in individuals and in institutions."[49] It is always marked by a diremption (that is dualism), such as those between law and ethics, legality and morality, which perpetually gives rise to an abiding temptation for philosophy and social theory[50] to ensure "a forced reconciliation of that which they have made residual by their exclusive accentuation . . ."[51]

Not surprisingly therefore she characterizes philosophic readings of works from Plato through to Marx as deterministic, "closed conceptual structures, colonising being with the garrison of thought . . ." while contending they could equally have borne analysis aporetically, by considering the "gaps and silences in the mode of representation."[52] It is this latter approach that for Rose characterizes successful negotiations of the middle for it recognizes that philosophy is always working with the irresolvable. The real problems arise in the attempt to *resolve* this gap because it obviates the more natural response of residing within the various antinomies for it is here that she locates an all-important, mediating third term, the universal-which recognizes the devastation wrought in the middle; hence she argues "The aporia or gap is the Janus-face of the universal."[53]

---

48. Brittain, "Leo Strauss and Resourceful Odysseus": 158.

49. Rose, *Broken Middle*, xii. Rose is referring here to Aristotelian categories, refer Rose, *Mourning Becomes the Law*, 9. Here she also compares it to Platonic types and archetypes.

50. Rose notes "Even when philosophy and social theory retain their relatively distinct identities, this pattern of the diremption of law and ethics paradoxically keeps philosophy and social theory close, because it appears *within* philosophy and *within* social theory as well as between them . . . ," before providing some examples. Rose, *Broken Middle*, xiii, emphasis original.

51. Ibid., xii. Lloyd notes that for Rose, "In the absence of an absolute, the way we react to what is left, to the 'broken middle', is with anxiety." Lloyd, "On the Use of Gillian Rose," 699.

52. Rose, *Mourning*, 7–9, for this discussion, the quotes are from p. 8 and p. 9 respectively.

53. Ibid., 10.

Culture in a Post-Secular Context

This alternative strongly reflects her Hegelian background for by it she is effectively promulgating the efficacy of dialectic. For Rose, residency within the tension of competing polarities is not a static affair but is characterized by a constant process of negotiation that is always reaching towards discovery. The discovery process represents what she calls "experience," the learning that occurs "between what interconnected actors posit as independent of them and their difficult discovery of those positings..."[54] This experience is phenomenologically described and dialectically oriented. Hence, "Without any necessary assumptions of linearity or progression, this alternative description of mutual positings and their breakdown also reopens the way to conceive learning, growth and knowledge as fallible and precarious, but risk-able."[55] What Milbank and like-minded scholars are presenting appears to be an escape from this rough, experiential requirement but it is no escape at all for the underlying diremption still exists and remains in need of negotiation, whether this is acknowledged or not.

A Landscape of Ashes: Aporetic Mourning

Perhaps the most accessible presentation of the broken middle comes in her description of the painting "Landscape with the Ashes of Phocion" by Poussin, itself based on Plutarch's "Life of Phocion," a description she provides in her book *Mourning Becomes the Law*.[56] This painting depicts the ashes of Phocion, an Athenian general and statesman, being tended by his wife. The poignant background to this painting is a story of the political betrayal of a virtuous long-serving leader of Athens now relegated in death to an ignominious pile outside his beloved city, amongst the aliens, unable to gain entry because of his "treason." The central focus of the painting is his wife, bent over on her knees gathering the ashes while being attended by a long suffering friend or companion who is keeping watch for fear the act of love being committed by her friend might be discovered.

The temptation, Rose avers, is to render the foregrounded act of Phocion's wife a gesture of perfect, redeeming love that contrasts sharply with and overcomes the unjust, tyrannical actions of the backgrounded city of Athens. But, she notes, "In this presentation of the rational order in itself as unjust power, and the opposition of this domination to the pathos of

---

54. Ibid., 13.
55. Ibid.
56. Ibid., 22–26. Note this description of the painting is the one accompanying the plate presented as Figure 2 on p. 24. On p. 23 this same painting is entitled by Rose "Gathering the Ashes of Phocion."

redeeming love, I discerned the familiar argument that all boundaries of knowledge and power, of soul and city, amount to illegitimate force, and are to be surpassed by the new ethics of unbounded community."[57]

For Rose, the "magnificent, gleaming classical buildings" in the background bespeak not malignant intent but perfect Athenian architecture. It is not the structure of Athens itself, or power, reason, or anything else of this ilk, that is corrupt but the specific purposes they are at times put to: "they [the Athenian buildings] present the rational order which throws into relief the specific act of injustice perpetrated by the current representatives of the city..."[58] There is therefore no inherent structural problem presented, despite even an endemic propensity for problems. The political thrust of this painting is entirely different for the roots of the problem are elsewhere, in specific acts perpetrated in the name of structure, though now revealed as only ostensibly so.

The corollary of the temptation to blame Athens is the equally abiding temptation to then "fix" the structural problem, to amend the Athenian structure that first gave rise to this injustice. Such commentators propose this fix, Rose is suggesting, by rendering Phocion's wife a paragon of redeeming, overcoming love. This love is conceived as communal in nature, personable, and diametrically opposed to the structured evil that gave rise to and perversely nurtured it. But, Rose goes on to argue, "To oppose the act of redeeming love to the implacable domination of architecture and political order—her purpose, individual love to the impure injustice of the world—is completely to efface the politics of this painting."[59] The fix is wrong because the initial diagnosis has missed the point and therefore the real problem remains completely untended. A perpetual cycle of inherently violent structure versus love is then entered into, between which is always the untended and broken middle.

This is precisely the charge Rose brings against postmodernity. Far from obviating the modern pattern, as its literature suggests, postmodernity instead repeats it: philosophy is again revalued around dichotomies;[60] though now the overarching paradigm is dominance or violence. "These

---

57. Ibid., 25. The reference to "unbounded community" recalls her previous discussion of "Community Architecture," ibid., 15–20.

58. Ibid., 26. Refer also to her discussion at p. 25 and pp. 103–4 for similar reflections. In this latter section she advocates the need of mourning, of resisting the temptation to posit "cherished good" against "public ill" in order to avoid mourning.

59. Ibid., 25.

60. Ibid., 1. "From Marx to Heidegger (and before and beyond), it has become *de rigueur* to charge your predecessor with adherence to 'metaphysics,' and to claim your 'new method' to be, exclusively and exhaustively, the overcoming of the tradition."

moves, which characterize post-modern thinking, would mend the diremption of law and ethics by turning the struggle between universality, particularity and singularity into a general sociology of control."[61] But this leaves the "broken middle" untended and therefore continues to perpetuate it. The broken middle, for Rose, is endemic to the human condition; but so too is the temptation to mend it, *a la* modernity and postmodernity and, in its turn, a "triumphant ecclesiology, as the sociology of the over-controlled secular is inverted into the sociality of the saints."[62] Her problematic can be summarized in the recognition that "In fact we have here middles *mended* as 'holiness'—without that examination of the *broken* middle which would show how these holy nomads arise out of and reinforce the unfreedom they prefer not to know."[63]

The sacral "fix" promulgated by Milbank and Taylor is, in the final analysis, a mere balm, an illusory whitewashing that mends in appearance only.[64] Instead of dwelling in brokenness, guided by Kierkegaardian anxiety, these proposals proceed in ignorance, unwittingly continuing the cycle by unknowingly importing into themselves insidious seeds of internal deconstruction. As Rose warns,

> This rediscovery of the holy city, pagan, nomadic, Judaic, these mended middles over broken middle, at the end of the end of philosophy, may be witnessed as the post-modern convergent aspiration which, in effect, disqualifies the third, the middle, on which they would converge. This very converging corrupts—for in figuring and consecrating its city, this holiness will itself be reconfigured by the resource and articulation of modern domination, knowable to these post-modern ministers only as mute and monolithic sedimentation.[65]

As this infers, post-secularities unwittingly retain the broken middle because of its apparent harmlessness for it is in appearance mute sedimentation. However, this appearance is entirely deceptive. Far from mute it corrosively rises through the layers, corrupting the entirety of these projects from the inside out. It does not use overt tactics that are either ingratiating or coercive in nature; instead it is always already insinuated in the projects, hence it distorts by processes of internal reconfiguration. Rose finishes her analysis with a warning to these projects:

61. Rose, *Broken Middle*, xiii.
62. Ibid.
63. Ibid., 284.
64. Ibid., 299 for an interesting discussion of the whitewash effect.
65. Ibid., 284.

Milbank, Violence, and Idealization

The two new kinds of political theology—the theological "imagination in action" and the architectural imagination "in practice"—would resist "domination" by solidarity in irenic community, whether configured in the mind of God or the mortar of man. They succeed, however, in legitimizing new absolute sovereignties, which reinforce the diremption left unknown but reconfigured at its source. This political theology aspires to overcome law and its charted positions without the labour to recognize its own formation and implication and persisting diremption. Legality, whether in theology or architecture, understood to be violent *per se*, reappears as violent in holy or royal authority.[66]

In the end, she suggests, these various strategies only repeat, however differently organized they may seem, previous modern and post-modern efforts, thereby becoming a part of the chain inaugurated by the turn to the modern, albeit now adducing sacral sanction to the effort. Unfortunately, according to Rose, all such efforts will ultimately fail because "The more the middle is dirempted the more it becomes sacred in ways that configure its further diremption."[67]

A Tale of Four Cities

It is perhaps best to finish this discussion with an example drawn from Rose's work that may make more obvious some of the more abstract moments in her analysis; namely her frequently used cities metaphor.[68] In its usual form she portrays philosophic history as a tale of two cities,[69] sometimes as a

---

66. Ibid., 307. The preceding discussion developed an example from architecture involving Prince Charles based on the book *Community Architecture: How People are Creating Their Own Environment*. Refer pp. 303–7 for this and Rose, *Mourning*, 16–20.

67. Refer also to the discussion of this quote in Lloyd, "On the Use of Gillian Rose," 701. He notes its misuse by Graham Ward. Rose depicts here a disquieting prospect: "that which these post-secular projects purportedly overcame or 'mended' still remains, though now hidden beneath a balm that itself exacerbates and quickens the continuing diremption: . . . the more the middle is eroded, the more its illusion proliferates." Rose, *Broken Middle*, 297.

68. She uses other metaphors as well but they are not as convincing as the city analogy. Refer, for example, to her discussion of Facism and representation in Rose, *Mourning*, 42ff. This is prefaced by the "owl of Minerva" metaphor, p. 42. See also Rose, *Broken Middle*, xi.

69. Rose, *Broken Middle*, 277ff.

tale of three cities,⁷⁰ but most comprehensively as the story of four cities.⁷¹ The first city is the corrupt polity of old Athens, the nemesis of Phocion to whom many are uncritically resigned, as partially indicated by the woman accompanying Phocion's wife. Those who are not so resigned, per Phocion's wife, seek to overcome Athens by the redemptive, sacral love of a New Jerusalem, the second city. But, this "New Jerusalem, the new ethics, has been developed from a dangerously distorted and idealized presentation . . ."⁷² The overcoming is never real, it ever only remains apparent.

The root of the attraction for and seeming necessity of the New Jerusalem is the existence of the fourth city: Auschwitz⁷³—"the measure for demonic anti-reason."⁷⁴ The basic argument is that Athens left alone inevitably results in the horrors of Auschwitz (Phocion's ashes being perhaps representative) a result that must therefore, at least for those not simply resigned to it, be overcome. But, Rose argues, this depiction of Auschwitz is "too exculpatory" for it provides a "blanket condemnation" that obviates a necessary but painful process of analysis.⁷⁵ Instead of Athenian resignation or Judaic escapism, both exhibiting a refusal of analysis, Rose suggests the need for critical engagement in which we

> do not see Auschwitz as the end-product and telos of modern rationality . . . [but] . . . as arising out of, and as falling back into, the ambitions and the tensions, the utopianism and the violence, the reason and the muddle, which is the outcome of the struggle between the politics and the anti-politics of the city. This is *the third city*—the city in which we all live and with which we are too familiar.⁷⁶

The "third city" describes a situation of active engagement in which the breach perpetrated by Auschwitz is appropriately mourned in a process that avoids evasion and resignation: "mourning becomes the law. Mourning

---

70. Rose, *Mourning*, 15ff.

71. Ibid., 26ff.

72. Ibid., 26.

73. Rose also calls this the "City of Death," refer for example Rose, *Broken Middle*, 293.

74. Rose, *Mourning*, 26, 33. Refer pp. 26–34 for a discussion of Auschwitz. Rose chooses it as a city partly because it was chosen by the German hierarchy to be a "major German city . . . the administrative centre for the Germanification of eastern Upper Silesia, in the Nazi version of the medieval German ambition to civilize the Slav lands by colonizing the territories between the River Oder and the River bug." Ibid., 31.

75. Ibid., 33–34.

76. Ibid., 34. Elsewhere in *Mourning* she describes the third city as "the just city and just act, the just man and the just woman." Ibid., 26.

draws on transcendent but representable justice, which makes the suffering of immediate experience visible and speakable. When completed, mourning returns the soul to the city, renewed and invigorated for participation, ready to take on the difficulties and injustices of the existing city."[77]

Lloyd is particularly helpful when thinking through a theologically oriented metaphysical shape for this third city in suggesting the work of Rowan Williams as an exemplar.[78] Williams, like Rose in part because inspired by her, "emphasizes human fallibility," the recognition that error characterizes our relations. This does not foreclose the possibility of ethical action but to act this way "is to renounce the possibility of a final true judgment yet not to renounce the possibility of acting. It is to act knowing that one will act in error yet to continue acting."[79] We are to enter into the difficult negotiations demanded by the middle rather than obviate them through placebos. Quoting Williams, Lloyd comments "it is 'not the facile and tempting question of law's relation to grace, but the harder one of how the very experience of learning and negotiation can be read as something to do with God.'"[80] Lloyd points to William's metaphor of "supreme disinterestedness" which, when carefully described and circumscribed, is the embodiment of this lineage of thought. He suggests that William's theology is appropriately negative here: "God does not mend the middle but echoes its brokenness."[81]

Lloyd then goes on to argue that while Williams accepts "Rose's problematic: the unavoidability of the difficult work of the broken middle . . ."[82] he does not then take the next step of considering the solution Rose offers. Rose is not just advocating a metaphysic position but an ethically inclined one. The practice of theological virtues, such as faith and love, within the brokenness of the middle, within the law, Lloyd suggests, offers fruitful possibilities. In short he is suggesting "Rose offers an alternative to the secular colonization of the sacred and the theological colonization of the secular."[83]

Overall this is a powerful challenge to all postures purportedly "rediscovering ineluctable Revelation—as a singularity, Event, difference,

---

77. Ibid., 36. The rest of *Mourning* can be read as a series of worked examples that attempt to explain the mourning that characterizes the third city. Her discussion of the Potters field is a poignant instance, refer, pp. 101–23.

78. Lloyd, "On the Use of Gillian Rose," 704.

79. Ibid. Rose describes the characteristic of the third city as *activity beyond activity*, refer Rose, *Mourning*, 121–23 and 38 for a summary of its relationship to the third city.

80. Lloyd, "On the Use of Gillian Rose," 704. He is quoting Williams, "Between Politics and Metaphysics," 9.

81. Lloyd, "On the Use of Gillian Rose," 704.

82. Ibid., 705.

83. Ibid.

whether in a Gnostic or a negative or . . . in a positive theology . . ."[84] It indicts Milbank for a "theological colonization of the secular," albeit through a positive theology, because despite all efforts this seemingly remains, even if unwittingly, trapped within the problematic of the middle. Mythic originary violence is not finally overcome; instead Milbank participates in the perpetuation of an illusory repetitious patterning that only ever *apparently* overcomes violence.[85] A full comprehension of the diremption of law and ethics is never actually entered into for it is finally avoided, and therefore proposals like Milbank's continue to refract an original Kantian breakage.

> The dualities issuing from this breakage beg to be "overcome" as culmination of "Western metaphysics," to be "deconstructed" as "difference" and to be celebrated as post-aesthetic sublimity or holy theopathy. *The pathos of this concept is this cyclical repetition.* Such overcoming, with its singular, antinomian aconceptuality, betrays the diremption it will not address. Diremption, unlearnt and unchanged, demands the gratuity of being mended in origin and in perpetuity.[86]

The central charge being prosecuted by Rose against Milbank is the avoidance of equivocation and anxiety by naming the broken middle "violence" and then translating it into holiness.[87] Also implicit in this charge is an indictment of the institutional structure he has built upon the middle for it is in this space that the middle expresses itself.

> Ethics and domination, the good and violence, the community and the law, do not belong to two worlds, to two cities, to two different methodologies. The counter-distinction of ethics from politics is itself the effect, the result, the outcome, the mediation, of the relation between the negotiated meaning of the Good, whether ancient virtue or modern freedom, and the historical actualities of institutional configurations.[88]

It is too simple to conceive the broken middle as politically manifesting between ideal and actual configurations yet this gives the flavor of Rose's argument. Following the young Marx she locates the origins of "the breaking of the middle" in the political revolution initiating the transition from

---

84. Rose, *Broken Middle*, xiii.

85. As Rose notes, "violence at the beginning persists when it is meant to be overcome by the elevation and extension of the 'divine milieu.'" Ibid., 309.

86. Ibid., 308, emphasis mine.

87. Ibid., 296.

88. Rose, *Mourning*, 88.

feudal to state politics.[89] As she comments, this transition was predicated upon a tragic diremption for "The breaking of the middle is exposed here in its main configuration: the fact and fiction of the 'individual' who emerges split—naturalized as 'egoism' and allegorized as 'ethical.'"[90] Contrary to Marx therefore, who saw it as a necessary step for revealing the underlying but hidden conflict, Rose laments the transition.

> For "the perfection of the idealism of the state was at the same time the perfection of the materialism of civil society." . . . In feudalism, statuses, privileges, guilds, formed the middle of legal estate, and determined individuals as their particulars, as members of the middle, which corporatively faced the separated state; with the dissolution of this feudal middle, the individual emerges with two separate lives: merely particular existence outside any middle, and yet bearer of the universalist aspirations, of citizenship, enjoyed by each—enjoying, that is, the arbitrary fate of civil society, and "active" in the increasingly imaginary state.[91]

This brief delineation of Rose's exposition cannot possibly do justice to her many nuances however it is suggested that it describes the main patina of her argument. At this point a decision is required as to how to tackle Rose's critique. Milbank never directly refutes Rose but instead maintains a complex relationship with her writings. She was influential in his early development and has retained this influence. He attributes much of his essay "A Critique of the Theology of the Right" to her and later takes on board her account of diremption, though not in any simple sense.[92] Against this must be noted his immediate linkage of diremption with what is for him the concomitant ability to separate this from the rationalist determinism characterizing Hegel's metaphysics.[93] This is an arguable contention but one he nevertheless entertains.

At the level of metaphysics there is real potential for bringing Rose's account of diremptive tension into discussions with Milbank's Vichian analysis of metaphoric tension. In this type of analysis Milbank would join with Rose in the desire to retain the inherent tension as against collapsing

89. Rose, *Broken Middle*, 301–4. The reference to "young Marx" reflects the presence of subsequent change in his views. The focus upon the conflict between civil society and state as reflecting the split within humanity between their particularity in activities and universality in ethics present here is later related to economic factors.

90. Ibid., 303.

91. Ibid.

92. John Milbank, "A Critique of the Theology of Right," 28, refer esp. p. 35 n. 36.

93. He also suggests this same ability in his later essay Milbank, "Out of the Greenhouse," 260.

the terms of the metaphor into a dualism. As Rose notes "The fundamental categorical contraries which are said to capture the differences at stake, such as, repetition/contradiction, description/constitution, and, lately, structure/event, do not only imply and depend upon each other, but, on examination of their jurisprudential claims and connotations, display a deeper mutual involvement, an identity and non-identity, which is historically discernible."[94]

On the other hand, attention to the primordiality of metaphor would expose to view the way Rose had herself partially collapsed the metaphor of origins into immanence (her Judaic sensibility perhaps mitigating this Hegelian move, but not completely forestalling it). Space however precludes these thoughts being given free reign as the intent behind this chapter is to arrive at a practical statement of Milbankian ecclesiology that answers not only Rose but the collocation of critiques her view has been taken as representative of. In view of this the following pursues questions more closely related to the pragmatic implications of Rose's critique, or more particularly, to the resources Milbank could bring to bear in response to it.

It is therefore tempting to proceed directly to a Milbankian rebuttal, arguing that his notion of "Gothic space" provides a direct counter to the practical implications stemming from Rose's position, a process mirroring in fact her own feudal nostalgia. This would be an inauspicious leap however as it implies her critique completely lacks pragmatic currency, when it does not; the situation is much more complex. It will be suggested instead that Rose does have a point but that it does not represent the thoroughgoing disavowal she suggests; partly because she misunderstands aspects of Milbank's position and partly arising from logic internal to her argument. On the other hand, she does make it clear that Milbank is insufficiently attentive to the practical application of his ecclesial proposal. To this extent it is perhaps feasible to suggest Rose's broken middle, in appropriately modified form, may augment Milbank's perspective in such a way as to anchor his project in the realities of daily life. Lubricating this augmentation are the presence of congenial albeit nascent elements in his thought, evidences that the broken middle is not an entirely foreign object within the panorama of his radically orthodox thinking.

A Different Tale: Milbank's Three Cities

This section of the discussion begins with a concession: Milbank idealizes the church in both structure and practice. So, for example, he renders it somewhat obscurely "a space (a space whose boundaries are properly

---

94. Rose, *Dialectic of Nihilism*, 208–9.

ill-defined) . . ."[95] It reflects the "absolute social harmony of heaven" and is the "exemplary form of human community."[96] Further, as Rose noted, Milbank considers it to be "the city of God on pilgrimage through this world"; "'a nomad city' (one might say) for it does not have a site, or walls, or gates."[97] At other points he ramifies this idealization by a noticeable suspicion of the institutional church; arguing, for example, that the institutional church has achieved its purpose only "in faintly traceable actuality . . ."[98] Even more damning is his indictment of the church for its complicity in the rise of both liberalism and nihilism; for failing in its task and unleashing thereby "a hellish anti-Church . . . [caught] . . . within the cycle of the ceaseless exhaustion and return of violence."[99]

The church portrayed by these representative selections appears amorphous and displaced;[100] the body of Christ depicting and embodying perfect harmonious relationships but somehow divorced from institutional expression and therefore earthly place. In short, the Milbankian understanding of church would seem to be that of an escapist phantasm that allows one to believe in perfection and perfectibility without any real sense of it being a grim task or one pursued in mourning; the dark night is flooded by the light of the Son and all becomes harmony—perhaps representing a sort of sophisticated francophone, theologically-attuned prosperity doctrine (to crudely but effectively put the matter). To an extent there is undeniably an element of this in his thought, but not just or even primarily this. Taking the preceding references in isolation leads to a reading almost exclusively generated off the surface of his writings that consequently fails to pay attention to the undercurrents they are in fact irrevocably linked with.

Closer attention to his work demonstrates the need to marry these erstwhile thoughts with other perhaps stronger gestures that point towards a balancing perspective that might even bridge the respective projects of Milbank and Rose. This does not deny the need for more explicit attention to the question of the broken middle by Milbank as it will be suggested that a stronger "negative theology" should weave its way through Milbank's thought. Rose provides just such a balance however a straightforward attempt to marry the two projects is apparently debarred by her consistently negative assessment of his project—from the foundations up. Yet against

95. Milbank, *Theology and Social Theory*, 422.
96. Ibid., 412 and 388 respectively.
97. Ibid., 392.
98. Ibid., 417.
99. Ibid., 433.
100. Picking up here Graham Ward's notion of the displaced body of Christ.

this can be noted hints that perhaps her assessment is overly negative and that the two proposals converge more than Rose allows. To explore this it is necessary to first return to Rose's key metaphor and consider it again relative to its expression in Milbank.

Milbank helpfully delineates his thought in one place through a metaphor that readily compares with the framework outlined by Rose. He comments:

> One could say that Christianity denies ontological necessity to sovereign rule and absolute ownership. And that it seeks to recover the concealed text of an original peaceful creation beneath the palimpsest of the negative distortion of *dominium*, through the superimposition of a third redemptive template, which corrects these distortions by means of forgiveness and atonement. This is all very well, but what of the persistence of the second text, and the way the Church compromises with it and continues itself to write it? This is the problem that Christianity can scarcely claim to have resolved.[101]

On the surface Milbank discerns three templates, or what Rose calls cities. The first may perhaps be called Eden, representing an "original peaceful creation" and drawing on Genesis 1–2.[102] The second accords with Athens but should be understood, in Milbankian terms, as founded in Cain though perhaps perpetuated most by Jove.[103] The third can be labeled Jerusalem, though only with the accompaniment of several caveats. First, it is a variant of Rose's "new Jerusalem" but one qualitatively different from the escapist construct implied by her; second, it incorporates but is not exhausted by a version of what Rose calls "new Jerusalem"; and third the unexhausted remainder is an earthly component loosely termed salvation city, though at this stage to be taken without any of the amorphous connotations usually associated with this way of describing it.

Eden refers transparently to the prelapsarian description provided in Genesis 1–2. In the shadows of this biblical account, behind the emphasis

---

101. Milbank, *Theology and Social Theory*, 417.

102. Rose is at pains to ensure a correlation between existing cities and their metaphoric application, refer for example to her discussion of Auschwitz in which its Germanic future as a city is carefully charted before it is brought to bear upon the situation she is explaining. Rose, *Mourning*, 26ff. This present discussion necessarily breaks this symmetry, for no comparable prelapsarian alternative existed—at least to our knowledge.

103. This invokes Ballanche's interpretation of the story of Cain and Abel in which "Cain's civic destiny at once perpetuates and 'contains' the economy of sacral violence which he has inaugurated." Refer Milbank, *Theology and Social Theory*, 69.

Milbank, Violence, and Idealization

upon Adam and Eve, there appears room to consider the growth of human sociality. Aquinas, for example, implicates these "other" shadowy figures in this very way when he seeks to support a stronger notion of artifice in the "consensual erection of convenient frameworks for human life" than is offered by the proposals generated by either Augustine or the stoic Seneca.[104] Both of these latter scholars, by contrast with Aquinas, had espoused a form of "natural rule" based in intellectual and moral superiority.[105] This removes the consensual element from view because it obliterates it hence the sense of communal growth is similarly obviated.

Athens is familiar from the work of Rose but distinguishable in important ways. Milbank is very close to Augustine when describing this city, equating it almost exactly to *civitas terrena*. He describes it as built on the presumption of sin and therefore as inherently in need of regulation. This regulation is structured towards peace but only as a "bare compromise between competing wills." It corresponds with the exercise of worldly *dominium* and represents a nascent liberalism.[106] It is therefore not surprisingly characterized by a notion of personhood as self-ownership that is also linked with the notion of unrestricted freedom within one's own domain, evident even in the stoic resignation embodied by the *cosmopolis* citizen.[107] Integral to this description is the lack of an Auschwitz. The fourth city, at least in the sense propagated by Rose, is not necessary for Milbank because it represents just one of several plausible, logically inherent conclusions to be drawn from the historical tapestry woven by Athens. Auschwitz and metaphoric cognates are included within and endemic to Athens. Their presence is overt at times, glimpsed through periodic ruptures, but generally they remain hidden within the crucible of *dominium* and *imperium*.

The real difference to be noted in this analysis however is the role and character of Jerusalem. On one level it can be seen to accord quite directly with the description provided by Rose. It is the heavenly city, Augustine's *Civitas Dei*, in which "true society" resides; it represents the idealist construct noted above. "True society implies absolute consensus, agreement in desire, and entire harmony amongst its members . . ."[108] However, despite

---

104. Refer, for example, to this discussion in ibid., 407.

105. Ibid., 406.

106. Ibid., 401–2.

107. Cf. Ibid., 408ff, esp. 410 for discussion of a fundamental individualism being present "within heroic ideals of antiquity . . ."

108. Ibid., 402. The remainder of the quote can be read as indicating an earthly position for this description however it is better read as presenting the *telos* to which the earthly city is working. This will become clearer as the earthly/divine relationship is further elaborated.

the exalted nature of this description it is not thereby able to be simply mapped onto the description provided by Rose. Milbank can arguably be considered to have blocked such a maneuver by his defense of Augustine against a similar charge. He notes Augustine is accused, in part, of understanding "the true Church, the *Civitas Dei*, as the collection of elect true believers, known only to God. This contention is, however, almost totally erroneous."[109] It misrepresents Augustine's understanding of both the state and the church, presenting a distortion that understates the extent to which Augustine is attuned to political reality.[110] Milbank tackles R. A. Markus in this regard, using Augustine's discussion on the Donatists to demonstrate that "while Augustine is certainly at pains to stress that many true members of the city of God lie outside the bounds of the institutional Church, just as many of the baptized are not true members at all, this does not mean that he regards institutional adherence as a secondary and incidental matter."[111]

As this indicates, Augustine, and more particularly Milbank, is to be read with the institutional church as an indelible background. Milbank is not arguing for some vague, "universal," amorphous conception of church but for a reconfigured earthly one whose inner core is rethought and restated (as will be seen below). In Milbank's thought the "earthly" aspect of the church is a complexly construed one suspended upon divine, corrupt, and properly worldly elements. Some explanation of Milbank's core ecclesial thought is required to explicate this network but before this it is important to note the shape of Milbank's proposal relative to that implied in Rose's analysis.

Rose imputes to Milbank Auschwitz as a result, it shall be argued here, of neglecting Eden. The loss of original paradise in her thought causes her to rely on precisely what Augustine, and following him, Milbank, finds most divinely incongruent—ancient virtue. Rose observes "Phocion's condemnation and manner of dying were the result of tyranny temporarily usurping good rule in the city."[112] She is arguing that Auschwitz represents this usurpation and that Milbank is guilty of simplistically, and therefore ineffectively, positing love against injustice: "to see ourselves as suffering but good, and the city as evil."[113] Against this she claims loss; the loss of mourning: "we are

---

109. Ibid., 400.

110. As Milbank notes, the use of the term "state" here is anachronistic but useful. Ibid.

111. Ibid., 402.

112. Rose, *Mourning*, 103.

113. Ibid.

no longer able to chant with Antigone: 'Because we suffer we acknowledge we have erred.'"[114]

Central to this argument is the underlying presence of good rule, a structurally neutral construct that may be directed in either appropriate or inappropriate ways. It is here that Rose is most susceptible to a Milbankian and Augustinian critique. Contrary to this view Augustine develops, and Milbank sharpens, a perspective in which precisely this "rule" is found to be structurally, not just directionally, inadequate because it draws from *civitas terrena*. Augustine does develop a concessionary role for earthly princes who are also Christian: they make *usus* of the peace of the world. But this is not optimal; relying on an at best ambiguous foundation that will always ultimately fail because it does not find purchase in divine charity and the forgiveness of sin.[115] In this can be seen part of the reason why Milbank is as theoretically inclined as he is; practice is derived from and ordered by mythological and ontological underpinnings.[116] These must first be revealed and then new ones articulated before a counter-practice can ensue. It is therefore necessary to briefly outline the "ideal" church Milbank is promulgating before delineating how this flows into practical applications.

The Ontological Foundations of Milbankian Ecclesiology

At the heart of Milbank's understanding of the church is both its conceptualization as a new form of society and its (re)statement through an Augustinian social ontology; the former following ineluctably from the latter. This ontology is described in the following terms:

1. micro/macro cosmic isomorphism;

2. the non-subordination of either part to whole or whole to part;

3. the presence of the whole in every part; and

4. positioning within an indefinite shifting sequence rather than a fixed totality.[117]

---

114. Ibid.

115. This will be developed further below but the specific discussion in mind here can be found in Milbank, *Theology and Social Theory*, 407, but see also 408–11, esp. 411.

116. Refer, for example, to his discussion of Augustine's charge that the Romans lacked true virtue "because they knew no real peace—either at the level of practice, *or at the level of mythological or ontological conception.*" Ibid., 363, emphasis original.

117. Ibid., 409, refer 404–6 for an elaboration of these themes.

Culture in a Post-Secular Context

The notion of isomorphism is a key to understanding this ontology. The background for this discussion can be found in Milbank's explanation of how Christianity overcomes various antinomies of antique reason: *polis/oikos; polis/psyche; gods/giants*.[118]

At the heart of his discussion is an Augustinian overcoming of the antinomy of *polis* and *oikos*. Milbank argues, using Plato and Aristotle as exemplars, that the ancients were trapped within a *mythos* that could not conceive justice and public peace as extending into the domestic sphere without thereby violating its integrity.[119] Plato rather than Aristotle wanted "to make the *polis* a real *oikos* as far as possible: an imitation of the lost, divine, 'pastoral' rule."[120] But he could not break from the governing *mythos*: "The thought of a domestic, tribal rule that would be peaceful without civic law did not occur to them."[121] In contradistinction Milbank argues the Old Testament already embodies this thought, initiating practices such as the protection of Cain, amongst many others, that "do not, in principle, require supplementation by a law founded on place."[122]

In the Christian dispensation the antique relationship between *polis* and *oikos* is radically subverted by *ecclesia*. In ecclesial perspective the *polis* is the *oikos* and the *oikos* is the *polis*: "every household is now a little republic . . . and the republic itself is a household . . ."[123] This establishes the central point in his analysis of ecclesiology.[124] At root, Milbank argues that all the various social relationships *should* refract, and be an extension of, both internally (interior organization) and externally (publicly visible), the individual/community relation. Community is here taken in its largest possible sense, as the entirety of individuals.

In this construct each individual is free to choose their locale but only one location results in harmonious peace, not just for the individual but for all individuals—each exercise of freedom being indivisibly related. Perhaps the best sense of what Milbank is describing can be gleaned from a point perhaps strangely absent from this summary so far: his discussion of difference. Milbank argues that

> the whole is only a series, and is thereby itself entirely effaced in favor of the *differentia* of the parts, where each particular

---

118. Ibid., 362–76.
119. Ibid., 364–69 for this discussion and esp. 368 for these points.
120. Ibid., 368.
121. Ibid.
122. Ibid.
123. Ibid., 403.
124. Ibid., 403–6, esp. 403.

Milbank, Violence, and Idealization

difference is defined by the position of all the other differences. The goal of the *ecclesia*, the city of God, is not collective glory, as if the city itself were a hero, any more than it is the production of heroic individuals. Instead it really has no *telos* properly speaking, but continuously *is* the differential sequence which has the goal beyond goal of generating new relationships, which themselves situate and define "persons."[125]

For Milbank, despite appearances, this is not simply *theoremata* without *pragmata* for it has an earthly impact. He comments "True society implies absolute consensus, agreement in desire, and entire harmony amongst its members, and this is exactly (as Augustine reiterates again and again) what the Church provides, and that in which salvation, the restoration of being, consists."[126]

In thinking through the question of harmony and peace Milbank also provides resources for thinking through how this ontology outworks itself in the practicalities of life. He argues from a critique of virtue, and concurrent advocacy of forgiveness, for a truly non-coercive and therefore harmonious societal order.

Virtue in a Clash of Ontologies

His critique of virtue is aimed at an antique profile in which it was thought citizens may, through appropriate *paidea* into "certain practices and states of character, regarded as objectively desirable goals for human beings as such . . . ,"[127] aspire to and eventually attain a natural mode of humanity that is also the objectively right way to be human.[128] The ancients were therefore attentive to the disciplining of unruly social elements, a process ultimately founded on coercion and dominance and expressing an arbitrary ordering and compulsion. At this point Milbank is able to set up a contrast between ancient and Christian perspectives.

He argues the presence of a "fundamental individualism" in these "heroic ideals" that "is necessarily present, because whole and part are turn and turn about subordinated to each other, and the part/whole ratio is given

---

125. Ibid., 405, the metaphor of series is drawn from Augustine's elaboration in *De Musica*.

126. Ibid., 402.

127. Ibid., 326.

128. Milbank critiques Aquinas here for distinguishing between natural and supernatural virtues such that he cannot conceive of a single virtue that may be redirected or transformed by Christianity, refer ibid., 409.

predominance over the relational sequence..."[129] The antique construct is founded on an ontology utterly at odds with the Christian ontology Milbank is presenting. Countering this is "the Christian social ontology, linked to the idea of an emanative procession of all reality from a single divine source..."[130] He argues that justice is founded in harmonious sociality and therefore is intimately connected with peace, itself grounded in a charity pre-eminently expressed in Jesus Christ.

These are, then, two fundamentally opposed approaches operating on the basis of distinctive, diametrically arrayed ontologies. It is therefore not as simple as presenting Christianity as the fulfillment of ancient virtue for much more is at stake. Milbank notes "Augustine asserts that, for us, the approach to divine perfection cannot be by any achieved excellence of virtue, but only through forgiveness."[131] It is at this point that Milbank begins to marry his "outnarration" with a supporting and substantiating praxis. He comments "the only thing really like heavenly virtue is our constant attempt to compensate for, substitute for, even short-cut this total absence of virtue, by not taking offence, assuming the guilt of others, doing what they should have done, beyond the bounds of any given 'responsibility.'"[132] In short, forgiveness.

Forgiveness

The discussion of forgiveness is pursued most fully in his treatment of coercion. Backgrounding this examination is an Augustinian account of how *Civitas Dei* relates to *civitas terrena*.[133] Augustine argued that the church was to make *usus* of the "peace of the world"; the "Christian emperor" being paradigmatic. By operating as if their "political function" was an exercise in pastoral care, treated as if it were an "inner ecclesial" function, the Christian emperor could bring earthly peace into subordination to Christian charity.[134] But there is a problem, or what Milbank terms an ambiguity: "The implication of this must be that insofar as *imperium* lies outside *ecclesia*, it

129. Ibid., 410.
130. Ibid.
131. Ibid., 411.
132. Ibid.

133. Milbank is careful to note the anachronism involved in terming this "a 'state' in the modern sense of a sphere of sovereignty, preoccupied with the business of government. Instead this *civitas*... is the vestigal remains of an entire pagan mode of practice stretching back to Babylon." Ibid., 406.

134. Ibid., 407.

is an essentially *tragic* reality, involved in a disciplining of sin, which constantly threatens to be (even, in fact, *always is*) itself nearer to the essence of sin as the self-exclusion of pride from the love of God."[135]

For Milbank the central mistake is ontological. Augustine denied any place for *dominium* in *ecclesia* but violated it by providing sacral authority to punishment, albeit for positive purposes. All punishment involves the exercise, at some level, of arbitrary or "pure" violence that "has an inherently negative, privative relationship to Being, and cannot therefore, by Augustine's own lights, escape the taint of sin."[136] It is the wielding of power over another *as if* it were the exercise of divine judgment, and therefore inherently involves the initiating or institution of spiritual inequality (not least because the "other" does not have access to our sins).

Milbank's Augustinian framework presents harmonious sociality as the hallmark of divine rule; its contrary counterpart is therefore a lack of peace articulated as isolation. Solitariness is here depicted as the inevitable consequence and therefore corollary of sin. In light of this he suggests "The only finally tolerable, and non-sinful punishment, for Christians, must be the self-punishment inherent in sin."[137] Importantly he urges that Christians not resign themselves to sinfulness but actively overcome it by acting in anticipation of heaven. Regarding sinners he argues that "there is only one way to respond to them which would not itself be sinful and domineering, and that is to anticipate heaven, and act as if their sin was not there, by offering reconciliation."[138]

In at least the realm of forgiveness Milbank has attempted to present a particular, pragmatic application in support of his ontological foundations, one that concurrently operates as an acknowledgement of the need to engage the world as it really rather than ideally is. Against the charge that it still appears impractical Milbank may reasonably reply that the solution must be envisaged before it can be enacted. Yet he offers much more than this for it is central to his project that "there can only be a distinguishable Christian social theory because there is also a distinguishable Christian mode of action, a definite practice. The theory explicates this practice, which arose in certain precise historical circumstances, and exists only as a particular historical development."[139]

---

135. Ibid., 419, emphasis original.
136. Ibid., 420, this whole discussion drawing from 417–22.
137. Ibid., 421.
138. Ibid., 411.
139. Ibid., 380.

He is offering orthodoxy informed by pre-existing orthopraxy. However hard it may be to envisage its practical application this cannot detract from the need to initially posit it and then to follow this up with an attempt to outwork it.[140] Christians are to follow the example set by Jesus.

The question now arises as to whether Milbank has offered here a response to Rose. In an important way he has. As a preliminary statement it is important to note that the need for forgiveness necessarily implies preceding action requiring it, and therefore the presence of a space in which it operates. The "broken middle" is the label Rose uses for this space. Within it Milbank argues the church should "be an *asylum*, a house of refuge from its operations, a social space where a different, forgiving and restitutionary practice is pursued."[141]

The Broken Middle in Milbank

While not determinative it is interesting to note that at certain important junctures Milbank's language in TST quite directly disputes Roses (re)construction of his proposal as escapist Jerusalem. For example, he presages his discussion of counter-ethics by noting

> An abstract attachment to non-violence is therefore not enough—we need to practice this as a skill, and to learn its idiom. The idiom is built up in the Bible, and reaches its consummation in Jesus and the emergence of the church. By drawing our attention to sacrifice, Girard helps us to articulate part of this idiom. However, it is given a more social form if one contrasts (like Ballanche, as we saw in chapter 3), a way of life based on the victimization of others and *one where we choose voluntarily to bear each others burdens*.[142]

To use Rose's language, Milbank is gesturing here towards an acknowledgement of the middle. He is suggesting that Christian life should embrace the middle rather than escape or avoid it: "How does it help though (one might protest) to imagine a state of total peace, when we are locked in a world of deep-seated conflict which it would be folly to deny or evade?"[143] His response is revealing. It is not something to run from, or fantasize away, but is something that stimulates thought and action: it

---

140. Refer, for example, Matthew 19:26.
141. Milbank, *Theology and Social Theory*, 422, emphasis original.
142. Ibid., 398, emphasis mine.
143. Ibid., 411.

demonstrates human implication in perpetuating the presumed necessity of violence and then highlights a way by which it can be overcome; a way designated "forgiveness of sins."

Forgiveness, restitution, and atonement are woven together into a single process of Christian response to be enacted from within the broken middle.[144] "Here we *do* echo God, not in punishing, but in suffering, for the duration of the *saeculum*, the consequence of sin, beyond considerations of desert and non-desert."[145] Interestingly this suffering is bearing the burden not only of the perpetration of sin, the external action characterizing the middle, Rose's usurping tyranny, but more so the church's necessary complicity in it through (as a minimum) its own adherence to sin perpetuated through punishment. Against Rose Milbank is arguing that this does not have to be, Christians do not have to just bear the burden for action is possible and required; another way is open to the church—the path of true forgiveness.

Returning to Rose, Milbank's Augustinian critique of virtue despoils the "good" she relies on. Athens is not ruled well and then usurped by the tyranny that bequeaths Auschwitz, Athens is altogether implicated in Auschwitz from the start, structurally, hence Auschwitz is an expression of nothing more than a logical Athenian conclusion. The heroic ideals of virtue are laid bare by Augustine: "an individualism both of public *imperium* and private *dominium* . . . when deconstructed, finished up by celebrating the greater strength shown by the polis or the soul in its control of its members or its body."[146]

The foregoing highlights the feasibility of reading Milbank in a way that not only answers Rose's problematic but which also highlights difficulties in her own constructive proposal. Milbank argues "it becomes possible to consider ecclesiology as also a 'sociology.' But it should be noted that this possibility only becomes available if ecclesiology is rigorously concerned with the actual genesis of real historical churches, not simply with the imagination of an ecclesial ideal."[147]

But Rose's critique was constituted by more than a charge of idealization. It was also directed at the political, a sphere in which Milbank still stands accused of obviating the middle. In this there is more substance. As already noted Milbank finds his central theme, "harmonious peace," readily

---

144. Refer for a discussion of Ballanche to ibid., 69–70. His work teases out these various threads and is somewhat of a forerunner of Milbank's own proposals.

145. Ibid., 422, emphasis original.

146. Ibid., 410–11.

147. Ibid., 380.

traceable in aspiration but only "faintly traceable" in actuality.[148] This points to a problem in implementation that cannot be ignored: in TST there is little evidence of a specifically corporate, political response. But there is some evidence, and it points to a possibility that while only hazily indicated in TST is developed further in other works by Milbank.

Dwelling in the Equivocal Middle: Gothic Space

While developing his social ontology Milbank at one point argues it was "precariously present during the middle ages . . . [as] a unique and distinctively structural logic for human society."[149] A little later he notes the further presence of this same impetus in the French socialism associated with Pierre Buchez and followers, who articulated a patristic if overly positivistic socialism bearing structural similarities to medieval guilds.[150] In both of these scenarios the line between church and state is depicted as hazy; interrupted by comparatively independent, spiritual groups forming a cohesive structure "of many complex and interlocking powers . . . [that may] . . . forestall either a sovereign state, or a hierarchical Church."[151]

These themes first developed in TST are further expanded and taken in a particular direction in WMS, especially through Milbank's essay "On Complex Space."[152] In this essay Milbank tackles two targets pertinent to present concerns: enlightenment "simple space" and the totalizing tendencies of much of the "complex space" discussion in Catholic Christian socialism.[153] Threading between these two competing visions Milbank elucidates a description of complex space he terms "Gothic space," and promulgates this as an antidote to the two discourses he is disputing. In the course of this he also articulates a framework useful for the continuing consideration of the broken middle being undertaken here.

148. Ibid., 417.
149. Ibid., 406.
150. Ibid., 408 for this discussion.
151. Ibid., 408.

152. Milbank, "On Complex Space." This is a revised version of a lecture given at a Von Hügel Institute conference on *Rerum novarum* in 1991 and first appeared in McHugh and Natale (eds) *Things Old and New*, 1992. It therefore belongs to a similar temporal milieu as TST when thinking in terms of the development of Milbank's thought. It should also be noted that some of these same themes are developed in his essay "Out of the Greenhouse," esp. 258–59. This was also published as John Milbank, "Out of the Greenhouse," *New Blackfriars* 74.867 (1993).

153. He is also taking on Liberation theology but this discussion is of tangential interest and is therefore not covered in the ensuing discussion.

Milbank, Violence, and Idealization

To make explicit the connections being made it is necessary to begin at the end of the essay, where Milbank comments "If we wish, in the few years of a century that remain to us and the new millennium to come, both to face up to the modern predicament and yet not succumb to resignation, then I suggest we must re-think the sources of twentieth-century disaster along the lines I have proposed, and consider again the claims of the 'Gothic vision' in its socialist, Christian, variant."[154]

Milbank is here attempting to negotiate the broken middle, seeking a critical engagement entailing neither escapism nor capitulation. He is "in the mix" so to speak, advocating an immanent encounter of law and ethics, not to mend the break but to live in it, fully cognizant of the disjunction but acting anyway; "insofar as socialism has to take a wager on justice, on the possibility that we live in a universe where we can be the vehicles for just acts, whose 'characteristic' shape we will continuously *come* to know."[155] The instrument of this engagement is Catholic Christian Socialism and the locale is Gothic complex space. This conjunction requires some explanation. Milbank describes two contending positions he is equally wary of:

> Here we have the outlines of competing totalitarianisms: on the one hand complex space hierarchized, and recruited to the service of crude mythologies, whose quasi-religious yet essentially *secular* imaginings of untrammeled energy obliquely disclose that corporatist fantasy has not really obliterated the formal emptiness of the modern state and market. On the other hand, simple space articulated between the controlling centre and the controlled individuals, an articulation whose supposedly "social" character barely disguises the fact that this is *still* the simple space of liberal modernity.[156]

In contrast to either of these postures Milbank argues Catholicism needs to consider engaging a "specifically socialist variant" of "complex space" for it is only through this path that one can avoid resigning oneself to liberal capitalism while avoiding the series of illusory postures normally offered as alternatives.[157]

> Socialists and liberals who partook of the Gothic fascination in the nineteenth century were clearly not simply subject to romantic nostalgia: their mediaeval interests were selective, and what mainly concerned them was not hierarchical authority, but

154. Milbank, "On Complex Space," 285.
155. Ibid., 283.
156. Ibid., 272, emphasis original.
157. Ibid., 274.

> rather a pervasive legal constitutionalism orientated to consensus beyond mere mutual expediency or contractual obligation; orientated also to the diversification of sources of power, and to a guild organization permitting a measure of economic democracy and collective preservation of standards of excellence.[158]

Milbank frames this discussion around two central "chronotopes":[159] enlightenment "simple space" and Gothic "complex space." The former argues "that political reality is a 'simple space' suspended between the mass of atomic individuals on the one hand, and an absolutely sovereign centre on the other."[160] This represents an "organically" oriented construal of the political, whether constructed through the artifice of contract or naturally pertaining through providence. By contrast the latter presents a construct that is considerably more complex.

Gothic space represents the interpellation of intermediate organisms that have a group personality and mutuality of relations across the socius such that they together resist subordination to any whole.[161] These "parts" are themselves "wholes," repeating here the ontology spelled out above. Milbank points to Gothic building as representative: "Just as in Gothic architecture, the basic structural unit—for example the arch—is multi-functional, such that it can be infinitely enlarged or infinitely diminished, itself the total context, or linked with similar features to form a wider context, so also the social unit . . . can be very small or very large, self-standing or conjoined with other entities."[162]

He notes that this space is inherently sacred rather than secular; built on mutual decisions about the "good, true and beautiful." In this sacred space, on a Pauline construal of the church as the "body of Christ," he locates his macro/micro isomorphism discussed above; a social Christological ontology underlying a specifically Christian understanding of Gothic space.

This conception of political space is not simply ideal for it has historical precedence; at various times certain forms of manifest actualization can

---

158. Ibid., 279.

159. Milbank uses this term, borrowed from Michael Bakhtin, to express types built around a complex interplay between spatial and temporal images, or what he terms "co-articulations of space and time." It is not that one is spatial and the other temporal but that varying degrees of both are present. Refer ibid., 274–75.

160. Ibid., 275.

161. This is a negative statement of the proposal that is necessitated by the current dominance of 'simple space' and therefore is tacit recognition of the need to define, at least to some degree, relative to this pre-existing condition rather than strictly positively, on its own terms.

162. Milbank, "On Complex Space," 278.

be pointed to.[163] The origins are in medieval structures but these, and subsequent manifestations, are not "decisive" in themselves. Their ability to physically express the underlying ideal is to be doubted for they are tainted "and yet in this very 'ruined' condition as disclosing certain yet-to-be-attained possibilities."[164] These possibilities have not yet found concrete expression but there is hope, according to Milbank, in the general tenor of Catholic social teaching.[165] This teaching proclaims a form of Christian socialism that articulates the need for complex space. Unfortunately he finds it heavily tainted; a hybrid that is "always likely to be flawed, since the *ecclesiastical* structure it upholds, itself exhibits troublingly hybrid features."[166] Better instead, he suggests, a specifically Christian socialist paradigm that articulates a complex "Gothic" space.

At one point Rose argues "The counter-distinction of ethics from politics is itself the effect, the result, the outcome, the mediation, of the relation between the negotiated meaning of the Good, whether ancient virtue or modern freedom, and the historical actualities of institutional configurations."[167] In her introduction she comments she is negotiating soul, city and the sacred along with the universal, particular and singular. It is suggested that Gothic space presents itself as a viable tool for this negotiation; an actual configuration that deals with the underlying diremption between law and ethics.

In Gothic space there is no longer a simple mediation between sovereign law and private ethics or civil society and state, or any of the other dichotomies characterizing enlightenment interactions. Neither is there an ecstatic holy middle empowered by an irenic discourse plundering eschatology. Instead there exists a real engagement. It is conducted in light of the eschatological peace of Jerusalem but occurs entirely in the realm of this world. Through it underlying diremption is "mended." Mending in this context is not in appearance alone, as if some balm of holy peace had descended. Here there is no façade but reality. Ethics is no longer set against law but a complex negotiation ensues that can only be conducted under the auspices of the divine. As Milbank notes, early socialist formulations were concerned with "a pervasive legal constitutionalism orientated to consensus beyond mere mutual expediency or contractual obligation; orientated also

163. Milbank finds it present in Germanist (Grimm) and Romanist (Savigny) thought; in thinkers such as Maitland, Gierke, Vinogradoff and Figgis; as noted above, in French socialism; and in the Catholic Church, amongst many others.
164. Milbank, "On Complex Space," 279, emphasis original.
165. Refer especially *Centesimus Annus*.
166. Milbank, "On Complex Space," 284.
167. "Midrash," Rose, *Mourning*, 88.

to the diversification of sources of power, and to a guild organization permitting a measure of economic democracy and collective preservation of standards of excellence."[168]

Such ideals are no longer in the realm of autonomous reason for they imply a need to communally adjudicate what is "right, true and beautiful," to determine order in a context of "irreducible diversity." This is no longer the prerogative of a sovereign center but is dispersed throughout the socius.

These responses from virtue, forgiveness and Gothic space do not constitute a complete answer to Rose's problematic for they still remain too abstract. Nevertheless they go a long way towards mitigating the force of her observations; gesturing towards the praxis of the broken middle even if finally lacking the empirical force of concrete actualization. Despite this it can be seen that Milbank does provide resources for such actualization, even if Rose's critique compels recognition of the need for more explicit recognition and development of these. In his most recent foray on ecclesiology something of this type of clarification can be discerned for Milbank begins to call on these resources in a way he has not previously, demonstrating something of a turn towards something like the empirical description being asked for.

In his essay "Stale Expressions: the Management-Shaped Church" Milbank forms an argument against what he sees as a widespread Protestant tendency that perversely fills the only remaining gap in capitalist methodology. Capitalism is defined by him as a profit-based tension between objectifying and subjectivizing tendencies: "The contest of the market is the struggle of individuals to augment their subjectivity and decrease their objectivity. On either side of the struggle profit is generated: the objectivization of some human beings means profits for others; the subjectivization of human beings means an increased capacity for initiative and so for investment."[169]

The freedom to attain subjectivization is sharply circumscribed by the requirement for gaining the requisite number of "objects" needed to support "promotion" into the realm of subjectivizing (so, for example, there must be a certain number of workers available to contribute towards the income of the employer before someone can enter into that capacity). This eminently capitalist program is perfected, Milbank argues, in certain Protestant strains of church that have uniquely harnessed an objectification that does not thereby strip subjectivity. By pursuing the harvest of souls rather than an appropriate display of *caritas* or exhibition of God's love, these particularly evangelical strands of Reformational thought have bought into and logically

---

168. Milbank, "On Complex Space," 279. The ensuing discussion is informed by the explanation offered by Milbank on the same page and following.

169. Milbank, "Stale Expressions," 118.

extended the subjectivizing economy just described by a process involving the production of Christians through the creation of a commodity that is also a subject. Milbank notes with heavy irony that the only close business approximation is the slave trade, though here it becomes a Pauline parody.[170]

Milbank's countervailing suggestions are revealing. He advocates instead of this the seminal importance of parish based ministry or, more accurately, geographically anchored churches. Church is not, he suggests, oriented around a collection of the likeminded in the comfort of their preferred surroundings, but instead a genuine human community of *all* "in one specific location," irrespective of interests, gifts, and so on.[171] He argues that the tendency to plant churches "in various sordid and airless interstices of our contemporary world, instead of calling people to 'come to church,' is wrongheaded, because the refusal to come out of oneself to *go to* church is simply the refusal of church *per se*."[172] It simply promotes the various dysfunctionalities endemic to sectarianism. What is instead important about institutional church is found in its deliberate associating of itself with "the accidental givenness of place" hence "The real, universal Church is found *always* paradoxically in one place, within one circumscribed boundary and in one sacred, consecrated building, for very good theological reasons."[173]

For Milbank "sacred place" is prioritized over "liturgical mobility" because it is only geographic givenness that allows for human assembly *without* exclusion and for a diachronic continuity that counteracts the disjunction of contemporary synchronic priority. He suggests therefore that geography is not a purely secular concern but an integral aspect of church life for the universal gathering of the faithful is only truly realized when congregating at specific locales. Conversely he argues that cultural space should not be viewed as amenable to any and all constructions of it. Some realizations are antithetical to the Christian ethos and this should be recognized. Particular attention should be paid to the disembodied or rebellious spaces, though not by simplistically exporting the church into them, thereby tacitly fostering and condoning the underlying sectarianism and disjunction.

Judicious Narratives

This response to contemporary Protestant ecclesial manifestations is in many ways a remarkable one for Milbank because he has previously

170. Ibid., 120.
171. Ibid., 124.
172. Ibid., 124, emphasis original.
173. Ibid., 124, emphasis mine.

provided only an ambiguous pattern of empirical ecclesiological observations. When responding to Rowan Williams charge of idealization and the construction of history according to ideal types, Milbank seems to demur. He posits the church as time, gift, and promise rather than any particular "place" that might be arrived at and inhabited. He adds further to this empirical ambiguity by avowing the church is not a "real society" but an "enacted, serious fiction" only sustainable in the Eucharist, which is not a site but is rather "memory and expectation."[174] Yet it is transmitted, he all too opaquely avers, and hence it necessarily has discernible historical manifestations. A charting of these however is difficult because the sheer "microtemperality" or obscure, privateness of its myriad expressions are lost in a "narrative essentialism" that can only be guarded against by resisting the urge to break with the formalism of his description.[175] There is here a necessary tension that the church has always lived with.

It is on these terms that Milbank argues "the last chapter of *Theology and Social Theory* requires (infinite) supplementation by judicious narratives of ecclesial happenings which would alone indicate the shape of the church that we desire."[176] What is really refused here is paradoxically an idealization of the church: raising a specific, contingent shaping of the church as "the" shaping of the church, the mere act of reporting on which would constitute a complicit contribution to just this phenomenon. The notion of judicious here is not to be taken as a spatial limiting but instead as a qualitative condition. It is not primarily the paucity of "ideal" ecclesial expression in mind *per se*, though of course there is an element of this, but the need to ensure the expression is truly *mimetic*, imaging forth the body of Christ.

The work of Christian Scharen seems to embrace what Milbank is proposing, providing a possible exemplar for future treatment. Scharen suggests ethnography be used to make Milbank's ecclesiology "more recognizably real." Ethnography is initially described by him in social scientific terms, as "direct, qualitative observation of situations or settings using the techniques of participation observation, intensive interviewing, or both."[177] This ostensibly sociological delineation is however importantly supplemented, and thereby sociologically (or secularly) subverted, by a dogmatic adaptation. Here he draws from Nicholas Adams and Charles Elliott who take seriously the claim that no observation is neutral. This allows them to propose the insight, colorfully glossed by Scharen, that "a full metaphysically shaped eye is all anyone

---

174. Milbank, "Enclaves or Where Is the Church?" 341–42.
175. Ibid., 343.
176. Ibid., 344.
177. Scharen, "Judicious Narratives," 125.

Milbank, Violence, and Idealization

has to look with, and for a theologian theism simply implies a God-shaped eye."[178] Scharen then undertakes just such a jaundiced analysis (for it can only be such), using the rubric of identity as his path through to what Milbank might consider a "judicious narrative" of the church.

What must be avoided in such descriptions however is the type of idealization the formalism characterizing Milbank's disputed ecclesial descriptions sought to avoid, for there is a paradoxical idealization historically accompanying the empirical practices of the church. This has arisen whenever the church has allowed itself to settle, to engage in a process of sedimentation or whenever it has been lulled into taking residence within and then universalizing certain institutional structures. According to Milbank's logic the church has over time allowed itself to inhabit specific structural instantiations that have then been allowed to hold the church captive, limiting it to singular expressions of itself when in reality myriad possibilities exist. Rather than this singularity Milbank suggests a need to recognize and acknowledge the almost infinite variety of ways by which the church might genuinely express itself, a task that requires a more flexible theoretic. This of course courts the very danger his critics accuse him of, of an amorphous unidentifiable church, but perhaps this needs to be the case while the church is adapting anew to its context. Perhaps also the long term possibilities immanent in this approach are worth waiting for.

In the meantime there is without doubt a disjunction between Milbank's theoretical construct and his ability to empirically substantiate it. But, the apparent *aporia* this seems to imply in his project—for example, between polarities such as particular site and universal giftedness—do not constitute the metaphysical gap his detractors (friendly and hostile alike) envisage, rather they amount to a lacuna in description. As his work proceeds further examples of what he has in mind are beginning to emerge. From what has already been commented on it can be noted that Milbank's argument against the "soul harvesting" mentality of many evangelical churches firmly placed the church in specific locations, granting this element of the church sacral character. Scharen's ethnographic analysis found the possibility of granting it also to identity. In both cases the supposed lacuna wrought by formalism was overcome on the basis of empirical evidence. Milbank's church is indeed construed through formalism but this does not rob it of empirical reality, it instead protects its specificity in the face of a more powerful and totalizing formalism.

More than this however, the foregoing discussion has found that the church, as the ideal liturgical expression of culture, exists, and not just

---

178. Ibid., 130.

theoretically but empirically. It is not present as a mere balm despite its formal articulation in Milbank for it acts within and through the brokenness of human life. It is a physical presence formed by identity engendering rituals that express through its encounter with divinity what culture was always meant to be. In immanent terms this is revealed as a participation in a human *poesis* that is anchored in the Trinity, one that gives rise to the *praxis* by which the church engages the world at large. It is in this state that the phenomenological attraction of the church subsists; though this is really a reflection of its imaging of Christ, the true source of its formal and empirical constitution. Of course this is all too imperfectly displayed in practice, as the various iterations of history amply testify to, but there is nonetheless hope in this description for it includes an account of how the church is slowly (asymptotically) bending itself towards its teleologically ordered goal.

The foregoing concludes the discussion of Milbank's account of culture, this chapter in conjunction with preceding ones having outlined in some detail his description, charting its main theoretical and pragmatic moments. Having now done so it becomes clear a central characteristic of his articulation is its encompassing comprehensiveness. Milbank provides an alternative intellectual history that funds a counter-modernity, one that is definitively Christian but one also inherently wedded to a particular, participatory form of Christianity. This of course raises the question of whether this specific delineation of Christ is the only resource upon which a specifically Christian account of culture may be based. Is Milbank's perspective on Christ the only possibility for envisaging and articulating a theological account of culture or are there other possibilities in the theological panoply? This question is turned to in the next chapter.

Chapter 5

Karl Barth and a Theological Alternative

THE PRECEDING CHAPTERS HAVE subjected the neutral presumption cloaking social scientific definitions of culture to a rigorous examination, challenging in the process the cogency of the secular account of reality it is built on and the immutability of its legitimating structures. It was suggested that "the secular," rather than building on some bedrock of inalienable truths, was instead trafficking in speculative forays legitimated by no more than an imaginative depiction of reality grounded in and arising from a preference for immanent rather than transcendent explanations. Its foundations were constructed rather than discovered, embedded in a particular narrative construal of reality rather than any objective depiction of reality as it in all actuality is. Its rise to prominence therefore did not reflect an underlying consonance with reality (however much it seemed to) but was instead a refraction of the ability of its adherents to persuade, a skill founded in equal part on the convincing nature of the underlying rhetoric and their ability to mask its quasi-theological roots and hence entirely contingent nature. This finding does not by any means obliterate or necessarily denigrate the secular option of course, but it does chasten it, highlighting the element of sheer contingency behind its argument.

Acknowledging a reduced, chastened understanding of the secular creates in its wake space for envisaging other possibilities; for finding alternative foundations on which descriptions of culture might be based perhaps offering even better explanations of the phenomenon. In its constructive mode the preceding discussion presented one such account, finding in Milbank's framework significant resources for building a viable description of culture funded by a Christian articulation of reality. The specific articulation provided by Milbank arose from a poetic stream within the Christian tradition that emphasized human making and hence culture, but which contrary to the (modern) variant expounded through Bacon, Descartes, and Hobbes followed a distinctively Vichian Christian formulation that understood making to coincide with knowing, perfectly in God but imperfectly in humanity who therefore correspondingly imperfectly partake in divine making.[1] This partial participation in Divine making is possible only because of the presence of the Divine within humanity, and this consummately so in liturgy. On this foundation Milbank built a theological description of culture narrating a different story, with a distinctive genesis, processes and structure. It was a story that imbued culture with a peaceable rather than violent teleology.

The discussion then concluded with a question: having established this possibility is it then also necessary to accept the accompanying implication that Milbank's neo-platonic, Gothic construal is the only viable Christian account? Certainly Milbank himself leaves little room for negotiation here, strongly advocating the primacy of his position, but this cannot be allowed to deflect from asking whether he is simply trying to occupy unopposed what should be contested territory. Is his neo-platonic version of poetic theology really the sole repository of resources within the Christian tradition available for funding and constructing meaningful descriptions of culture? The question needs to be asked at a practical level as well since Milbank also implies that a Gothic construal of the ecclesia is the only viable way of conceiving the best of culture in its empirical reality. Is this the only way of constructing the relationship between Christ, his bride and humanity, or are there alternatives? The field of possibilities is admittedly thin because culture has rarely come before theology in quite this way, nevertheless alternatives are available.

At the end of the previous chapter it was pointed out that within the broader RO corpus one such alternative impulse existed in the writings of James K. A. Smith. His Reformed sensibility, guided by an incarnational rather than neo-platonic inflection, was found to have opened up some congenial space within the RO *oeuvre* for envisaging culture in a very different way. Unfortunately his project remains unfinished, although it is just now progressing with the recent release of the second installment of a planned triptych on culture. If the initial release is a fair indication of his overall approach then it promises to be an informative and insightful liturgical analysis of culture quite different to the Reformed response famously pursued

---

1. For a discussion of the two alternative *verum-factum* traditions mentioned here refer Miner, *Truth in the Making*.

since Abraham Kuyper. Nevertheless it still remains in its formative stages. However, this does not mean the rich pickings offered by the Reformed tradition have been exhausted for in Karl Barth, it is suggested, a particularly insightful and powerful alternative paradigm can be found.[2]

This is perhaps a quite surprising assertion given, as Robert Palma acknowledges, that

> Barth's position on culture has had a bad press involving oversimplification, reductionism and even the denial that Barth gave us any theology of culture. It has too often been assumed that Barth did little more than express a loud "No" against human cultural endeavors and products. Moreover, there is the idea that once Barth had placed culture under the severe judgment of God, he had nothing else to say.[3]

Palma argues the contrary view, suggesting Barth's theological thought, both early and mature, displays a considerably more complex relationship with culture that actually affirms it. Barth's positive engagement with culture went considerably deeper than the love of Mozart he is usually ascribed with, the supposed exception proving the rule. Barth's understanding of culture is, in short, much more intricate and multifarious than most scholars suggest, forming what amounts to a richly endowed storehouse of cultural insights that can usefully be gathered together as a coherent and consistent theological description of culture.

The first step towards this goal is dealing with a well-known objection to a supposedly core element of culture by Barth—worldview. On closer examination his objection to this key element of much Reformed engagement with culture is more ambiguous than is usually acknowledged. His perspective displays a subtlety of thought that richly nuances his overriding desire to correctly characterize and adequately delimit human endeavor. It becomes evident that his work has been caricatured (not always without provocation it must be admitted) by this desire to limit the human element, however an emphasis on this risks distortion because it misses the way Barth places the desire at the service of his larger project. Barth wants to present the true place of humanity before God but must first deal with the human proclivity to disfigure it. To take this critical element as his terminal

---

2. The decision not to pursue a study of the Kuyperian tradition was made for a number of reasons. Barth's critique of worldview presented below provides good insight into some of them, given that this is an offshoot of the Dutch program. Essentially this tradition is taken to refract rather than mitigate, let alone get around, modern presuppositions, hence failing to offer a truly post-foundationalist response.

3. Palma, *Karl Barth's Theology of Culture*, ix.

position is to misunderstand him quite markedly for it is but a step in the process towards an accurate presentation of the Divine/human relationship.

Arguably this represents his broader agenda regarding culture. Barth is undertaking necessarily critical engagements with the concept of culture to all the more clearly posit his positive view of it. In this positive goal can be detected something of his broader strategy for dealing with humanity before God, and this not coincidentally since they are inter-related moments in his analysis. In CD 3 for example, Barth places humanity in the cosmos, then in relationship with each other and then considers how both the cosmos and humanity are to be thought of in relation to God. At all points Barth is concerned to ensure that despite sin it is understood that God is "for" the creation but especially that He is "for" humanity, that He is always, even when saying no, ultimately involved in a yes to humanity. It is the proclivity for humanity to spurn the need for dependence that necessitates the no, and it is in the effort to address this that the critical agenda surfaces, but it really arises only at the service of God's yes to humanity. To begin to demonstrate this effect the following begins with Barth's views on worldview.

Worldview

Barth provides his most comprehensive and cohesive statement on worldview in Volume IV of *Church Dogmatics*. It occurs during a discussion of the doctrine of reconciliation that is concerned with describing various aspects of the relationship existing between God and humanity. His particular interest at this specific moment within his overall argument is with the battle humanity finds itself in between good and evil. He pursues this theme using the related biblical metaphors of life and light. So, for instance, he constructs part of his argument on the idea that a light shining in the darkness is a light that the darkness *cannot* overcome. He sets the environment for this battle as the world in all its various facets, and the key fact of the encounter is that Jesus is Victor.

Importantly Jesus' victory is achieved in a particular fashion. It is not as if he were leading one of two equally situated opposing forces, nor as if he were a monistic monarch, but rather he proceeds through 'dynamic teleology'[4] The end has been set because it has already been won, hence Barth comments, "A history is here taking place; a drama is being enacted; a war waged to a successful conclusion."[5] However, this does not mean all resistance has been quashed, on the contrary. The battle must still be en-

---

4. Barth, CD 4/3/1:168.
5. Ibid.

gaged precisely because stubborn resistance is still being mounted. Barth suggests there are three intra-human elements offering this resistance, each operating as instruments of darkness in direct opposition to the light of the Word of grace.

The first, initial resistance involves simply ignoring the Word, as if it were of little consequence or were going to soon pass out of sight. This strategy does not resist very well when placed under pressure hence it does not rest easily for long. The second and more powerful method of opposition is the construction of a "little prophecy," a counter-construct designed to turn aside the light of life. This is the tactic Barth terms worldview. The third approach is to accept the Word, though only in appearance. This is a ploy that turns aside the supposedly stringent requirements of acceptance by proffering the ostensible advantages of nominal adherence.

As this so clearly indicates, Barth begins his discussion of worldview in entirely negative terms, elaborating it as a method of direct opposition to the Christian acceptance of Jesus as Victor. The reasons for his complete disavowal of worldview thinking are formally elaborated through five points, though a number of associated, subsidiary arguments provide important aspects of augmentation. In summary form, Barth first turns his attention to an objectifying argument granted wide currency by Heidegger's similar perspective, though with a distinctive theological twist. Barth argues that worldview thinking casts humanity as subject and everything else as object, including the Word of grace itself. People are able to contemplate the Word from a certain distance, as if it were something they could grasp hold of and analyze. This, he charges, subverts God's sovereignty. Second, and in continuation of this subversion, it attempts to construe the world in its entirety. A place may be given to God, but it is an allocated one. The exclusive claim of God is, however subtly enjoined it may be, relegated.

Third, in a move that deepens the subversive effects of worldview thinking, he notes its effect in relativizing the particular. There will often be a place for the contingent or unique, "but every world-view will insist that it is unique only in its own way, and it will thus co-ordinate it with and interpret it by a corresponding and ultimately comprehensive generality, instead of adopting the crude and arrogant process—which no world-view would ever do—of setting the generality in the light of this particular event. In world-views it is the principle which counts and not any one thing, even though it were the most important."[6]

---

6. Ibid., 256.

Clearly in mind here for Barth is the particularity of Jesus Christ, a single "event" that would nonetheless, contrary to the generalities of worldview thinking, seek to orient the world around Himself.

Fourth, this placement of the particular within the principle allows for comparative engagement, but to detrimental effect. Each worldview is now just one of many, as if it is *an* orientation instead of *the* orientation. Asserting the supremacy of one over the others finally collapses into a "First among equals" melee. As Barth contends, the Word of grace is not this type of doctrine, "It is a declaration and a summons: the declaration of a decision already taken, and the summons to orientation by this, since only obedience or disobedience is possible in relation to it."[7] Finally, the fifth objection is that worldview thinking merely represents the human propensity for sovereign mastery. It is an expression of the attempt to understand ourselves by way of ourselves. By contrast, the Word "strikes" us from without and above, and it is only from within this "foreign" Word that a proper understanding of ourselves is revealed. We can only understand ourselves to the extent we are understood.

Barth summarizes by proposing that worldview is the temptation of philosophical thought.[8] Jesus Christ may exist within worldviews, but only in a deformed way, present only as the abstract man, the historical Jesus, or the Christ-idea. Worldviews "offer plenty of pictures, panoramas, generalities, doctrines, human attempts at self-understanding. But His voice—and this is the decisive reason why we so easily resort to them—is not heard in any of them."[9] Philosophical thought is here reduced to or equated with an impulse springing from a human anthropology founded on immanence rather than transcendence, and so the element of sheer preference is again brought to the fore as it was also through Milbank.

Barth not only establishes opposition to worldview in its own right but adds another nail to the coffin by connecting worldview with the third element of resistance offered by a humanity seeking to oppose the Word of grace. He situates it as part of the domesticating process that finds the Word accepted, absorbed and promulgated in such an innocuous form that "the divine Yes has become curiously like the Yes which man is always about to say to himself, and it has become a kind of world-view . . ."[10] As he goes on to describe it, the Word has been immunized, tamed and harnessed.

---

7. Ibid. See also Barth, *Romans*, 39.
8. Barth, CD 4/3/1:257.
9. Ibid., 258.
10. Ibid., 259.

"Everything will still sound great and august and holy. But it will no longer be the indicative and imperative which impinge incisively upon the present."[11]

Elsewhere in his CD, during a summary of "The Christian Doctrine of Providence" in 3/3, these points are further clarified in a section that needs to be read in conjunction with the CD 4 analysis set out above. In this earlier analysis Barth sets out an argument that clarifies what will later appear as a thoroughgoing disavowal of worldview in CD 4, for here he acknowledges that there is a proper albeit subdued place for worldview thinking. Barth begins in CD 3/3 by presenting his own definition of worldview, contending "What is a world-view if it does not consist in the contemplation of a world rule, and therefore of a reality which is superior to the world and all its contemplation and interpretation, and can effectively order and co-ordinate world-occurrence?"[12]

By its very nature, therefore, the Christian perspective is "worldview," or what Barth terms the "Christian view of things."[13] But there is a significant difference in this way of stipulating the matter. Worldview under Barth's gaze is not a comparative term as it tends to be when normally invoked. It is not as if it were *a* worldview, first amongst equals, but rather that it is *the* worldview, or better yet, the *one true way* of viewing and understanding world-occurrences.

This formulation implies that perspectives emanating from outside of this "Christian view of things" concerning world-occurrences, or the aspects of creation, are necessarily explained through reference to creaturely aspects, ascribing to these immanent perspectives the status of "world-rule." But, "From world-occurrence as such there are obviously only arbitrary and highly debatable ways to a world principle . . ."[14] a concise explanation for the proliferation of worldviews. These world orientated perspectives enter into a struggle for explanatory supremacy, and any Christian viewpoint predicated upon similar foundations simply joins this competitive pantheon, constituting little more than one further exposition jockeying for primacy.

But the world is not as these worldviews describe it, for in these observations "We are confronted by the necessary impotence of all systems which radically or practically, primarily or subsequently, abstract from God's work of grace and the kingdom of Jesus Christ";[15] a concise and particular statement

11. Ibid.
12. Barth, CD 3/3:55.
13. Ibid.
14. Ibid.
15. Ibid., 54.

of the more general eschewal of philosophic systems undertaken by Barth. Instead of such systems, the world is to be understood as the creation of God, with all that is entailed therein. Everything emanates from, and is oriented by, this single truly "Archimedean" point. Here humanity is confronted by the reality of what post-modern accounts term Alterity or the Other.

Yet this does not leave humanity without resources for articulating a view of the world. He comments, "there can be a contemplation of the divine world-rule, and therefore of world-occurrence under this rule, and therefore a Christian view of things, only in the movement of faith itself from within outwards, and in the concrete realization of its perception."[16]

It is only as God reveals Himself to humanity that humanity gains the capacity to start to understand the world. It is therefore only through the operation of faith, and this through the power of the Holy Spirit, that humanity is placed in a position to see, even if only dimly, what the world truly is like.

Within this point Barth notes the important caveat of humility, of the human realization of its creaturely status. Humanity can only ever see partially and therefore always only provisionally interpret the world; the gift of faith that enables interpretation is a constantly refreshed gift of the Holy Spirit. He warns however that there is always a danger here: "The establishment of a fixed Christian view, of a lasting picture of the relationship between Creator and creature, would necessarily mean that in taking to-day the insight given him to-day man hardens himself against receiving a new and better one to-morrow."[17]

God is constantly active in the world, but He is not always active in the same way from day-to-day. It is only because of His faithfulness "That tomorrow as to-day He will give creaturely occurrence its function, *telos* and character..."[18] Everything garnered in the course of Christian contemplation and under divine inspiration is therefore entirely provisional, held only lightly in recognition of the creaturely limits within which humanity operates.

Barth therefore sets out an extremely modest notion of worldview, one that takes the form of a partial "series of promising standpoints" separated by many "reservations and gaps." It does not have the character of grandiosity he discerns in other descriptions of worldview for its purpose is not to explain "larger or total issues," instead it remains always provisional and highly particular. It is nonetheless binding, representing the fullness of current revelation, but is not thereby either stagnant or impregnable; it

16. Ibid., 55.
17. Ibid., 56.
18. Ibid.

remains entirely conditional upon this revelation in its teleologically ordered unfolding.

As revelation grows so too does understanding, but this understanding does not finally equate to comprehension for this is solely a divine prerogative, but instead it amounts to the much more humble notion of apprehension. Barth's worldview remains a view of the world that is sufficient for the warp and woof of life; adequate for human purposes but it is not *ultimately* defining of purpose, life or world. It is a guiding light emanating from faith in the Lord God, in whom alone ultimate belief is to be vested. It is therefore a distinctly hermeneutic rather than ontological model of worldview.

It should be noted that Barth is not alone in drawing back from the metaphysic implications of worldview in order to promulgate a more subdued hermeneutical articulation. Others have effectively developed the same position albeit deriving it through quite different analyses. Heidegger has already been mentioned in this regard but others have developed it further.

Roger Ebertz is one such scholar. He comments that any worldview articulation is necessarily promulgated from a specific perspective. As he argues, "it is impossible to identify a single, ahistorical worldview we can label as the Christian worldview. Because all human thought is historically, culturally and linguistically conditioned, one can only grasp and express a particular Christian worldview, that is a view from one's own perspective."[19]

He further charges "that worldview thinking succumbs to the modern passion to find foundational formulations of truth which are unshakeable and upon which all Christian thinking must rest."[20]

To address these problems Ebertz suggests the hermeneutical model. In articulating this model he avails himself of five key Gadamarian insights. First, the resurrection of a positive understanding of "prejudice," or in other words, of prejudice as the preconceptions each of us brings to bear upon an interpretive situation. Allied to this is a positive rehabilitation of tradition and authority. Second, prejudices stem from the various traditions we are all embedded in, traditions that we are not by any means available able to step outside of; we are all caught within the ambit of the language and history that precedes us. It is inherent to the human condition to be so situated. Third, it is our prejudices that make understanding possible in the first place. "Experiencing the world requires a point of view from which it is experienced."[21] These form our guiding frameworks. Fourth, these

19. Edertz, "Beyond Worldview Analysis," 10.
20. Ibid.
21. Ibid., 13.

frameworks are not closed systems but are necessary foundations for what is "new." Finally, any act of interpretation represents a fusion of horizons between ourselves and some *other*.

The final result is that the small space for a more truly hermeneutical rendering of worldview left by Barth has been expanded by a Gadamarian framework that renders it an enlarged (even if only slightly) hermeneutical model. This enlarged space does not equate to the grandiose schema proposed by Kuyperian and associated scholarship but it constitutes one that nonetheless does justice to the central insight being acted on in this scholarship, even if now in a highly chastened form. For Barth the concept of worldview is not painted in the entirely negative way his popularly conceived inclination towards *Diastasis* would seem to indicate. Certainly placing an emphasis on the CD 4 discussion would support the contrary view however careful attention to other points at which he discusses worldview, hence also CD 3, allows a better depiction to emerge. Barth is not against worldview *per se* but is instead against its use as either a tool of divine objectification or as an instrument wielded in the absence of an appropriate humility. When neither of these conditions is breached then he sees a properly hermeneutic role for it.

Given this, it is *not* feasible to present his worldview discussions as in themselves examples of some anti-cultural bias in his corpus. His concern, it is suggested, is not with the pursuit of an anti-cultural agenda but with the need for an appropriate understanding of what human creaturely limits are in the recognition that humanity endemically seeks to surpass or overcome these limits. Barth works hard to ensure that humanity understands the need to avoid transgressing these divinely granted limitations in favor of operating in full recognition of them for it is only by doing so that humanity achieves true, authentic human being. This of course moves quite beyond the discussion of worldview engaged above, serving instead as an introduction to the idea of culture as it is positively exposited by Barth.

Before this positive agenda is considered however, it is necessary to examine how Barth's readers have understood his work. If there is indeed some sort of general perception that his writings embrace an anti-cultural bias then there are presumably identifiable catalysts for this perspective. In the following some of his closest and most sympathetic interlocutors are turned to in an effort to identify the roots for this view. This then provides a platform for more carefully considering whether this thesis of bias has validity, for determining whether it is a cogent reading of his project.

An Anti-Cultural Bias in Barth?

The notion of Barth providing a positive description of culture is not normally affirmed by many commentators.[22] If anything he is most often associated with the contrary perspective, and not without reason. Hans Urs von Balthasar's influential commentary on Barth's theology argued that the "monism of the Word of God, which invades the hostile world and is expressed in such Idealist categories . . . threatens time and again to swallow up the reality of the world. Though the world (which does after all stand in relation to the Word of God) is certainly something and not nothing, it looks so forlorn and hopeless under this harsh glare that one might just as well wish it did not exist."[23]

Something of this is most clearly evident in Barth's preface to the second edition of his famous *Römerbrief* where he comments "if I have a system, it is limited to a recognition of what Kierkegaard called the 'infinite qualitative distinction' between time and eternity, and to my regarding this as possessing negative as well as positive significance: 'God is in heaven and thou art on earth.'"[24]

Eberhard Jüngel clarifies the depth of the disjunction opened between heaven and earth here by noticing the attention Barth initially gave to the negative injunction in the wake of his efforts to deal with liberal theology, especially in both Schleiermacher and the excessively historicizing effect of the historical-critical method of biblical exegesis. McCormack characterizes this as Barth's "effort to overcome historicism and psychologism in theology."[25] Barth's aggressive critique of the first target in particular was the catalyst for many in the early days to indelibly mark his theology as anti-cultural.

For Jüngel, the Kierkegaardian negative injunction was radicalized by Barth in light of his reading of Franz Overbeck and the two Blumhardts (the father Johann Christoph and the son Christoph).[26] From Overbeck especially he learnt the need to keep "the distance between God and humanity,

---

22. See, for example, the discussion surrounding Barth as an anticultural theologian in Vahanian, "Karl Barth as Theologian of Culture."

23. Balthasar, *The Theology of Karl Barth*, 94. Barth referred to Balthasar as "The shrewd friend from another shore . . ."; see Barth, *Humanity of God*, 44.

24. Barth, *Romans*, 10. This has sometimes been rendered by commentators through the slogan "God is everything, humanity nothing." For a critical engagement of this rendering see Jüngel, *Karl Barth*, 132.

25. Jüngel, *Karl Barth*, 59–60; McCormack, *Orthodox and Modern*, 81.

26. For Barth's own recording of these influences, along with Kutter, Leonhard Ragaz and Dostoevski see Barth, *Humanity of God*, 40.

between the coming Kingdom and present world reality."[27] This expressed itself, as Jüngel notes, in the thoroughgoing eschatological cast of Barth's theology.[28] It also came to fruit in his paradoxical and sophisticated expression "the impossible possibility." Here the impossibility of human effort and the requirement for Divine intervention (hence the possibility) are conjointly emphasized, a formulation that only heightens the already firmly established distance between God and humanity.

Colin Gunton perhaps best brings out the nature of the engagement Barth had entered into during this period, providing in the process a general rubric for understanding Barth's supposed anti-cultural bias. He argues the situation between Barth and liberal theology is best understood by considering it a dispute between rival types of theology, types that have consistently recurred through the tradition. Schleiermacher represents a supposed theology of culture (Tillich is Gunton's specific example but the illustration still works), hence an approach "that tries to make peace with the culture in which it lives; it tries to mediate between itself and the world around." By contrast Barth pursues a theology of crisis whereupon it is responding to "something critical happening of such a kind that theology has to respond, in a sense, by throwing a radical message at the people and the church of its time . . ."[29]

Barth, by extolling a theology of crisis, can be seen as initiating through his Romans commentary (especially from the second edition onwards) what would become a sustained attack on theologies seeking to promulgate any kind of entanglement between culture and Christianity. It is then just a short step from this sort of view of Barth to the seemingly associated premise that he is against culture, a perspective granted further credence by the monism Balthasar discerns or, in terms clearly invoking the Kierkegaardian formulation noted above, when Gunton announces in Barth "a dualism operating here between the world of time, where religion takes place, and the world of eternity, which is God's world."[30] This firmly places the locus of dispute *as* (not in) the world of *time* (not religion, a vital distinction to be covered just below). Barth's 1926 assessment of Schleiermacher certainly

---

27. Jüngel, *Karl Barth*, 66. Refer pp. 58ff for discussion of Overbeck and the two Blumhardts.

28. Ibid. The quote he most closely links it with is an editorial addition brought in through the second edition: "If Christianity be not altogether thoroughgoing eschatology, there remains in it no relationship whatever with Christ." Refer Barth, *Romans*, 314.

29. Gunton, *Barth Lectures*, 29. Note he takes Irenaeus and Origen as his classical exemplars.

30. Ibid., 30.

does nothing to dispel this thought: "He forced Christianity, *solely for the sake of culture*, into a position where the whole was already surrendered."[31]

The clear impression emerging from these observations is of a fundamental bias against culture in Barth's writings. Myriad other pieces of evidence could be gathered in support of this contention, many of which Robert McAfee Brown manages to summarize in his succinct synopsis of a common American response to Barth:

> So much does [Barth] stress the uniqueness of Christian revelation, so vehemently does he reject natural theology and the insights of "religion," that he seems to isolate the Christian, placing him in a private world of his own where he can learn nothing save what he hears directly from God's Word. There is no path from culture to Christ, which would appear to suggest that there is no path from Christ to culture. The isolation of Christian thought from all other thought would seem to result.[32]

It seems that at various points, in multiple ways, almost right across the board, Barth indulges in a consistent and persistent separation of the divine from the worldly that exalts deity in such a way as to render whatever is of humanity negligible, if not actually nothing. Whether taken from the perspectives of culture, religion or natural theology (his infamous *Nein* to Emil Brunner ringing loudly here) it appears that Barth is faithfully asserting the Kierkegaardian trajectory. Or so it seems.

Barth himself disagrees. At least as early as 1939 he was actively contesting this perspective, claiming

> The abstract, transcendent God, who does not take care of the real man ("God is all, man is nothing!"), the abstract eschatological awaiting, without significance for the present, and the just as abstract church, occupied only with this transcendent God, and separated from the state and society by an abyss—all that existed *not* in *my* head, but only in the heads of my readers and especially in the heads of those who have written reviews and even books about me.[33]

---

31. Barth, "Schleiermacher," 198. Emphasis mine.

32. As quoted in Vahanian, "Karl Barth as Theologian of Culture," 38. Emphasis original. R. H. Roberts notes something like this characterizes the American view, as opposed to the sheer indifference of the British and the rather positive perspective of the Scottish. Refer Roberts, "The Reception of the Theology of Karl Barth."

33. Quoted in Vahanian, "Karl Barth as Theologian of Culture," 39. Emphasis original.

Culture in a Post-Secular Context

How can this complete disavowal be reconciled with the various pieces of evidence either alluded to or explicitly noted above? Perhaps the best way to tackle this question is to return to the source material in order to consider a representative passage in detail. A good example comes during his consideration of Romans 3:27–28 in his commentary on Romans. Here there arises the clear assertion that "Men are righteous only when their righteousness proceeds from God, and from Him continuously. From this presupposition it is possible to adopt a critical attitude to the law, to religion, to human experience, to history, to the inevitability of the world as it is, in fact, to every concrete human position."[34]

This establishes a "critical attitude" towards culture (i.e., law, religion, human experience, history, and world) that is founded on the thought that it is "moving in a secular and relative context, which is in itself ultimately meaningless."[35] However this assertion does not simply make culture into something completely and utterly meaninglessness because Barth also manages to retain a sense in which culture is "a parable of the wholly other world . . . a parable, a witness, and a reminiscence, of God."[36]

Yet, he goes on to suggest, there is within culture nevertheless something that truly is "altogether meaningless and incomprehensible," namely "all confusing of time and eternity . . . all improper notions of immanence, every non-radical idea of transcendence, every kind of relative relation between God and man, every divinity which presents itself as being or having or doing what men are or have or do, every human figure which calls itself in any way divine. When all this middle-realm between God and man is clearly recognized, it must be discarded."[37]

There are three key moments to be registered in this discussion. The first is his establishment of a limiting condition, namely that righteousness comes from God and must be continuously renewed. The second appears to be somewhat obscure (at least for now) for he seems to be implicitly claiming that culture lacks such righteousness (being secular) and hence is meaningless, except that it is also a parable of the other world, in which case it has meaning. There is then, third, also an identifiable intra-culture negative irruption of mediation that must be discarded.

There is clearly evident here, in his treatment of the irruption, a characteristic anathematizing of mediating positions between God and humanity, the latter position often being referred to by Barth through the cipher of

---

34. Barth, *Romans*, 107.
35. Ibid.
36. Ibid.
37. Ibid., 108.

"religion." Gunton, for example, captures this feature of Barth's perspective when he characterizes Barth during this period as presenting a "theology against religion," religion being equated to the Schleiermacherian understanding in which humanity is thought to be "viewing and feeling the infinite in the finite. . . . Religion is the finite with capacity for the infinite (*capax infiniti*)."[38] In 1924 Barth would comment that "Jesus simply has nothing to do with religion."[39] Actually, while this Schleiermacherian formulation might well have been uppermost in Barth's mind throughout this time his deployment of "religion" really enjoys a far wider currency since he applies it to the whole of the "middle-realm," of which Schleiermacherian religion constitutes just one example.[40]

It is worth pausing a moment to note that Barth's relationship with Schleiermacher is much more complex than is often thought. In his early, post World War I writings, Barth certainly sought to distance himself from Schleiermacher, conceiving him as the foundation that gave rise to the German church's abominable theological affirmation of German war policy. In 1923 therefore Barth argued "I have indeed no reason to conceal the fact that I view with mistrust both Schleiermacher and all that Protestant theology essentially became under his influence . . ."[41] Yet this comment was made in preparation for a serious engagement of Schleiermacher precisely because of his theological genius. He was a figure to be thought through rather than one already transcended; a gifted theologian and historical figure worthy of close attention.

By 1968 this attitude might seemed to have softened even further, with Barth declaring he was "at odds" with Schleiermacher only "with reservations." This uncertainty stems from the hope that in some way he has misread Schleiermacher, that he might "perhaps be understood differently so that I would not have to reject his theology, but might rather be joyfully conscious of proceeding in fundamental agreement with him . . ."[42] As Barth notes, "old love never fades," and this, it might be suspected, is the nature of the otherwise forlorn hope he is holding out here: that despite decades of engagement, the fundamental character of the disagreement, and the ongoing dispute with those pursuing projects even implicitly linked to Schleiermacher, that somehow Barth might have misread him and "that means that all along the line

---

38. Barth, "Schleiermacher," 176–77. See also McCormack, *Orthodox and Modern*, 23ff.
39. Quoted from Jüngel, *Karl Barth*, 59.
40. See for discussion von Balthasar, *Theology of Karl Barth*, 87ff.
41. Barth, *The Theology of Schleiermacher*, xv.
42. Ibid., 275.

I am not finished with Schleiermacher, that I have not made up my mind, whether on the positive or even on the negative side!"[43]

To return to the unfolding argument however, Gunton goes on to note that methodologically Barth is pursuing a dualist Kierkegaardian dialectic in which the two poles are neither synthesized nor sublated (the former proposal being a populist rendering of, the latter the more properly technical conception of, Hegelian dialectics) but rather, and paradoxically so, brought together solely and only in Jesus Christ.[44] This leads him to conclude by commenting, "And so, in the presence of Jesus, all that men are and have and do is perceived to be complete unreality, unless, bowed under the negation of God, they await His divine affirmation. All that men are and have and do is naught but the righteousness of men, and, in the sight of God and men, remains illusion, unless under the judgement of God, it ceases to be the righteousness of men."[45]

The critical stance noted above is here represented by the provisional aspect of culture stemming from its position under Divine rather than human judgment. When viewed from this angle it is now easy to see how Barth can argue for there to be elements within culture that constitute parables and then elements within it which are to be discarded. Still difficult to understand however is his assertion that culture represents a "secular and relative context" which is "in itself ultimately meaningless." How is this seeming obscurity to be accounted for?

Much later, in 1956, Barth gives what amounts to an explanation for this confusion. In his essay on "The Humanity of God" he provides a seminal outline of his more mature theological anthropology drafted on the basis of a significant *Wendung* (change in direction).[46] More specifically, Barth had come to realize that the range of positions he so heavily chastised in his earlier writings might be accorded "greater historical justice than appeared to us possible and feasible in the violence of the first break-off and clash."[47] This is not at all a denial of the efficacy of the original challenge for he still argues that "Evangelical theology almost all along the line, certainly in its representative forms and tendencies, had become *religionistic, anthropocentric,* and in this sense *humanistic.*"[48] Theology had "gone overboard" in the

---

43. Ibid., 277.

44. For this analysis refer Gunton, *Barth Lectures*, 26–36. Note also the critique this dialectic attracted, most prominently in von Balthasar, *Theology of Karl Barth*, 81ff.

45. Barth, *Romans*, 109.

46. Refer Barth, *Humanity of God*, 35–65. This records the text of a lecture he delivered on 25th September 1956 entitled "The Humanity of God."

47. Ibid., 39.

48. Ibid. Emphasis original.

nineteenth century and his coming against it represented a timely and necessary corrective.[49] Nevertheless he was only "partially right" in "the same sense in which all preponderantly critical-polemical movements, attitudes, and positions, however meaningful they may be, are usually only partially in the right."[50]

What Barth had neglected in this earlier challenge was the element of truth subsisting within the German liberal position he was so assiduously demolishing. In particular he was now concerned that he had in the process of his earlier critique paid insufficient attention to how the deity of God was related to humanity, and in the process had constructed God such that He was "this 'wholly other' in isolation, abstracted and absolutised . . ." who was then set over man "in such fashion that it continually showed greater similarity to the deity of the God of the philosophers . . ."[51] What was missing from these earlier formulations, he suggests, was a Christological grounding for it is precisely in Christ that the apex of communion between God and humanity is reached, and it is therefore here that the deity and humanity of God co-exists.[52] It is in the very moment that the deity of God is first encountered that there is also encountered the humanity of God for it is exactly here that God is "for" humanity. As Barth defines it, the humanity of God is "His free affirmation of man. His free concern for him, His free substitution for him . . ."[53]

This humanity must also be understood to be that which is gifted to individuals and by which they are characterized, and this is so notwithstanding the effects of the fall because the individual is elected by the grace of God, and this not because they deserve it, but rather gratuitously and freely by Divine will.[54] It is at this central point in his argument that the key reflection for culture arises because for Barth the logic behind his formulation of the humanity of God extends beyond the existential human being and on into the cultural being and from there on into human culture itself. This is so because for Barth culture is "the attempt of man [sic] to be to be man [sic] and thus to hold the good gift of his humanity in honour and to put it to work . . ."[55] This gift can and is frequently perverted and put to ill use such

---

49. Ibid., 19.

50. Ibid., 42.

51. Ibid., 44–45.

52. For an interesting analysis of these themes see the extended Christological discussion of Barth's "royal man" in Jüngel, *Karl Barth*, 127–38.

53. Barth, *Humanity of God*, 51.

54. Ibid., 52–53.

55. Ibid., 54.

that it habitually appears subverted, yet structurally it is not for it always remains the good gift of God. Culture as the gift of God is structurally good, even if bent for nefarious purposes "all along the line."

The next stage of his 1956 argument is an interesting development that seems to muddle the waters for the thesis being pursued here in that he sets about distinguishing a category called *"theological* culture" from culture, treating it almost as if it were a distinct subset of culture as more generally understood. He argues "Since God in His deity is human, this [*theological*] culture must occupy itself neither with God in Himself nor with man in himself but with the man-encountering God and the God-encountering man and with their dialogue and history, in which their communion takes place and comes to its fulfillment."[56]

This seems to depart somewhat from his previous statements, however it is illuminating to note that Barth moves from this statement directly into establishing that theology is *therefore* to "think and speak only as it looks at Jesus Christ and the vantage point of what He is."[57] When theology attains to this goal it has reached, and therefore Barth is describing the proper task and parameters of, "cultivated" theology. On the 8th January 1957 he gave an address on "Evangelical theology in the Nineteenth Century" that helps to clarify this point. In this address he argues regarding theology that "A very precise definition of the Christian endeavor in this respect would really require the more complex term 'The-anthropology.' For an abstract doctrine of God has no place in the Christian realm, only a 'doctrine of God and of man'..."[58]

From this analysis it appears most logical to suggest that Barth is using "theological culture" in a technical sense, as a synonym for "theology" in order to capture what he intends by the more complex synonymous conjunction of "The-anthropology." In essence this is a Christologically-derived formulation that attempts to capture the need to avoid separating deity and humanity in view of Christ's perfect conjoining of them. As he argues "In Jesus Christ there is no isolation of man from God or of God from man.... Jesus Christ is in His one Person, as true God, man's loyal partner, and as true man, God's."[59] It is therefore fair to suggest that Barth is concerned with properly defining theology relative to its rightful Christological subject, stance and purpose. In this respect he is not elaborating some distinctive aspect of culture, or sub-culture in contemporary parlance, and neither is he

---

56. Ibid., 55.
57. Ibid.
58. Ibid., 11.
59. Ibid., 46. Emphasis original.

developing a distinct theological description of culture along the lines being entertained by this thesis. Rather, he is properly identifying the nature and task of the discipline called theology.

This suggests it is feasible to argue that by logically and consistently extending his Christological formulation of theological anthropology Barth can be seen to have derived a specifically theological foundation for, and initial theological articulation of, culture. His earlier emphasis on *Diastasis* and the wholly otherness of deity had clouded this in his Romans work although it was, as the preceding discussion demonstrated, nevertheless present within it. This does not of course deny the seminal role played by his "turn to Christ" for it was really here that he found a coherent and consistent framework to permanently connect what he had otherwise only tentatively and sporadically joined together.

Having examined some overtly critical perspectives arguing the presence of a negative view of culture in Barth it is now necessary to consider a more recent treatment that ostensibly seeks to assert Barth's affirmation of culture. Only a couple of commentators have in recent times set out to describe Barth's positive theological description of culture in book length treatments.[60] The first is Robert Palma's 1983 *Theology of Culture: The Freedom of Culture for the Praise of God*, while the second is Paul Metzger's 2003 *The Word of Christ and the World of Culture: Sacred and Secular through the Theology of Karl Barth*. In what follows careful attention will be paid to Palma's proposal, while Metzger's analysis will be considered a little later.

There is a particular difficulty associated with the task of describing Barth's understanding of culture peculiar to the present age, namely the danger of conflating the anthropological and theological perspectives, a temptation especially enticing given that the social scientific position constitutes the scholarly status quo. This temptation births a tendency to treat the concept of culture as if it really was an inherently neutral construct, and Barth's commentators are not immune to it. For example, Palma at one point argues "Granted that materially and methodologically we have in Barth a paradigm directly determinative only for theological culture and theologically significant culture, its extensive and comprehensive character requires that it be considered as a context applicable to and consequential for the whole spectrum of cultural activity."[61]

---

60. Others have integrated to varying degrees elements of his thinking on culture into their projects, although always for other purposes and hence their treatment has been correspondingly limited. Perhaps the best example of this is Gorringe, *Furthering Humanity*.

61. Palma, *Theology of Culture*, 5.

Palma's use of the phrase "theological culture" falls into the category of "sub-culture" rather than the technical use to which Barth put it (as just described) and hence it betrays a questionable prevarication that borders on a bifurcation. Unfortunately Palma does not step back from this boundary but breaches it, strongly suggesting the possibility that a (secular) realm of culture might exist which is able to be bracketed off from theological or religious considerations, and indeed Palma describes the situation as one of bracketing off the theological dimension.

Palma a little later argues that Barth queries any "culture that would not be termed explicit theological culture but which is still responsible for and answerable to the Word of God."[62] The deliberate use of the term "culture" in this sentence rather than, for example, "cultural activities," is important. It establishes in Palma's thought the possibility that culture might actually consist of two distinctive realms, the one secular and the other theological. What Palma seems to be dallying on the fringe of is collapsing the ontological and hermeneutical or, in more directly Reformed terminology, structure and direction distinction. There is validity in what he is saying at the hermeneutical or directional level but not in terms of the structural or ontological foundation of culture. He has after all only just finished commenting that for Barth the church knows nothing but a concrete, particular sinful person,[63] necessarily implicating thereby all culture, a point he explicitly acknowledges just a little later, "all culture . . . is finally for him theologically determined and conditioned."[64] The problem comes with the "all."

If there is "a culture" that can be "bracketed off" from the general notion of culture otherwise thought to be under the sway of the Word of God then it is not actually under its sway at all. The ontological category "culture" either does or does not encompass all instances. By contrast, the way various elements of culture (i.e., "cultural activities") are (mis)directed is an altogether different issue since it is quite plain that the immanent and contingent choices of a fallen humanity have full play. Perhaps the main point behind Palma's desire to bracket off a theological understanding is his argument that a certain slant inhabits Barth's view of culture, one arising directly from Barth's historical situation.

For example, Barth talks of a higher and lower view of culture, though the exemplars of culture he aligns with his technical category "theological

---

62. Ibid., 10.

63. Barth describes the central point thus: "On the basis of the eternal will of God we have to think of *every human being*, even the oddest, most villainous or miserable, as one to whom Jesus Christ is Brother and God is Father; and we have to deal with him [sic] on this assumption." Barth, *Humanity of God*, 52–53.

64. Palma, *Theology of Culture*, 12.

culture" is revealing: "Yes, along with pyramid building, pre- and post-Kantian philosophy, classical poetry, socialism, and theoretical and practical nuclear physics there is also theological culture."[65] His son Markus argues that Barth uses the term "culture" in contradistinction to "civilization" (correlated with the "way of life" meanings more familiar to contemporary understandings of culture) to mean "the very acme, the summit of human possibilities for which we yearn, which we can never define, which occurs in a great work of art, or in Mozart, or in great persons."[66] It is fair to suggest that Barth often has this in mind except for at one point—the properly theological (or in philosophical language, ontological) determination of culture. Here he is adamant, time and again, that culture speaks of the totality of human activity and relations. So, for example, he comments "What is culture in itself except the attempt of man to be man and thus to hold the good gift of his humanity in honour and to put it to work?"[67] The sense of good achievement is certainly present but it is altogether dominated by the notion of totality, a pattern maintained throughout his writings.

In short Palma's general thesis that Barth sometimes brackets off the theological dimension must be considered unsustainable. This would then seem to bring into question a whole section of Palma's discussion that may now seem untenable. Yet this is not the case for it is recoverable in the sense that rather than seeing Barth as bracketing off the theological dimension in order to admit admiration for Mozart, Leibniz, Botticelli and Grünewald it is more accurate to see him as delineating impressive expressions of culture that reach farther towards the divine purpose of culture.[68] Culture for Barth embraces the totality of human activity but not all of this activity is well directed or undertaken to a very high standard. Barth is not so much bracketing off these exemplary instances, as Palma wants to suggest, but is instead acknowledging their pre-eminence.

One of Palma's other central themes is that Barth's view of culture is multiplex in nature, a description he uses to encapsulate two separate but interconnected thoughts.[69] First, he uses the term to convey a sense of transition in Barth's thought, trying to indicate thereby the impact of Barth's now well established (if still controversially structured) turn towards

---

65. Barth, *Humanity of God*, 55.

66. Barth, "Response," 53.

67. Barth, *Humanity of God*, 54.

68. Despite his earlier theory Palma is approaching something like this view in his later considerations. Refer for example Palma, *Theology of Culture*, 42ff.

69. Ibid., 2–5.

analogy, as noticed especially by Balthasar.[70] In particular Palma wants to suggest a gradual softening of Barth's early emphasis on *Diastasis*, notably present in his *Epistle to the Romans* and furthered by his attention to dialectic, and the emergence of a view guided by analogy and diffuse parabolism. Yet if the topic under consideration is culture then it would seem that some of the observations outlined earlier in this chapter, relating to the *Romans* period, belie this. These suggest that Barth may in fact already have been unconsciously developing this through the internal logic of his argument by at least the second edition of *Romans*, though perhaps even in the first.

Palma actually starts to confirm this when he notes that Barth's attention in *Romans* was focused particularly on the question of religion rather than culture (as was independently argued above), a point he finds confirmed by T. F. Torrance in his introductory comments for Barth's book *Theology and Church*. Torrance argues that "the intention of *Romans* was by no means an attack on culture as such, but rather the opposite."[71] Unfortunately Palma does not carry on with the quote because the fuller quote conveys much more clearly the true location of Barth's emphasis. Torrance continues directly on from above as follows: "upon a bogus mystification of culture which required to be disenchanted of this secret divinity before it really could be human culture."[72] He explains more completely just a little further on when he suggests

> Already there is apparent in the *Romans Commentary* that immense emphasis upon *humanity*, as that to which God has directed his saving love, and to which we also in obedience to God must direct our attention in the humanity of our fellow men, but in the polemic to achieve a proper distance or Diastasis the negative emphasis appeared, perhaps inevitably, greater than the positive.[73]

The background against which Barth was writing is important for understanding this because his critical engagement is targeted here. He wanted very specifically to counter the "immanentism and pantheism" that accompanied the way Christianity had been assimilated by European culture.[74]

---

70. This is now a very contentious argument since Bruce McCormack's controversial overturning of Balthasar's thesis. Refer von Balthasar, *Theology of Karl Barth*, esp. 93ff. See also McCormack, *Critically Realistic Dialectical Theology*.

71. Cited in Palma, *Theology of Culture*, 86 n. 8.

72. T. F. Torrance, "Introduction," 22.

73. Ibid.

74. Barth comments that "Evangelical theology almost all along the line, certainly in all its representative forms and tendencies, had become *religionistic, anthropocentric,*

Barth's target was not culture *qua* culture but the particular manifestation of it he encountered around him. Primary here of course, as already seen above, is his relationship with Schleiermacher's writings in which Christianity was quintessentially expressed in terms of accommodation, and had therefore become thoroughly anthropocentric. As Torrance suggests, such a theology "had no positive word to say to culture which that culture did not already know and had not already said to itself in ways more congenial to it."[75]

Barth's early "no" was therefore no simple broadside on culture *per se* but was instead a judicious targeting and indictment of German *Kulturprotestantismus* (and cognates wherever and whenever they appear) and is therefore to be understood in that very movement of criticism as intimately concerned with achieving a "right" understanding and articulation of culture. Barth was all along concerned with adumbrating the relationship of humanity with God in a way that accorded to each "partner" their rightful role and place, balancing appropriately therefore the relative intertwining of the deity and humanity of God. In this the twin issues of human sociality and human engagement with the world must necessarily be engaged in both positive and negative ways. In a sense it is not far off the mark to suggest Barth was clearing the house with his critical assertions in order to prepare for his constructive positive proposals (albeit he would not consciously recognize this until much later, per comments already noted above).

The second way Palma understands Barth's views as multiplex rests on the premise that Barth does not always approach culture in the same way. Palma suggests instead that Barth adopts one of three different postures at various times. The first he describes as dogmatic, the second as critical, and the third as constructive. This subtly differs from the central premise of this book, namely that Barth always maintains an emphasis on the purely theological nature of culture and that all his statements on culture therefore gain their bearings from this central consideration. But, with a light tweak, this formulation proves a useful tool for understanding some of the different foci Barth has recourse to when describing his understanding of culture.

The second posture, the critical (or analytical one), is easily recognized since it straightforwardly equates to the counter-cultural perspective so popularized in the secondary literature.[76] It is an over emphasis on

---

and in this sense *humanistic*." Barth, *Humanity of God*, 39, emphasis original. In a similar vein he elsewhere characterised nineteenth century theology as 'religious anthropocentrism'. Barth, *Humanity of God*, 28.

75. Torrance, "Introduction," 16.

76. See for example the treatment of Barth in Bevans, *Models of Contextual Theology*.

this perspective that is being disputed in this present chapter. Palma then goes on to argue that Barth can at times be seen to be operating in the less clearly discernible dogmatic (or descriptive) and constructive (or normative) modes. It is here that his suggestion needs to be tweaked because Palma's goal is the assertion that these are interdependent yet therefore relatively independent moments. In reality however, they tend to collapse into each other since the dogmatic or descriptive account is always of culture as it is theologically and therefore ideally, and therefore as it is described by the normative or constructive mode. There is of course a certain nuance Palma correctly discerns but this is very subtle and not highly informative.[77] It is better to see Barth as adopting a two-fold schema that is on the one hand critical and the other constructive (normative).

It is then in this (expanded) normative mode that Barth's true understanding of culture is most clearly evident since the critical agenda is only advanced in order to clear the way for, and to act in support of, the constructive purpose. Barth's theological understanding of culture, grounded in his understanding of the humanity of God even as early as his *Romans* commentary, albeit appearing there without the formal and systematic exposition it would later be endowed with, provided him with the means and impetus to deconstruct the prevailing notions of culture he confronted in his daily life. The nascent and ill-formed formulation of his Christological grounding for culture, coupled with the enthusiasm accompanying his apparent denial of all things human, were without doubt critical factors in the popular view that he entertained no underlying positive assessment of culture. Nevertheless this view is inaccurate. Barth was all along inhabiting a constructive proposal, one that has so far been only partially described. It is now time to more fully delineate this understanding, a process best undertaken with the aid of his clearest statement on culture—his lecture entitled "Church and Culture."

Barth on Culture

> The problem of the Church has a historical-sociological aspect as well as a theological. If we wish to define the Church in that aspect, we should have to omit mention of God and his Word, of faith and obedience. We should then have to speak of "that sociological group which is concerned with religion," or more

77. Palma, *Theology of Culture*, 2–4.

specifically of a community or a number of communities which share more or less the same religio-ethical convictions . . ."[78]

Here, in a lecture delivered on the 1st June 1926, is an anticipation of some of the central ideas Milbank would later use in his critique, as outlined in chapter 2.[79] Barth distinguishes between two ways of viewing the church, the one theological and the other sociological, which he then sets against each other: to select one is to denigrate the true intention embodied by the other, and neither is it possible to go part of the way with one as if the other could then supplement it. They represent instead a genuine duality between which there can only be choice, and for Barth the Christian option can only be found in the theological alternative. The sociological perspective he equates with "religion" which as has already been discussed and for those reasons, is an anathema to him.

Barth does go on to recognize a degree of validity in historical-sociological descriptions of the church that would seem to militate against the duality he has established, not least because he allows they are not only theologically permissible but also somewhat informative. They describe or give a certain insight into human aspects of the church, providing a particular account of behavior and structure that can be interesting. But it is important to recognize the nature of the claim he is making here for he is not trying to suggest these descriptions enter into the discussion at the ontological/structural level but rather that they provide guidance and assistance in a hermeneutical/directional mode. In this respect it might be said that he accords some value to theologically interpreted ethnography. This usefulness is entirely relative however because it is always subservient to the larger and deeper theological claim, rendered acquiescent to the overarching requirement for theological explanation.

There are substantial and enlightening parallels here between Barth and Milbank since in the latter's view historical-sociological descriptions were birthed in a milieu that had already largely established itself outside of Christian theological parameters, and which were therefore already well on the way to developing for themselves alternative accounts of origin (and hence an alternative theology). Milbank's archaeological unearthing of these is instructive, revealing the mixed pagan and heretical Christian parentage of the sociological child. These roots, long since hidden, give rise to an

78. Karl Barth, "Church and Culture," 334.

79. This is rendered even more visible in his 1957 essay discussion of Evangelical theology in the nineteenth century whereupon the post-Kantian religious realm is described as shrinking to "only a small realm . . ." He then later affirms that what could be considered positive in this theology was attributable to Herder and the Romanticists. Barth, *Humanity of God*, 13, 28.

innate tendency to usurp Christian theological primacy because, in Milbankian terms, sociology is guided by an all-encompassing secular theology (or anti-theology) that constantly and consistently seeks to assert itself. Barth, well before Milbank, is deeply concerned by these structural inclinations and hence is likewise not interested in allowing them a foothold.

For example, Barth argues that insights generated from sociological sources might be informative in select ways but only regarding aspects that necessarily belong to secondary externalities. Whatever information is offered does not enter into the fundamental, which is to say theological, internal reality around which these secondary features cohere for this reality has its source, impetus and structure given to it by God rather than humanity. As Barth argues, "These [secondary] concepts, separately and together, relate to a decisive event occurring between God and man.... Apart from the actuality of this event, these concepts would be empty."[80] This is a decisive comment for it grants no ontological foothold to sociology. It is also not far from Scharen's Milbank inspired notion of "prudence in description" (per the previous chapter), or a limited ethnography taken as dogmatics (the Barthian background to this in Scharen should of course be noted).

According to Barth therefore, anything that purports to provide an account of the church in the world must deal primarily with the fact of Jesus, and every implication that flows from his life, death, and resurrection. The principal defining characteristics of the church and the world are theological; every depiction necessarily emanates from this root, however it may articulate itself. For Barth there would be no world or church available for description if there was no God, and no relevant descriptive categories available if Jesus had not been.[81] But He is, and God did create, and consequently all things cohere under God and must be depicted with reference to this primary fact. In view of this it is arguable that Barth has not gone far enough for in conceding the possibility of sociological description that he must then delimit, he necessarily grants positive space to exactly that which he wants to excise. Better, given his schema, to have acknowledged the efficacy of certain of the tools currently deployed by sociology than to have granted it any possibility of such a foothold.

Barth in a way acknowledges the difficulties here when he argues that terms like "church" can and have been defined without reference to theology but that this has been disabling and idolatrous. On the same note he wants to suggest that "culture" is similarly disposed. If it is defined without reference to

---

80. Barth, "Church and Culture," 335.

81. "The normal pattern is that the world exists, therefore we know that God exists. That's the wrong pattern isn't it? . . . Barth says . . . that we know the world exists because God does." See Gunton, *The Barth Lectures*, 251–52.

Karl Barth and a Theological Alternative

the central fact of Jesus, for example along the lines of French *civilization* and German *Kultur*, and if such definitions are taken as determinative, then they can only attract a negative and polemical assessment from the church; standing as examples of idolatrous error.[82] Tacit within this stance, it can be suggested, is recognition of the ultimately confessional foundations of the "social" Milbank was to reveal some seventy years later. As Barth notes, "The Church sets the Word of God at the beginning and the end, above all empirical or transcendental principles, as the sole, supreme event which gives law."[83] The church, in stating its self-definition, is declaring something; a confessional foundation that orients everything, even the notion of culture.

And the re-orientation of culture implied here is a total one. Culture, Barth argues, means humanity, but it currently expresses the fundamental problem of humanity. Humanity lives in brokenness, lacking a synthesis, living with an "annihilating incongruity"; the rift brought about by sin. "Whatever deserves the name culture has in some fashion originated from this rift and this problem."[84] *But sin has not obliterated the original claim of God upon humanity, the dual promise of affirmation and of fellowship with God.* Sin has certainly scarred the claim, in that people have forgotten both the affirmation and the desire for fellowship, but it has not completely eclipsed it; God did not and will not forget. Through Jesus Christ He has restored not only the promises but also the means of their fulfillment.

In a helpful schema Barth delineates this restoration through three perspectives. The first is creation, whereupon culture is promise. It is *"the promise originally given to man of what he is to become."*[85] Here a teleological ordering begins to emerge into view. Palma notes that Barth's understanding of culture "has a pronounced teleological and, rightly understood, even instrumental character"[86] This is evident here, and as Palma goes on to argue, it forms the basis on which Barth constructs his various positive affirmations. So, for example, it guides his personal choices as when he decides "for" socialism in terms of economics (albeit he vacillates here) but is politically inclined towards democracy, and so on. More importantly, for Barth the eschatological framing posits and gives life to the very nature of the distinctive Christian engagement with society.

Barth therefore argues that "With this eschatological anticipation, the Church confronts society. Not with an undervaluation of cultural

82. Barth, "Church and Culture," 337–38.
83. Ibid., 338.
84. Ibid., 338–39.
85. Ibid., 341, emphasis original.
86. Palma, *Theology of Culture*, 56.

achievement, but with the highest possible evaluation of the goal for which it sees all cultural activity striving. Not in pessimism, but in boundless hope."[87]

This teleological argument can and should be supplemented however by an appropriate description of the relationship subsisting between God, humanity and creation for the doctrine of creation is equally foundational for Barth's understanding of culture (though he does not address it through this essay). For example, in CD III Barth explicitly ties the teleological and creation elements together, along with the mediating element of divine providence, when he argues

> Because God loves the creature, its creation and continuance and preservation point beyond themselves to an exercise and fulfillment of His love which do not take place merely with the fact that the creature is posited as such and receives its existence and being alongside and outside the being and existence of God, but to which creation in all its glory looks and moves, and of which creation is the presupposition.[88]

The second perspective is that offered by reconciliation, thereby bringing culture into dialogue with the kingdom of grace. Looked at in this light, *"culture is the law in reference to which the sinner, sanctified by God, has to practice his* [sic] *faith and obedience."*[89] This enters into the process by which the promise of becoming given to humanity is actualized. It is about humanity affirmed by God and sustained through a positive relationship with God. This is the established norm that sinners have lost sight of but which is restored to their consciousness through justification. It is therefore also the content of sanctification, the goal towards which humanity works in faithful obedience. It is not fully attainable on earth, for it is hidden in Christ, which in turn is what makes it true obedience. As Barth notes, "Therefore, sanctification, election for God, doing the will of God, is always in content being human."[90]

Again there is a corresponding entry in CD III that expresses in more dogmatic terms what he has just traced through in terms of culture, hence:

> The ordaining of salvation for man and of man for salvation is the original and basic will of God, the ground and purpose of His will as Creator.... God creates, preserves and overrules man for this prior end and with this prior purpose, that there may be

---

87. Barth, "Church and Culture," 349.
88. Karl Barth, CD 3/1:95–96.
89. Barth, "Church and Culture," 344, emphasis original.
90. Ibid., 346.

a being distinct from Himself ordained for salvation, for perfect being, for participation in His own being, because as the One who loves in freedom He has determined to exercise redemptive grace...[91]

Finally, therefore, human culture can be viewed through redemption. In creation human culture was promise, in reconciliation it is the law, and in redemption it is the limit set for humanity. Culture in redemptive view is more than creation, for it is a new creation, and it is more than reconciliation, for it is given manifest form. Human culture is a "*formed* reality and *real* form, which is not already here but is in process of becoming."[92] In this it is a limit. Both negatively and positively it defines our situation before God and over against God. It sets our parameters and marks us out as who and whose we are. It is with this hope, this eschatological certainty, that the church engages culture. The church is therefore *for* culture, calling it to be what it was always intended to be: the fulfillment of humanity.

In terms of the underlying doctrine of Creation this is grounded in, Barth supremely affirms that "Divine creation is divine benefit.... We cannot understand the divine creation otherwise than as benefit.... It shows us God's good-pleasure as the root, the foundation and the end of divine creation."[93] It is in His good pleasure that He creates and maintains an autonomous creaturely occurrence that is good *as created*.[94] Importantly however this occurrence "has a significance outside itself. It is not moving in circles, but moving towards a destiny which is posited and given from without.... The creature itself cannot decide either why it moves or whither it moves. This decision belongs to God who rules the creature. It is His action which determines the world-process in its true and definitive form."[95]

Autonomy is granted but in the context of subordination of the creature to the Creator for contrary to what the world thinks this lowly dependency does not result in "degradation, depreciation or humiliation" but rather in exaltation. The creature "is rich in this poverty.... To exist in any other way but in this relativity towards God would mean misery and shame and ruin and death for the creature. Its full and perfect salvation consists in this subordination to Him..."[96]

91. Karl Barth, CD 4/1:10.

92. Barth, "Church and Culture," 348, emphasis original.

93. Barth, CD 3/1, 330–31.

94. See for example von Balthasar, *Theology of Karl Barth*, 110–11. On the goodness of creation refer Barth, CD 3/1: §42.3 Creation as Justification.

95. Barth, CD 3/3:170.

96. Ibid., 171.

Palma, when attempting to describe the emergence of Barth's "truly free theology of culture" uses T. F. Torrance: "Therefore the *Diastasis* which Barth was concerned for so many years to reveal between theology and culture was not only in the interests of good theology but in the interests of good culture, that is to say, of the proper fulfillment and enjoyment of full creaturely being and activity in its own determinate reality and truth."[97]

This "reality" is variously described by Barth but perhaps "free" is the most frequent label Barth turns to.[98] This captures best, it might be suggested, something of the sheer joy and complete peace Barth envisages as the accompaniment accruing to a person living just as God intended, in full recognition of their inherent creatureliness.[99]

In this culture is not only the promise of a state of being, of creaturely humanity in fellowship with God, but is also a present task. It is *"the task set through the Word of God for achieving the destined condition of man in unity of soul and body."*[100] Culture is therefore verb and noun, activity and state. As verb or activity it implies a dual account of state. The state of being, engaged in activity, is not just oriented around teleology but is descriptive as well, refracting contemporary conditions. There are therefore three postures in this formulation: the present, incorporating the past; the near future, or the work to be done; and the distant future, the final goal.

At this point Barth circles back to a key theme left unattended earlier in his essay. The external aspect of the church must now be given its due, and elucidated in its rightful place. The church, at least in its visible reality, is itself a human institution, organization, or voluntary association. In this theologians like Kathryn Tanner are accurate as to brute fact. As Barth notes "It knows that its behaviour, its will and deed, its thought, its speech, is not fundamentally different from that of men [sic] in general; that its special concern, 'religion' so-called, is liable to the same doubts and suspicions as is all human existence, and that its special activity is under the same exigencies as all human activity."[101]

---

97. Palma, *Theology of Culture*, 21.

98. Ibid., 32–33.

99. For Palma, Barth primarily thinks of freedom as *to* and *for* (the positive pole of culture) and only secondarily as freedom *from* (the negative pole). Ibid., 33ff. His discussion of exactly what culture is free for occurs at pp. 63ff. He later contends that such freedom is ultimately founded "in God's positive freedom exercised and revealed in Jesus Christ." Refer p. 60 for the quote and 59–63 for a broader panorama. See also Barth's own views, set out in summary form, in "The Gift of Freedom: Foundation of Evangelical Ethics" in Barth, *Humanity of God*, 67–96.

100. Barth, "Church and Culture," 337, emphasis original.

101. Ibid., 350.

Karl Barth and a Theological Alternative

It is no different than other organizations when examined in anthropological or sociological terms, at least as far as putatively "objective" ethnographic research is concerned. In short, it is a cultural activity, and this cannot be simply elided. But it must be appropriately understood.

The church is a cultural activity that speaks of creation, reconciliation and redemption. It is rooted in a confessional, or what Barth terms a "hidden," foundation against which it must always "judge itself and determine its direction . . ."[102] This is not just for its own sake, but also on behalf of wider society. Whatever it wills to do, and whatever it does, can be, in Christ, a transparent and meaningful symbol that partakes of the original promise while pointing to its ultimate eschatological fulfillment. It stands between the "can" and the "is," the "now" and the "not yet." The church, by being human, and by reminding society of eternity, discharges its duty here on earth. "Upon the knowledge of the limit depends also the knowledge of the promise and the law."[103]

This description locates culture, in its contemporary anthropological, sociological, and cultural studies guises, in a specific theological space. Culture, as portrayed by these and associated disciplines, represents the promise of God in hamartiological relief, a distorted reflection of a misshapen promise. Not only is the content thereby labeled culture misidentified, a divine predicate (re)constructed in human likeness, but the instruments of labeling are deformed. These two influences interact in interdependent ways such that together they present a wholly inadequate depiction of what culture really is. What emerges is a creaturely parody or caricature of a Divine truth.

Quite a different portrayal emerges from reflection on Barth's eschatological framing. Culture is both the task of humanization and the state of being human. In this it reflects the inextricable relationship subsisting between God, humanity, and the created order, in Christ. It is first task. Timothy Gorringe usefully summarizes Barth here by commenting, "Theologically understood, culture is the name of that whole process in the course of which God does what it takes, in Paul Lehman's phrase, to make and to keep human beings human. Culture, in this sense is, under God, 'the human task.'"[104] "The human task" reflects the current influence of redemption, or what is normally termed sanctification. The imprint of sin and idolatry or, as Gorringe argues, alienation and ideology, on culture is not inextricable. It is already removed, and is being removed, because of redemption through the risen Christ.

---

102. Ibid., 351.
103. Ibid., 354.
104. Gorringe, *Furthering Humanity: A Theology of Culture*, 4.

Because of this activity culture is not left bereft of hope, it stands under a theology of hope; hope fulfilled in redemption but worked out through sanctification. This hope reveals culture as state, not the present state of sinful inclination away from God but the future state of communion with Him. Already revealed in Jesus Christ, and awaiting final consummation in Him, culture is the state of being truly human. It reflects the worshipping and praising presence of humanity within God's presence. It is tasted only lightly and fleetingly now but shall soon be partaken of fully, each eating in the process their fill of the goodness of God. As Robert Palma's title suggests so well, Barth is describing "The Freedom of Culture for the Praise of God."[105]

Barth argues, "Creation is one long preparation, and therefore the being and existence of the creature one long readiness, for what God will intend and do with it in the history of the covenant."[106] This enters into the heart of Barth's creation architectonics, most often elaborated according to his now famous formula, "Creation is the external basis of the covenant and the covenant is the internal basis of creation."[107] By this he means to suggest that "the covenant is the goal of creation and creation the way to the covenant."[108] Barth most colorfully depicts this through a temple analogy whereupon "It describes creation as it were externally as the work of powerful but thoroughly planned and thought out and perfectly supervised preparation, comparable to the building of a temple, the arrangement and construction of which is determined both in detail and as a whole by the liturgy which it is to serve."[109]

The world was therefore created with purpose, as the location in which the covenant relationship of God with humanity, supremely mediated by Jesus Christ, would unfold, eventually to culminate in an eschatological fulfillment. Culture must also be understood in these liturgical terms for as Barth argued in 1926 "The Word confronts man with the problem of his existence. And that problem is precisely the problem of culture. Culture

---

105. Palma, subsidiary title of *Theology of Culture*.

106. Barth, CD3/1:231. Elsewhere he argues that God "wills and posits the creature neither out of caprice nor necessity, but because He has loved it from eternity, because He wills, not to limit His glory by its existence and being, but to reveal and manifest it in His co-existence with it." Barth, CD 3/1:95.

107. Refer for example to his section headings in Barth, CD3/1, under §41 Creation and Covenant. He elaborates the external basis through section 2, pp. 94–228; and the internal basis in section 3, pp. 228–329. Note also the exegetical basis Barth relies on for this distinction, with the P document of Gen. 1:1—2:4 providing his foundation for the external basis and the J account of Gen. 2:4b-25 the internal basis. Gunton, *The Barth Lectures*, 243ff.

108. Barth, CD3/1:97.

109. Ibid., 98. He later describes creation as "a true sacrament." Ibid., 232.

Karl Barth and a Theological Alternative

means humanity."[110] In as much as humanity can be said to participate in this creational teleology, which it does intimately, so too does culture.

Having briefly outlined a fairly full description of culture according to Barth it is now important to consider its plausibility. To what extent might reliance on this framework be considered legitimate? Presupposed within this question are a plethora of issues associated with determining exactly what is meant by the term "legitimate" in this context. As already described in the introduction, a certain sort of definition is provided by the rationality that has permeated post enlightenment Western thinking, a form holding sway through its role as the legitimating function of the secularist confession. In contradistinction to this Milbank turns to the poetic operation of rhetoric, finding under the sway of linguistic idealism his legitimating function. But what may be posited for Barth?

This question begins to probe the central distinction noted at the end of the previous chapter, and also above, between Barth and Milbank. Whereas Milbank argued on the basis of a neo-platonic ontology Barth, it was earlier suggested, provided what James K. A. Smith was really after, an incarnational alternative. This so-called incarnational perspective in scholarship on Barth is usually termed something like his Christological concentration or his Christocentric emphasis.[111] In his early Christological period Barth did not always consistently uphold this emphasis, sometimes allowing for the possibility of other foundations. This is particularly true for the essay just now analyzed, "Church and Culture." Palma, under advisement from Emil Brunner, notes the presence in this essay of an element of natural theology, an instance of *via cognoscendi*. Barth argues for "the possibility that culture may be revelatory, that it can be filled with promise."[112] He would later, as Palma also acknowledges, recognize and withdraw from this position.

Despite occasionally slipping from this ideal, there is no doubt that Barth intended his writings to pulse with Christological emphasis. The discussion of creation just undertaken demonstrates that creation is at all points orientated by the covenant, and therefore by Christ the divine mediator. Paul Metzger therefore explicitly orients his analysis of confessional legitimacy

---

110. Barth, "Church and Culture," 338.

111. See for example von Balthasar, *Theology of Karl Barth*, 30. Note also Gunton, *Barth Lectures*, 10. For a somewhat contrary view refer Hunsinger, *How to Read Karl Barth*, 7ff. He does not deny the centrality of Christology, but does argue against it as a monolithic characterization of Barth. The clearest point at which Barth renders both the church and the world "in Christ" is CD 2/2:566–83, 631–61, 719–26 per Cioffi, "Developing a Political Theology," 19 n. 19.

112. Barth, "Church and Culture," 344.

similarly, around an elaboration of the central Christological analogue.[113] Palma, by comparison, pays more attention to the general analogical case Barth relies on, providing an important analysis of his deployment of *analogia fidei*, *analogia gratiae* and *analogia relationis*.[114] Unfortunately Barth's use of this structure is facing increasing criticism. Peter Oh, for example, persuasively argues that Barth's repudiation of *analogia entis* was seriously misconstrued, a point Barth came to begrudgingly recognize (*pace* Palma). Oh contends *analogia fidei* and *analogia entis* are actually complementary notions, one the flip side of the other. In this view Barth's construal of *analogia fidei* can act as a corrective of post-Thomist Catholic developments to bring contemporary articulations of *analogia entis* back in line with Aquinas' original intentions, as both Eberhard Jüngel and Balthasar argue.[115] It is therefore to Metzger's account of Barth's legitimating structure that the following turns.

Barth's Confessional Foundations

According to Metzger, Barth's is a subtly nuanced model of culture anchored in two inter-related Christological languages. The first is Chalcedonian Trinitarianism.[116] At the center of Barth's Christological model is an attempt to convey not only *unio personalis*, the union of divinity with humanity in one person, but a concomitant demarcation that recognizes *finitum non capex infiniti*, with its consequent asymmetry of relationship mediating the *genus majestaticum*, hence avoiding the Lutheran mistake.[117] Jesus is therefore both fully divine and fully human, *homoousios*, yet one inseparable personality. There is a mutual interchange of attributes, *communicatio idiomatum*, but this communication is indirect as regards the ascription of divine attributes to the human nature, and direct vice versa.[118]

---

113. As indeed Palma acknowledges, refer Palma, *Theology of Culture*, 28.

114. For his analysis of this analogical structure refer Ibid., 21–27.

115. Oh, *Karl Barth's Trinitarian Theology*, 3–16.

116. For discussion of its explicit and implicit presence throughout CD refer Hunsinger, *How to Read Karl Barth*, 185–88, 201–18.

117. For an explanation of the notion of asymmetry, applied in terms of double agency, refer Ibid., 204.

118. *Communicatio idiomatum* is used here, in accord with the historical record, as the general description for this theory. It also acts as the expression of a particular element within it; hence the general theory expresses a three part formulation of *communicatio idiomatum* (impartation of essences), *communicatio gratiarum* (the address to the human essence within this) and *communicatio operationum* (actualisation). Refer Karl Barth, CD 4/2:73.

This bare statement is in need of nuance at several points, but most notably regarding the idea of "person" implied by *personalis*. There is a double problematic. In the first instance, the notion of "person" originated as an imprecise metaphor which, Barth using Augustine argues, was applied in the absence of "a really suitable concept." Barth suggests,

> The more the distinction of Persons is regarded as taking place and being grounded in the divine essence itself, the more conceivable in fact becomes the inconceivability of this distinction: this distinction participates in the inconceivability of the divine essence, which would not be the essence of the revealed God, if it were conceivable, i.e. apprehensible in the categories of *usitatum eloquium*. Neither *persona* therefore nor any other concept can do the service of rendering this concept really conceivable.[119]

In the second place, it intersected in modern times with the idea of personality such that the attribute of self-consciousness became attached to person. This offered the possibility of formulating the Trinity according to one of two structures—the one ancient and the other contemporary however, Barth notes, both paths have historically shipwrecked in light of the fundamental inadequacies attending both notions.[120] He argues instead that "mode of being" and "mode of existence" both constitute better descriptions.[121]

The Chalcedonian formulation, because it echoes by its very name the various developments of older dogmaticians, also needs adjustment in other ways to account for his peculiar deployment of it. Barth develops his doctrine specifically against this historical record, arguing for example that the Reformed application of *finitum non capex infiniti* to the *communicatio idiomatum* formulation was not intended to dispute the doctrine as such, but to address the strong possibility it would lead to arbitrary and non-biblical results, such as "that 'God died' ('O ill most dread, that God is dead'), or that 'the man Jesus Christ is Almighty.'"[122] But, Barth argues, this possible danger should not then also disrupt the ability to boldly proclaim the positive thesis this formulation seeks to express.

What is particularly in danger here is the ability to assert, as is most needed, that God has determined and willed, in complete freedom, to become man such that "The actuality of the incarnate Son of God, the union

---

119. Karl Barth, CD 1/1:408–9.

120. Ibid., 409–12. Barth earlier argues "'Person' in the sense of the Church doctrine of the Trinity has nothing directly to do with 'personality.'" Refer p. 403 for this avoidance of tritheism.

121. Ibid., 413ff.

122. Barth, CD 4/2:76.

of the two natures in Him, is the direct confrontation of the *totality of the divine* with the human in the one Jesus Christ."[123] This also confutes the Lutheran desire to draw back from attributing all of the divine attributes to Jesus (such as eternity or infinity) because "Is not each perfection of God itself the perfection of his whole essence . . ."[124] The totality of the divine is unchanged *and* given particular form in the specific man Jesus Christ such that the divine and the human aspects remain precisely what they are. Barth concludes therefore that "*Communicatio* is supposed to mean that even the human nature of Jesus Christ . . . is in full possession, and capable of full use, and participant in the full glory of the divine . . . so that the last and solemn declaration of the doctrine is that we must worship and adore His humanity with and like His divinity . . ."[125]

Barth is therefore not simply repristinating these constructions; rather he carefully examines them relative to their historical developments, especially as mediated through the Reformers, in order to refract them through his Christological lens. His application of "Chalcedonian Trinitarianism" must therefore be understood in this light, as indeed does the second language through which Barth describes his conception of the incarnation (his legitimating foundation), namely the technical formulation supposedly developed by Leontius of Byzantium—the doctrine of *anhypostasis*.[126] The human nature that Christ takes up is *anhypostatos*, lacking personal existence outside of the union, but is *enhypostatos* in that it has a personal subsistence *in* the divine person. This needs careful articulation since Barth has a specific formulation of this doctrine in mind.

As should be quite clear, but is nonetheless in need of certain statement, Barth is here working with the incarnation, using in particular the ancient construction of *unio hypostatica* (or *unio personalis* as he sometimes avers).[127] He argues that this expresses "direct unity of existence of the Son of God with the man Jesus of Nazareth . . ." and is correspondingly what has

123. Ibid., 85. Emphasis mine.

124. Ibid., 85.

125. Ibid., 77, see also p. 88 for a reiteration of this same theme in the language of the older dogmaticians.

126. See Metzger re its development, and its origins for Barth in Protestant scholastics, through John of Damascus, per Metzger, *The Word of Christ and the World of Culture*, 38 n. 5, also p. 45 n. 25 for contrary views of this formulation. For critical engagements refer in particular to Davidson, "Theologizing the Human Jesus," Shults, "A Dubious Christological Formula." In essence the debate centres on syntactical and derivation issues but does not significantly disturb the legitimacy of the proposal being presented here.

127. For a lengthy discussion of other nomenclature or analogical candidates and their inadequacies refer Barth, CD 4/2:52–60.

been called *enhypostasis*.[128] However, "as distinct from us He is also a real man only as the Son of God, so that there can be no question of a peculiar and autonomous existence of His humanity."[129] What, then, does the *anhypostasis* subsist in? Here Barth opens up into a wide ranging discussion that for now only need be summarized, hence "In Jesus Christ it is not merely one man, but the *humanum* of all men, which is posited and exalted as such to unity with God."[130]

The deployment of this framework allows Barth to maintain both a distinction within singular unity and the asymmetry of interaction at the heart of his theological project, and it is consistently repeated through the alternative but parallel formulation of *logos asarkos* and *logos ensarkos*. This is used by Barth to refer to the particular divine-man Jesus Christ rather than some universal, amorphous Christ.

The Legitimacy of Barth's Confessional Foundations

This schema is broadly accepted in what follows as the central logic empowering Barth's Christological project, elaborated as it is at central points throughout his writings.[131] It must be noted however that it has attracted some significant critiques, of which two in particular are worth paying attention to. They have been usefully summarized in an article by Anthony Buzzard.[132] Most notably Barth is charged with a form of crypto or soft Docetism in that he subtly depreciates the humanity of Jesus. The key point of contention is whether the notion of *anhypostasis* really allows for *unio personalis* or whether it actually involves two personal centers. As Buzzard notes, Barth meets this charge with the rejoinder that the Son of God did not take on an individual human personality because the human nature had no existence independent of or outside of Him, as the *anhypostasis* description given above clearly demonstrates.[133]

George Hunsinger acknowledges that "the relationship between divine being and human being is one of the most vexed topics in Barth interpretation . . ."[134] He essentially directs his book to elaborating this theme, finally

128. Ibid., 51.
129. Ibid., 49.
130. Ibid.
131. See for example ibid., especially his discussions at pp. 51–60 and p. 91. See also Karl Barth, CD 1/2:163.
132. Buzzard, "Some Questions."
133. Ibid., 34.
134. Hunsinger, *How to Read Karl Barth*, 4.

concluding that "The two life acts united in him [Jesus], that of God and that of the creature, are held together by the Chalcedonian pattern."[135] What Hunsinger adds in particular to this discussion is insight into what is gained from the construct Barth is using here; and the benefits are quite substantial. On the flipside of the Chalcedonian patterning can be found Barth's ability to speak of the mysterious notion of being "in Christ." As Hunsinger essentially argues, the logic of this Chalcedonian structure means that both God and humanity are objectively self-involved in Christ. By arguing God's presence in "unity and entirety" in Jesus Barth is able to show that "There is no God apart from, beyond, or behind God as God is in Jesus Christ."[136]

As Barth argues, "that human nature elected by Him and assumed into unity with His existence is implicitly that of all men.... In Him not only we all as *homines*, but our *humanitas* as such—for it is both His and ours—exist in and with God Himself."[137] That it is only implicitly all people has a double meaning, one in that all humanity is potentially present, and a second in that some certainly are (a potential modification of the first possibility). Barth goes on to contend that those "in Christ" are a second form of His body or existence such that Jesus Christ "was and is and will be this *totus Christus*—Christ and Christians."[138]

Barth, when discussing the Nicean creed in his *Dogmatics*, describes a "dialectic of revelation" such that in Christ we see "the hidden and the manifest God, and yet the hidden God is none other than the manifest, the manifest none other than the hidden ... as Christ is in revelation, exactly so is he antecedently in himself."[139] In his *Credo* he affirms regarding Jesus "Here the hidden, the eternal and incomprehensible God has taken visible form.... Here in His Son, in the revelation of His Name and Word, the one God has shown Himself as differentiated in Himself, so that we can hear Him, so that we can say 'Thou' to Him ..."[140]

Of particular interest to the present discussion however is the corresponding move he makes with regard to humanity. Just as for divinity, then so too humanity (per Colossians 3:3) is never independent of Jesus since "Our true humanity is to be found not in ourselves but objectively in Him."[141] This is of course an eschatological statement available only through faith; nonethe-

---

135. Ibid., 230.
136. Ibid., 37.
137. Barth, CD 4/2:59.
138. Ibid., 60.
139. Barth, CD 1/1: 490.
140. Barth, *Credo*, 46.
141. Hunsinger, *How to Read Karl Barth*, 37.

less it is also an objective reality in the here and now. By this means "The transitory and sinful creature is lifted up in Jesus Christ to an eternal life of love and freedom in and with the Trinity."[142] There is, then, a dialectic of "already but not yet" mediating the dialectic of revelation for humanity.

Potentially more telling is the second charge Buzzard brings, levied in two forms. First, that Barth has stepped outside of sound exegetical practice by allowing his presuppositions to direct his exegesis such that it is really eisegesis. In a sense there is validity in this charge however only in as much as it is levied at all such efforts since there is no firm exegetical position here, the textual analysis is always mediated by an "external" decision in light of the mystery of the event of incarnation and the elusiveness of Scripture regarding it. In fact the entire Trinitarian discussion can be seen as similarly infected, making Barth's rendition of both the incarnational and Trinitarian facets a special case of this larger problem.[143] Where this charge has the potential to gain more purchase is in the suggestion that Barth has moved outside of the tradition in his particular formulation of the Chalcedon pattern. Ironically Barth is just as often charged with repristination. But, for present purposes, as the discussion briefly outlined above demonstrated, Barth does step out of the Chalcedonian framework. What is critical, however, is that he does not do so in quite the way his detractors suppose.

Perhaps a more tenable and serious allegation is found in the related (second) form of the charge: that Barth has founded his theology on tendentious exegesis. Buzzard for example notes the extent to which Barth's interpretation of John 1:14 exercises control over his understanding of the Johannine prologue, a centerpiece of his exegetical legitimation that consequently accords it a central role in this exegetical decision.[144] A similar accusation arises from Barth's consideration of the Gospel of Luke, where Buzzard suggests Barth opts *a priori* for a Chalcedon rather than exegetically developed Lukan "conception Christology."[145] In terms of Hunsinger's categories this might read as a clash between the motifs of particularism and objectivism, with the latter being accorded priority. But there is an anomaly in both the Lukan conception narrative (as to whether there is a causal link) and the Johannine Logos (as to whether the Logos was impersonal or not prior to verse 14) that must in any case be resolved by the application of

---

142. Ibid., see 27–42, 42 for the quote.

143. Buzzard does implicitly acknowledge this, for example when noting Schillebeeckx's claim that there is no Johannine evidence to support the scholastic notion of the procession of the Son from the Father, but does not allow it sufficient play in his analysis. See Buzzard, "Questions," 41.

144. Ibid., 36ff.

145. Ibid., 39ff.

exterior considerations hence this does not amount to a decisive critique even if it were sustainable.[146]

Something of the stakes involved in Barth's Johannine and Lukan decisions are considered by Colin Gunton when he examines Barth's use of the language of *Logos asarkos* (Word unfleshed), asking in essence whether it is possible to see Barth conceiving of such a possibility. He suggests Barth does not because he ties Jesus Christ and the Word together so tightly, arguing, for example, that it was not simply the Logos that was present to Abraham.[147] For Gunton, arguing other than this is to leave the door open for the possibility of a sense in which God can be known other than through Jesus Christ. "What Barth is saying is that there is no Christ who isn't Jesus Christ in some way or other."[148] Bruce McCormack argues to this same point through Barth's account of election, commenting that Jesus is the elected and electing God and is therefore both the subject and object of election, which is "to bid farewell to the distinction between the eternal Word and the incarnate Word."[149]

McCormack offers what might arguably be the best discussion of Barth's use of the Chalcedonian pattern, albeit he presents a controversial description of it.[150] His argument is that while Barth certainly used the form of Chalcedonian patterning, by the end of CD it was unrecognizable relative to its original shape at the crucial point it is deployed. The decisive difference came through Barth's doctrine of election as he wrestled his way from a substantialist to actualist ontology.[151] By the time Barth was writing his doctrine of reconciliation McCormack argues that a focus on what constituted the nature of things (the substantialist ontology), characteristic of metaphysics ancient and modern, had given way to an altogether different emphasis. It is worth quoting McCormack at length here: "Barth preserves the theological values registered in the Chalcedonian formula but . . . he has done so by fundamentally altering the theological ontology in which those values find their home. He has replaced the language of 'natures' with the concept of 'history,' and he has integrated the concept of 'history' into his concept of 'person.' The result is that Jesus Christ is still seen as truly God,

---

146. For a discussion of Barth's Cyrillian view of the conception refer McCormack, *Orthodox and Modern*, 209–10.

147. Gunton, *Barth Lectures*, 170.

148. Ibid., 168.

149. McCormack, *Orthodox and Modern*, 217.

150. Ibid., See esp. pp. 201–33 and then the supplementary analysis of pp. 235–60.

151. Ibid., 213ff. Hunsinger very succinctly defines actualism by noting "Being is always an event and often an act . . ." Hunsinger, *How to Read Karl Barth*, 4.

Karl Barth and a Theological Alternative

truly human, and is both in a single Subject. But he is seen to be all of this under quite different ontological conditions."[152]

The key to this framework is therefore the notion of history, which he describes in the following manner:

> The history which constitutes the being and existence of the human Jesus belongs to the history of God in the second of God's modes of being (as "Son"). If, in Jesus Christ, God has elected to become human, then the human history of Jesus Christ is constitutive of the being and existence of God in the second of God's modes to the extent that the being and existence of the Second Person of the Trinity cannot be rightly thought of in absence of this human history.[153]

The effective impact of this can be seen most clearly by considering the most recent objection to an understanding of the *extra Calvinisticum* supposedly owing its structure to Barth's antecedent framework. Myk Habets contends this lineage "undermines the whole point of the incarnation—that the Son of God became man so that as man and not as God, he could freely offer his human life to the Father as a loving sacrifice for our sin."[154] In his view the Barthian option ends with the humanity of Jesus becoming an "instrumental shell" and the Trinitarian communion shattered. Gunton suggests a riposte by asserting that unlike Moltmann, "Barth goes back to God's freedom. God is free in the exercise of his omnipresence: the true God is obedient as true God."[155] This is the argument Barth develops from Colossians 2:9, as was noted above.

McCormack turns to the same section in Barth in a move that resonates deeply with the architectonics of Barth's proposal. He suggests God does not ever cease to be God when engaged in this act of divine Self-humiliation because He has eternally elected Himself precisely for this act in a prior act that also eternally determined Him.[156] "Thus God is never seen more clearly as the God that he truly is than when he suffers death on a cross. Here is where his true being is disclosed."[157] This relies on a primal decision in God to be one Subject in three modes which is "an *event* in the being of God which *differentiates* the modes of God's being . . ."[158] The notion that

152. McCormack, *Orthodox and Modern*, 229.
153. Ibid., 223.
154. Habets, "Putting the 'Extra' Back into Calvinism," 454.
155. Gunton, *The Barth Lectures*, 169.
156. On this see the discussion in Barth, CD 4/2:85.
157. McCormack, *Orthodox and Modern*, 225.
158. Ibid., 218, emphasis original. He later contends "Thus, for Karl Barth, 'essence'

a distinction can be made between an eternal Christ and temporal Jesus is here obliterated because the two are in fact identical, hence McCormack can speak of "Karl Barth's historicized Christology." "God *is* in himself, in eternity, the mode of his Self-revelation in time—God as Jesus Christ in eternity and God as Jesus Christ in time—thus guaranteeing that the immanent Trinity and the economic Trinity will be identical in content."[159] God is therefore a suffering God, not abstractly but concretely, in reality. As Barth comments, "God gives Himself, but He does not give Himself away . . ."[160]

This actualist account has significant implications for the notion of culture being advanced by this chapter since, as Metzger argues, for Barth, "one only understands human concepts and patterns of relation in the creaturely sphere, including that of church and broader culture, in light of God's commandeering of flesh and language in the incarnation."[161] He goes on to suggest "For Barth, the Word serves as the basis or backdrop for the perichoretic relation of various tandems such as time and eternity, God and the world, Christ and culture. The use of *perichoresis* still presupposes a view of the person centering relations between distinct entities. However, there is a sense here in which for Barth the entities in question actually *interpenetrate* one another *ontologically*, albeit dialectically in and through the mediation of the person of Christ."[162]

The ontological penetration is dialectical in that there is an asymmetrical penetration from the divine to the human; but the human to divine communication is mediated through the person of Christ.[163] The election of the particular person Jesus Christ is of universal relevance because it involves humanity itself since humanity is "chosen in Him," or in other words, because human essence or true being has been established by and in Christ.[164] As Metzger notes

> All humanity is elected in Christ, who is the elect of God throughout eternity and in history. The divine Word, second person of the Trinity, in whom an anhypostasized, that is a potential human nature is enhypostasized, is the one in whom all

---

is not something that is fixed and immovable in itself, a metaphysical substructure or 'substance' that guarantees to God or to the human Jesus identity with himself, . . . 'essence' exists nowhere—neither in eternity nor in time—in abstraction from the concrete material 'determination' which makes it to be what it is." Ibid., 239.

159. Ibid. Emphasis original.
160. Ibid., 225–26.
161. Metzger, *The Word of Christ*, 58–59.
162. Ibid., 132 n. 39.
163. cf. McCormack, *Critically Realistic Dialectical Theology*, 47–48.
164. See McCormack, *Orthodox and Modern*, 239–40.

those possessing human nature are elect, that is, *constituted* as truly human persons. *And by analogical extension*, not only the church, but also human culture generally, is inseparably related to Christ, having no existence apart from him (*anhypostasis*).[165]

Most succinctly, "Election involves humanization."[166] McCormack distinguishes between "essence" and "existence" at this point, arguing that the human essence is an eschatological reality and goal for humanity that is distinct from the human existence in the here and now.[167] In the reality of everyday life it is possible to reject the significance of this essence in the sense that people are free to choose to live in conformity with it or not.[168] Here the thesis presented by Barth in his essay "Church and Culture" is given solid ontological anchoring and allocated its appropriate place within his overall schema. Culture is associated with human existence but has its teleology grounded in the human essence that is therefore its proper and fitting goal.

It is worth registering two objections to Metzger's proposal in this last quote from him. First, he seems to be working with a definition of anhypostasized at odds with Barth's own proposal since there is the real danger of perceiving here the "peculiar and autonomous existence" Barth expressly excluded, as was noted above. Second, Metzger is perhaps too quick to suggest an "analogical extension" into culture generally. It was noted above that *totus Christus* was formulated through the relation of Christ and Christians but that extension to all humanity was uncertain. There is in this formulation room really only permission to envisage two tiers of humanity—those in Christ and those not.

Overall, the McCormack account of Barth as actualist in his ontological foundation resonates with the framework set out above, and hence with the reading of Barth presented by this book, however it is not without problems. Most notably, for many commentators the very notion of actualist ontology is problematic, something Barth was well aware of. McCormack is frequently at pains to suggest the real problem with most of these criticisms is the degree to which they explicitly or, more often, implicitly begin from a foundation already committed to the presently dominant paradigm of substantialist ontology. In this approach the respective foundations become as ships passing in the night. Before such criticisms can gain currency therefore they need to do the hard work of overcoming the strangeness of the alternative foundation Barth presents because as McCormack argues

---

165. Metzger, *The Word of Christ*, 88. Emphasis original.
166. Ibid., 93.
167. McCormack, *Orthodox and Modern*, 247.
168. Ibid., 240.

"however incomprehensible it may be to think in this way, so long as there is a genuine necessity for it, then even doubts about its possibility cannot finally be made decisive."[169]

The main identified problem with the presentation so far outlined does not relate to this actualist foundation however but to the problem of a supposedly weak pneumatology. Earlier it was argued that Barth suggests the Word confronts humanity and in this there also occurred a confrontation with culture since "Culture means humanity."[170] It was therefore also suggested that culture participates in the creational teleology outlined above to the same extent as humanity itself does. But it is just at this point of a creational teleology that a significant critique is launched in that Barth is accused of a weak pneumatology that sabotages his teleological perspective on creation.

Barth and Creation: A Weak Pneumatology?

As Barth would have it, "the creation is the outer or external basis of the covenant, that is, the covenant of reconciliation."[171] This is meritorious in that creation has no existence outside of Christ; humanity is not depicted independent of the covenant; and history is the stage upon which redemption is played out. Metzger points out a central tension though, in that for Barth "creation, the fall, and reconciliation stand within election in the crucified."[172] The doctrines of creation and redemption are here collapsed towards each other such that while Barth affirms the goodness of creation, creation nonetheless stands in need of redemption. Metzger goes on to state the problem thus: "*The creation is good as created. But its* perfection *rests with its ultimate redemption. Thus, although the creation is not fallen from its inception, it is created* in order to *be redeemed.*"[173]

Colin Gunton takes the issue to be one endemic to post Augustinian and hence Western theology. The divorce in Barth between creation and redemption derives from "the strong protological, as distinct from eschatological, drive of his doctrine of election." Similarly, "the heart of the Western weakness can be seen as a whole to derive from a stressing of the protological over against the eschatological, the christological against the pneumatological . . ."[174] The resulting imbalance is most often corrected

169. Ibid., 246.
170. Barth, "Church and Culture," 338.
171. Metzger, *The Word of Christ*, 104–5.
172. Ibid., 109.
173. Ibid., 110, emphasis original.
174. Gunton, *The One, the Three and the Many*, 159–60 n. 5. See also, for a

Karl Barth and a Theological Alternative

by a reversal of emphasis however this simply subordinates creation to the opposite polarity, a solution Gunton suggests is present in Pannenberg's eschatological proposal. At root the problem revolves around finding a way to maintain the essential and necessary tension between these two extremes, the task modernity has been unable to achieve. Since its most prominent divorce in Augustine the tradition has been marked by competing conceptions "of a christological and pneumatological mediation of the creation, and a conception centering on a structure of timeless forms."[175] In this history it has been the Platonic version that has maintained the stronger grip on the tradition.

Both Gunton and Metzger suggest recourse be made to Irenaeus as a corrective to these inclinations in Barth. Irenaeus, according to Gunton, achieves a unique unity in which each aspect—creation, fall, redemption, and eschatology—plays its distinctive role in an interrelated rather than separated way. He suggests Irenaeus "has a dynamic teleological drive which conceives the end as something more than a return to the beginning."[176] Hence the static element of protological determination is balanced by an eschatological emphasis that imbues creation with the requisite dynamism in its teleology. This is achieved by ensuring a sense of continuing communion between God and creation through an economy of interactions guided by both the Son *and* Holy Spirit. Christology contributes the centrality of embodiment and the idea of created particularity as something inseparable from divine will, while it is through the Spirit that God comes into ongoing relationship with the world, a relationship that respects "otherness" and which therefore protects the particularity of each element of creation.[177]

This would seem to indicate why it is possible for Metzger to suggest that for Barth "both the bird and Mozart . . . simply by making music, by simply being what they in fact are *as created* by God . . . glorify God,"[178] while in apparent opposition to this statement McCormack can also assert that according to Barth "in him [Jesus] human essence was 'set in motion' and lifted above its creaturely and fleshly limitations."[179] Gunton and Metzger are perhaps right to suggest Barth fails to resolve this tension. Yet in resolving this some account must also be given of the fundamen-

---

restatement of this critique in relation to Barth Gunton, *The Barth Lectures*, 253–54.

175. Gunton, *The One, the Three and the Many*, 56.

176. Ibid., 160 n. 5.

177. Ibid., 53–55. Refer also pp. 182ff. for a fuller discussion of the role a proper pneumatology plays in upholding particularity.

178. Metzger, *The Word of Christ*, 115, emphasis original.

179. McCormack, *Orthodox and Modern*, 247.

tal difference subsisting between the rest of creation and humanity since humanity is "in Christ" in a way the rest of creation is not.[180] There is certainly some validity to the claims by Metzger and Gunton but a distinction can and must be made between its relevance for creation qua creation and culture qua humanity.

Sitting alongside this critique is Gunton's associated accusation that Barth renders creation an almost entirely instrumental element within the economy of redemption.[181] Yet this is a stark description of the situation since Barth is able to argue that taking creation as the external basis of the covenant means creation is described "as it were externally as the work of powerful but thoroughly planned and thought-out and perfectly supervised preparation, comparable to the building of a temple, the arrangement and construction of which is determined both in details and as a whole by the liturgy which it is to serve."[182]

And this liturgical goal is centered on Jesus Christ because he is "the beginning (the beginning just because He is the goal) of creation."[183] Hence "Whatever objections might be raised against the reality of the world, its goodness incontestably consists in the fact that it may be the theatre of His glory, and man the witness to this glory. We must not desire to know *a priori* what goodness is, or to grumble if the world does not correspond to it. For the purpose for which God made the world it is also good. 'The theatre of His glory, *theatrum gloriae Dei*,' says Calvin of it."[184]

In this series of quotes the instrumental nature of creation is therefore certainly to the fore but accompanying it are hints of a sacramental, liturgical perspective that Barth unfortunately does not allow a stronger role in his theological paradigm. What is critical in this however is that it is directly applicable to humanity and thence to culture for the liturgy is enacted by humanity and is therefore in some sense culture.

It can of course be argued that this response does not take the critiques seriously enough, but on the contrary it takes them very seriously by ensuring they are attached to the appropriate doctrines. This is no simple elision of the problems for lurking within the Gunton critique in particular is a similar and potentially equally penetrating assertion of a pneumatological

---

180. As noted above, this statement may require nuance in light of the two tiers of humanity identified above. It is beyond the needs of this thesis to resolve this since the core point of a difference between creation and humanity is established on other grounds anyway.

181. Gunton, *The Barth Lectures*, 253–54.

182. Barth, CD 3/1:98.

183. Ibid., 232.

184. Barth, *Dogmatics in Outline*, 58.

weakness in how Barth envisages humanity and hence culture operating in the mode of existence. Unfortunately there is not space to pursue this any further however in a fuller treatment the implications involved in this accusation deserve attention, however it is now time to conclude this examination of Barth's account of culture.

Culture as a State and a Task

Culture is often described by commentators working through Barth's earlier categories as the state of being human and the task of humanization. As the preceding demonstrates this is accurate yet in need of nuance. In particular the notion of "being" in this statement requires comment since it tends to buy into a substantalist metaphysic Barth would later object to. As McCormack notes, the actualist framework did not fully emerge until Barth was working on his doctrine of election—well after the "Church and Culture" essay forming the heart of the discussion set out above.[185] In terms of this later construct then, the description of culture could still stand but only if "being" is accepted in an actualist sense, as referring to an "essence" only found "in Christ" (hence invoking the doctrine of participation, and pointing towards the *totus Christus*) rather than as some independent, abstract essence.

If this actualist stance is taken then it also influences the task of humanization since "being" is always also an "act," one that such a task necessarily participates in. In this way being and act are not set over against each other as independent moments heading towards a single goal but as interdependent modes of human living instead. As already hinted above, and seen previously with Milbank, it is in the church that the humanity/culture nexus comes to specific theological expression and here Barth also envisages the being/act breakdown just described. The church's "act is its being, its status its dynamic, its essence its existence."[186] He argues further, "The Church *is* when it takes place, and it takes place in the form of a sequence and nexus of definite human activities."[187] It has a certain "special" visibility susceptible to human historical and sociological inquiry as one human activity amongst many, one "earthly-historical" element amongst others with the abiding temptation to succumb to this two-dimensional description.

However, "What Christianity really is, the being of the community as the 'living community of the living Lord Jesus Christ,' calls for

185. McCormack, *Orthodox and Modern*, 201ff.
186. Barth, CD 4/1:650.
187. Ibid., 652, emphasis original.

the perception of faith, and is accessible *only* to this perception and not to any other."[188] The glory of humanity is hidden in Christ and hence is invisible to the world precisely because it is accessible only through faith; faith in Jesus Christ. This is not to suggest the presence of two different churches, one visible and one invisible, but "one is the form and the other the mystery of one and the self-same Church."[189] As he argues, "The community is the earthly-historical form of existence of Jesus Christ Himself . . . His body, created and continually renewed by the awakening power of the Holy Spirit."[190] This Christological statement, pregnant with insights, anchors his ecclesiology in his confessional foundation as a refraction of the *totus Christus* framework. It also records the teleological shape of his perspective, as the "Church and culture" essay outlined above had already described. In these crucial respects it is clear the later *Church Dogmatics* add to rather than alter the prior essay.

Finally, while this treatment has of necessity been extremely brief, it is worth mentioning a disjunction within his proposal that emanates from his confessional foundation. Earlier it was argued that Metzger was too quick to suggest an "analogical extension" between church and human culture because the extension of *totus Christus* to all humanity was uncertain (although clearly desired by Barth). In his discussion of church in the Dogmatics this tension becomes prominent as he struggles to uphold the singularity of the community of Christ against the universal intent of Christ. On the one hand he argues *credo sanctam ecclesiam* suggests differentiation from the surrounding world yet "as the body of Christ it has to understand itself as a promise of the emergence of the unity in which not only Christians but all men are already comprehended in Jesus Christ."[191] The implicit universalism of this statement and the drift of his intentions throughout §62 leave this dynamic unresolved. Barth reads this as teleology, and conceives this as a resolution to the problem; however this just shifts the emphasis, placing significant questions at the door of the Church within history. This remains an unsatisfactory element of his proposal in need of further exploration, although it does not fundamentally affect the efficacy of his proposal for the purposes of this present chapter.

Having so briefly established the feasibility of positing a Western alternative to Milbank's project it now remains to ask whether such Western

188. Ibid., 656, emphasis mine.
189. Ibid., 669.
190. Ibid., 661.
191. Ibid., 685 for the differentiation perspective and p. 665 for the assimilation thrust.

theological accounts of culture are the only possibilities, hence whether a rigorously theological description of culture is the sole prerogative of non-foundational Western thinking. Both Milbank and Barth have prosecuted their cases against the backdrop of modernity, which may be described as the distinctive child of a peculiar collocation of Western (rather than any other) interests that therefore stems from and reacts back upon the particularities inhering in this specific cultural identity. In a global context such an identity is specific, and its intellectual products equally so, however much globalization may have projected them around the world. There arises therefore the question of whether theologians from other contexts have negotiated this same question in some alternative way. This possibility seems worth exploring.

It is suggested that Kwame Bediako, a Ghanaian theologian, offers one such possibility. His proposal is birthed in West African soil but is couched in terms given him by his Western education; hence it is not expressed in a way completely foreign to a Western audience. As will become clear, whereas Milbank and Barth constructed their frameworks against the backdrop of modernity, Bediako is not so constrained. In fact, it is central to much of his writing that the contemporary African context bears a marked similarity to the early second-century church and hence some of the insights generated then, pre the rationalist cloaking of Western history, infecting even Greek philosophy such that its always religious overtone is lost to view, is a valuable resource for African theology.[192] It may even, via this route, become once again a more pertinent source of insight for the contemporary post-modern and now increasingly post-secular frameworks. The next chapter therefore will turn its attention to Africa and to the task of determining whether Bediako offers an alternative, equally viable theological model of culture.

---

192. It is worth pointing out that religion is used in its general sense from now. It is only with Barth that it is rendered a more technical term with specific anti-theological connotations.

Chapter 6

Kwame Bediako and an African Alternative

> Cultural identities are temporary, serving to yield us as Christians to the fullness of our identity with Christ. Paradoxically, culture snatches us away from Christ, it denies that we are His; yet when it is best understood, at its meeting with Christianity, culture drives us to Christ and surrenders us to Him, affirming us to be permanently, totally and unconditionally His own.[1]
>
> JOHN MBITI

UP TO THIS POINT discussion has concentrated on Western descriptions of culture. In the contemporary global context it is increasingly recognized that such a focus is too narrow. While the output from Western theologians still holds a dominant literary position on the global stage it is now only doing so in an increasingly specific and particular way. The belatedly recognized "southwards shift" in the international Christian constituency certainly reflects a significant numerical shift, whereupon the decline within the Christian community in the West has been more than offset by, for example, the explosive growth in "third-world" Pentecostalism.[2] But ac-

---

1. John Mbiti quoted in Bediako, *Jesus and the Gospel in Africa*, 75.

2. Refer for example Walls, "Gospel as Prisoner and Liberator of Culture," 23ff. Walls argues at p. 23 "First, let us recall that within the last century there has been a massive southward shift of the center of gravity of the Christian world, so that representative Christian lands now appear to be in Latin America, Sub-Saharan Africa, and other

companying this rapid population change are some important effects. For example, Western thinking is finding it much more difficult to command the global Christian audience in the way it has in the past, especially in the wake of a militant de-colonizing project that has spawned an associated de-westernizing impetus (which also has roots in the postmodern attention to otherness and subalterns).[3] The process of globalization currently sweeping the globe is possibly a countervailing influence although it too plays its part in the southern rise, spreading throughout these regions the tools necessary for future engagement with the West (such as education).

What follows seeks to take advantage of the opportunity this shift offers to explore a theological determination of culture from within a context to which the religious character of culture is not strange, and in which the cultural character of religion is also widely acknowledged. Generations of African scholars have received their intellectual training in Western schools that have built their institutions around a denial of the former position, yet this has not resulted in an enfeeblement of the traditional patterns such students were exposed to in their youth.[4] On the contrary, it has birthed a wrestling between the imported ideals inculcated during Western education and the customary sensibilities, and it is in this debate that an exciting, sometimes sharp but nevertheless productive dialogue occurs. It sometimes becomes derailed, as when scholars inhabit a romantic nostalgia regarding traditional patterns or entertain an unhealthy focus on the new. By and large however it is generally recognized that both positions err in their extremity for, as will be seen below, African culture is indelibly a mixture of the two. The key is to recognize gradations of influence from both sources, rather than succumb to simplistic assertions of the primacy of one or the other.

What this means for this chapter is the need to clearly delineate the various lines of thought to be encountered, and this in turn necessitates an extended introduction to the African theological context. As will become clear, each element of the African context is contentious. Even the descriptor "Africa" is embroiled in debate, not least because of the variety of cultural expressions it seeks to encompass. The sheer magnitude of what is termed "Africa" is problematic. Its intellectual landscape is rich, diverse, and vast, so much so that any attempted summary runs the risk of flattening the panorama. The following confronts this formidable challenge in

---

parts of the southern continents. This means that Third World theology is now likely to be the representative Christian theology. On present trends (and I recognize these may not be permanent) the theology of European Christians, while important for them and their continued existence, may become a matter of specialist interest to historians..."

3. For a mission perspective refer to Weerstra, "De-Westernizing the Gospel."
4. See for example Bediako, *Jesus and the Gospel in Africa*, 63ff.

the time-honored way of specificity. It is quite beyond the work of a single chapter to encompass such a wide field of enquiry hence what follows is a consideration constructed on the basis of specific interests. In particular, it takes its lead from scholars primarily, though not exclusively, born in West Africa. Even this represents a wide sweep of different people groups claiming distinctive heritages hence there is a deliberate concentration on Ghanaian writers.

The task of this chapter is quite ambitious. It forms a companion to the preceding chapter in that it too offers a critique of the apparent hegemony of Milbank's Christian account of culture, though one drawing from resources outside of the Western framework. At the same time its foundation in such a different framework offers the chance to consider the neutrality of culture from a very different perspective, one that brings a distinctive inter-cultural light to bear on the issues involved. The chapter therefore falls into two distinct though closely related parts. The first is largely negative in that it reconsiders the neutrality of culture, highlighting the core arguments involved in an African critique. The second is positive in that it sets out, on the basis of the findings from the first section, one African theological description of culture. This perspective forms both the counterpoint to the two theological accounts of culture already presented by Milbank and Barth and the culmination of the critique established in the first section of the chapter.

The final introductory element needing attention is the recognition that "we can never apprehend another people's or another period's imagination neatly, as though it were our own. The falsity of it is that we can therefore never genuinely apprehend it at all. We can apprehend it well enough, at least as well as we apprehend anything else not properly ours; but we do so not by looking *behind* the interfering glosses which connect us to it but *through* them."[5]

The following is inevitably shaped by the prejudices and proclivities of the author although it is to be hoped that by looking through rather than from behind these necessary hermeneutic glosses something of the richness of the underlying subject might emerge.

An African Critique of the Neutrality of Culture

Engaging the African philosophical context raises a lot of preliminary issues, each in and of itself sustaining a significant volume of scholarship. The

---

5. Bell, "Understanding African Philosophy," 198. Here he is following Geertz, "Found in Translation," 799, emphasis original.

label 'Africa' may be taken as an example: its use and definition is notoriously difficult. Kwame Anthony Appiah comments:

> if we could have travelled through Africa's many cultures in those years—from the small groups of Bushman hunter-gatherers, with their stone-age materials, to the Hausa kingdoms, rich in worked metal—we should have felt in every place profoundly different impulses, ideas and forms of life. To speak of an African identity in the nineteenth century—if an identity is a coalescence of mutually responsive (if sometimes conflicting) modes of conduct, habits of thought, and patterns of evaluation; in short a coherent kind of human social psychology—would have been "to give to aery nothing a local habitation and a name."[6]

In similar vein Jean-Marie Makang argues that what is commonly termed "African" tradition amounts to little more than gleanings from a "disbursed series of insular tribes" occupying a broad physical space. Ethnological description should therefore be, and often is, inherently tribal; descriptive of discrete tribal entities rather than nations or larger tribal groupings. These larger conglomerations only emerged as a result of later "institutionalized violence" rather than arising as a reflection of natural configurations or the choice of the peoples involved. African unity is therefore a later development, one not predicated, at least initially, on any positive expression of self-identity but on the negative passions engendered by their colonizeability.[7] "Africa" in this perspective is an imposition, an artificial Euro-centric construct that belies the reality it purportedly represents.[8]

Some, like Lucius Outlaw, suggest the possibility of alternative labels, such as his preferred nomenclature "Africana." Central to this concept is the underlying notion of a "dispersed *geographic race*" based on "shared lines of descent and ancestry" with "a relatively distinct gene pool."[9] Eze critiques this proposal because it binds African philosophy to a distinctive raciation that denigrates the substantive influence, in terms of both method and content, of non-African thinkers like Placide Tempels, Robert Horton, and Gary Hallen.[10] Africa as it is today does not just reflect indigenous African factors; it refracts myriad influences. At the very least many aspects and

---

6. Appiah, *In My Father's House*, 282.

7. Makang, "Of the Good Use of Tradition," 329.

8. A number of recent works have explored and investigated the implications and possibilities of challenging this construct, most notably Masolo, *African Philosophy*, Mudimbe, *The Invention of Africa*.

9. Outlaw, "African, African-American, and Africana Philosophy."

10. Eze, "Introduction," 4.

features of African life betray a continuing, sometimes muted but often still powerful, colonial influence.

Safro Kwame argues in contrast to Outlaw that an African philosopher is anyone who "is a person of whatever sex, race, or color who brings his or her peculiarly African experience (of, say, language, examples, topics, or beliefs) to bear, significantly, on the treatment of a philosophical question, issue or problem."[11]

This description nicely balances several contentious points arising from the postcolonial context, especially the oft exercised tendency to highlight the ethnic locatedness of African thought. Such indigenizing tendencies bring to the fore aspects of the postcolonial nature of the discourse but downplay the impact of others. The need to reflect insights generated by diaspora scholars, and the abiding place of uniquely influential Western thinkers, are particular victims of this approach.

Eze has some sympathy for Outlaw's position but like Kwame ultimately finds it inadequate, especially for dealing with "the multiplicity and pluralism of 'African/a' philosophy within (and, for some, outside of) Outlaw's conceptual 'umbrella' . . ."[12] Kwame's definition is wider but for Eze does not yet get to the heart of the matter. Eze instead offers a provocative suggestion: explicitly recognizing the notion of "(post)colonial" as the key definitional pivot. He argues that while this cedes central status to the colonial context it nonetheless reflects a simple but enduring fact: *"the single most important factor that drives the field in the contemporary practice of African/a philosophy has to do with the brutal encounter of the African world with European modernity*—an encounter epitomized in the colonial phenomena."[13]

This is a decision he does not take lightly for it moves to the center of attention an "indescribable crisis disproportionately suffered and endured by the African peoples in their tragic encounter with the European world . . ."[14] To sustain this argument he takes the term "colonial" to be a "clustered concept" that designates each of several realities of suffering endured by the various African peoples. No single effect is therefore determinative; rather the overall impact in all its dispersed variations is sought, though without thereby minimizing any individual reality of suffering. Further, he does not limit this suffering to the "episodic" view espoused by some, who want to limit colonial impact to the single generation generally defined as "colo-

---

11. Kwame, "Introduction," xxiv, but refer also xvii–xxv, and esp. xxii–xxv.
12. Eze, *Postcolonial African Philosophy*, 4.
13. Ibid., 4, emphasis original.
14. Ibid., 4.

nial times," contending instead that it coincides with the "age of Europe," a period he argues covers the timeframe between 1492 and 1945.[15]

This extension of timeframe is important for it allows Eze to highlight a more pervasive sense of racialism in European thinking than is often thought or acknowledged. In particular he is able to demonstrate how intimately connected with European views of reality these racial perspectives are. Eze suggests "The aims and intentions, the questions and the problems, that preoccupy twentieth-century African philosophy are stalked by a singular and incisive Occidental model of man."[16] The core argument developed by Eze is relatively simple. European self-identity was developed in the context of an "other," an "other" which legitimated a pervasive sense of superiority built on the back of scientific, technological and presumed cultural advancement. From within this self-identity European history is recounted not just as the emergence of European humanity but as *the* history of "humanity"; the rise of humanity *en toto*.[17] Eze, with Kant firmly in mind,[18] argues "the very condition of the possibility of European modernity as an Idea was the explicit metaphysical negation and theoretical exclusion of Africa and the African, archetypally frozen as 'savage' and 'primitive' . . ."[19] Africans are the negative other of Europe and its Idea of self, constituting what Tsenay Serequeberhan describes as its speculative core.[20]

For Serequeberhan this speculative core is founded on a "pre-text" of "a singular humanity or the *singularization* of human diversity by being forced on a singular track of historical 'progress' grounded on an emulation and/or mimicry of European historicity . . . [or] the Occidental surrogate for the heterogeneous variance of human historical existence . . . [which] is the shrine at which the great minds of Europe (past and present) prayed and

15. Ibid., 6; refer also to p. 17 n. 6.

16. Ibid., 13.

17. "Kant, Hegel, and Marx have been shown to originate in, and to be intelligible only when understood as an organic development within, larger sociohistorical contexts of European colonialism and the ethnocentric idea: Europe is *the* model of humanity, culture, and history in itself." Ibid., 6.

18. For a critique of Kant and his pervasive influence regarding the question of race refer Eze, "The Color of Reason."

19. Eze, "Introduction," 13.

20. "Broadly speaking, Eurocentrism is a pervasive bias located in modernity's self-consciousness of itself. It is grounded at its core in the metaphysical belief or Idea (*Idee*) that European existence is qualitatively superior to other forms of human life. The critique of Eurocentrism is aimed at exposing and destructuring this basic speculative core in the texts of philosophy. This then is the critical-negative aspect of the discourse of contemporary African philosophy." Serequeberhan, "The Critique of Eurocentrism," 142.

still pray."[21] The central task of the African de-structuring critique for both Eze and Serequeberhan is therefore a de-centering of this anthropology.

For both scholars this de-centering begins with an engagement of the chief constructor of the "Idea," Kant. Central to this (re)construction is the question of how Kant understood humanity, and here the issue of a non-religiously centered culture begins to problematically emerge. Serequeberhan notes "for Kant, 'the value of existence itself,' which is ontologically and/or metaphysically proper to human life, is manifested in the rational control of nature, both in the human being and in nature as such."[22] European expansion is not vindicated on the basis of economics, politics, or military power but on inherent elements of European self-identity. Imperial expansion was therefore not "an accidental or extrinsic aspect of his [Kant's] historical thinking—an easily excusable 'blemish.' It is rather, as I have argued in this paper, the effect of his universalistic and universalizing discourse grounded on the *Idee* that European history is the 'transcendentally obligatory' meeting point of all particular histories."[23]

What Kant constructs is "the Idea of 'rational control' best incarnated in European humanity and lacking in the non-European world."[24] Serequeberhan understands this to be a central point of the European philosophic tradition and consequently as an essential colonial fact to be dealt with. It is part of the shared European heritage transmitted through colonial occupation and a still continuing process of educational fortification. He therefore suggests the task ahead "presupposes the critical de-structive labor of seeing how the truth is skewed and skewered by the partiality it justifies and in which it is enmeshed."[25]

This task is not centered on Eurocentrism *per se* but on a specific conceptualization of Eurocentrism. More specifically, beneath the veneer of economic, technological, scientific, and other dominances taken as reasons for superiority "in and of themselves" there lurks a truer account, one in which Western superiority arises because they have "discovered *the* way

---

21. Ibid., 146, emphasis original. The shrine reference picks up a comment by Joseph Conrad in his *Heart of Darkness*, 7, where he talks of bowing before and offering a sacrifice to an idea; and Nietzsche's reference against Hegel in *The Advantage and Disadvantage of History for a Life* where one prostrates oneself before the idea.

22. Ibid., 150.

23. Ibid., 153. This includes a comment from Castoriadis, "The Greek Polis and the Creation of Democracy," 100 (no further details available).

24. Ibid., 154.

25. Ibid., 155.. Earlier Serequeberhan had made it clear that the notion of destruction here is borrowed from Martin Heidegger and is used in this specific sense. Refer particularly p. 157 n. 4.

of life appropriate to all human society."²⁶ Here a key impetus behind the rationalist framing of culture as being inherently neutral is placed on full display. It is then this hegemony of the Idea and the metaphysical superiority it engenders that forms, or should form, according to Eze and Serequeberhan, the target of African critique. Serequeberhan defers to Jose Rabasa for a summary of this position: "I must emphasize again that by Eurocentrism I do not simply mean a tradition that places Europe as a universal cultural ideal embodied in what is called the West, but rather a pervasive [metaphysical] condition of thought. It is universal because it affects both Europeans and non-Europeans, despite the specific questions and situations each may address."²⁷

Eze argues that this explains the enduring importance, despite heavy critique,²⁸ of Placide Tempels' *Bantu Philosophy*. It was an historic moment, a point of African unshackling. Against the anthropological (and hence rationalist cultural) trend

> Tempels spoke of *philosophy*; and because philosophy, to the Western mind, is the honorific term symbolizing the highest exercise of the faculty of reason, the book's title amounted to an admission of the existence of an African philosophy, the existence of African reason, and hence—following this logocentric European logic—African humanity. This notion flew in the face of the entire intellectual edifice of slavery and colonialism, which was built precisely on the negation of this possibility.²⁹

Tempel's work has had far reaching consequences quite outstripping the strict confines of its contents; perhaps even in spite of this content as Eze sometimes suggests. Many scholars are now tackling the "pervasive condition of thought" Serequeberhan refers to from a number of angles. One particular example is offered by Sandra Harding in her *Is Modern Science an Ethnoscience? Rethinking the Epistemological Assumptions*. Here she argues modern science was built on the basis of a specific cultural paradigm and must therefore be recognized as a cultural product.³⁰ She comments "since

26. Ibid., 156, emphasis original.

27. Ibid., 155. The square brackets were added by Serequeberhan and the initial quote came from Jose Rabara, *Inventing America* (London: University of Oklahoma Press, 1993), 18.

28. Refer for example Makang, "Good Use of Tradition," 329; Mudimbe, *The Invention of Africa*, 139–46; and Masolo, *African Philosophy in Search of Identity*, 57–59.

29. Eze, "Introduction," 11. Refer also p. 19 n. 24 for critical engagement.

30. "A central focus of recent work in the social and cultural studies of science and technology (SCSST, for short) has been to show how modern sciences have been constituted by their practices and cultures, not just externally enabled by them in ways that

Culture in a Post-Secular Context

the perception of scientific claims as universal, objective, and rational is itself locally constructed, not an internal, transcultural feature of any truly scientific process, any appeal to such notions should carry no more authority than the claims can command on other grounds."[31]

The core premise here has already been well established by internal Western critiques emanating from a "postpositivist, anti-internalist, socially located epistemology..."[32], or what Harding characterizes as a 'Northern' sensibility. What is new is the way it is being challenged now by a 'Southern' discourse based in comparative analyses.[33]

The basic distinction these latter critiques pursue is that existing between science and what is often called "ethnoscience," or what amounts to the pseudo-science emanating from other cultures. The core argument is that there remains a latent claim to "superiority" in even these post-positivist articulations, a claim that actively militates against positions that are "for treating all cognitive systems on a par as belief systems, thereby refusing to recognize the usual epistemological distinctions between real knowledge and mere local belief."[34] Harding argues that once these "epistemological distinctions" are broken down it becomes clear that the "modern sciences" are no more than European ethnosciences. However useful their findings may be they do not constitute transcultural "human" sciences. Even the central requirement of value neutrality is now recognized as a distinctive European cultural value; "when modern science is introduced into other cultures, it is experienced as a rude and brutal *cultural* intrusion because of this feature..."[35]

Here Harding establishes a critique of the value neutrality empowering Western notions of culture, but she then makes a perhaps surprising claim that begins to align her thought closely with the position being advocated by this book. Harding suggests that far from aiming "to provide ... just another, culturally local account on an epistemological par with

---

leave no marks on their cognitive cores." Harding, "Is Modern Science an Ethnoscience?" 45. Refer also pp. 65–66 n. 1 for a comprehensive outline of studies in this vein.

31. Ibid.

32. Ibid., 60.

33. The comparative argument described here does not exhaust the constituency of the "Southern" sensibility; Harding notes that in addition to it there are distinctive feminist and postcolonial views that can be explicitly linked to it. The term "Southern" is therefore not a geographic label so much as it is representative of several loosely collegiate 'schools' of thought. Refer ibid., 66–67 n. 4 for comments and an extensive bibliography of the respective constituents.

34. Ibid., 46, refer also p. 66 n. 2 for further references.

35. Ibid., 56.

Eurocentric, single-stream histories of science and technology . . ." these Southern perspectives are really aiming for "an account that is *more* objective and rational."[36] The inherent logic of these alternative paradigms is manifestly clear: "at some moments in history and culture, certain locally generated cultures and practices can provide knowledge of interest far beyond the locations where it was generated . . . it travels in a determinant historical relationship to other knowledge claims: it overtly contests them, claiming that they lack maximal accuracy and comprehensiveness. It claims greater objectivity, in that it can identify distorting or limiting features of the claim it contests."[37]

The European scientific enterprise represents one such specific historical trajectory that has admirably explored and exploited the particular aspects of the potential field of knowledge conducive to its own exploratory devices and socially constituted requirements. But this surveys only one portion of the available field of discovery. Other frameworks drawing on alternative methodologies and social constructs are entirely feasible. "This raises the possibility that in different historical situations and contexts sciences very different from the European tradition could emerge. Thus an entirely new set of 'universal' but socially determined natural science laws are possible."[38]

In this statement, appropriately transposed into philosophy, can be discerned something like the intent expressed by both Milbank and Barth, although now radicalized by the addition of a cultural element neither had entertained.[39] Space has been opened up not only for a distinctive cultural contribution, but also for a specifically religious one. This final claim emerges because of the African context Harding had in mind when developing her thesis. It now remains to demonstrate the cogency of this suggestion by considering what is meant by "African Philosophy."

The Non-Western Character of African Philosophy

As already noted, "African philosophy" is not a settled category of discussion, representing instead a maelstrom of conflicting perspectives rigorously

36. Ibid., 59. Emphasis mine.

37. Ibid.

38. Ibid., 63. Here she is quoting from Goonatilake, "Project for our Times," 229–30 (no further details provided).

39. This transposition into philosophy is stated here ahead of the proof that any such claim could be substantiated. The next section sets out on the task of legitimating this claim.

debating the fundamentals of philosophy and life.[40] This is not surprising given that "African philosophy" is a catalyst and conduit for postcolonial discourses and as such has been very interested in terminological clarifications. In this vein the phrase "African philosophy" has been dissembled, rearranged, disputed, discarded, deconstructed and vaunted through a variety of discussions that interweave in a complex and always complicated manner. Taking cognizance of these often intricate maneuvers would quickly exhaust the limited parameters of this chapter and therefore a fairly straight path is made for the central point relevant to this book.[41]

Safro Kwame provides an initial conceptual, albeit not chronological, starting point. He posits a continuum, suggesting that contemporary understandings of African philosophy draw from either of two main emphases. The first "looks back to the pre-colonial, traditional, African society for African philosophy. On this view, African philosophy is contained in, found in, or constructed out of the proverbs, folklore, art, aphorisms, fragments, rituals, traditions and collective wisdom of the African people; and African philosophy so discovered or constructed is comparable to Western philosophy (without necessarily being, significantly, the same)."[42]

The second he articulates as two interlinked streams: the first a critique of the "tradition" position outlined above, criticizing it for being little more than "ethnography with philosophical pretensions or, in short, ethnophilosophy";[43] and the second as a refraction of contemporary African and Western thought, Kwame following Wiredu at this point in discerning a still nascent but nevertheless rapidly developing array of philosophical reflections on present-day African experience. The relative positions of several important philosophers are then described across this tradition-contemporary continuum.

At the root of the underlying debate is a central question highlighted by the structure of Kwame's argument: What is the status of African traditional beliefs for African philosophy? This is in fact the fulcrum of this whole chapter, with the answer directly bearing on Harding's just noted proposal and on the perspective offered by this chapter. The relevance of traditional thinking in African philosophy is therefore a central and abiding question.

40. African philosophy is perhaps unique in its concentration on both legs of the philosophy and life dualism, a focus lost in the West except for in isolated cases such as Bourdieu. Refer the introduction for this discussion.

41. For an excellent survey of Anglo-African philosophy, encompassing many of the figures drawn on below, refer Hallen, "Contemporary Anglophone African Philosophy."

42. Kwame, "Introduction," xvii.

43. Ibid.

The main argument it turns on is the claim by traditionalist philosophers that traditional beliefs represent philosophy. This is commonly claimed in terms of a direct assertion of comparability, even if not accompanied by an overt declaration of this. In this respect these beliefs are said to present conclusions stemming from reconstructible premises that accordingly articulate second-order reflections upon life.[44] In short, they are, even by standard Western procedures of legitimation, philosophical statements. Often this claim is bolstered by adherents pointing to similarities with seminal moments in the development of Western philosophy, the Socratic tradition being most notably referred to in this regard.[45]

By contrast the contemporary school understands traditional beliefs to be, and this is at best, a set of initial premises; the starting point for a critical engagement that itself constitutes true philosophy.[46] The more stringent of the contemporary scholars sharply critique the philosophic status of traditions for three main reasons: as lacking the dissensious construct of critical reflection; for having no written record; and because they constitute no more than the articulation of "beliefs." The central point they argue is that these beliefs do not fulfill the requirements for philosophy because they do not adhere to the rationalist foundation underlining philosophy in the West. Often this translates into the suggestion that traditional African thinking is not Western and hence is not philosophy.

The seminal work of typology in this field is a 1978 presentation by Henry O. Oruka in which he outlined a fourfold categorization that has dominated subsequent discussions. Over the course of time these four positions have been considerably refined, although the central thrusts have remained unchanged. They can be succinctly described, according to Kaphagawani, in the following terms.[47]

44. Ibid., xxi–xxii.

45. Oruka, "Sage Philosophy," 102–3. Here he quotes Bell who argues that on the basis of the Socratic tradition oral argumentation is as much philosophy as literary productions.

46. Kaphagawani describes a similar two-fold division but characterizes the contemporary school in less dichotomized terms "as a joint venture and product of traditional as well as modern trained philosophers . . ." Kaphagawani, "What Is African Philosophy?" 87. For reasons that will become apparent in later discussions this description is inadequate. It fails to properly characterise a number of scholars who hold to a more universalist position.

47. Development of the Orukan framework has not halted over the years. Oruka himself, before his death, added two more trends to the list provided above, namely the hermeneutic and the artistic or literary trend. He comments, "The former consists of the philosophical analysis of concepts in a given African language to help clarify meaning and logical implications arising from the use of such concepts." Oruka, "Sage Philosophy," 101. Others have added further categories, Gale Presbey noting in particular

Culture in a Post-Secular Context

Professional philosophy is, broadly speaking, the work engaged in by professional philosophers steeped in the Western philosophic tradition. This can be further refined by noting the dominance of the analytic tradition. The categories of discussion reflect this background by centering on well attested Western topics such as logic, metaphysics, ethics and the history of philosophy. To a large extent adherents are interested in providing an African contribution to the ongoing international dialogue in "general philosophy," as well as engaging the contemporary African context. It is this model that most closely resembles the contemporary school outlined by Safro Kwame above.

Nationalistic-ideological philosophy is a pragmatic category chiefly concerned with the question of liberation and the development of political theory to advance this concern. It is uniquely African in that it is self-confessedly an attempt to remain rooted in the traditional social context of Africa, seeking from this foundation to elaborate a political philosophy. These African philosophers tend to take an active role in changing the political landscape, forming the vanguard of social and political reorganization. Its significant "other" is the colonial influence; hence it tends to split history into a tripartite pre, post, and colonial schema. In terms of an African philosophy it is beleaguered by variety, the sheer diversity of ethnic groupings and their associated social and political structures presenting a bewildering array of possibilities.

Ethnophilosophy, or what is sometimes termed "cultural philosophy," originated in francophone Africa and is most commonly associated with Placide Tempels, John Mbiti, and Alexis Kagamé. Its goal is to discern the underlying metaphysics of the folk tradition of African societies. There are a number of assumptions guiding this view, two of which have become particularly important for subsequent discussions. First, it assumes the validity of oral tradition, touting it as the equal of the discursive practice common in the West. Second, it is based on "a holistic approach to the analysis and exposition of world outlooks implicit in most, if not all, African cultures."[48] As Kaphagawani notes, it tends to be orientated towards the preservation of this tradition.[49] The notion of ethnophilosophy is sharply criticized for a

---

that Sophie Oluwole "added negritude, Egpytologists and "the historical group," "critical traditionalists," "the universalists," those who want to deconstruct the myth of inferiority, and the socialists who think philosophy is meant to change the world." Presbey, "Syllabus for an African Philosophy and Culture Course."

48. Kaphagawani, "What Is African Philosophy?" 91.

49. Ibid., 88. He goes on to comment that the Orukan framework has clear "affinities with the framework introduced to the subject of African oral literature by Okpewho, and as alluded to by Anthony Nazombe (1983: 45–36). The indebtedness to Nazombe's

number of reasons, most commonly for lacking a literature; its reliance upon a collective perspective, or what has been termed "groupspeak"; its lack of systemization; its inadequate use of ratiocinative methods; its loose definition of philosophy; and for an inability to properly distinguish between the alleged philosophy of the society being studied and that which is imposed upon it by the observer in question.

Sagacity Philosophy is comparatively new, constituting part of Oruka's enduring legacy to African philosophy. The core of this school is the position of the sage within traditional culture; someone endowed with a deep knowledge of tribal wisdom and its application. Oruka distinguishes between sages and prophets, and then suggests a distinction between sages and philosophic sages, noting the latter have recourse to a form of rational, critical enquiry that accords with the standard philosophic practice of second order reflection.[50] In a number of ways the description of sagacity philosophy displays clear affinities with ethnophilosophy, a point strengthened if analysis is pursued through the language of cultural philosophy. "Culture philosophy is, in this case, the first order system with its dogmatic truth claims and absolute ideas, whereas philosophic sagacity is a second order system, a metaculture philosophy which analyses critically the validity of the truth claims made in the first order system."[51]

This quote brings the focus of the debate into sharp relief for the central point, as will be demonstrated below, is whether this first/second order distinction is appropriate. Is it really the case that "culture philosophy" is dogmatic and hence not philosophical or is it simply deemed so through the application of a parochial Western structure with universal pretensions? In this question can be seen shades of the critiques of Milbank and Barth for at stake here is the question of whether religious considerations enter into the philosophic realm. As will then be seen, this is closely tied to a consideration of the religious nature of culture, a discussion that sets up for the second half of the chapter in which just such a Christian understanding of culture is presented.

---

rendition is quite apparent."

50. "A person is a sage in the philosophic sense only to the extent that he/she is consistently concerned with the fundamental ethical and empirical questions relevant to the society, and has the ability to offer insightful solutions to some of those issues." Oruka, "Sage Philosophy," 100.

51. Kaphagawani, "What Is African Philosophy?" 94. Kaphagawani highlights apparent connections with the framework promulgated by Alfred Tarskian, a categorisation that would quite explicitly link sagacity with ethnophilosophy such that the former is "a second order system of ethnophilosophy, a meta-ethnophilosophy, analytical and critical—as are all meta-systems—of ethnophilosophy." Kaphagawani, "What Is African Philosophy?" 94.

The Inherently Religious Nature of African Culture and Philosophy

In his article, "The Parochial Universalist Conception of 'Philosophy' and 'African Philosophy,'" Polycarp Ikuenobe argues "debate regarding the nature and existence of African philosophy has culminated in two camps, which I shall call the universalists and the particularists."[52] The universalist (or African analytic philosophers) advocates the role of formal philosophy, understood as a universally applicable systematic and rational theoretic.[53] Within this schema contingent philosophic thought arising from engagement with particular contexts (such as Africa) does not give rise to systematic and universal principles; instead such thought either provides a contribution to or always already arises from within the pre-defined universal context. Either way it does not constitute an alternative possibility and hence the particularist case does not escape the ambit of the universalist one. Africa therefore has no distinctive philosophy but is instead just a different cultural location at which universal philosophical concepts can be deployed.

Something like this approach can be found, in terms of the Orukan framework outlined above, in Africa's professional philosophers, those working within the Western traditions and who are therefore articulating a formal philosophy in line with the universal categories of Western philosophy.[54] However even this praise is diluted by the observation that these attempts are still in process and "No African individual or group of philosophers *ex hypothesi* has such a reasonable volume of writings that is profound enough on such philosophical topics to warrant serious study as philosophers or as African philosophy ... it is rather rudimentary."[55]

Despite this Ikuenobe is keen to suggest the possibility that such a body of work might yet emerge and that African philosophers are on their way to achieving this. Part of the problem, he suggests, is that the formal philosophy of the universalist has always been defined through "an ideal conception of philosophy (what the universalist think philosophy in general ought to be), which has led to the distinction between formal and folk philosophy ..." but that this "does not reflect the real nature of philosophy

---

52. Ikuenobe, "The Parochial Universalist Conception": 189.

53. Ikuenobe summarizes the main features of the universalist perspective as universal conceptualization; rigorously scientific adversarial methodology; ideas of individuals; and a written corpus, ibid., 201.

54. Ibid., 195–99.

55. Ibid., 198.

(what philosophy is or has been), if it is viewed holistically from the perspectives of all the traditions and periods of Western philosophy."[56]

Instead of talk about African philosophy being conducted through the dichotomy of folk and formal categories he suggests attention be paid to the historical development of Western philosophy. It can, he argues, be reconstructed in terms of its own past such that it becomes clear that African philosophy, in its ethnophilosophical and sagacity philosophical modes, are the same types of precursors one might consider mediaeval philosophy to be; a preparation for later developments.[57] He suggests "one could argue that African philosophy exists—in terms of its subject matter and method—in a form comparable to the ancient, mediaeval, and modern periods of Western philosophy."[58] It is in these periods of Western philosophy that one can discern the unsystematic, collective and dogmatic characteristics with which African philosophy is generally described. Importantly, it is plausible to see philosophy in this precursor period as both an activity and "a system of beliefs, ideas, ways of seeing, and thoughts that have been structured by culture, different experiences, time, and history."[59]

This might seem to suggest an idealization of the Western system in that he appears to concede the nature and form of rationality to the Western depiction of it. This is heightened by his suggestion that Safro Kwame's eschewal of the meta-philosophical approach is not authentically African because it lends credence to the notion "it is not African to be rigorous and critical of beliefs . . ." a view he argues tacitly leaves Africans "bereft of intellect."[60] But his argument is much more subtle than this for as he at one point comments, "I agree that the universalists' search for a 'universal' ideal criterion may be legitimate for harmonizing the discipline of philosophy, but the conception of this criterion, which precludes the non-Western or traditional African paradigm(s), is parochial. There could be a universal sense of philosophy, but it must be stressed that this sense has to be a synthesis of the various essential elements of the thought systems of different peoples."[61]

He does not go on to express what this might look like although he does argue that "the worldviews and beliefs of traditional African people

---

56. Ibid., 195.

57. Ibid., 204.

58. Ibid., 202.

59. Ibid., 204. He follows Wiredu in explicitly noting that philosophy has always been "culture-relative in various subtle ways . . ." Refer p. 201.

60. Ibid., 206.

61. Ibid., 203.

could be precursors of the kind of contemporary analytic philosophy that the universalists are looking for in Africa."[62] Yet in this he is really wanting to affirm, in common with Kwame Appiah, that the African intellectual enterprise should seek some sense of rigorous activity that honors the nature of philosophy, or in other words that seeks "to find something with dignity that Africans will want to call their philosophy."[63]

Peter Amato, in "African Philosophy and Modernity," comes at the problem of an overarching account of philosophy from a quite different angle, using Serequeberhan's well-known historico-hermeneutical approach. As he notes, "Here, the contemporary reconsideration within Western thought of some of the central assumptions of classical modern philosophy is invoked in order to make sense of the intercultural situation of understanding."[64] Serequeberhan argues, using Heidegger and Gadamer, that all philosophical inquiry and discussion is governed by pre-judgments or prejudices. The key in intercultural dialogue, the specific ambit of philosophical discussion he is concerned with, is to bring these underlying foundations to the fore; part of the task Amato sets himself in this essay.

Amato's specific target is the international hegemony of a "mythology" propagated and nurtured by Western rationalism, namely the "universal horizon of development." He argues "all intellectual forms and forms of discourse that may have existed in any culture were subsumed into an economic and political metanarrative."[65] His intention is to deconstruct this rhetoric of domination in order to allow a positive reconstruction of it, a reinscription that prefigures a different "universal horizon." "Rather than a rhetorical device that allows one cultural tradition to subsume the individuality of all others in a homogenous and self-serving narrative of supposed intellectual and material progress, the idea of a universal human horizon may become simply the generalized location for the overlapping conceptualizations of human nature that our different intellectual cultures may produce through real dialogue."[66]

Throughout his article Amato is concerned with articulating one central thought. He argues "It has been a fundamental premise of the modern philosophical attitude to place religious and social values outside of what it

62. Ibid., 204.
63. Ibid., 206.
64. Amato, "African Philosophy and Modernity," 71.
65. Ibid., 75. See also Janz, "Alterity, Dialogue, and African Philosophy," 222. Janz sugggests "If the universalistic philosophy does claim to represent all human experience, it is because that experience has been coerced or forced into the point from which generalization has occurred."
66. Amato, "African Philosophy and Modernity," 75.

considers legitimate philosophical thought."⁶⁷ The basic explanation being "philosophical reason must, or in any case can only ever truly, operate independently of some basis in the mythic or religious life of the community."⁶⁸ As a consequence, "religious-inspired conceptions of reality and mythic conceptions of reality have been seen as merely the elements of superstition and obfuscation, having no place in philosophical reason."⁶⁹

Not surprisingly therefore "The key statements of modernism assert that philosophy is a liberated and liberating discourse. It is liberated in relation to myth, superstition, tradition, political power, rationality, passion, etc."⁷⁰ Yet there is a curiously paradoxical moment in this meta thesis for "Modern thought does not escape the mythic dimensions of its own cultural setting."⁷¹ And neither can it. Like all such metanarrative discourses it originates in particularity; is embedded within a specific cultural context that has an effect. The "modernist call to regard all religious authority, myth, and tradition as having only a negative influence on thought refuses to recognize the extent to which this has never been possible."⁷²

The cry for liberation from the authoritative claims of traditional authorities bred a "tendency to bracket or exclude tradition and culture from knowledge . . . [in an] attempt to overcome them."⁷³ The path of modernity blazed through Plato, Locke, Descartes, Hume, and Kant was forged by the ability to narrowly circumscribe the field of endeavor; a process that limited sharply the questions falling within the purview of rational thought. "Unsurprisingly, these forbidden questions are all the areas most involved in myth and religion, and most deeply inscribed in cultural tradition—cosmology, psychology, and theology."⁷⁴

These questions, concerned with the *noumenal*, were placed instead or surfaced anyway, within the realm of metaphysics, "the repository for . . . ill-conceived projects of reason venturing into and trying to satisfy the demands of cultural traditions. Reason must abandon such projects to find itself and fulfill its promise. It can do this once it has cleared intellectual culture of the dialectical illusions fostered by religion and scholasticism."⁷⁵

67. Ibid., 76.
68. Ibid.
69. Ibid.
70. Ibid., 77.
71. Ibid., 78.
72. Ibid., 84.
73. Ibid., 83.
74. Ibid., 85.
75. Ibid.

Amatos' genealogical plotting of this discussion from Plato, through the so-called dark ages and the Renaissance, to Hobbes and beyond "models the intellectual path of early modernism, from a narrative which it conveniently takes to be natural and for which it accepts no responsibility, to the extension of that idea to include all humanity; from its own horizon it deduces a universal horizon."[76]

A key metaphor for this model can be found in Locke and is traceable in both Descartes and Kant, namely understanding the soul as a *tabula rasa*. Per Locke, the modern autonomous self is a blank slate upon which our experiences discursively mark out their course. Amato does not fully develop this theme because though foundational for his argument it is not the central point he is trying to put across. He does however comment significantly for present purposes that "this way of thinking about the soul is at the center of the controversy regarding the status of culture and tradition in regard to the modern autonomous self. If we are, as Locke believed, blank slates to be written on by experience, then there is an irreducible and culture-free core or center, which can be regarded as the seat of reason. . . . This center is the heart of reason as ahistorical and non-cultural."[77]

As he goes on to note,

> If this self can be conceived to exist in some respect or form, whether it be logical or temporal, then there is a hope for the Classical Modern conception of reason as unsituated and purely autonomous; there is a ground zero for reason. But if there is no constituted self without culture and history, without language and experience, without physicality and situatedness, then there cannot be a conception of reason that relies upon a cipher or an irrational posit: i.e., the Lockean self. Hegel seems to have realized this in his rejection of Kantian abstract reason.[78]

In Hegel we arrive at Amatos' Western hope, though not the only hope for he recognizes in particular the role Heidegger's project plays in releasing the shackles of modernist rationalism. But it is in Hegel that he locates "recognition that, to some extent, reason is situated in some kind of history and is entwined with, while perhaps not being reducible to, the trajectory of perspectives that are accessible to humans in time."[79] Unfortunately, "despite the many clear ways in which modernism has taken leave of key pre-Hegelian assumptions, and despite the broad-scale questioning

---

76. Ibid., 81.
77. Ibid., 96 n. 34.
78. Ibid., 97 n. 34.
79. Ibid., 87.

of rationality that this has sparked within Western philosophy itself, it is also clear that there has yet been no coherent accomplishment of a post-Hegelian philosophical perspective that successfully fuses the plurality of perspectives that is generated in the abandonment of the Kantian ahistorical ideal of knowledge."[80]

The void this situation leaves has spawned a number of "post" articulations of Western philosophy that are united by their joint quest to decipher the future direction of Western thinking. In the meantime however Western rationalism is still being propagated by Western educational facilities wherein local and international scholars alike are continuously educated in Western philosophical premises. This apparently benign legacy of colonial interaction, carefully cultivated in a context of soft evolutionism, has proven a highly seductive means of furthering the core enlightenment project. As Amato notes, "it has been difficult for scholars educated in the traditions of Western philosophy to easily recognize that cultural productions and forms of thought from beyond its self-imposed boundaries can be legitimately philosophical, rational, or even modern, in an important sense."[81]

Further, the perpetuation of the norming mythology of modernity no longer relies upon inherent credibility but on sustained recitation garnished with scientific, technological and economic advantages. In this regard the aggressive advance of late capitalism; the flow of aid dollars; IMF policies; and a legion of other well documented devices have leveraged a space for modernity in "developing" countries around the world. But what kind of space is this? Amato argues that "modernity" is "only the particular label by which we have come to identify the most lively and enduring element of the Western European philosophical *tradition*, rather than a normative category applicable to other cultures, measuring the degree of their escape from their own traditions."[82]

Here, from an intercultural perspective, Amato has established a critique of Western modernism that from a different angle makes the same point as Milbank. For Amato however this is the precursor to a considerably more positive description of traditional African philosophy than Ikuenobe is able to manage, one he articulates through a consideration of the relationship existing between "Sagacity and Hermeneutics." His guiding thought would seem to be a post-Hegelian movement towards "an idea of knowledge

---

80. Ibid.
81. Ibid., 86.
82. Ibid., 78.

that does not forswear its own roots in the history, tradition, and culture of a people."[83]

Amato begins by considering the ethnophilosophic critique promulgated by Oruka. As noted above Oruka distinguishes three positions in opposition to ethnophilosophy, namely "philosophic sagacity"; "nationalist-ideological philosophy"; and "professional philosophy." Amato argues Oruka thought ethnophilosophy presented a unique conception of philosophy based on a "wholly customs dictated" foundation that meant it acted also as a conserver or protector of tradition, and which therefore represented a position bound to the mythic formulations of the social collective. In contrast to this view, he suggests, Oruka sought to clearly distinguish the second order reflection on the African condition embodied by his preferred option of "philosophic sagacity." The basic point Oruka is making, according to Amato, is that "Sagacity is or can be philosophical when it is closely connected to individual or dialogical reflection in distinction from religion and other non-reflective aspects of culture."[84] Therefore "The crucial difference between [sic] sage and a philosopher is that the former is a vessel for tradition and the latter accepts only that part of traditional belief that can satisfy rational scrutiny."[85]

Amato is suspicious of this formulation and makes two pertinent observations. First, there is a curious disjunction in the way "the philosophical sage is to develop a 'rational' departure from prevailing wisdom which is, nonetheless, not a departure from the prevailing *mythos*, or general philosophy of the people."[86] Amato goes on to comment "The second order, philosophical and rational, seems fairly deliberately defined in opposition to the first order, which is mythicoreligious and 'traditional.'"[87] The internal logical difficulty this points to is quite obvious and the second observation he makes also involves an inherent difficulty in the formulation itself. Amato comments "One must, in this context, take care that the 'development' *toward* philosophy on the *basis* of sagacity does not end up as a movement away from the particularity of real traditions with roots in a lived to way of life toward a purported universality outside and independent of any tradition with roots in an Enlightenment dream."[88]

---

83. Ibid., 87.
84. Ibid., 88.
85. Ibid., 89.
86. Ibid.
87. Ibid., 90.
88. Ibid., 91, emphasis original.

Here a direct critique of and yet paradoxical fulfillment of Ikuenobe's position is registered. On the one hand, the shift toward a horizon dominated by analytic philosophy is disputed, while on the other hand, the shift towards a multi-cultural horizon of particular philosophies is affirmed. In line with this latter goal therefore Amato finishes by contending for a position in which "the movement that is based on sagacity should become a conscious movement from one particularity toward an inclusive plurality of particularities seeking convergences."[89] This is a stance that necessarily engenders humility in philosophic descriptions emanating from individual cultures for, as he comments,

> To become conversant with other traditions in lieu of having been formed by them should become a working model for intercultural understanding, rather than the requirement that all aspire to speak with no dialect, or that legitimate philosophy only consider certain specific topics. Both within any culture and between any two cultures, understanding is a matter of bringing traditions into active correspondence, not pretending to "speak reason," and waiting for the Other to learn its language.[90]

Pieter Coetzee builds on Amato's thesis in two major respects. First by moving forward the program of creating space for African philosophy within international philosophic discourse; and second by continuing the emphasis upon a recovery of ethnophilosophy, albeit a more mature version of it. His approach is to outline a comprehensive cultural model of philosophic interaction that is rooted in biological isomorphism and targeted towards the universal human horizon outlined by Amato above.

In a programmatic statement Coetzee argues,

> each epoch in philosophy deals with particular linguistic presentations of problems rooted in a set of social conditions and each employs preferred traditions of reasoning from among a competing set. The preferred traditions of rationality are the ones which successfully transcend the limitations of their predecessors and rivals, such advances being measured in terms of their ability to resolve incoherences, anomalies and inconsistencies—advances measured in relative and not absolute terms.[91]

He extends this to include not only intra-cultural but inter-cultural discussions. Undergirding this proposal is a specific understanding of

---

89. Ibid.
90. Ibid., 92.
91. Coetzee, "Uncovering Rationality," 64.

culture, which he defines as "a complex of shared meanings that people in a given society derive from or attach to their experiences, the ground by which they understand themselves and interpret their experiences."[92]

For him Western modernity inculcated a communocultural understanding of culture based in a syllogistic disjunction, a foundation that could not help but depict cross-cultural interactions as inherently conflictual encounters because it took homogeneity as its basic premise. By contrast he proposes a conjunctural conception of culture where culture is the product of *both* indigenous and "alien" cultural elements. These alien elements come from multiple sources and over time meld together with both each other and the indigenous elements such that all of them become *equally* constitutive of the culture in question. Each element becomes an integral aspect of the cultural tradition. There is, therefore, no need to assume that "the elements of a people's tradition are all autochthonous in their genesis."[93]

This redefining of cultural encounters is important for Coetzee and indeed African philosophy more generally, because it allows for the possibility of cultural borrowing. The African context, as noted above, is fundamentally defined by its colonial experience. Europe has had a significant and enduring impact upon the African continent, penetrating at some points to its conceptual sub-structures. Contemporary Africa is not therefore best understood by its autochthonous features but by its peculiar mixture of indigenous and colonial elements.

Coetzee recognizes that the conjectural proposal cannot simply stand by itself, it requires a supporting apparatus. This is provided by two sub-theses regarding language and social context. The first is the language thesis. He argues that each language is constructed on unique conceptual structures that are nonetheless highly translatable. While there are some barriers to cross-cultural understanding they are not so effective as to significantly impair translatability; there is instead an essential adequacy in translation that allows cultures to effectively engage in dialogue for mutual understanding. Adequacy, however, does not mean complete translatability hence a level of remainder is implied in any cross-cultural exchange. This is essentially an effect of particularity.

Coetzee is not blind to this effect and refers to examples given by Wiredu from his work on the difficulties involved in translation between the Akan and English cultures. Wiredu argues that Placide Tempel's infamous use of "force" "was radically misstated by the use of an inapplicable

---

92. Ibid., 63. Here he is quoting Gyekye, *Tradition and Modernity*, 107.

93. Coetzee, "Uncovering Rationality," 64. He is quoting Gyekye, *Tradition and Modernity*, 227.

Western category of thought, namely, the concept of being as existentially construed."[94] The application of this specific category effectively skewed the Bantu framework, giving it a distinctive Western flavor that belied its underlying structure. For Coetzee this is an example of misrepresentation rather than incompatibility since the use of an alternative category might have better translated the underlying notion. By contrast, the conceptualization of truth in the Akan and English contexts is an example of incompatibility, and it is for this reason that the social thesis becomes an important element of this proposal.

The social thesis, succinctly stated, argues "Any adequate philosophical thesis is also an adequate cultural and/or social thesis, which by their very nature as conceptual theses have transcultural conceptual import, i.e., they do not remain restricted to the milieu in which they originated."[95] Philosophic discussion always emanates from and is consequently grounded within specific social contexts. This has a number of implications, two of which are important. First, each context is irreducibly a particularity; hence there will often be an element of remainder in any specific cross-cultural translation. Second, there is an inbuilt impetus towards change in philosophic discussions as and when underlying social conditions change. Philosophic outputs are therefore likely to be malleable, to some degree at least, though the process of change implied here is of course slow and deliberate. Coetzee calls it "development."

Social change does not bear a simple relationship to philosophic change; instead there is a complex transition that occurs over time in a somewhat Kuhnian fashion. In this respect the reigning philosophic construct purportedly represents the best explanatory framework for the social context it is directly engaged with, but is not thereby the only feasible proposal. There may be a number of different frameworks jockeying for position, each attempting to lay claim to the status of ascendant explanatory model. Over time, and in the face of social change, the particular framework considered most coherent changes. This may occur in several ways, such as: a restructuring of the existing dominant paradigm; or the emergence of an entirely new conceptualization; or perhaps the rise to ascendancy of a previously subjugated position.

The theoretical structure of Coetzee's theory is best understood through attention to how he understands universality and particularity to relate. He suggests that the human condition is best characterized by a situation in

---

94. Coetzee, "Uncovering Rationality," 67. He is quoting Wiredu and Oladipo, *Conceptual Decolonization in African Philosophy*, 174.

95. Coetzee, "Uncovering Rationality," 68.

which there exists a universality that creates "sameness" but which is not thereby thoroughgoing, hence the universal is mediated by cultural distinctions. This allows him to argue for the presence of a universal human horizon, and the associated occurrence of cross-cultural commonalities, while concurrently contending for a fundamental diversity in cultural elements and conceptual structures; a point highlighting the importance of particularity. It is central to his framework that the universal and the particular are dialogically related; always existing in a state of tension that is never simply resolved into one pole or the other.

Coetzee refers to this tension as the route of interpretation mediating between "lived conditions and theory."[96] It mediates because reliance on a hegemonic theory claiming universal status is not sufficient for this nullifies both the particularity out of which the theory emerged and the essential particularity of other cultures. It is also inadequate to posit a fundamental relativism for this violates, at the very least, the biological commonality of humanity and ushers in a radical form of incommensurability that belies the "irreducibly dialogical" nature of a philosophy drawn from disparate contexts. Both extremes express important elements of his theory but an overdetermination in one direction or the other is detrimental, causing a disastrous collapse of the model.

So far Coetzee's model has been discussed by way of underlying principles and necessary supports. It is now time to outline in more detail the major thrust of his argument. On the foregoing foundations Coetzee builds a concept of reconstructible rationality. For him rationality stems from human commonality and is therefore grounded in a basic notion of rationality, one common to all cultures. But this does not necessarily connote a single rational construct; rather he posits or recognizes a plurality of rationalities. This is not an unfettered plurality for each has a basis in some quite specific tradition and hence represents a communally shared structure and content of meaning. Amato's "universal horizon for humanity," as presented by Coetzee, therefore becomes the "generalized location for the overlapping conceptualizations of human nature that our different intellectual cultures may produce through real dialogue."[97] It represents a philosophical "dialogical zone" that emerges at the intersection of various reconstructible rationalities each emanating from a specific tradition and expressing the mores of individual communocultural reflections upon lived human experience. Just as Africa is an equal partner in this meta-interchange so too is the West.

---

96. Ibid., 70.
97. Ibid., 64.

Coetzee presents this model as a way through the so-called double-bind of having to articulate philosophy either so similar to the West that had it no distinctive voice or so different from it that it lacked credentials for voicing its perspective.[98] In this he might be said to have succeeded however in doing so he has left unspecified the nature of the universal human horizon towards which he is pointing. His essay goes so far as to perhaps indicate it represents an evolving construct of human design, although it could also be understood as an unspecifiable final fullness of understanding. What is important however is that it sets the scene, providing a framework for the discussion to follow. Amato began by noting the tendency to bracket out both African religion and African tradition, understood by him as being indelibly religious, from philosophic discussions. The problem was that this decision did not reflect an inherent requirement of philosophy but arose from the dominance of an ultimately parochial Western mythology that sought to subsume particularities within the ambit of its specific description of the rational. His strategy for subverting this was to advocate the need for philosophy to acknowledge a "plurality of particularities" converging on a universal horizon, a place in which traditions engaged in genuine dialogue.

Coetzee filled out this framework in important ways. He argued that the dialogical framing of the "plurality of particularities" is based in both a fundamental human commonality and the existence of "adequate" cultural translatability. Culture is the purveyor of difference, and is philosophically expressed through distinctive traditions. He therefore described general philosophy as the result of the dialogue occurring between various traditions of thought. Such philosophy should not and indeed could not truly be mediated by any specific parochial construal but needed to reflect instead points of convergence and leave open the various gaps between these agreements. Unfortunately the embracing nature of this structure meant the character and content of this universal human horizon was left ill-defined. It is effectively a negotiated space open to all the foibles of human interactions, most particularly the endemic power relations characterizing such

---

98. Bernasconi, "African Philosophy's Challenge to Continental Philosophy," 188. From within a Continental framework Bernasconi makes use of Lucius Outlaws' essay "African 'Philosophy': Deconstructive and Reconstructive Challenges" to make a similar point, refer p. 194 n. 21. He suggests that Outlaw argues the notion of African *philosophy* challenges the notion of *Philosophy*, defining the latter as representing the dominant Western tradition and the former as a critical self reflection engaging that tradition. The former is deconstructive of the latter by the simple event of its historical condition. It is both the same as and different from that within which it is constituted and therefore "'African philosophy' as a term functions, in ways that a reader of Derrida's 'Violence and metaphysics' would recognize, to expose the limits of the dominant framework as they are enshrined within the double-blind, and thereby to displace them."

interactions. It is feasible to suppose that this space has in fact been operative this whole time, the scene of a particular set of negotiations in which the Western tradition grabbed the initiative and carved the space in its own likeness, buttressing it firmly against the intrusion of other traditions. It is therefore against this edifice that the assertions of particularity discussed above are slowly chipping away.

What is critical in this whole discussion for the purposes of this chapter however is the space that has been opened up for conceiving of philosophy as a social and religious construct. For both Amato and Coetzee there is the real possibility of envisaging reality through ethnophilosophy and the African religious heritage. Amato argues that sagacity philosophy finally deconstructs into ethnophilosophy once the need for a critical element based in Western rationality is removed. Coetzee is implicitly resistant to this given his advocacy of analytic philosophy but this is unsatisfactory and unconvincing in the face of his concurrent support of reconstructible rationality. If the African heritage is inherently religious then his theory either collapses under the weight of an intolerable tension or is pressured towards either an analytic or reconstructible resolution. Given his overall framework it is unlikely that the analytic would, or in fact should, survive, despite his personal predilections.

It will be recognized that this emphasis on ethnophilosophy cannot be conceived in simple isolation from the other options, not least because each of the Orukan types present themselves as viable alternatives. On the same grounds just argued it is equally possible to suggest the plausibility of pursuing the hermeneutic or political-nationalist options, amongst others. An early foreclosure on which of them *should* be alternatives is neither warranted nor advisable in this formative stage of the theory. It is worth noting however the extent to which each of these alternatives builds on or presupposes important elements of the perspective offered by ethnophilosophy, a point that becomes clearer once an appropriate understanding of this approach is developed. This suggests the foundational character of the ethnophilosophical approach and hence the need to particularly focus attention here.

There now remains the need to discuss, before specifically considering the religious character of this ethnophilosophy, how it relates to Western philosophy. Theophilus Okere begins to open this up, albeit he is working with the formal/informal structure eschewed above, when he suggests "philosophy must always deal with the non-philosophical features of lived experience and its expression, whether that be religion, culture, or even the irrationality of certain presuppositions."[99] For Okere the non-philosophical

---

99. Janz, "Alterity, Dialogue, and African Philosophy," 224. He is referring here to

refers to "the non-reflected, that unreflected baggage of cultural background . . ."[100] By beginning from this foundation he is attempting to assert that African philosophy is unique; it "can make use of all the rational tools that any other philosophical tradition assumes as essential," yet remain "rooted in a particular tradition of non-philosophy."[101] In this case hermeneutics becomes the bridge between culture and philosophy.

Janz suggests that Okere's analysis is ultimately problematic for two reasons. First, it does not allow room for a self-reflection that brings its own prejudices to the fore. Second, it has an overly simplistic account of uncovering meaning, meaning that may have been established through a now hidden violence.[102] Janz then brings Tsenay Serequeberhan and his work *The Hermeneutics of African Philosophy* into the discussion, arguing the core difference between Okere and Serequeberhan is that "Okere wants a hermeneutic method (he says as much in taking Ricoeur's path) which will *apply to* the African situation. Serequeberhan wants a hermeneutic that *grows from* lived African experience."[103] Janz considers neither author to have adequately dealt with essential aspects of particularized hermeneutics. He avers "While I have been arguing all along that theory bears the marks of its own history, the answer is not to adjust the parts of the theory that are inconvenient. This is to regard hermeneutics as a method, with a particular set of assumptions and outcome. But if Gadamer is right, hermeneutic philosophy begins exactly where method ends."[104]

As Janz later comments, "The either/or of African tradition vs. Western modernity cannot be solved simply by reversing the binary opposition and favoring tradition over modernity."[105] What is needed instead, this suggests, is a critical engagement that recognizes the hegemony of Western modernity, acknowledges the force of some of its insights, yet avoids according it the privileged position it has previously arrogated.

Robert Bernasconi also takes up the question of foundations. He notes that while the African critique will be similar to the internal critique of European philosophy it will always be different, and this difference is to the extent of the differing existential situations. He picks up Masolo's point that

---

Okere, *African Philosophy*, 82ff.

100. Janz, "Alterity, Dialogue, and African Philosophy," 224. Referring to Okere, *African Philosophy*, 88.

101. Janz, "Alterity, Dialogue, and African Philosophy," 224.

102. This follows in the footsteps of Hountondji, "Comments on Contemporary African Philosophy."

103. Janz, "Alterity, Dialogue, and African Philosophy," 226, emphasis original.

104. Ibid., 228.

105. Ibid., 229.

philosophy begins from experience and is therefore a personal perspective. Africans were originally relegated to the pre-philosophical. "However, once it is recognized that all philosophies draw on pre-philosophical experience, the old dream of scientific philosophy is *ausgeträumt*, it is exhausted. According to Heidegger, what necessitated fundamental ontology to proceed by existential analysis was the recognition that philosophy arises from and returned to pre-philosophical experience."[106]

He contends that while Derrida tends to overlook this, Levinas does not. "Levinas has also recognized both the pre-philosophical and the non-philosophical sources of his own philosophy . . . [and] shows how the particular experiences of a people, experiences often enshrined within a tradition, can constitute its universal significance."[107]

In this respect it becomes important to recognize the Heideggerian destructive in the pre-colonial and thereby the significance of ethnophilosophy, sage philosophy and the nationalist-ideological philosophy.[108] He goes on to note "the ideas of pre-philosophical and non-philosophical experience as expounded by Heidegger and Levinas open Continental philosophers to the particular value of critiques of Western philosophy written from Africa."[109]

What now remains missing from the account so far given is the promised description of the religious character of the philosophical and cultural situation in Africa. At many points above this was explicitly stated or at least strongly intimated, but it has not yet been given formal expression. In a seminal discussion John Mbiti, in *African Religions and Philosophy* argues that "Africans are notoriously religious, and each people has its own religious system with a set of beliefs and practices. Religion permeates into all the departments of life so fully that it is not easy or possible to isolate."[110]

He later comments "in traditional life there are no atheists."[111] In a similar vein K. A. Busia argues in *Africa in Search of Democracy* that the

---

106. Bernasconi, "African Philosophy's Challenge to Continental Philosophy," 191.

107. Ibid.

108. Cornel West, a former Rorty graduate student at Princeton, has noted the existence of four "major historicist forms of theoretical activity" providing resourcing for "black cultural workers": "Heideggerian *destruction* of the Western metaphysical tradition, Derridean *deconstruction* of the Western philosophical tradition, Rortian *demythologization* of the Western intellectual tradition and Marxist, Foucaultian feminist, antiracist or antihomophobic *demystification* of Western cultural and artistic conventions." West, *Keeping Faith*, 21.

109. Bernasconi, "African Philosophy's Challenge to Continental Philosophy," 192.

110. Mbiti, *African Religions and Philosophy*, 1.

111. Ibid., 38.

cultural heritage of Africa is "intensely and pervasively religious . . ." and that "in traditional African communities, it was not possible to distinguish between religious and nonreligious areas of life. All life was religious."[112] G. Parrinder in *African Traditional Religion* notes that many colonial administrators made reference to the Africans as "this incurably religious people . . ."[113]

A picture emerges, from both African and colonial figures alike, of Africans as traditionally being indelibly religious and, implicitly, of this still being so in the contemporary milieus of Africa. The thesis that this situation still pertains today on a widespread basis is not easy to establish for against this view must be weighed the perspective offered for example by Gyekye in his essay "Philosophy, Culture, and Technology in the Postcolonial." Here he argues "Yet, despite the alleged religiosity of the African cultural heritage, the empirical orientation or approach to most of their enterprises was very much to the fore. I strongly suspect that even the African knowledge of God in the traditional setting was, in the context of the non-revealed religion of traditional Africa, empirically reached."[114]

But here the qualifier 'non-revealed' becomes extremely important because there is a strong implication here of it arriving in some religious guise, a prospect he could very easily have removed by using more direct language. His point rather becomes something more like that it did not arrive through anything akin to one of the formal religions like Christianity or Islam. A great deal in fact hinges on how he understands and therefore uses the term 'empirical' since he seems to intend it as a phenomenological statement; however it could, as currently stated, easily be understood from within a religious context.[115] That he is relying on a humanist perspective is clearly

---

112. Busia, *Africa in Search of Democracy*, first quote p. 1 and second quote p. 7.

113. G. Parrinder, *African Traditional Religion*, 9.

114. Gyekye, "Philosophy, Culture, and Technology in the Postcolonial," 27. See also Gyekye, *Tradition and Modernity*, 24ff. The idea of empirical knowledge guiding Gyekye here is inextricably Western in character, especially when compared with African "grass roots" understandings in which "empirical" or concrete referents become the catalyst for reflections on God and Jesus. Kwame Bediako's example, based on the "spontaneous adoration of Jesus by an illiterate Ghanaian Christian woman, Christina Afua Gyan, better known as Afua Kuma . . ." illustrates this. She develops a theology predicated on images like grinding stones, cutlasses, hunters, lions, water, vipers, and so on. Bediako, *Theology and Identity*, 8–15.

115. Which is precisely what Kwame Bediako argues with respect to John V. Taylor's very similar argument that "the African primal world [does not] need a transcendent God. It is *this* life, *this* existence and its concerns, its cares, its joys which are the focus of African primal religions." Emphasis original. Refer Bediako, *Jesus and the Gospel in Africa*, 91. At p. 92 he shows how this can be reconciled with a religious perspective in a way that makes sense also of the argument presented by Gyekye.

evident from the generally anti-religious tenor of his surrounding argument, but despite this he nonetheless struggles to emphatically articulate the phenomenological point such that the possibility of an inherently religious foundation to African social life becomes completely removed from view.

Given this equivocation in the countering position it is not surprising, other than to Western eyes, to see a growing consensus emerging around the notion of the presumed religiosity of the African, of philosophy and also of culture. Those philosophers conceiving of philosophy as a second order discipline are not surprisingly disputing this conception of the situation; however their articulate rebuttals struggle to deal with the empirical question Gyekye stumbles over. In counterpoint to these proposals theologians such as Kwame Bediako are constructing their projects on the first order lived religious experience of the African people and it is therefore his project that the remainder of this chapter describes.

Kwame Bediako
and an African Christian Account of Culture

In 1992 Kwame Bediako published his 1983 doctoral thesis under the title *Theology and Identity: The Impact of Culture upon Christian Thought in the Second Century and in Modern Africa*. As the title highlights Bediako is interested in juxtaposing contemporary African Christianity and second-century Christianity with a view to exploring what he perceives to be their congenial cultural and religious frameworks. His interest is in understanding how the interaction of the gospel and culture is conceived within these two theological landscapes, a goal Bediako pursues by considering how Christian identity is shaped and expressed in these contexts. The category of identity is therefore his hermeneutical key. The most obvious question this conjunction raises, given the presence of a strong and enduring Christian church in the West, is why Bediako would consider second-century Christianity the best dialogue partner for engaging with modern African Christian scholarship.

It will be argued here that perhaps the main reason for this choice is how each context conceives of and therefore defines the notion of culture. Importantly, it is recognized that Bediako does not explicitly argue this specific point because he is writing for altogether different purposes, nevertheless it is suggested that the view is integral to his argument—woven into its very fabric. The following therefore begins with a close analysis of the argument he does pursue in order to determine what it reveals about his underlying understanding of culture. There is a particular concentration of material on this topic within the introduction and first chapter; hence these will form the initial focus of investigation. From there the flow of his argument, as it relates to this question, throughout the remainder of his book will be briefly examined before attention is turned to his other published works bearing on this question.

What this analysis will highlight is that the underlying reason for Bediako selecting the second-century context as a foil for the African one is their similar conception of the religious character of culture. While the two contexts understand this framework in different ways they are nonetheless joined in their explicit avowal of a religious underpinning. The second-century espousal of this will only be examined to the extent it deals with this specific proposal since the primary interest of this chapter is in the African perspective. What concurrently emerges from this analysis is an understanding of how Bediako conceives of culture and this quite naturally leads into a discussion of his theological framework for culture. Bediako begins on the basis of the philosophical schema just outlined and then builds his case from there.

In terms of his doctoral dissertation then, from early on Bediako seeks to distinguish the work of African theologians from that undertaken by their Western counterparts in the same way as many of the authors described above did. His introduction begins with two juxtaposed claims. The first draws on a comment by Adrian Hastings that "the chief non-Biblical reality with which the African theologian must struggle is the non-Christian religious tradition of his own people . . ."[116] The second is that despite claims "About the links between African theology and Western theology, the departure of the modern African theological interest from modern Western theology could not be more pronounced."[117] In large part the reason for this departure was the failure of European academics to take seriously the importance of the African religious tradition.

Bediako then comments,

> even though Africa's theologians would make use of categories of description inherited from the Western Christian theological tradition, they were obviously setting themselves to give to the African pre-Christian religious heritage an interpretation which the European missionary understanding of Africa was, on the whole, unable to achieve. The real significance of modern

---

116. Bediako, *Theology and Identity*, 1.
117. Ibid., 2.

African theological writing lies in the attitude that is taken towards the African religious past.[118]

This is a programmatic statement for Bediako's attitude towards the Western Christian theological tradition. At one level, evidenced throughout his writings, Bediako is deeply concerned about the effect of European attitudes, especially those that gave rise to the specific missiological approaches employed during missionary engagement with African culture (the dominant trend of the 1910 Edinburgh World Mission Conference being a notable example). Beneath this trenchant critique however can be found a deeper, tacit concern with the "spirit of the times"; namely with a widespread Western theological deferral to social theories predicated upon enlightenment ideals.

In light of this it can be suggested that his support of certain statements made by other theologians speaks more deeply into the Western theological consciousness than is generally thought. For example, he agrees with Bishop Bengt Sundkler that "A theologian who with the Apostle is prepared to become to the Jews as a Jew, to them that are without the law, as without law, and *therefore*, unto Africans as an African, must needs start with the fundamental facts of the African interpretation of existence and the universe."[119]

He therefore affirms efforts at "rehabilitating Africa's rich cultural heritage and religious consciousness" conducted as "self-consciously Christian and theological" efforts for these reflect "the true character of African Christian identity." The key is therefore in how this "true character" is defined. For Bediako it is not in the traditional socio-anthropological cultural terms endemic to Western discourse, but rather in the language of religion, and inherently so. Bediako argues "the traditional religions of Africa belong to the African religious past; but this is not so much a chronological past as an 'ontological' past."[120]

African identity is therefore anchored by him in a religious ontology that expresses the 'religious consciousness' of Africans. When conjoined with the Christian profession of faith this becomes a single articulation of faith and life, at once cultural and historical. The African Christian therefore accounts for their faith in terms of both these aspects, creating thereby a genuine "unity of self" founded on an essential "integrity in conversion." But what does he mean by "unity of self" and how can this be related to the African religious heritage as an ontological foundation? According to Bediako this cannot be described in any terms other than theological ones. He suggests that

118. Ibid.
119. Ibid., 3, emphasis original.
120. Ibid., 4.

> it is precisely on the question of the validity of applying Christian theological categories to the elucidation of African religious experience, that the debate over "African Theology" has been most intense. Thus, whereas sociological, anthropological, as well as purely phenomenological approaches have generally been welcomed, theological perspectives have tended to be treated with suspicion.[121]

Bediako does not simply jettison the various devices of Western scholarship for he does recognize their usefulness. Like Barth however, they are not assigned the ontologically grounded role they normally enjoy in Western intellectualism but rather take on a much reduced hermeneutic application, much like Scharen's deployment of ethnography in the wake of Milbank or Barth's model of worldview. For Bediako it is central to his case that such devices lack ontological grounding in the way the secular West would normally conceive things since, following Harold Turner, the appropriate foundation for Africa is a distinctively religious one.

The presupposition that the world is grounded by a religious ontology is the basic fact that orients all of his discussion, forming the central bridge linking his two contexts. He argues that identity in second-century Greco-Roman culture was built on the same basic premise and for this reason offers a truly comparable model for comparison. By turning to this religious and cultural stratum he is effectively bypassing the effects of secular presuppositions. By concentrating on original documents from this period he is also able to mitigate somewhat the influence of secular perspectives conveyed through associated secondary scholarship. Having established this framework he then turns his attention to a consideration of his key question, namely an examination of "the Christians response to the religious past as well as to the cultural tradition generally in which one stands, and the significance of that response for the development of theological answers to the culturally rooted questions of the context."[122]

When stated in this way an underlying confusion in Bediako's work is brought to the fore that must first be negotiated. There is evident in this quote a bifurcation between culture and religion, one that occasionally surfaces throughout his corpus. This is difficult to explain because it is clear that the majority of the time he wants to hold them as inseparable elements constitutive of the same reality. Perhaps the best explanation for this can be found in his background for he received a thoroughly Western education that included two doctorates. The first he received from the University

121. Ibid.
122. Ibid., 7.

of Bordeaux in France and his second from the University of Aberdeen in Scotland, the latter being completed under the tutelage of Andrew Walls.[123] With this extensive exposure to Western thought patterns in mind it is plausible to suggest some slippage from time to time into key tenets of the Western intellectual milieu that informed his thinking for so long, however much he may have sought to exorcise its excesses.

Nevertheless, it will become clear in the ensuing discussion that this is indeed a slippage, an aberration relative to the weight of evidence from across his corpus that his intent was to hold the poles of culture and religion together. Perhaps the key discussion that brings this out occurs when he considers issues related to the question of how superstition and religion relate to each other. He notes that Suetonius and the younger Pliny pejoratively labeled the nascent Christian movement *superstitio*. Initially Christianity enjoyed the protection afforded by Jewish identity because the Romans considered it a sect of Judaism. Over time this began to change because Christianity continued to grow, in the process of which it also began to establish a distinctive identity. For a number of reasons to be covered soon this became problematic. The genesis of pagan hostility towards Christians, according to Bediako, as demonstrated by the sanctions imposed for allegedly causing the fire of Rome in AD64, can therefore be traced to the emergence of a particular religious identity.

The key in this argument for present purposes comes when he is explaining the importance of the Roman distinction between superstition and religion for this emergent Christian identity. Bediako launches an inquiry into the Roman understanding of *superstitio* that necessarily requires a treatment of the underlying religious sensibility of the Roman Empire giving rise to it. This in turn means he discusses at some depth the basic structure of a culture grounded by a religious ontology. Bediako begins by observing that Roman society was structured by a religious ontology that meant religious observance could never be a matter of personal belief or values. Second century piety had both a public and personal element, as Cicero reflects when he argues "No-one shall have gods to himself, either new gods or alien gods, unless recognized by the State. Privately they shall worship those gods whose worship they have duly received from their ancestors."[124]

The importance of this public element to the religious structure of Rome is exhibited by the Romans' national pride in their superior reverence for the gods over the other nations. Hence, "Roman religion was . . .

---

123. For a good but brief background on Bediako refer to the outline provided in Visser and Bediako, "Introduction."

124. Bediako, *Theology and Identity*, 21.

associated with the Imperial mission of Rome, affording sacral sanction for Roman values, *Romanitas*, and its proper observance having far-reaching consequences for the prosperity and advancement of the Commonwealth founded upon the fortunes of the Eternal City."[125]

As this shows, coupled with the notion of maintaining a conjoint sacral and societal alliance was a commitment to the importance of ancestral piety. It was within these broad parameters that the Roman distinction between religion and superstition developed. Bediako comments "In terms of the argument, therefore, true *religio*, right 'reverence for the gods', hence also genuine piety, set forth the appropriate devotion to the traditional gods in accordance with the ideals and social virtues which had been passed on from one generation to the next for centuries."[126]

Here the link between religion and culture is rendered very explicit with religion providing the culture with both its ideals and virtues. Bediako suggests this effectively equates to a variant of what Varro calls a "civil theology" hence the existence of philosophical or other cultural factors are not simply obviated by this proposal, rather it more simply recognizes the primary role that can be attributed to the religious element when trying to understand and describe second-century Roman society.

Having prepared this ground Bediako now begins to consider in more depth the question of superstition and its application to Christians in the Roman Empire. For a general statement of the relationship subsisting between religion and superstition Bediako turns to the writings of Plutarch, especially his *On Superstition*. It is revealing that Plutarch is guided by more "than the social and cultural differences between Graeco-Romans and barbarians, and the divergences in their religious practices." Instead of this generally neutral position he is useful precisely because of his "deep feeling for religion and his broad sympathies with every well-held religious tradition, wherever it may be found . . ." which means he is described as "a persistent defender of the claims of the inherited religion and piety . . ."[127]

Plutarch argues true religion can be distinguished from the "cognate evils" of atheism and superstition, both of which are grounded in an essential ignorance regarding the gods. While cognates, these associated evils are nonetheless distinguishable in that atheism is an intellectual error whereas superstition is associated with unnecessary emotion and hence is further vilified. This does not affect the end ruling in the sense that because

---

125. Ibid., 22. Refer in support of these assertions regarding the cultic practices and beliefs of the Roman Empire to Trebilco, *The Early Christians in Ephesus*.

126. Bediako, *Theology and Identity*, 23.

127. Ibid., 25 for all quotes in this paragraph.

true religion is linked with practical ethical ends both are ultimately to be charged with impiety. As Bediako notes, this charge "is at one with the general Roman suspicion of religious groups whose practices were at odds with Roman ancestral custom and so were considered not to promote genuine religion."[128] He approvingly notes Robert Wilkin's comments that the terms superstition and impiety carried both cultural and religious overtones, forming together an inherent aspect of the prevalent public religion.

It is against this background of Roman religion and piety that Bediako considers the specific situation of the Christians within the Empire. He notes that from the Roman point of view the Christians were susceptible to both charges through their denial of the ancestral gods, as evidenced by their lack of participation in the cult of the Emperor. The historical continuance of these charges is evidence of the continuing prevalence of this same cultural religious affection. He notes second-century examples such as Celsus, who "was no cold rationalist, and his opposition to Christianity arose out of the philosophical strand of Graeco-Roman religious piety which accepted the existence of a supreme God along with a host of subordinate supernatural powers without seeking to reconcile them."[129]

Here again Bediako's concern to safeguard the religious character of the culture is clearly evident. The quote highlights the way philosophical critiques were founded in a rationalist framework but *not* one congenial to contemporary secular understandings. They were instead initiated from within an overwhelmingly religious context, albeit this represented a form of cultural or state religion. He finds affirmation of this thesis in the work of J. Vogt, who argues "in the final analysis the eventual state persecution of Christians could be fully understood only in terms of the nature of Graeco-Roman 'religiosity' . . ."[130]

Bediako also engages a discussion of this theme from the Christian perspective, from which point of view an essential similarity can be found in that the conjoining of national identity and religion is presupposed. The experience of conversion for Christians was not the comparatively simple transfer of values so characteristic of contemporary Western examples but instead "a vindication of the dimension of the distinctiveness of personality in Christ, and a radical challenge to the 'ontocracy' of Graeco-Roman *religio*. The Christian stance, therefore, amounted to confrontation of the

---

128. Ibid., 27.

129. Ibid., 28.

130. Ibid., 29. Bediako goes on to note "Religion in Graeco-Roman paganism . . . existed as an intrinsic aspect of social organization . . . its essential element was the practice and the sanctity of custom hallowed by preceding generations." Ibid., 30.

spirit of classical Paganism, the religion of culture, with the culture of religion."[131]

This last point is fundamental both for Bediako and for this chapter. What Bediako is driving at is the need to recognize that the Christian challenge to the Roman Empire arose as a direct result of its distinctive *Christian* identity. What was so important about this identity however was not that it represented a new *polis, oikos,* or other social structure *per se* but that it presented an alternative religious understanding that framed the world in an entirely different religious way.[132] In this respect it is not really the case that "the religion of culture" is being confronted by the "culture of religion" but that two distinctive religions are coming into conflict.[133]

This same underpinning logic can be seen in the way Christian identity was expressed through a tripartite schema in the second century. Bediako explicitly takes this up when discussing the Christian movement as the third race. Paul in 1 Corinthians 10:32 divides humanity into three divisions: Jews, Greeks, and the people of God, the latter representing an embracing of the previous two in as much as it represents the new grade of humanity, though it also thereby provides a contrast. The Gospel of John describes it slightly differently. From John 4:21 onwards John describes humanity according to a tripartite division that divides according to Samaritans (those lacking true understanding and knowledge); Jews (those with access to understanding but an erroneous and/or inadequate conception of it); and finally, Christians (who worship the Father in spirit and in truth). Notably, irrespective of the specifics of the formulation referred to "It is this triple division, *on the grounds of religion and worship,* which comes to form the basis for the development of Christian self-consciousness in the Graeco-Roman world."[134]

That this framework remains a self-conscious element of Christian identity in the second century is clear from surviving records. Three important writings from within early Hellenistic Christian apologetics point to this: the anonymous *The Preaching of Peter,* especially given the way Clement

131. Ibid., 31–32.

132. "[T]hat the historical development of the Christian religion during the early centuries witnesses to more than the interaction of Graeco-Roman and Christian *ideas* ... [it was] ... to establish an authentic Christian identity within their culture, meaningful both for them and for the world as it was then known." Ibid., 33, emphasis original.

133. His use of the phrase "religion of culture" here is understandable, both for its value as rhetorical embellishment and as a convenient summary of a certain lineage of thought, however it also constitutes "slippage," as noted earlier, into one of the Western categories he is otherwise working hard to resist. It therefore represents a less than ideal formulation of the point.

134. Bediako, *Theology and Identity,* 36. Emphasis mine.

of Alexandria uses it; *Diognetus*; and the *Apology of Aristides*. These would also seem to form the background of a positive conception still present in the Latin Christian literature of the mid-third century, namely the Pseudo-Cyprianic tract, *De Pascha Computus*. Bediako infers from this that "There is no question of separation from the rest of mankind, but of distinction from erroneous and misguided conceptions of Deity and worship. Christians are not fundamentally alien to the world, neither are they opposed to society as a whole. They simply believe differently about God and they conduct themselves differently, that is, with moral excellence and love."[135]

Christians did not always use the term in this positive manner however. By the third century Tertullian was forced to argue against notions of a *tertium genus* because it was being used as a term of abuse against Christians. However even within this pejorative context it is important to note that the underlying religious thrust remained the same. Bediako notes "The term was therefore employed to distinguish Christians from devotees of Roman religion and from Jews . . ."[136]

Bediako finishes off these initial discussions by considering the problem of Greek philosophy. Central to his argument once again is the religious background in which both Christian and philosophic thinking was embedded. He argues the early apologists came to present a Christian faith that was philosophic in nature however the conception of philosophy at play here is best understood with reference to the earlier distinction between religion and superstition. In the background there lingers the attempt to reconcile the Christian faith to the Greco-Roman religious foundations in a way that allowed the Christians to present themselves as the purveyors of true piety.

Hence Bediako comments "The goal of the Christian effort became essentially identical with the philosophical religion of Lucius Annaeus Seneca: 'Philosophy's sole function is to discover the truth about things divine and things human. From her side, religion never departs, nor duty, nor justice, nor any of the whole company of virtues which cling together in close united fellowship. Philosophy has taught us to worship that which is divine, to love that which is human . . .'"[137]

Philosophy is here depicted, in *both* its pagan and Christian conceptions, as always at the service of divine thinking. Rationality and philosophy in this milieu are not forerunners of contemporary Western secular

---

135. Ibid., 37. He further argues, underscoring the point already previously made that "the distinctions are made on the basis of religion—specifically, the conception of Deity and the manner of worship." Ibid., 38.

136. Ibid., 39.

137. Ibid., 42, quoting Seneca.

understandings for they emanate from and express an altogether different cosmology, one very similar to the African conceptualization outlined above. Both contexts display similar degrees and structuring of religious affections, and together differ markedly from the modern Western framework at precisely this point.

Bediako explicitly states this when he comments that these attempts to reconcile Christian thinking with Hellenistic philosophy "were still operating within a unified framework of the religious quests of their time, since the philosophy they meant was virtually a religion—the religion of the educated and thoughtful people."[138] The patristic material is therefore considered very relevant to the African context by Bediako, but not because it forms a link for envisaging some primitive conception of philosophy and theology through which Africa must travel in order to achieve a Western style framework as Ikuenobe had suggested (refer above). Instead it forms an exploitable link because it presents a description of one way in which a Christian community had developed a properly theological response to its own pre-Christian heritage; a response that "has tended to be assessed by the criteria of social anthropology, and so has been generally misunderstood."[139]

This perspective underwrites a substantial portion of Bediako's critical views on Western scholarship and his positive affirmation of certain African theological endeavors. He deplores, for example, the presumption of Western value setting that has guided so much of the faith engagement with Africa, a point he underscores through an analysis of Raoul Allier.[140] The target here is European evolutionary thinking as it has pervaded the African experience of the social sciences and, through this mechanism, Western theology. Of course tacit in this is a wider objection to the European understanding of reality when it is posited as the appropriate guide for African descriptions; it wrongly traffics in a disputable universality.

For Bediako reliance on this framework proved historically disastrous for Africa in that the missionary encounter with Africa was structured around an overly simplistic application of this model. He effectively suggests that, using a broad characterization admittedly, the encounter stumbled because the Christian faith was equated to a Western civilization that already had the seeds of secular subversion implanted deep within it.[141]

138. Ibid., 436.
139. Ibid., 438.
140. Ibid., 235ff.

141. This is a point that recurs throughout Bediako's corpus, one whose cumulative effect distorts by its lack of balance. For example he elsewhere identifies three reasons for the problematic, first the initial, "dark" image of Africa propagated by the first European explorers; second the intellectual frame of reference permeating European

From the numerous problems this approach engenders he singles out one for particular attention. If conversion to Christianity meant also a Westernization then the prospects of developing a genuinely African Christian identity, one understood to be an indigenous articulation of faith building on and reacting back upon an underlying African identity, are bleak.

This line of thinking is most readily evident in his consideration of the African theologian Bolaji Idowu. Bediako argues on the basis of his work

> that the essential and constitutive element in an authentic African Christianity is not found in the latter's historical connection with European or Western Christianity, missionary history notwithstanding. Rather, it is to be found in the direct, deliberate and self-conscious appropriation of Jesus Christ as a living and present reality experienced in African terms. This principle sets aside the "tyranny of structural heredity" exercised by Western traditions of Christianity over those African Christian communities which have come into existence through their instrumentality.[142]

For Bediako the heart of Idowu's theology is his understanding of Africans, "*who in all things* are religious"[143] In Idowu's writings the center of culture is not as it appears in Western descriptions but is instead located in the inherently religious nature of what the term culture is describing, and especially of African culture. At its core this culture is religious and must accordingly be addressed in these rather than other terms. Bediako comments, "By reducing the culture he is intent on vindicating to its core—religion, Idowu is able to identify this fundamental element as African Traditional Religion..."[144]

The explanation of this religious background by Idowu reads something like a modified Vichian Judaism. Rather than African traditional religions perpetuating some form of polytheistic religious background, as is so often thought, Idowu suggests they offer a modified form of monotheism, a

---

thinking at the time; and third, the pervasive self identification of Europe as Christendom. Refer Bediako, "Biblical Christologies," 82–84. There does need to be some balance in this analysis though, see both Newbigin, "The Enduring Validity of Cross-Cultural Mission," 50, and Kaplan, "The Africanization of Missionary Christianity," 166–67. They argue the need for recognizing positive elements in the encounter that are often neglected in the overly pessimistic readings of mission history by many scholars. For a similar point though argued differently, providing also a very challenging critique of even these positive "moments" see Sanneh, "The Horizontal and the Vertical in Mission."

142. Bediako, *Theology and Identity*, 276.
143. Ibid., 284, quoting Idowu, emphasis original.
144. Ibid., 284.

diffused monotheism. This means that the multitude of divine beings in the African pantheon actually represent various refractions of the one Supreme Being. Idowu is not content to simply predicate this of his own Yoruba background but is instead intent upon locating it within the broader ambit of continental Africa's religious consciousness. It is revealing in this respect that African Traditional Religion is most often framed in the singular, although this question remains an enduring query within African religious research. Bediako therefore argues, along with Mbiti, that "the Christian Gospel, far from being opposed to African religious ideas is, in fact, the crowning fulfillment of African religiosity."[145]

Mbiti also contends that African life is permeated by a religious consciousness that is its ground, constituting force and sustaining influence. Mbiti has argued extensively against the tendency for African life to be depicted according to the mores of Western secular scholarship as embodied by the work of anthropologists and sociologists. For the African, he argues, life is inherently religious and must therefore be described theologically rather than anthropologically. Bediako comments, with reference to Mbiti's important book *African Religions and Philosophy* that "Mbiti posits the methodological principle that "a study of these religious systems is therefore, ultimately, a study of the peoples themselves in all the complexities of both traditional and modern life."[146]

For Bediako it is therefore the case that this record of religion is really an account of the African within their cultural context. An enforced separation of religion from culture in this context is by the very nature of the case impossible; a bifurcation that completely destabilizes its respective terms. The depth of the African religious sensibility is for Bediako captured somewhat in Mbiti's book *Concepts of God in Africa* where Mbiti asserts rather than feels forced to prove the presence of this sensibility. For Mbiti it is the case that "religion is probably the most profound and the richest part of the cultural heritage of the African peoples."[147] Mbiti goes on to note that while the African traditional religions and their associated concepts have not been codified in the way Western religions have been there is nonetheless overwhelming evidence of spiritual literacy.

Bediako quotes Mbiti to this effect: "To assert, however, that they have 'no faith' in God, would be absolute nonsense, and there are no atheists in traditional African societies. An Ashanti proverb seems to summarise the

---

145. Ibid., 310.
146. Ibid., 318.
147. Ibid., 321.

situation well; it says, 'No one shows a child the Supreme Being,' because even the child knows of God almost automatically by instinct."[148]

Not surprisingly this leads both Mbiti and Bediako to elucidate a theme already covered by the earlier discussions on Barth. Bediako asserts that Jesus Christ "came to make man so totally and absolutely religious that no department of man should be left untouched by His Lordship, no department should be left outside the relationship between creature and Creator, between man and God, between the child and the heavenly Father."[149]

At all points therefore the central engagement of the African with the gospel is not one between humanity and religion, as it is so often depicted in the West, but between African humanity in the fullness of its ongoing religiosity and Jesus Christ. African theologians are therefore not generally approaching African Traditional Religions in the same way an anthropologist or the historian of religion does. For them it is a living element of their culture that appropriately calls them to adopt theological language and to follow a specifically theological perspective when describing it.

It is clear from the preceding that the religious nature of culture is a pervasive theme in Bediako's doctoral thesis, one he continues to return to in his later writings as well. For example he has pursued it quite vigorously in his book *Jesus and the Gospel in Africa*, offering there a similarly concentrated focus to that sketched out above. The essays forming Part II, "Theology and Culture" are notable in this regard; most of which directly and explicitly seek to advance ideas first set out in his doctoral thesis. For example his essay "Understanding African Theology in the Twentieth Century" begins by critiquing the view put forward by Adrian Hastings that the notion of an African traditional religion predating the modern Christian era reflects an unhealthily introspective recounting of an imagined past.[150]

Once again the hermeneutical rubric by which he navigates this is identity and the ontological foundation he relies on is the religious nature of humanity, and hence culture. So also the same target is engaged, namely

---

148. Ibid.

149. Ibid., 330, quoting from Mbiti here. See also p. 345 n. 156 where Bediako includes an extensive quote from p. 1 of John Mbiti's article "Christianity in East African culture and religion": "The whole of African life as a religious phenomenon, and every person who comes into this world is, *ipso facto*, a religious being: he cannot run away from that, and he cannot reject it because he belongs to a religious phenomenon and a religious community. Long before he is born, at his birth, through has initiation rites, in marriage and procreation, at death and burial, and in the life after death—all through this long journey, he is involved in a religious drama. His vocabulary, has thought-forms, his actions, and every portion of his life, is a participation in a religious experience."

150. Bediako, *Jesus and the Gospel in Africa*, 49.

a Western predilection for religious neutrality that must be understood to enter the African context only as an extraneous factor for "Once it is granted that African theology's investigations into African primal religions are qualitatively different from the observations of anthropologists, it becomes possible to appreciate how, by its fundamental motivation, African theology may have been charting a new course in theological method."[151]

In this he discerns a further potential task for African theology in reacting back upon the West by reminding it of its own primal heritage "For the African vindication of the theological significance of African primal religions may indicate that the European primal heritage was not illusory, to be consigned to oblivion as primitive darkness."[152] He tellingly concludes this discussion by commenting "The primal world view may turn out to be not so alien to the West after all, even in a post-Enlightenment era."[153] Bediako points to the resurgence of the occult as an indicator that this heritage may not be as distant from the contemporary West as scholars tend to suggest, to which might be added the internally consistent philosophical "turn to religion" evident in Derrida (as covered in the introduction).

Culture as Life, Lived Religiously

Contemporary African culture is at all points, for Bediako, animated and oriented by a religious core in the same way that second-century Roman society was. Just as modern Western scholars tend to minimize or sideline this Western heritage, so too they try to obviate the African religious tradition. He argues this tendency must be resisted because it obliterates the most significant feature of African culture. In contradistinction to this trend he advocates recognition of the inherent importance of the religious perspective and of the need for adopting a fundamentally theological perspective on culture. The use of identity as his hermeneutical key points to this, demonstrating how the religious factor enters into the very heart of the human existential and social condition.

For Bediako living necessarily entails "living religiously" hence "Because primal world-views are fundamentally religious, the primal imagination restores to theology the crucial dimension of living religiously for which the theologian needs make no apology. The primal imagination may help us restore the ancient unity of theology and spirituality."[154]

151. Ibid., 53.
152. Ibid., 59.
153. Ibid., 59, see also p. 95.
154. Ibid., 95.

Culture in a Post-Secular Context

Any analysis of culture must of necessity recognize this factor, a requirement that can only be fulfilled by adopting a thoroughly theological perspective on culture, as indeed Bediako, Barth, and Milbank each suggest.

Conclusion

THEOLOGICAL AND MISSIOLOGICAL PROJECTS from a variety of backgrounds have tended to use the concept of culture as if it were a theologically neutral concept, an approach that effectively devolves into the appropriation of secular definitions of culture. In many cases these projects were unwittingly building into their analyses an underlying preference for an immanent understanding of reality antithetical to their own emphasis on a transcendent perspective. That this has occurred without much debate or even, in most cases, without recognition of the disjunction involved or the associated difficulties accruing from this, is worrying. This book sought to address the situation in two ways: first, by suggesting the need for distinctively theological models of the concept of culture, and second, by noting the presence of three existing theological models that could act as exemplars for this task.

The key model was John Milbank's. He argues for a poetic theology, a theology that takes seriously the metaphoric origins of human language, history, and law (to borrow categories from his analysis of Vico) or, in short, culture. He further argues that God can be approached through one of three ways: ontology (the God who is), epistemology (the God who knows), and culture (the God who is infinite poetic utterance and reciprocity). The avenue of culture is accessed through two divine transcendentals (only within infinite divinity are metaphors not foreclosed; this latter error being the key characteristic of the philosophic transcendentals). The first is *verbum*. This is to do with human making and production, encompassing all that humanity creates. Milbank conceives this as human participation in the infinite *poesis* of God such that culture is intrinsically anchored in divinity, or more properly, in the Trinity.

This Trinitarian anchor reflects the relational character of both divine and human making, as well as the necessarily relational character of *donum*, the second divine transcendental. Culture is also human participation in infinite reciprocity; hence the idea of gift exchange is central. As with *poesis*, so too with reciprocity, the human effort inherently reflects what is infinitely occurring within the Godhead. The concept of culture, in this view, originates in God and is always moving towards its consummation in God. It is therefore teleological, always oriented towards the infinite possibility constantly opening before humanity as a result of god's gift of *poesis* and reciprocity to humanity.

In short, the concept of culture captures what it is to be human; what it is to be made in the image of God and also what it is to live this image out in light of an eschatological horizon. Culture is everything that humanity does; an "everything" that always flows in some way from the initial gift of life bestowed by Creator God. In other words, it reflects human attunement towards and effort to express the divine, however inadequately this may actually be achieved. For Milbank the truest expression of culture is therefore found in the church, although more particularly in liturgy, for it is here that humanity and divinity commune, that Christ is imaged most clearly. From this source there springs a *praxis* that reaches into the community at large, both as an expression of "true" culture and as a reading of all human cultural efforts.

Perhaps one way to describe Milbank's ecclesial framework is to borrow somewhat from the framework offered by Lesslie Newbigin. The church, it might be suggested, can be seen as an anticipation of the eschatological community and is therefore a foretaste of it. It is also therefore a sign in two senses. First, it is teleological hence always pointing towards the future perfect consummation of humanity. Second, it is always pointing towards the triune God that is its source and sustenance. The church is also an instrument, enacting in this world true community, as best it can, in such a way as to influence human communities to embrace their true identity— relational beings in the image of their Creator. For Milbank the empirical expression of this is problematic in that it is often such a dim refraction of the authentic and true. Yet, ideally, and somewhat sporadically in practice, the church represents and hence refracts true culture. Culture, as this demonstrates, is something that Milbank cannot conceive of or understand except as a response to Divinity, hence it is an intrinsically theological topic only accessible to theological investigation, although certain traditional social scientific analyses can play a useful, subsidiary empirical role.

When stated in this way it becomes clear that Milbank and Barth are not as different from each other as they may first appear. To mention just a few of the various possibilities, there is in Milbank an essential affirmation of what Barth fundamentally seeks to convey—the sheer creatureliness of humanity and the appropriateness of this status in the face of human efforts to escape it. Allied to this are their respective assertions regarding foundations: that the church rests on a confessional foundation fundamentally orientating every created thing, or in other words—the whole world. It is even possible to argue for a potential cross-over in their understanding of how pagan religiosity comes to expression. Milbank's reliance on Vico's metaphoric analysis of Jove and therefore pagan religiosity comes very close to the admittedly deleted analysis of the gods of other religions as the "offspring" of the true God for Barth.[1]

Karl Barth's account of culture is grounded in the sheer creatureliness of humanity and the relationship to God this implies. In his schema culture is humanity and humanity is culture, as it also was for Milbank. Culture is currently subjected to the claims of sin but Jesus Christ has broken into this situation by restoring to humanity its original status within creation. Through His reconciling work humanity and therefore culture have had the promises inherent in creation restored to them and a consequent teleology renewed. Humanity has been restored, reflecting its true current status, and is being restored, representing its present task. Culture is heading towards its eschatological perfection (redemption offering both assurance and limit—certainty of attainment and the nature of what is to be attained, magnificent creatureliness).

The instrument deployed for this task is the church, the body of Christ, understood not in a substantialist sense but through an actualist ontology. As the church acts, so it is in its essence. Its activity is susceptible to earthly-historical enquiry, however this reflects only part of what the church is since it has an invisible component or activity discernible only through faith—the activity of Christ on earth. In this respect, as the actualist ontology already suggests, the church is the earthly-historical existence of Christ. Humanity is hidden in Christ and hence the church is culture already en route to what it is "in Christ." To fully flesh out Barth's actualist stance it is probably best to argue that culture as state is culture as task, albeit the task remains unfinished despite being already eschatologically determined.

There is in this proposal, as in Milbank's, a clear presumption of the universality of the Christian confessional foundation. Culture in both cases is understood as presently subject, to an undetermined degree, to the "annihilating incongruity" of sin, and it is really this aspect of culture that secular instruments of understanding are most attuned to. By contrast, in the

---

1. An analysis of this appears in the unpublished paper presented to a Karl Barth Society annual meeting by Wolf Krötke, "A New Impetus to the Theology of Religions from Karl Barth's Thought." In a section entitled 'Barth's phenomenology of the "gods"' (pp. 9ff.) he draws on material Barth presented during his lectures but which he then decided not to publish—the original §42 of *Church Dogmatics*. The reasons for this deletion, as Krötke suggests, are not known. My thanks go to Paul Metzger for facilitating access to this paper.

proposals outlined in this book, culture is seen as both reconciled and being reconciled, with the church acting as an instrument for this latter aspect by both its work in the world and its example. At this stage it is possible to outline a preliminary Western Christian proposal for understanding culture.

In some respects an outline such as this is not very different from the various socio-cultural definitions of culture considered in the first chapter. For example, definitions examining culture as the "meaning dimension" of humanity, or as the totality of human engagement with the world, or everything that humanity does, or which use myriad other possible constructions of similar generality, are all feasible ways of describing culture even as a theological category. By their very generality they are useful, acting as a vulgar categorization in the vein of Raymond Williams, or as a topical category such as was advocated by Vico and then Milbank. They are ways of organizing the material.

Beyond this point, the situation begins to change markedly from that usually promulgated by the social sciences, whose categories are reinscribed, filled with theological rather than secular content. For example, culture could be examined across three interdependent contexts. First, there is the church in all of its visible and invisible complexity, as manifested through its empirical and idealistic expressions, across temporal and geographic contexts, across its unities and divisions, in recognition of its role as the instrument set apart by God for His purposes here on earth in anticipation of eschatological consummation as the bride of Christ. The church is the purveyor of true humanity, of human participation in triune relations. This is of course a stumbling and weak participation, but it is one that is nonetheless authentic in desire and it is one graced to ultimately succeed, by the mercy of God. This is culture in its redeemed mode, still imperfect on earth and hence in transition towards what it will become, what it eschatologically already is.

Second, there are a range of other human interactions and arrangements that operate within the realm of reconciliation. This refers to a host of human activities involving some form of direct dialogue with the church and with God, though they are not in form or substance church as such. These arrangements and interactions are affirmed and sustained by God, heading towards the heavenward goal and hence partaking of authentic humanity to a significant degree although expressing it very differently from the church. Here there are interminglings with church of various kinds, perhaps oriented around, for example, joint interests in social justice, economic equity or other such similar goals.

There is then a third context, consisting of all other human engagements and social configurations. These are no less authentic in their search for true

Conclusion

humanity or in their desire to live as they were created to be, however there is a stumbling block set between them and their goals—the "annihilating incongruity" described by Barth. Yet in this state there are two core affirmations that hold out hope for understanding—the goodness of creation and the certainty of teleological ordering. These are the ones the church is reaching out to, fulfilling its calling to help humanity towards its true self.

This is but one possible, tentative schema, largely built around categories drawn from Barth although Milbank's category of participation cannot be read as absent or distant from this way of conceiving culture. The process of theologically defining culture is of course a significant and complex task that will take some time and effort, as history so aptly demonstrates. What is set out here is no more than a speculative beginning hinting at some initial, potentially suggestive possibilities. This book primarily sought to establish the possibility that culture might be a theological category in need of theological conceptualization and analysis. The very achievement of this also establishes however, the need for moving this agenda forward through further theoretical and empirical engagement, an undertaking beyond the confines of this present discussion. The task of theologically defining culture therefore remains the primary unfinished element of this book and the central work towards which it points.

It now remains to consider the global context and the possibilities outlined in the discussion of Kwame Bediako and his various suggestions. The controlling paradigm of Bediako's outlook is the inherently religious character of the African life. He describes a world in which culture is grounded by a religious ontology. It is this emphasis that explains his predilection for second-century Latin thinking rather than contemporary Western scholarship as a comparative tool for his examination of the African context. In his investigation of this ancient framework he pays particular attention to true *religio*, essentially arguing it represents what in contemporary Christian Africa amounts to right reverence for God. This he see as core to culture, a point his attention to identity formation makes especially clear. Christian identity, oriented around true *religio*, necessarily structures the world in a particular way. No aspect or element of life is left untouched by religious convictions. Jesus is all in all and is through all.

On the face of it there seems a remarkable continuity between the Western theological proposals set out above and Bediako's suggestion. In both cases culture is examined as a necessary predicate of human identity, an identity understood as grounded, in some sense, in and by a Christian sensibility that permeates everything. All that humanity does therefore falls under the sway of this sensibility and should be considered in this light. There is what some may consider an exclusivist perspective at play, although it is really an acknowledgement of the universal implications inherent in the event of Jesus Christ. What happened in and through this particular divine man is of consequence for the entire world.

There are many points of divergence however but for the purposes of the present analysis it is worth focusing on one specific (potential) divergence. This apparent discontinuity arises because on the face of it Barth eschews the notion of "religion," a construct that Bediako, by contrast, has placed at the very center of his analysis. This would initially seem to suggest a significant disjunction between the two proposals; however appearances can be deceptive. The term "religion" is complex, representing a keenly contested concept. Without delving too much into the debate, this book takes a position that contests the concept structurally, as will be briefly described below. One of the key implications of this for present purposes is the suggestion that Barth and Bediako may not be as distant from each other in their underlying intent as the terminology they deploy might at first suggest. Some observations are in order.

First, it is not obvious that Barth and Bediako are necessarily invoking the same content when using this word. For Bediako it acts as a positive term, describing an inherent human turning towards transcendence. For Barth, it ostensibly embraces a negative connotation, an expression for one aspect of that which within the human sets itself against Yahweh. Second, for Bediako the underlying intent is to describe humanity as being by nature religious rather than to place humanity within religion *per se*, whereas for Barth there is a specific concern with the implications of religion in this second sense. There is more than mere semantics involved in this differentiation.

As Krötke argues, religion for Barth takes its place alongside the idea of worldview.[2] In other words, it facilitates the human objectification of God, providing humanity with a way to domesticate and thereby (in a sense) construct Him. For Bediako however the intent is to express that within humanity which is orientated towards the transcendent object, towards God or gods. It reflects the human concern for and relative alignment with transcendence. Barth was being guided in his thinking by (or, perhaps better, was reacting to) Western intellectualism whereas for Bediako it was African conceptualizations. It would necessitate a chapter in its own right to develop this further however some indication of the issues involved can be briefly chartered with reference to an important study in this field.

Timothy Fitzgerald's *Discourse on Civility and Barbarity: A Critical History of Religion and Related Categories* treats the concept of religion in a way analogous to the treatment of culture in this book. His core concern is

2. Ibid.

writing "a critical history of 'religion' as a category, in the hope of showing that far from being a kind of thing or an objective and observable domain around which an industry of scholarship can flourish, religion is a modern invention which authorises and naturalises a form of Euro-American secular rationality. In turn, this supposed position of secular rationality constructs and authorises *its* 'other,' religion and religions."[3]

No doubt there is slippage in Bediako's treatment of the African religious sensibility in the sense of embracing something of this constructed category; however his general intent, signaled clearly by his decision to use second rather than twenty-first-century thinkers, is to elucidate the endemic presence of transcendence in human life rather than analyse or exploit an object called religion.

Barth's position is much more complex since he is actively engaged in a direct way with the Western construct of "religion" that Fitzgerald is seeking to deconstruct. Barth seeks to subvert or sublimate the term but strikes difficulties in doing so. Some sense of the difficulties involved can be gleaned from his most comprehensive treatment of the concept, *On Religion: The Revelation of God as the Sublimation of Religion*. In this book Barth argues at one point that there is "a relationship between the name Jesus Christ and the Christian religion from the standpoint of its sanctification. It is not by the laws and powers inherent in human religion and therefore in man but rather by virtue of divine endowment and appointment that this particular existence and this particular form will become an event in the midst of the world of human religion."[4]

Just prior to this he had argued "We said that in seeking the basis for asserting the truth of the Christian religion we could, to begin with, only look past the religion itself to the act of God on which it is based . . ."[5] Clearly Barth is wanting to get behind the category of religion, as it were, in order to discern and bring to the fore that which is at the back of it in the Christian case, namely Jesus Christ. His problem is that he remains entangled within the category precisely because of his reliance on it as a construct for conducting the argument in the first place. In this respect Bediako sits closer to Fitzgerald in a way that Barth needs to in order to more fully achieve his purposes.

At this point it should be clear that a potentially significant discussion could usefully be engaged between Barth, Fitzgerald and Bediako on the very idea of religion. There is not space to undertake it here however the

3. Fitzgerald, *Discourse on Civility and Barbarity*, 6, emphasis original.
4. Barth, *On Religion*, 122.
5. Ibid., 123.

material presented above does usefully advance the argument being presented here because the divestment of religion from culture is no longer necessarily the case. Arguably, Bediako's African context provides him with an advantageous understanding, one that the others could usefully deploy in the pursuit of their own projects. The Western propensity for treating culture and religion as separate objects, let alone the tendency to use religion as a way to objectively examine (and thereby control) any transcendent impulses, is no longer a necessary correlate of theological engagement with topics like culture. The two concepts can, and should, be examined together, as seamless rather than cleaved aspects.

This outline of the three proposals would not be complete without also recording the presence of sometimes significant areas of weakness in their suggestions. Milbank is accused of promulgating an optimistic and idealized framework that struggles to find a point of connection with empirical reality. This is most clearly evident in his ecclesiology where the church seems to only very weakly point the way forward for humanity. Scharen begins to address this problem but much more work is still needed here. This might also be affected by what appears to be a weakened Christology in that Milbank downplays the "in Christ" formulation so important to Barth. It is Christ that both ideally and empirically points the way for humanity and by somewhat lessening the emphasis here Milbank correspondingly struggles to articulate how Christ manages this.

Barth, on the other hand, is very good at demonstrating this Christological emphasis but has been accused of the opposite problem, namely a theological determinism. Most critical engagements of Barth locate the problem in his doctrine of election because here he seems to foster an at least implicit universalism, a claim given further credence by his professed agnosticism on the question of universalism. Colin Gunton refers to this as a residual Platonism but points also to the complexity involved in this claim in that Barth at times seems to support the realized eschatology this view requires, while at other times he does not.[6] When this feature of his theology is combined with his weak pneumatology then, as Gunton goes on to argue, following in the footsteps of his mentor Robert Jenson, Christ becomes "a sort of timeless Platonic principle . . ."[7] At this point it can be seen that Barth arrives in a somewhat similar location as Milbank, sporting a similarly weak ecclesial framework with which to drive the empirical expression of temporal culture. Having said this Barth is certainly stronger here than Milbank for he is more optimistic regarding the church and at

---

6. Gunton, *Barth Lectures*, 198–200, 203–5, 226–28.

7. Ibid., 200.

Conclusion

least provides room for the possibility of a more robust doctrine of the Holy Spirit.

Bediako's weaknesses are difficult to determine given the unsystematic nature of his treatment. Despite this gap a few observations are possible. For example, there is a decided tendency towards anthropocentrism that is arguably in need of a full-bodied Christology and pneumatology to support it. Bediako's proposals are developed within and largely also limited to the rubric of identity and while this is an important theological category it lacks the universal application of categories like gift, Christ, and so on. There is also his lack of attention to ecclesiology for it is here that the effects of his concentration on identity will be felt and the implications for culture established. In fairness however, it needs to be recognized that while his proposal appears, in a systematic sense, embryonic relative to the others it also refracts the mores of a context for which systematic reflection is secondary to lived experience. In this respect it deserves to be treated on its own terms.

What clearly emerges from this summary of weaknesses is the need for developing a robust ecclesiology capable of explaining how the church can and should enact its theological framing of culture, as well as its engagement with the understanding of culture presented by the social sciences and allied disciplines. In terms of the former in particular, it would appear the undue attention paid to the secular definitions in the past has diverted Christian resources from the ecclesial task, leaving the church with an impoverished understanding of both its cultural mantle and the practical implementation of it. Scharen's ethnographic proposal presents itself as one feasible way of beginning to address this concern though it remains only a beginning.

This book has traced the ecclesiology of Barth through his most ecclesial moments, concentrating on the points at which he is most involved with the concrete, visible church. There is no slippage into the invisible paradigm for he firmly shuts this door; however it is not entirely clear the extent to which the church is granted a concrete role in the work of God. Stanley Hauerwas is particularly clear on this, using the work of Joseph Mangina to argue that for Barth the church as a social configuration does not seem to make much difference regarding the task of witnessing to Christ. As he notes, Barth at one point argues that the world would certainly be lost without Christ but not necessarily so without the church.[8] The *totus Christus* thesis described earlier would seem on the face of it to address this; however this requires further analysis.

Finally, the question of how these observations are relevant for missiology can be addressed. Most often theology and missiology have both

---

8. Hauerwas, *Grain of the Universe*, 192–93, see also 144–45.

framed their analyses along the lines of a Christ and culture relationship, thereby framing the entire discussion such that these concepts appear to be independent conceptualizations that must somehow, in a separate movement, be related to each other. There is a sense in which this may prove a useful academic tool at some level however it does not and cannot be taken as an expression of the nature of the case. This represents instead the natural inclination of the neutrality thesis which at its very best can only envisage some sort of interdependent dynamic between them.

Contrary to such a view, this book has sought to reflect on culture as a specifically theological category. Christ and culture are not entirely separate or only distantly related concepts since mention of one necessarily invokes and involves the other. Culture, it has been suggested, is humanity, which in turn is "under Christ." Understanding culture necessarily involves specifically theological categories such as Christology, theological anthropology and ecclesiology. Exactly how these are related to the concept and to each other, and how the empirical realities are granted appropriate space within this schema, can only be speculated on at the moment. Certainly the secular efforts at defining were forged over generations so it would be presumptuous to presuppose any lesser timeframe. What this book hopefully makes clear is the possibility that culture might now be set before theology and missiology as a subject to be engaged and a task to be undertaken. Culture now takes shape as a specifically theological topic, one best viewed through an appropriately shaped "theological eye."

Bibliography

Allen, R. Michael. "Putting Suspenders on the World: Radical Orthodoxy as a Post-Secular Theological Proposal or What Can Evangelicals Learn from Postmodern Christian Platonists?" *Themelios* 31.2 (2006) 40–53.
Amato, Peter. "African Philosophy and Modernity." In *Postcolonial African Philosophy: A Critical Reader*, edited by Emmanuel Chukwudi Eze, 71–99. Cambridge: Blackwell, 1997.
Appiah, Anthony. *In My Father's House: Africa in the Philosophy of Culture.* Oxford: Oxford University Press, 1992.
Barth, Karl. "Church and Culture." In *Theology and Church: Shorter Writings*, 334–54 New York: Harper & Row, 1962.
———. *Church Dogmatics. 1/1: The Doctrine of the Word of God: Prolegomena to Church Dogmatics.* Translated by G. T. Thomson et al. Edinburgh: T. & T. Clark, 1936.
———. *Church Dogmatics. 1/2: The Doctrine of the Word of God.* Translated by G. T. Thomson et al. Edinburgh: T. & T. Clark, 1956.
———. *Church Dogmatics. 3/1: The Doctrine of Creation.* Translated by J. W. Edwards et al. Edinburgh: T. & T. Clark, 1958.
———. *Church Dogmatics. 3/3: The Doctrine of Creation.* Translated by G. W. Bromiley et al. Edinburgh: T. & T. Clark, 1960.
———. *Church Dogmatics. 4/1: The Doctrine of Reconciliation.* Translated by G. W. Bromiley et al. Edinburgh: T. & T. Clark, 1956.
———. *Church Dogmatics. 4/2: The Doctrine of Reconciliation.* Translated by G. W. Bromiley. Edinburgh: T. & T. Clark, 1958.
———. *Church Dogmatics. 4/3/1: The Doctrine of Reconciliation.* Translated by G. W. Bromiley. Edinburgh: T. & T. Clark, 1961.
———. *Credo: A Presentation of the Chief Problems of Dogmatics with Reference to the Apostle's Creed.* London: Hodder and Stoughton, 1964.
———. *Dogmatics in Outline.* Translated by G. T. Thomson. London: SCM, 1949.
———. *The Epistle to the Romans.* Translated by Edwyn C. Hoskyns. 6th ed. London: Oxford University Press, 1968.
———. *The Humanity of God.* London: Collins, 1961.
———. *On Religion: The Revelation of God as the Sublimation of Religion.* Translated by Garrett Green. London: T. & T. Clark, 2006.
———. "Schleiermacher." In *Theology and Church*, edited by Karl Barth, 159–99. New York: Harper & Row, 1962.

Bibliography

———. *The Theology of Schleiermacher: Lectures at Gottingen, Winter Semester of 1923/24*. Translated by Geoffrey W. Bromiley. Edited by Dietrich Ritschl. Edinburgh: T. & T. Clark, 1982.

Barth, Markus. "Response." *Union Seminary Quarterly Review* 28.1 (1972) 53–54.

Bartholomew, Craig G., and Michael W. Goheen. *The Drama of Scripture: Finding Our Place in the Biblical Story*. Grand Rapids: Baker Academic, 2004.

Bediako, Kwame. "Biblical Christologies in the Context of African Traditional Religions." In *Sharing Jesus in the Two Thirds World: Evangelical Christologies from the Contexts of Poverty, Powerlessness and Religious Pluralism*, edited by Vinay Samuel and Chris Sugden, 81–121. Grand Rapids: Eerdmans, 1984.

———. *Jesus and the Gospel in Africa: History and Experience*. New York: Orbis, 2004.

———. *Theology and Identity: The Impact of Culture Upon Christian Thought in the Second Century and in Modern Africa*. Milton Keynes, UK: Regnum, 1999.

Bell, Richard. "Understanding African Philosophy from a Non-African Point of View: An Exercise in Cross-Cultural Philosophy." In *Postcolonial African Philosophy: A Critical Reader*, edited by Emmanuel Chukwudi Eze, 197–220. Oxford: Blackwell, 1997.

Bernasconi, Robert. "African Philosophy's Challenge to Continental Philosophy." In *Postcolonial African Philosophy: A Critical Reader*, edited by Emmanuel Chukwudi Eze, 183–96. Oxford: Blackwell, 1997.

Bevans, Stephen B. *Models of Contextual Theology*. 2nd ed. Maryknoll, NY: Orbis, 2002.

Black, Max. *Models and Metaphors: Studies in Language and Philosophy*. New York: Cornell University Press, 1962.

Bodley, John H. *Cultural Anthropology: Tribes, States, and the Global System*. Mountain View, CA: Mayfield, 1994.

Bosch, David Jacobus. *Transforming Mission: Paradigm Shifts in Theology of Mission*. Maryknoll, NY: Orbis, 1991.

Bradley, Arthur. "Derrida's God: A Genealogy of the Theological Turn." *Paragraph* 29.3 (2006) 21–42.

Breyfogle, Todd. "Is There Room for Political Philosophy in Postmodern Critical Augustinianism?" In *Deconstructing Radical Orthodoxy: Postmodern Theology, Rhetoric, and Truth*, edited by W. J. Hankey and Douglas Hedley, 31–48. Aldershot, UK: Ashgate, 2005.

Brittain, Christopher Craig. "Leo Strauss and Resourceful Odysseus: Rhetorical Violence and the Holy Middle." *Canadian Review of American Studies* 38.1 (2008) 147–63.

———. "The 'Secular' as a Tragic Category: On Talal Asad, Religion and Representation." *Method and Theory in the Study of Religion* 17 (2005) 149–65.

Brumann, Christoph. "Writing for Culture: Why a Successful Concept Should Not Be Discarded." *Current Anthropology* 40 Supplement: Special Issue: Culture: A Second Chance? (1999) 1–13.

Bultmann, Rudolf. *History and Eschatology: The Gifford Lectures 1955*. Edinburgh: Edinburgh University Press, 1957.

———. *Theology of the New Testament: Volume Two*. Translated by Kendrick Grobel. London: SCM, 1955.

Burrell, David B. "An Introduction to Theology and Social Theory, Beyond Secular Reason." *Modern Theology* 8.4 (1992) 319–29.

Busia, K. A. *Africa in Search of Democracy*. London: Routledge, 1967.

Buzzard, Anthony F. "Some Questions about the Chalcedonian Christology of Karl Barth." *A Journal from the Radical Reformation* 5.2 (1996) 31–43.
Caputo, John D. *Philosophy and Theology.* Nashville: Abingdon, 2006.
Cauchi, Mark. "The Secular to Come: Interrogating the Derridean 'Secular.'" *Journal for Cultural and Religious Theory* 10.1 (2009) 1–25.
Cioffi, Todd V. "Developing a Political Theology: Some Considerations for the Church." *The Princeton Theological Review* 11.1 (2004) 14–19.
Cochran, Elizabeth Agnew. "'At the Same Time Blessed and Lame': Ontology, Christology and Violence in Augustine and John Milbank." *Journal for Christian Theological Research* 11 (2006) 51–72.
Coetzee, Pieter. "Uncovering Rationality: A Perspective in African Thought." *South African Journal of Ethnology* 23.2/3 (2000) 63–82.
Conn, Harvie M. *Eternal Word and Changing Worlds: Theology, Anthropology, and Mission in Trialogue.* Grand Rapids: Zondervan, 1984.
D'Costa, Gavin. "Seeking after Theological Vision." *Reviews in Religion and Theology* 6.4 (1999) 354–59.
Davidson, Ivor. "Theologizing the Human Jesus: An Ancient (and Modern) Approach to Christology Revealed." *International Journal of Systematic Theology* 3.2 (2001) 129–53.
de Vries, Hent. "'The Miracle of Love' and the Turn to Democracy." *The New Centennial Review* 8.3 (2009) 237–90.
Eagleton, Terry. *The Idea of Culture.* Malden, MA: Blackwells, 2000.
Edertz, Roger P. "Beyond Worldview Analysis: Insights from Gadamer on Christian Scholarship." *Christian Scholars Review* 36.1 (2006) 5–20.
Erickson, Millard J. *Christian Theology.* 2nd ed. Grand Rapids: Baker, 1998.
Eze, Emmanuel Chukwudi. "The Color of Reason: The Idea of 'Race' in Kant's Anthropology." In *Postcolonial African Philosophy: A Critical Reader,* edited by Emmanuel Chukwudi Eze, 103–40. Oxford: Blackwell, 1997.
———. "Introduction: Philosophy and the (Post) Colonial." In *Postcolonial African Philosophy: A Critical Reader,* edited by Emmanuel Chukwudi Eze, 1–21. Oxford: Blackwell, 1997.
———, editor. *Postcolonial African Philosophy: A Critical Reader.* Oxford: Blackwell, 1997.
Firestone, Chris L. "Rational Religious Faith and Kant's Transcendental Boundaries." In *Transcending Boundaries in Philosophy and Theology: Reason, Meaning and Experience,* edited by Kevin J. Vanhoozer and Martin Warner, 77–90. Aldershot, UK: Ashgate, 2007.
Fitzgerald, Timothy. *Discourse on Civility and Barbarity: A Critical History of Religion and Related Categories.* New York: Oxford University Press, 2008.
Flanagan, Kieran. "Sublime Policing: Sociology and Milbank's City of God." *New Blackfriars* 73.861 (1992) 333–41.
Fox, Richard Gabriel, and Barbara J. King. *Anthropology Beyond Culture.* Oxford: Berg, 2002.
Friedman, R. Z. "Hypocrisy and the Highest Good: Hegel on Kant's Transition from Morality to Religion." *Journal of the History of Philosophy* 24.4 (1986) 503–22.
Gadamer, Hans-Georg, and Jean Grondin. "Looking Back with Gadamer over His Writings and Their Effective History: A Dialogue with Jean Grondin (1996)." *Theory, Culture & Society* 23.1 (2006) 85–100.

Bibliography

Gadamer, Hans Georg. *Truth and Method*. Translated by Joel Weinsheimer and Donald G. Marshall. 2nd ed. London: Continuum, 2004.

Gathje, Peter R. "A Contested Classic." *Christian Century* 119.13 (2002) 28–32.

Gorringe, Timothy. *Furthering Humanity: A Theology of Culture*. Aldershot, UK: Ashgate, 2004.

Greene, Theodore M. "The Historical Context and Religious Significance of Kant's Religion." In *Religion within the Limits of Reason Alone*, ix–lxxviii. New York: Harper & Row, 1960.

Grenz, Stanley J. *Theology for the Community of God*. Grand Rapids: Eerdmans, 1994.

Gunton, Colin. *The Barth Lectures*. London: T. & T. Clark, 2007.

———. *The One, the Three and the Many: God, Creation and the Culture of Modernity: The 1992 Bampton Lectures*. Cambridge: Cambridge University Press, 1993.

Gyekye, Kwame. "Philosophy, Culture, and Technology in the Postcolonial." In *Postcolonial African Philosophy: A Critical Reader*, edited by Emmanuel Chukwudi Eze, 25–44. Oxford: Blackwell, 1997.

———. *Tradition and Modernity: Philosophical Reflections on the African Experience*. Oxford: Oxford University Press, 1997.

Habets, Myk. "Putting the 'Extra' Back into Calvinism." *Scottish Journal of Theology* 62.4 (2009) 441–56.

Hallen, Barry. "Contemporary Anglophone African Philosophy: A Survey." In *A Companion to African Philosophy*, edited by Kwasi Wiredu, 99–148. Oxford: Blackwell, 2004.

Harding, Sandra. "Is Modern Science an Ethnoscience? Rethinking Epistemological Assumptions." In *Postcolonial African Philosophy: A Critical Reader*, edited by Emmanuel Chukwudi Eze, 45–70. Oxford: Blackwell, 1997.

Hauerwas, Stanley. *With the Grain of the Universe: The Church's Witness and Natural Theology*. Grand Rapids: Brazos, 2001.

Hedley, Douglas. "Should Divinity Overcome Metaphysics? Reflections on John Milbank's Theology beyond Secular Reason and Confessions of a Cambridge Platonist" *Journal of Religion* 80.2 (2000) 271–98.

Hemming, Laurence Paul. "Quod Impossible Est! Aquinas and Radical Orthodoxy." In *Radical Orthodoxy? A Catholic Enquiry*, edited by Laurence Paul Hemming, 76–93. Aldershot, UK: Ashgate, 2000.

Hiebert, Paul G. *Anthropological Insights for Missionaries*. Grand Rapids: Baker, 1985.

———. *Anthropological Reflections on Missiological Issues*. Grand Rapids: Baker, 1994.

———. "Missions and Anthropology: A Love/Hate Relationship." *Missiology: An International Review* 6.2 (1978) 165–80.

Hountondji, Paulin. "Comments on Contemporary African Philosophy." *Diogenes* 71 (1970) 109–30.

Hughes, Kevin L. "The Ratio Dei and the Ambiguities of History." *Modern Theology* 21.4 (2005) 645–61.

Hunsinger, George. *How to Read Karl Barth: The Shape of His Theology*. New York: Oxford University Press, 1991.

Hyman, Gavin. *Predicament of Postmodern Theology: Radical Orthodoxy or Nihilist Textualism?* Louisville: Westminster John Knox, 2001.

Ikuenobe, Polycarp. "The Parochial Universalist Conception of 'Philosophy' and 'African Philosophy.'" *Philosophy East and West* 47.2 (1997) 189–210.

Bibliography

Jackson, Ken, and Arthur F Marotti. "The Turn to Religion in Early Modern English Studies." *Criticism* 46.1 (2004) 167–90.

James, Allison, Jenny Hockey, and Andrew Dawson. "Introduction: The Road from Santa Fe." In *After Writing Culture: Epistemology and Praxis in Contemporary Anthropology*, edited by Allison James, Jenny Hockey and Andrew Dawson, 177–93. London: Routledge, 1997.

Janz, Bruce. "Alterity, Dialogue, and African Philosophy." In *Postcolonial African Philosophy: A Critical Reader*, edited by Emmanuel Chukwudi Eze, 221–38. Oxford: Blackwell, 1997.

Jenks, Chris. *Culture*. London: Routledge, 1993.

Jenson, Robert W. "Christ as Culture. 1, Christ as Polity." *International Journal of Systematic Theology* 5.3 (2003) 323–29.

Joas, Hans. "Social Theory and the Sacred: A Response to John Milbank." *Ethical Perspectives* 7.4 (2000) 233–43.

Johnson, Mark. "Introduction: Metaphor in the Philosophical Tradition." In *Philosophical Perspectives on Metaphor*, edited by Mark Johnson, 3–47. Minneapolis: University of Minnesota Press, 1981.

Jüngel, Eberhard. *Karl Barth: A Theological Legacy*. Translated by Garrett E. Paul. Philadelphia: Westminster, 1986.

Kallenberg, Brad J. *Live to Tell: Evangelism in a Postmodern World*. Grand Rapids: Brazos, 2002.

Kaphagawani, Didier N. "What Is African Philosophy?" In *The African Philosophy Reader*, edited by P. H. Coetzee and A. P. J. Roux, 86–98. London: Routledge, 1998.

Kaplan, Steven. "The Africanization of Missionary Christianity: History and Typology." *Journal of Religion in Africa* XVL.3 (1986) 166–86.

Kerr, Fergus. "Simplicity Itself: Milbank's Thesis." *New Blackfriars* 73.861 (1992) 305–10.

Kraft, Charles H. *Anthropology for Christian Witness*. Maryknoll, NY: Orbis, 1996.

———. *Christianity in Culture: A Study in Dynamic Biblical Theologizing in Cross-Cultural Perspective*. Maryknoll, NY: Orbis, 1979.

Kroeber, A. L., and Clyde Kluckhohn. *Culture: A Critical Review of Concepts and Definitions*. Papers Vol. 47.1. Cambridge: The Museum, 1952.

Krötke, Wolf. "A New Impetus to the Theology of Religions from Karl Barth's Thought." *Cultural Encounters* 7.2 (2011) 29–42.

Kuper, Adam. *Culture: The Anthropologists' Account*. Cambridge: Harvard University Press, 1999.

Kwame, Safro. "Introduction: African Philosophy and the Akan Society: An Introduction." In *Readings in African Philosophy: An Akan Collection*, edited by Safro Kwame, xv–xxix. Lanham, MD: University Press of America, 1995.

Lash, Nicholas. "Where Does Holy Teaching Leave Philosophy? Questions on Milbank's Aquinas." *Modern Theology* 15 (1999) 433–44.

Lawn, Christopher. "Wittgenstein, History and Hermeneutics." *Philosophy and Social Criticism* 29.3 (2003) 281–95.

Lindbeck, George A. *The Nature of Doctrine: Religion and Theology in a Postliberal Age*. Philadelphia: Westminster, 1984.

Lingenfelter, Sherwood G. *Transforming Culture: A Challenge for Christian Mission*. Grand Rapids: Baker, 1992.

Lloyd, Vincent. "On the Use of Gillian Rose." *Heythrop Journal* 48.5 (2007) 697–706.

Bibliography

Luft, Sandra Ruduick. *Vico's Uncanny Humanism: Reading the New Science between Modern and Postmodern*. Ithaca, NY: Cornell University Press, 2003.

MacIntyre, Alasdair. *After Virtue: A Study in Moral Theory*. London: Duckworth, 1981.

Makang, Jean-Marie. "Of the Good Use of Tradition: Keeping the Critical Perspective in African Philosophy." In *Postcolonial African Philosophy: A Critical Reader*, edited by Emmanuel Chukwudi Eze, 324–38. Oxford: Blackwell, 1997.

Malinowski, Bronislaw. *A Scientific Theory of Culture and Other Essays*. New York: Oxford University Press, 1960.

Masolo, D. A. *African Philosophy in Search of Identity*. Edinburgh: Edinburgh University Press, 1994.

Mazzotta, Giuseppe. *The New Map of the World: The Poetic Philosophy of Giambattista Vico*. Princeton: Princeton University Press, 1999.

Mbiti, John S. *African Religions & Philosophy*. New Hork: Praeger, 1969.

McClendon, James William, and Nancey C. Murphy. *Witness: Systematic Theology*. Vol. 3. Nashville: Abingdon, 2000.

McCormack, Bruce L. *Karl Barth's Critically Realistic Dialectical Theology: Its Genesis and Development, 1909–1936*. Oxford: Clarendon, 1997.

———. *Orthodox and Modern: Studies in the Theology of Karl Barth*. Grand Rapids: Baker Academic, 2008.

Mendieta, Eduardo, editor. *The Frankfurt School on Religion: Key Writings by the Major Thinkers*. New York: Routledge, 2005.

Metzger, Paul Louis. *The Word of Christ and the World of Culture: Sacred and Secular through the Theology of Karl Barth*. Grand Rapids: Eerdmans, 2003.

Middleton, J. Richard, and Brian J. Walsh. *Truth Is Stranger Than It Used to Be: Biblical Faith in a Postmodern Age*. London: SPCK, 1995.

Milbank, John. *Being Reconciled: Ontology and Pardon*. London: Routledge, 2003.

———. "A Critique of the Theology of Right." In *The Word Made Strange: Theology, Language, and Culture*, edited by John Milbank, 7–35. Oxford: Blackwell, 1997.

———. "Enclaves or Where Is the Church?" *New Blackfriars* 73.861 (1992) 341–52.

———. "Knowledge: The Theological Critique of Philosophy in Hamann and Jacobi." In *Radical Orthodoxy: A New Theology*, edited by John Milbank, Catherine Pickstock, and Graham Ward, 21–37. London: Routledge, 1999.

———. "The Linguistic Turn as a Theological Turn." In *The Word Made Strange: Theology, Language, Culture*, edited by John Milbank, 84–120. Oxford: Blackwell, 1997.

———. "On Complex Space." In *The Word Made Strange: Theology, Language, and Culture*, edited by John Milbank, 268–92. Oxford: Blackwell, 1997.

———. "Out of the Greenhouse." *New Blackfriars* 74.867 (1993) 4–14.

———. "Out of the Greenhouse." In *The Word Made Strange: Theology, Language, and Culture*, edited by John Milbank, 257–67. Oxford: Blackwell, 1997.

———. "Pleonasm, Speech and Writing." In *The Word Made Strange: Theology, Language, Culture*, edited by John Milbank, 55–83. Oxford: Blackwell, 1997.

———. "'Postmodern Critical Augustinianism': A Short Summa in Forty Two Responses to Unasked Questions." *Modern Theology* 7.3 (1991) 225–37.

———. *The Religious Dimension in the Thought of Giambattista Vico, 1668–1744 Part 1: The Early Metaphysics*. Lewiston, NY: Mellen, 1991.

———. *The Religious Dimension in the Thought of Giambattista Vico, 1668–1744 Part 2: Language, Law and History*. Lewiston, NY: Mellen, 1991.

———. "Stale Expressions: The Management Shaped Church." *Studies in Christian Ethics* 21.1 (2008) 117–28.

———. *Theology and Social Theory: Beyond Secular Reason.* Oxford: Blackwell, 1990.

———. *Theology and Social Theory: Beyond Secular Reason.* 2nd ed. Oxford: Blackwell, 2006.

———. "William Warburton: An Eighteenth Century Bishop Fallen among Post-Structuralists." *New Blackfriars* 64.757 (1983) 315–24.

———. "William Warburton: An Eighteenth-Century Anglican Bishop Fallen among Post-Structuralists – 2." *New Blackfriars* 64.759 (1983) 374–83.

———. *The Word Made Strange : Theology, Language, and Culture.* Oxford: Blackwell, 1997.

Milbank, John, and Catherine Pickstock. *Truth in Aquinas.* London: Routledge, 2001.

Milbank, John, Catherine Pickstock, and Graham Ward, editors. *Radical Orthodoxy: A New Theology.* London: Routledge, 1999.

Milbank, John, Graham Ward, and Edith Wyschogrod, editors. *Theological Perspectives on God and Beauty.* Rockwell Lecture Series. Harrisburg, PA: Trinity, 2003.

Miller, Carolyn R. "Genre as Social Action." *Quarterly Journal of Speech* 70 (1984) 151–67.

Miner, Robert C. *Vico: Genealogist of Modernity.* South Bend, IN: University of Notre Dame Press, 2002.

———. *Truth in the Making: Creative Knowledge in Theology and Philosophy.* New York: Routledge, 2004.

Mudimbe, V. Y. *The Invention of Africa: Gnosis, Philosophy and the Foundation of Knowledge.* Bloomington, IN: Indiana University Press, 1988.

Murphy, Nancey. *Beyond Liberalism and Fundamentalism: How Modern and Postmodern Philosophy Set the Theological Agenda.* Valley Forge, PA: Trinity, 1996.

Murphy, W. T. Review of *The Broken Middle*, by Gillian Rose. *The British Journal of Sociology* 45.1 (1994) 146–47.

Newbigin, Lesslie. "The Enduring Validity of Cross-Cultural Mission." *International Bulletin of Missionary Research* 12.2 (1988) 50–53.

———. *Foolishness to the Greeks: The Gospel and Western Culture.* Geneva: World Council of Churches, 1986.

Nicholls, Bruce. *Contextualization: A Theology of Gospel and Culture.* Downers Grove, IL: InterVarsity, 1979.

Nichols, Aidan. "'Non Tali Auxilio': John Milbank's Suasion to Orthodoxy." *New Blackfriars* 73.861 (1992) 326–32.

Niebuhr, H. Richard. *Christ and Culture.* New York: Harper, 1951.

O'Meara, Thomas F. *Church and Culture: German Catholic Theology, 1860–1914.* South Bend, IN: University of Notre Dame Press, 1991.

Oh, Peter S. *Karl Barth's Trinitarian Theology: A Study in Karl Barth's Analogical Use of the Trinitarian Relation.* London: T. & T. Clark, 2006.

Okere, Theophilus. *African Philosophy: An Historico-Hermeneutical Investigation of the Conditions of Its Possibility.* Lanham, NY: University Press of America, 1983.

Oruka, Henry. "Sage Philosophy." In *The African Philosophy Reader*, edited by P. H. Coetzee and A. P. J. Roux, 99–108. London: Routledge, 1998.

Ostry, Bernard. *The Cultural Connection.* Toronto: McClelland and Stewart, 1978.

Outlaw, Lucius. "African, African-American, and Africana Philosophy." *The Philosophical Forum* xxiv.1–3 (1992–1993) 63–93.

Bibliography

Palma, Robert J. *Karl Barth's Theology of Culture: The Freedom of Culture for the Praise of God*. Eugene, OR: Pickwick, 1983.

Parrinder, G. *African Traditional Religion*. London: SPCK, 1962.

Pickstock, Catherine. *After Writing: On the Liturgical Consummation of Philosophy*. Oxford: Blackwell, 1998.

Pilario, D. F. *Back to the Rough Grounds of Praxis: Exploring Theological Method with Pierre Bourdieu*. Leuven: Leuven University Press, 2005.

Presbey, Gail M. "Syllabus for an African Philosophy and Culture Course." *American Philosophical Association Newsletters* 00.2 (2001).

Putt, B. Keith. "Poetically Negotiating the Love of God: An Examination of John D. Caputo's Recent Postsecular Theology—A Review Essay." *Christian Scholars Review* 37.4 (2008) 483–97.

Reno, Russell R. *In the Ruins of the Church: Sustaining Faith in an Age of Diminished Christianity*. Grand Rapids: Brazos, 2002.

Roberts, R. H. "The Reception of the Theology of Karl Barth in the Anglo-Saxon World: History, Typology and Prospect." *Communio viatorium* 31 (1988) 13–30.

Robertson, Roland. "Review: The Recovery of Rhetoric: Persuasive Discourse and Disciplinarity in the Human Sciences." *Contemporary Sociology* 23.5 (1994) 765–66.

Rose, Gillian. *Broken Middle: Out of Our Ancient Society*. Oxford: Blackwell, 1992.

———. *Dialectic of Nihilism: Post-Structuralism and Law*. Oxford: Blackwell, 1984.

———. *Mourning Becomes the Law: Philosophy and Representation*. Cambridge: Cambridge University Press, 1996.

Rowland, Tracey. *Culture and the Thomist Tradition: After Vatican 2*. London: Routledge, 2003.

Sanneh, Lamin. "The Horizontal and the Vertical in Mission: An African Perspective." *International Bulletin of Missionary Research* 17.4 (1983) 165–71.

Scharen, Christian Batalden. "'Judicious Narratives', or Ethnography as Ecclesiology." *Scottish Journal of Theology* 58.2 (2005) 125–42.

Seitz, Jonathan. "A Review of Secularisms." *Journal for Cultural and Religious Theory* 9.3 (2008) 41–44.

Serequeberhan, Tsenay. "The Critique of Eurocentrism and the Practice of African Philosophy." In *Postcolonial African Philosophy: A Critical Reader*, edited by Emmanuel Chukwudi Eze, 141–61. Oxford: Blackwell, 1997.

Shults, F. LeRon. "A Dubious Christological Formula: From Leontius of Byzantium to Karl Barth." *Theological Studies* 57 (1996) 431–46.

Shumway, David R., and Ellen Messer-Davidow. "Disciplinarity: An Introduction." *Poetics Today* 12.2 (1991) 201–25.

Smalley, William A. "Anthropological Study and Missionary Scholarship." In *Readings in Missionary Anthropology*, edited by William A. Smalley, 3–13. South Pasadena, CA: William Carey Library, 1974.

Smith, James K. A. *Introducing Radical Orthodoxy: Mapping a Post-Secular Theology*. Grand Rapids: Baker Academic, 2004.

Soskice, Janet Martin. *Metaphor and Religious Language*. Oxford: Clarendon, 1985.

Taber, Charles R. *To Understand the World, to Save the World: The Interface between Missiology and the Social Sciences*. Harrisburg, PA: Trinity, 2000.

Tanner, Kathryn. *Theories of Culture: A New Agenda for Theology*. Minneapolis: Fortress, 1997.

Taylor, Charles. *A Secular Age*. Cambridge: Belknap, 2007.

———. "What Is Secularity?" In *Transcending Boundaries in Philosophy and Theology: Reason, Meaning and Experience*, edited by Kevin Vanhoozer and Martin Warner, 57–76. Aldershot, UK: Ashgate, 2007.

Torrance, T. F. "Introduction." In *Theology and Church: Shorter Writings 1920–1928*, edited by Karl Barth, 7–54. New York: Harper & Row, 1962.

Trebilco, Paul R. *The Early Christians in Ephesus from Paul to Ignatius*. Grand Rapids: Eerdmans, 2007.

Vahanian, Gabriel. "Karl Barth as Theologian of Culture." *Union Seminary Quarterly Review* 28.1 (1972) 37–49.

Vanhoozer, Kevin J. *The Drama of Doctrine: A Canonical Linguistic Approach to Christian Theology*. Louisville: Westminster John Knox, 2005.

———. "What Is Everyday Theology? How and Why Christians Should Read Culture." In *Everyday Theology: How to Read Cultural Texts and Interpret Trends*, edited by Kevin J. Vanhoozer, Charles A. Anderson, and Michael J. Sleasman, 15–60. Grand Rapids: Baker, 2007.

Vanhoozer, Kevin J., and Martin Warner. "Introduction." In *Transcending Boundaries in Philosophy and Theology: Reason, Meaning and Experience*, edited by Kevin J. Vanhoozer and Martin Warner, 1–14. Aldershot, UK: Ashgate, 2007.

Visser, Hans, and Gillian Bediako. "Introduction." In *Jesus and the Gospel in Africa: History and Experience*, edited by Kwame Bediako, xi–xvii. Maryknoll, NY: Orbis, 2004.

von Balthasar, Hans Urs. *The Theology of Karl Barth: Exposition and Interpretation*. Translated by Edward T. Oakes. San Francisco: Ignatius, 1992.

Walls, Andrew F. "The Gospel as Prisoner and Liberator of Culture." In *New Directions in Mission and Evangelization 3: Faith and Culture*, edited by James A. Scherer and Stephen B. Bevans, 17–28. Maryknoll, NY: Orbis, 1999.

Wan, Enoch. "A Critique of Charles Kraft's Use/Misuse of Communication and Social Sciences in Biblical Interpretation and Missiological Formulation." No pages. Online: http://ojs.globalmissiology.org/index.php/english/article/viewFile/120/346.

Ward, Graham. "Bodies: The Displaced Body of Jesus Christ." In *Radical Orthodoxy: A New Theology*, edited by John Milbank, Catherine Pickstock, and Graham Ward, 163–81. London: Routledge, 1999.

———. *Cities of God*. London: Routledge, 2000.

———. "John Milbank's Divine Commedia." *New Blackfriars* 73.861 (1992) 311–18.

———. "Radical Orthodoxy and/as Cultural Politics." In *Radical Orthodoxy? A Catholic Enquiry*, edited by L. P. Hemming, 97–111. Aldershot, UK: Ashgate, 2000.

———. *True Religion*. Oxford: Blackwell, 2003.

Watson, Patty Jo. "Archaeology, Anthropology, and the Culture Concept." *American Anthropologist* 97.4 (1995) 683–94.

Webber, Robert E. *The Church in the World: Opposition, Tension, or Transformation?* Grand Rapids: Academie, 1986.

Weerstra, Hans M. "De-Westernizing the Gospel: The Recovery of a Biblical Worldview." *International Journal of Frontier Missions* 16.3 (1999) 129–34.

West, Cornel. *Keeping Faith: Philosophy and Race in America*. New York: Routledge, 1993.

Whiteman, Darrell L. "Anthropological Reflections on Contextualizing Theology in a Gloablizing World." In *Globalizing Theology: Belief and Practice in an Era of World*

Bibliography

    Christianity, edited by Craig Ott and Harold A. Netland, 52–69. Grand Rapids: Baker, 2006.

Williams, Raymond. *Culture and Society 1780–1950*. London: Chatto and Windus, 1958.

———. *Keywords: A Vocabulary of Culture and Society*. London: Fontana, 1976.

———. *The Long Revolution*. London: Chatto and Windus, 1961.

Williams, Rowan. "Saving Time: Thoughts on Practice, Patience and Vision." *New Blackfriars* 73.861 (1992) 319–26.

———. "Between Politics and Metaphysics: Reflections in the Wake of Gillian Rose." *Modern Theology* 11.1 (1995) 3–22.

Williams, Thomas. "The Doctrine of Univocity Is True and Salutary." *Modern Theology* 21.4 (2005) 575–85.

Winthrop, Robert H. *Dictionary of Concepts in Cultural Anthropology*. New York: Greenwood, 1991.

Wiredu, Kwasi, and Olusegun Oladipo. *Conceptual Decolonization in African Philosophy: Four Essays*. Ibadan, Nigeria: Hope, 1995.

Wood, James. "Black Noise." *The New Republic*, 10 Nov 1997, 38–44.

Wright, N T. "How Can the Bible Be Authoritative?" *Vox Evangelica* 21 (1991) 7–32.

Index

Aesthetic necessity, 113–14
Africa, viii, 223, 225, 227, 229, 231, 236, 238, 240, 248, 252–53, 256–57, 263, 279–80, 285
African
   context, 223, 225, 236, 246, 263, 267, 273
   critique, 226, 231, 251
   culture, 33, 225, 236, 256, 264, 267
   humanity, 231, 266
   life, 228, 265–66, 273
   philosophy, 227–29, 231, 233–34, 236, 238–40, 245–46, 249–52, 280, 282–83, 285
   philosophy and culture, 8, 226, 236, 286
   primal religions, 253, 267
   religious past, 250, 255–56, 267
   religious sensibility, 265, 275
   theologians, 255, 266
   theology, 5, 223, 257, 267
   traditional religions, 253, 264–66, 286
African/s, 228–29, 234, 236, 239–40, 249, 252–56, 264–66, 285–86
Alterity, 35, 66, 75, 88, 90, 240, 250–51, 283
Amato, Peter, 240, 242–45, 248–50, 279
Anthropologists, 17–18, 33, 39, 50, 265–67, 287
Anthropology, 1, 15–16, 18–19, 22, 26–27, 29–31, 33, 38–39, 230, 280–82, 287
Anxiety, 144–45, 152

Aquinas, Thomas, 136, 157, 208, 285
Augustine, 24, 120, 126, 157–59, 161–63, 165, 219, 281
Augustinian, 115, 135, 138, 159–60, 162
Authority, 72, 80, 86, 183, 232

Balthasar, Hans Urs von, 185, 189–90, 196, 203, 207, 287
Barth, Karl, vii–viii, 3, 5–8, 55, 175, 177–223, 257, 266, 268, 270–71, 273–77, 279–81, 283–84, 286–87
   affirmation of culture, 193
   anti-cultural bias, 184–85
   christological model, 208, 211
   confessional foundations, 208, 211
   covenant, 206–7, 218, 220
   culture, 177, 191, 193, 201–2
   worldview, 177, 183, 257
Bediako, Kwame, 3, 8, 223–25, 227–29, 231, 233–35, 237, 239, 241, 243, 245, 247, 249, 251, 253–68, 273–75, 280, 282–83, 287
   true *religio*, 259, 273
Behaviors, 16–18, 23, 28, 30, 199
Being, 84, 93, 110, 127–28, 136, 161, 163, 202–4, 206, 214–15, 221, 247
   cultural, 191
   state of, 204–6, 221
   true, 215–16
   univocity of, 84
Beliefs, 16, 20, 60, 64, 228, 235, 239, 252, 259, 287
   traditional, 235, 244

289

Index

Bias, 35, 79–80, 184
Bildung, 40–41, 56
Bosch, David, 11–12, 37, 43–45, 280
Boundaries, 36, 71–72, 89, 109, 142, 147, 154, 194
Bourdieu, Pierre, 77–81, 234
　habitus, 77–78
Bradley, Arthur, 66–67, 280
Brumann, Christoph, 19, 38–39, 280
Bultmann, Rudolf, 12, 55, 280
Bultmann, Rudolph, 12
Buzzard, Anthony, 211, 213, 281

Caputo, John, 65–66, 84, 286
Cartesian, 53–54, 57, 74, 113
Cauchi, Mark, 58, 61–62, 66, 281
Christ, Jesus, 11–12, 23–25, 138–39, 155, 172, 174, 176, 180–81, 186–87, 190–92, 194, 202, 204–7, 209–18, 222, 224, 266, 270–72, 274–78, 283
　in, 207, 212, 220–21, 271
Christian, 3, 5–8, 11, 67, 69, 87–89, 91, 94, 133, 137, 159, 162–63, 167, 174, 176, 187, 256, 260–62, 281, 285
　culture, 70, 140
　faith, 55, 262–63
　identity, 254, 261, 273
　ontology, 125
　practice, 128
　reason, 5
　religion, 261, 275
　worldview, 181, 183
Christianity, 82–83, 85, 115, 119, 156, 160–62, 174, 186, 196–97, 221, 224, 253, 258, 260, 264
Christians, 11, 13, 21, 91, 163–65, 171, 212, 217, 222, 224, 258–62, 287
Christological, 193, 207, 218–19
Christology, 24, 207, 219, 278, 281
Church, ix, 12, 23–24, 91–92, 129–30, 138–41, 154–55, 158–59, 161–62, 164–66, 168, 170–74, 198–201, 203–5, 216–17, 221–22, 270–73, 276–77, 279, 284–87
　institutional, 155, 158, 171

Cities, 100, 121, 139, 142–43, 147–52, 154, 156–58, 161, 169
Coetzee, Pieter, 245–50, 281, 283, 285
Community, 23, 66, 92, 138, 152, 160, 199, 221–22, 241, 270
Confessional foundation, 83, 201, 222, 270
Contextualization, 20, 27, 31–33, 43, 285
Creation, 1, 12, 55, 109, 123, 125, 138, 171, 178, 181–82, 201–3, 205–7, 218–20, 271, 273
Creature, 6, 182, 202–3, 206, 212, 266
Cultural
　activity, 81–82, 193–94, 202, 205
　anthropology, 13, 15, 20–21, 26, 32, 38, 288
　differences, 15, 259
　forms, 18
　fundamentalism, 39
Culture, 13–14, 18, 32, 34–35, 39–40, 42, 44, 50, 69, 71, 116, 122, 128, 131, 191, 196–97, 203, 217, 222, 237
　anthropological understanding, 15, 27, 31, 81
　cultivation, 49–50
　deferral model, 13–14, 39, 45–46, 70
　definition, vii, 19, 21–22, 25, 28, 34, 37, 41–42, 51, 69, 197, 273
　neutrality of, 29, 91, 226
　pagan, 106, 118
　religious character of, 225, 237, 255, 266
　social scientific description, 69–70, 91, 93, 175
　theological description, vii–viii, 4–5, 14, 45, 110, 174, 197–98, 204, 223, 226

D'Costa, Gavin, 139–40, 281
Deity, 191–93, 197, 262
Derrida, Jacques, 57, 66–67, 84–85, 120–21, 123–25, 137, 249, 252, 267, 280
Dialectic, 103, 111, 146, 190, 196, 213
Diastasis, 3, 5, 184, 193, 196, 204
Dilthey, Wilhelm, 54–55, 57

290

Index

Disciplinarity, 71–73, 89, 286
Divine, 90, 94, 107, 114, 122–23, 128, 158, 160, 169, 176, 180, 183, 187–88, 190–91, 208, 210, 216, 219, 269–70, 274
Divinity, 106, 108–10, 130, 133, 136, 174, 188, 208, 210, 212, 269–70

Ecclesia, 138, 160–63, 176
Ecclesiology, 1, 4, 91–92, 129, 132, 140, 160, 165, 170, 222, 276–78, 286
Election, 202, 214, 216, 218, 221, 276
Engagement, theological, viii, 11, 14, 26, 40, 46, 276
Eschatology, 12, 219, 280
Essence, 25, 44, 89, 163, 192, 208–10, 214–17, 221, 271
 human, 208, 216–17, 219
Eternity, 185–86, 188, 205–6, 210, 216
Ethics, 29, 77, 114, 138, 145, 148, 152–53, 167, 169, 236, 285
Ethnophilosophy, 234, 236–37, 244–45, 250, 252
Ethnoscience, 231–32, 282
Eurocentrism, 229–31, 286
Europe, 229, 231, 246, 264
European, 229–31, 263–64
Evangelical theology, 190, 192, 196
Event, 71, 88, 151, 154, 179–80, 200, 213–15, 274–75
Exchange, 58, 128–30
Existence, 16–18, 50, 54, 92, 94, 150, 153, 202, 206, 210–12, 215, 217–18, 221–22, 225, 231, 249, 252–53, 256, 259–60, 264
 human, 123, 204, 217
Experiences, 44, 54, 56–57, 67, 76, 101, 146, 151, 239–40, 242, 246, 252, 260, 280–81, 287
Experts, 71–74, 79, 89
Eze, Emmanuel Chukwudi, 279–84, 286

Faith, 12, 32, 40, 44, 58, 60, 65–66, 68, 88, 91, 122–23, 125, 129, 182–83, 198, 202, 222, 256, 284, 287
Field, concept of, 12, 77–79, 81
Fitzgerald, Timothy, 275, 281

Flanagan, Kieran, 134, 281
Fore-understandings, 35, 39, 42, 45, 75
Forgiveness, 156, 159, 161–62, 164–65, 170
Freedom, 58, 170, 203–4, 213, 215
Fulfillment, 84, 162, 192, 201–4
Gadamer, Hans Georg, 8, 35–36, 49, 54–57, 60, 75–76, 80, 240, 251, 281–82
 interruption, 35–36, 91
 signal, 35–36, 39, 42
Game, 73–74, 78, 81
Glory, 202, 206, 210, 220, 222
God, 33–34, 59–60, 65–66, 76–77, 99, 101–2, 109–10, 122, 125, 176–79, 181–82, 185–88, 190–206, 209–12, 214–16, 219–20, 265–66, 269–75, 279–80, 285–87
 humanity of, 191, 197–98
Gods, 128, 258–59, 271, 274
Gospel, 32–33, 89, 213, 224, 261, 285, 287
Gospel in Africa, 224–25, 253, 266, 280, 287
Grace, 83, 115, 138, 151, 179–81, 191, 202
Graeco-Roman, 259–61
Gunton, Colin, 186, 189–90, 200, 206–7, 214–15, 218–20, 276, 282
Gyekye, Kwame, 246, 253, 282

Hamann, Johann Georg, 111, 114, 121–22, 137
Harding, Sandra, 232, 234, 282
Heaven, 24, 155, 163, 185
Hegel, Georg W F, 62–65, 67, 113–14, 137, 229–30, 242
Heidegger, Martin, 37, 55, 57, 75, 84–85, 137, 143, 147, 179, 183, 252
Hermeneutics, 35, 55–56, 65–66, 183–84, 194, 235, 250–51, 283
Hiebert, Paul, 27–31, 33, 282
History, 12, 54, 56, 77, 79, 86, 99–101, 112, 115, 121, 125–27, 137–38, 188, 214–16, 218–19, 229–30, 242, 280, 282–84, 286–87
 human, 88, 91, 122, 125, 129, 215

291

Index

Horizon, 75, 109, 115, 123, 184, 240, 242, 245, 248–49
Human
    beings, 18, 28, 81, 100, 109, 115, 117, 121, 161, 170, 184, 191, 194, 205, 211, 230
    experience, 188, 240
    nature, 16, 33, 70, 90, 208, 210–12, 217
Humanity, 49–50, 61–62, 65, 80, 89, 121–22, 176–80, 182, 184–89, 191–92, 195–97, 200–208, 210–13, 215–18, 220–22, 229–30, 261, 266, 269–74, 276
    sheer creatureliness of, 270–71
Humanity of God, 185, 190–91, 194–95, 197, 199, 204, 279
Humanization, 205, 221
Hunsinger, George, 207, 211–12, 214, 282

Idealization, 72, 140–41, 155, 172–73, 239
Identity, 23, 72, 139, 154, 173, 223–24, 227, 254, 257, 261, 266–67, 273, 277, 284
    cultural, 19, 223
Ikuenobe, Polycarp, 238, 243, 263, 282
Immanence, 55, 89–90, 92–93, 111, 154, 180, 188
Incarnation, 1, 57, 121, 137, 210, 213, 215–16
Irenaeus, 186, 219

Janz, Bruce, 240, 250–51, 283
Jenson, Robert, 23–24, 283
Jesus, 11, 91, 122, 128, 164, 178–79, 189–90, 200–201, 208, 210–12, 214–15, 219, 224–25, 253, 266, 273, 280, 287
    divine, 208, 210, 216
Jove, 101–2, 111, 156
Judicious narratives, 4, 92, 171–73, 286
Jüngel, Eberhard, 185–86, 189, 191, 283

Kant, Immanuel, 63–64, 67, 113–14, 137, 229–30, 241–42, 281–82
Kaphagawani, Didier, 235–37, 283
knowledge, 55, 60, 63, 72, 107, 109, 127–28, 146–47, 205, 233, 237, 241, 243, 261, 285
Kraft, Charles, 29–31, 33, 46, 283
Kultur, 15, 40–42

Language, 44, 56–57, 65, 74–75, 77, 83, 95, 97–103, 106, 113, 115–21, 125–27, 210, 214, 216, 237, 242, 245–46, 280, 284–85
    origins of, 117
    pagan, 101–2
Language games, 74–75
Law, 97, 102, 142, 144–46, 149–52, 160, 167, 169, 188, 201–3, 205, 256, 269, 275, 286
Law and History, 83, 95, 99–100, 115, 118, 121, 284
Lawn, Christopher, 74–76, 283
Levinas, Emmanuel, 143, 252
Life, ix–x, 16–17, 55–57, 59, 76, 78, 81, 161, 164, 178–79, 183, 200–201, 227, 230–31, 234–35, 252–53, 256, 265–67, 270, 273
    way of, 50, 87
Liturgy, 128, 139, 176, 206, 220, 270
Lloyd, Vincent, 143–45, 149, 151, 283
Love, redeeming, 146–47

MacIntyre, Alasdair, 8, 61, 73–74, 76, 82, 137, 284
Mbiti, John, 33, 252, 265–66, 284
McCormack, Bruce, 185, 189, 196, 214–17, 219, 221, 284
Metaphor, 19, 101–2, 106–8, 111, 118–20, 124, 142, 149, 154, 156, 161, 269, 280, 283
    original, 102, 120, 125
Metaphoric, 102, 106–8, 120
Metaphysics, 97, 99, 106, 108, 114, 126, 128, 147, 151, 153, 236, 241, 288
Metzger, Paul, 208, 210, 216–20, 222, 284

Index

Milbank, John, vii–viii, 1, 3–10,
    47, 52, 57, 61, 68, 70, 80–149,
    151–74, 176, 180, 199–200, 207,
    268–72, 276, 281, 283–85, 287
  charity, 102, 115–16, 138, 144, 162
  complex space, 4, 166–70, 284
  concealment, 84, 100, 112
  conceit, 105, 113
  critica, 104, 107
  cultural theology, 4, 96, 130, 132
  donum, 126–29, 269
  ecclesiology, 154, 159
  gift, 10, 102, 126–29, 171–72, 182,
    191–92, 270, 277
  gothic space, 154, 166, 168–70
  ideal church, 159
  inventio, 103–4
  iudicio, 103–4
  methexis, 126–29
  poetic cultural theology, 95, 110
  reciprocity, 269–70
  topica, 104, 106–7
  verbum, 125–29, 269
Milbank and Barth, 5–6, 8, 223, 226,
    233, 237, 270
Missiologists, vii, 1, 3, 13, 23, 26–27,
    29, 31–32, 46, 48, 68
Missiology, 26–27, 29–31, 33–34, 42,
    277–78, 282, 286
Mission, ix, 27, 42–43, 138, 264,
    280–82, 286–87
Missionaries, 27–28, 282
Modernity, 9, 15, 40, 52–53, 85, 93,
    131, 148, 229, 241, 243, 251
Modern Moral Order, 37, 58–59
Mythos, 87, 101, 160, 244

Natural Theology, 8–9, 187, 207
Neutrality, 2–3, 6, 8, 24, 26, 60, 93
Nicholls, Bruce, 32–33, 69–70, 285
Niebuhr, H. Richard, 2, 11–12, 25–26,
    46, 285
Nihilism, 80, 93–94, 108, 123, 142,
    154–55, 286

O'Meara, Thomas, 39–40, 44–45, 285
Ontology, 85, 89, 127, 129, 135, 140,
    159–60, 162, 168, 269, 281, 284
  actualist, 214, 217, 271
  religious, 256–58, 273
Origins, 61, 99–100, 112, 116, 118–19,
    121, 124, 152, 154, 169, 199, 210
Oruka, Henry, 235–38, 244, 285
Outlaw, Lucius, 227–28, 249, 285

Pagan, 83, 107–8, 120, 143, 148, 262
Pagan religiosity, 271
Palma, Robert, 177, 193–98, 201, 204,
    206–8, 286
Particularity, 8, 16, 53, 82, 148, 153,
    180, 219, 241, 244–48, 250
Perfection, 153, 155, 210, 218
Performance, 76–77
Perspective
  humanist, 60, 253
  religious, 47, 62, 253, 267
  theological, 3, 46, 49, 95, 98, 193,
    257, 266–68
Philosophers, 52, 78, 99, 107, 134,
    191, 238, 244, 254
Philosophic, 237, 247, 249, 262
Philosophical, 62, 81, 180, 237,
    243–44, 248, 251–52, 259, 283
Philosophy, 35, 39–42, 54–55, 62–63,
    66–67, 74, 100, 106, 127–28, 139,
    145, 147–48, 229, 231, 233–41,
    244–45, 248–54, 262–63, 265,
    280–88
  contemporary, 64, 127
  cultural, 236–37
  deconstruction, 65
  sagacity, 237, 244, 250
Phocion, 146–47, 150
Pickstock, Catherine, 73, 95, 130, 136,
    139, 284–87
Pilario, D. F., 74, 76–79, 81, 141, 286
Pleonasm, 116–25, 128, 284
Plutarch, 146, 259
Pneumatology, weak, 218, 276
Poesis, 128, 269–70
Polity, 23–24, 101, 142, 283
Postcolonial African Philosophy, 228,
    279–82, 284, 286
Postmodern, 19, 81, 89, 95, 130, 137,
    143, 284–85

293

Index

Postmodern Critical Augustinianism, 89, 112, 135, 284
Postmodernity, 85, 90, 112, 137, 147–48
Pre-cultural humanity, 113
Prejudices, 75, 127, 183, 226, 240, 251
Promise, 80, 135, 172, 176, 201–5, 207, 222, 241, 271
Prophecy, 118, 123, 125

Radical Orthodoxy, 88, 95, 116, 134, 139–40, 279, 282, 284–87
Rationality, 10, 55–56, 63, 79–80, 85–86, 92, 207, 239, 241, 243, 245, 248, 262, 281
Reality, empirical, 28–29, 173, 176, 276, 278
Reason, 62–65, 67–68, 79–80, 84, 88–89, 93, 98, 105, 109, 147, 150, 185, 189, 229, 231, 241–42, 254–55, 257, 280–82, 287
Reconciliation, 163, 178, 202–3, 205, 218, 272, 279
Redemption, 203, 205–6, 218–20, 271
Religion, 29, 40, 44, 58–67, 85–86, 98, 102, 186–89, 196, 198–99, 204, 223, 225, 241, 244, 250, 256–66, 271, 274–76, 279–84
  true, 62, 259–60, 287
Religious character, viii, 250, 252, 260, 273
Revelation, 44, 80, 109, 114, 144, 182–83, 212–13
Rhetoric, 57, 89, 102–3, 105–6, 207, 240, 280, 286
Righteousness, 188, 190
Roman Empire, 62, 258–59, 261
Roman religion, 258, 260, 262
Romans, 159, 180, 185–86, 188, 190, 196, 258–60, 279
Rose, Gillian
  architecture, 7, 147, 149
  Athens, 142–43, 146–47, 150, 156–57, 165
  Auschwitz, 150, 156–58, 165
  broken middle, 142–55, 164–65, 167, 170, 285–86
  diremption, 145, 149, 152–53
  middle, 144–45, 148–49, 151–53, 164–65
  mourning, 145, 147, 149–52, 155–56, 158, 169, 286
  third city, 142, 150–51
Rowland, Tracey, 46, 72–73, 80, 82, 89, 286

Sagacity, 244–45
Sage Philosophy, 235, 237, 252, 285
Salvation, 142, 161, 202–3
Scharen, Christian, 172–73, 200, 276, 286
Schleiermacher, Friedrich, 7, 55, 185–87, 189–90, 197, 279–80
Sciences
  modern, 231–32, 282
  natural, 9, 54
Scotus, Duns, 6, 84, 93, 135–36, 142
Secular, vii, 6, 57–61, 69–70, 82–83, 85, 87, 89, 94, 102, 132, 138, 151–52, 168, 175, 188, 194
Secular, as anti-theology, 132, 200
Secular Age, 6, 58–59, 61, 67, 84, 287
Secular autonomy, 136
Secularity, 6, 37
Secular reason, 10, 70, 83, 87, 90, 132, 285
Serequeberhan, Tsenay, 229–31, 240, 251, 286
Shumway, David, 71–73, 286
Signs, 23, 102, 120, 123–24, 270
Sin, 30, 138, 157, 159, 163, 165, 178, 201, 205, 215, 271
Site, 119, 142, 155, 172–73
Smith, James K A, 138–39, 176, 207, 286
Social sciences, vii–viii, 2–3, 9, 13, 22–24, 29, 32, 38, 56, 72, 87, 91, 129–30, 263, 272, 277
Social theory, 23–24, 26, 29, 57, 59, 70, 82–83, 85, 87–88, 94–95, 111, 113, 129–30, 140, 142, 145, 156, 159, 283, 285
Society, 16, 28, 30, 58–59, 86–87, 102, 130, 159, 187, 201, 205, 237, 262, 288
  civil, 99, 138, 153, 169
  true, 157, 161

294

Index

Sociology, 16, 38, 42, 74, 85–86, 148, 165, 200, 285
Socius, 88–89, 168, 170
Space, 4, 6–7, 58, 61, 65, 67, 81, 85, 90, 96–97, 108–9, 138, 144, 152, 154, 164, 168, 243, 245, 250
  public, 58–59
  simple, 166–68
Speech, 68, 116–17, 204, 284–85
State, 153, 158, 162, 166, 169, 187, 204, 206, 221, 258, 271, 273
Structuring, cultural, 29–30
Sub-culture, 192, 194
Superstition, 241, 258–59, 262
Supreme Being, 265–66
Systems, 22, 29, 71, 101, 120, 181–82, 185, 239

Tanner, Kathryn, 14–22, 42, 49, 70, 81–82, 86–90, 286
Task of humanization, 205, 221
Taylor, Charles, 6, 37–38, 58–61, 67, 84, 143–44, 148, 287
Teleology, 64, 89, 91, 121, 202, 204, 207, 217–19, 222, 270
Temptation, 146–48, 180, 193
Theologians, 1–5, 8, 13–14, 22–23, 25–26, 29, 33–34, 37, 42, 46, 48, 68, 72, 82–84, 134, 185, 204, 223, 256, 267
Theological colonization, 151–52
Theological culture, 192–95
Theological projects, 2, 13–14, 24, 69, 95, 135, 211
Theology
  liberal, 185–86
  poetic, 97, 130, 176, 269
  political, 83, 143, 149, 281
  positive, 152
  post-secular, 67, 286
Theology and culture, 266
Theology of crisis, 186
Torrance, T. F., 196–97, 204, 287
Totus Christus, 24, 212, 217, 221–22
Tradition, vii, 37, 49, 55–56, 64, 73, 75–76, 103, 111, 139, 147, 177, 183, 186, 213, 219, 234–36, 239, 241–45, 248–52
  cultural, 240–41, 246, 257

  preferred, 245
  religious, 255, 259
  theological, 255–56
Transcendence, 37, 55, 60, 84, 89–90, 111, 113, 180, 188, 274–75
Trinity, 57, 99, 116, 129, 174, 209, 213, 215–16, 269, 285–86
Truth, 53–54, 67, 72, 77, 85, 93, 95, 99–100, 105, 110, 113, 127, 134, 136, 176, 183, 261–62, 275, 280, 284–85
Truth claims, 54–55, 237

Universalists, 238–40
Univocity, 102, 118, 135–36, 288

Vanhoozer, Kevin J., 14, 20–22, 36, 64, 67–68, 76–77, 80, 281, 287
Vico, Giambattista, 4, 52–56, 61–62, 68, 95–113, 115–21, 125, 130–32, 136–37, 269, 272, 284
  acutezza, 105–6, 113
  ars critica, 52–53
  factum, 97–98, 105, 109–10
  verum, 105, 109–10, 113
Violence, 83, 101, 132–33, 135, 137–43, 145, 147, 149–53, 155, 157, 159, 161, 163, 165, 167, 169, 171, 173, 190, 280–81
Virtue, 69, 73, 76, 116, 130, 136, 161–62, 165, 170, 275, 284
  critique of, 161
Vulgar wisdom, 52–53

Warburton, William, 117–22, 285
Ward, Graham, 62–63, 88, 95, 133, 137, 139, 287
Western, 37, 58–59, 61–62, 222–25, 231–32, 234–36, 240, 248–49, 252–55, 258, 266–67, 275, 287
  modernity, 246, 251
  philosophy, 234–35, 238–39, 243, 250, 252
  theology, 218, 263
Williams, Raymond, 49–53, 58, 288
Wiredu, Kwasi, 239, 246–47, 288
Wittgenstein, Ludwig, 8, 37, 74–77, 79, 88, 283
Word of Christ, 193, 210, 216–19, 284

295

Index

Word of God, 185, 194, 201, 204, 279
Word of grace, 179–80
World, 11–12, 21, 31–32, 63, 89–90, 99, 101–2, 107–8, 143–45, 163–64, 178–83, 185–86, 188, 200, 206–7, 219–20, 222–23, 261–62, 270–75, 284–87
   cultural, 111
   natural, 37

World-occurrences, 181–82
Worldview, 5, 30, 33, 44, 177–84, 239, 257, 274
Worldview thinking, 179–80
Worship, 49, 77, 83, 210, 258, 261–62

www.ingramcontent.com/pod-product-compliance
Lightning Source LLC
Chambersburg PA
CBHW061431300426
44114CB00014B/1628